LINGUISTICS: AN INTRODUCTION

This book is a self-contained introduction to language and linguistics, suitable for use as a textbook and for self-study. Written by a team of distinguished linguists, it offers a unified approach to language from several perspectives. A language is a complex structure represented in the minds of its speakers, and this book provides the tools necessary for understanding this structure. It explains basic concepts and recent theoretical ideas in the major areas of linguistics (phonetics, phonology, morphology, syntax and semantics), as well as the applications of these to the study of child language acquisition, psycholinguistics, language disorders and sociolinguistics. The book is divided into three parts: sounds, words and sentences. In each of these parts, the foundational concepts are introduced along with their applications in the above fields, giving this book a clear and unique structure. Each section is accompanied by extensive exercises and guidance on further reading.

The authors all teach at the Department of Language and Linguistics at the University of Essex.

ANDREW RADFORD is the author of four best-selling textbooks: *Transformational Syntax* (1981), *Transformational Grammar* (1988), *Syntax* (1997), and *Syntactic Theory and the Structure of English* (1997), all of which are published by Cambridge University Press.

MARTIN ATKINSON is the author of *Explanations in Child Language Acquisition* (1982), *Children's Syntax* (1992) and *Foundations of General Linguistics* (with D. Kilby and I. Roca, 1988).

DAVID BRITAIN has published articles in *Language in Society* and *Language Variation and Change*.

HARALD CLAHSEN has written a number of books and articles on developmental language disorders, the acquisition of German as a second language, and child language acquisition.

ANDREW SPENCER is the author of *Morphological Theory* (1991) and *Phonology* (1996), and has contributed to the *Handbook of Morphology* and the *Handbook of Linguistics*.

Linguistics: An introduction

ANDREW RADFORD, MARTIN ATKINSON,
DAVID BRITAIN, HARALD CLAHSEN
and ANDREW SPENCER

CAMBRIDGE
UNIVERSITY PRESS

PUBLISHED BY THE PRESS SYNDICATE OF THE UNIVERSITY OF CAMBRIDGE
The Pitt Building, Trumpington Street, Cambridge CB2 1RP, United Kingdom

CAMBRIDGE UNIVERSITY PRESS
The Edinburgh Building, Cambridge CB2 2RU, UK   http://www.cup.cam.ac.uk
40 West 20th Street, New York, NY 10011–4211, USA   http://www.cup.org
10 Stamford Road, Oakleigh, Melbourne 3166, Australia

First published 1999

Printed in the United Kingdom at the University Press, Cambridge

Typeface Times MT 10/13pt   *System* QuarkXPress® [SE]

A catalogue record for this book is available from the British Library

ISBN 0 521 47261 X hardback
ISBN 0 521 47854 5 paperback

Contents

List of figures   *x*
List of maps   *xii*
List of tables   *xiii*
A note for course organisers and class teachers on the use of this
    book   *xv*

Introduction   *1*
Linguistics   *3*
Developmental linguistics   *7*
Psycholinguistics   *10*
Neurolinguistics   *12*
Sociolinguistics   *16*
Exercises   *19*

Further reading and references   *24*

Part 1   Sounds   *25*

1   Introduction   *27*

2   Sounds and suprasegmentals   *29*
Consonants   *31*
Vowels   *39*
Suprasegmentals   *45*
Exercises   *49*

3   Sound variation   *52*
Linguistic variables and sociological variables   *52*
Stylistic variation   *57*
Linguistically determined variation   *58*

Variation and language change   *61*
Exercises   *62*

4 Sound change   *66*
Consonant change   *66*
Vowel change   *69*
The transition problem: regular sound change versus lexical
    diffusion   *73*
Suprasegmental change   *76*
Exercises   *78*

5 Phonemes, syllables and phonological processes   *84*
Phonemes   *84*
Syllables   *88*
Syllabification and the Maximal Onset Principle   *91*
Phonological processes   *92*
Phonological features   *95*
Features and processes   *97*
Exercises   *101*

6 Child phonology   *105*
Early achievements   *105*
Phonological processes in acquisition   *106*
Perception, production and a dual lexicon model   *110*
Exercises   *117*

7 Processing sounds   *120*
Speech perception   *120*
Speech production   *125*
Other aspects of phonological processing   *130*
Exercises   *133*

Further reading and references   *135*
Appendix 1: The International Phonetic Alphabet   *137*
Appendix 2: List of distinctive features   *138*
Appendix 3: Distinctive feature matrix for English consonant
            phonemes   *141*

Part 2 Words   *143*

8 Introduction   *145*

9   Word classes   *147*
Lexical categories   *147*
Functional categories   *150*
The morphological properties of English verbs   *153*
Inflectional classes in Italian and Russian   *156*
Exercises   *160*

10   Building words   *162*
Morphemes   *162*
Morphological processes – derivation and inflection   *165*
Compounds   *171*
Clitics   *173*
Allomorphy   *175*
Exercises   *177*

11   Morphology across languages   *180*
The agglutinative ideal   *180*
Types of morphological operations   *186*
Exercises   *190*

12   Word meaning   *193*
Entailment and hyponymy   *194*
Meaning opposites   *199*
Semantic features   *200*
Dictionaries and prototypes   *204*
Exercises   *207*

13   Children and words   *211*
Early words – a few facts   *211*
Apprentices in morphology   *214*
The semantic significance of early words   *218*
Exercises   *223*

14   Lexical processing and the mental lexicon   *226*
Serial–autonomous versus parallel–interactive processing models   *226*
On the representation of words in the mental lexicon   *232*
Exercises   *240*

15   Lexical disorders   *243*
Words and morphemes in aphasia   *244*
Agrammatism   *245*
Paraphasias   *248*
Dissociations in SLI subjects' inflectional systems   *250*
Exercises   *252*

16 Lexical variation and change   *254*
Borrowing words   *254*
Register: words for brain surgeons and soccer players, hairdressers and life-
    savers   *256*
Biscuit or cookie? Variation and change in word choice   *257*
Same word – new meaning   *260*
Variation and change in morphology   *264*
Exercises   *271*

Further reading and references   *274*

Part 3 Sentences   *277*

17 Introduction   *279*

18 Basic terminology   *282*
Categories and functions   *282*
Complex sentences   *285*
The functions of clauses   *289*
Exercises   *290*

19 Sentence structure   *292*
Merger   *292*
Tests for constituency   *298*
Constraints on merger: features and checking   *300*
Exercises   *302*

20 Empty categories   *304*
Empty INFL   *304*
PRO: the empty subject of infinitive clauses   *310*
Covert complements   *312*
Empty constituents in nominal phrases   *313*
Exercises   *318*

21 Movement   *321*
Head movement   *322*
Operator movement   *325*
Yes–no questions   *331*
Other types of movement   *333*
Exercises   *336*

22 Syntactic variation   *338*
Inversion in varieties of English   *338*
Syntactic parameters of variation   *342*
The null subject parameter   *347*
Parametric differences between English and German   *349*
Exercises   *354*

23 Logical form   *357*
Preliminaries   *357*
A philosophical diversion   *359*
Covert movement and Logical Form   *364*
More evidence for covert movement   *371*
Exercises   *375*

24 Children's sentences   *378*
Setting parameters: two examples   *379*
Null subjects in early Child English   *381*
Non-finite clauses in Child English   *384*
Children's nominals   *389*
Exercises   *391*

25 Sentence processing   *394*
Click studies   *395*
Processing empty categories   *397*
Strategies of sentence processing   *399*
Exercises   *404*

26 Syntactic disorders   *406*
Agrammatism   *407*
Paragrammatism   *412*
Specific Language Impairment (SLI)   *413*
Conclusion   *416*
Exercises   *419*

Further reading and references   *422*

Bibliography   *424*

Index   *429*

Figures

1 The human cerebral cortex, with the functions of some areas indicated *13*
2 The human cerebral cortex, with Broca's Area (BA) and Wernicke's Area (WA) indicated *14*
3a Percentage of assistants using 'r' by store *22*
3b Percentage of assistants using 'r' by age and sex *22*
3c Percentage of assistants using 'r' by position in the word and speech style (repetitions are capitalised) *22*
4 Percentage of assistants using 'r' by store in 1962 and 1986 *23*
5 Cross-section of the human vocal tract *30*
6 Cross-section of the vocal tract, illustrating the articulation of [m] *33*
7 Cross-section of the vocal tract, illustrating the articulation of [n] *33*
8 Cross-section of the vocal tract, illustrating the articulation of [ŋ] *34*
9 Cross-section of the vocal tract, illustrating the articulation of interdental sounds *34*
10 Cross-section of the vocal tract, illustrating the articulation of labiodental sounds *35*
11 Cross-section of the vocal tract, illustrating the articulation of [j] *35*
12 Cross-section of the vocal tract, illustrating the articulation of palato-alveolar sounds *36*
13 The vowel quadrilateral (including only short vowels) *40*
14 The vowel quadrilateral (with long vowels) *41*
15 The vowel quadrilateral, including mid closed vowels *42*
16 The diphthongs of English *43*
17 The vowel quadrilateral, including central vowels *44*

18 Sound variation and speaker educational achievement: vowel
    assimilation in Teheran Farsi   *54*
19 Sound variation and speaker gender: the use of non-standard
    variants of (θ) in Detroit   *55*
20 Sound variation and speaker ethnicity: the use of [f] for (θ) among
    Italian, Greek and Anglo lower working class teenage boys in
    Sydney   *55*
21 Travel agency assistant's style shifting to clients: (t) glottalisation   *58*
22 (t)-flapping among news readers on two New Zealand radio
    stations   *63*
23 A vowel split in London   *71*
24 The Northern Cities Chain Shift   *73*
25 Preliminary model of child phonology   *108*
26 Lateral harmony as feature spreading   *112*
27 Lateral harmony: constructing the output UR   *114*
28 A dual lexicon model of child phonology   *114*
29 Matching input representation to syllable structure template   *115*
30 Results of an identification experiment for an [ɪ–ɛ]-series   *122*
31 Results of a discrimination experiment for an [ɪ–ɛ]-series   *123*
32 Results of an identification experiment for a [p–b]-series   *124*
33 Results of a discrimination experiment for a [b–p]-series   *124*
34 A simplified version of the scan-copier model of speech
    production   *128*
35 One view of the structure of the mental lexicon, illustrating the
    form of a lexical entry   *233*
36 A simple concept   *234*
37 Five conditions in a word/non-word recognition experiment   *235*
38 Differences between types of speech errors   *237*
39 Reported use of lexical pairs in New Zealand English   *258*
40 The adoption of British English by Canadian children: lexicon and
    phonology   *259*
41 The lexical attrition of *dwile* in East Anglia   *260*
42 Speaker sex and the use of (ing) in casual speech in three English-
    speaking cities   *266*
43a Social class and the use of (ing) in casual speech in Norwich   *267*
43b Speech style and the use of (ing) among upper working class
    residents of Norwich   *267*
44 Changes in the use of (ing) in Norwich across the generations   *268*
45 Ethnicity, levels of interethnic contact and the use of AAVE
    morphological features   *270*

Maps

1 Percentage use of [ɫ]-vocalisation among forty-five- to sixty-five-year-olds living in an area of Eastern England   *82*
2 Percentage use of [ɫ]-vocalisation among fifteen- to thirty-year-olds living in an area of Eastern England   *82*
3 The lexical attrition of the word *dwile* in East Anglia   *260*

Tables

1   IPA transcription for the English consonants   *31*
2   Consonantal sounds arranged by place and manner of articulation   *38*
3   The omission of [h] in Bradford   *53*
4   (th) and (ʌ) in the speech of two Belfast residents   *56*
5   Deletion of [t] and [d] in English   *59*
6   A hypothetical implicational scale   *60*
7   Social, contextual and linguistic variables from Labov's study of (r) in New York department stores   *62*
8   Percentage use of standard and non-standard variants of (ing) according to the sex of the addressee   *63*
9a Canadian children's acquisition of southern British English variants of (t)   *65*
9b Canadian children's acquisition of the southern British contrast between *Don* and *Dawn*   *65*
10 Spirantisation in Liverpool   *68*
11 Vowel changes in contemporary varieties of English   *70*
12 [aː] and [æ] in Standard British English (RP)   *75*
13 (t)-glottalisation in the speech of Milton Keynes children   *79*
14 Pronunciations of some simple words in a number of varieties of English   *79*
15 Vowel changes in an English dialect   *80*
16 Percentage retention of /j/ in Texas English   *80*
17 Percentage of vowel mergers in Texas English   *81*
18 The use of [ʍ] and [w] in Dunedin, New Zealand   *81*
19 The English phoneme inventory   *87*
20 A distinctive feature matrix for vowels   *103*
21 Personal pronouns in English   *152*
22 *parlare* 'to speak': first conjugation   *156*

23 *credere* 'to believe': second conjugation   *157*

24 *finire* 'to finish': third conjugation   *157*

25 *kod* 'code': Class I   *158*

26 *sonata* 'sonata': Class II   *158*

27 *kost'* 'bone': Class III   *159*

28 *bl'udo* 'dish': Class IV   *159*

29 Examples of derivational morphology in English   *167*

30 Equivalences between Modern English and other Germanic languages   *262*

31 The present tense forms of Modern English *help* and their equivalents in Old English and Modern German   *265*

32 Changes in the Old English suffixes *-inde* and *ingel-ynge*   *268*

A note for course organisers and class teachers on the use of this book

There are a number of points which teachers can usefully bear in mind when considering how to use this book.

Firstly, the division into three major parts (sounds, words and sentences), with the foundational concepts *and* the 'hyphenated' disciplines being covered in each part, provides some options which are not readily available in the context of more conventional structures. Specifically, the distribution of competence for small group teaching becomes a more manageable problem within this structure. The graduate student in phonology can take classes linked to sounds and give way to the morphologist when the course moves onto words, and the situation where hard-pressed assistants have to spend valuable time reacquiring basic material remote from their own research area is avoided. Additionally, as the three parts of the book are largely self-contained, each could be integrated as the introductory segment of more specialised courses in phonology, morphology or syntax. This might be particularly appropriate for students who have followed an introductory course which is at a somewhat lower level than that we are aiming at here.

Secondly, the book contains extensive exercise material at the end of each section, and it is intended that this should be helpful for small group teaching. We have distributed references to the exercises throughout the text, the idea being that when an exercise is referenced, students should be in a position to undertake it with profit. On occasions, these references cluster at the end of a section, indicating that the whole section must be covered before students can fruitfully tackle the exercises. Obviously, this gives class teachers some flexibility in deciding what proportion of a section will be required reading, and while this might be seen as disrupting the uniformity of the structure of the book, we believe that its pedagogical justification is clear.

Thirdly, we should mention a point about conventions. We have attempted to use bold face on the introduction of any technical or specialised vocabulary and thereafter use ordinary typeface unless particular emphasis justifies italics. There is always room for disagreement on what counts as technical or specialised and on the good sense of repeating bold face references, at least on some occasions. We wouldn't wish to say we've got it right but we have thought about it!

Finally, at the end of each of the major parts of the book, we have included some bibliographical material. The purpose of this is twofold: we provide guidance on further reading for the topics covered in the book and we also give references for the research on which we rely in our discussions. Usually, although not always, these latter works are not appropriate for a student's next step in the discipline, but providing references in this way gives us a means of acknowledging the work of the many colleagues whose ideas have influenced us. Throughout these sections, we use the author–date system, and at the end of the book full details of both types of publication – further reading and original research – can be found in a conventional bibliography.

Introduction

The major perspective we adopt in this book regards a language as a *cognitive* system which is part of any normal human being's mental or psychological structure. An alternative to which we shall also give some attention emphasises the *social* nature of language, for instance studying the relationships between social structure and different dialects or varieties of a language.

The cognitive view has been greatly influenced over the past four decades by the ideas of the American linguist and political commentator, Noam Chomsky. The central proposal which guides Chomsky's approach to the study of language is that when we assert that Tom is a speaker of English, we are ascribing to Tom a certain mental structure. This structure is somehow represented in Tom's brain, so we are also implicitly saying that Tom's brain is in a certain state. If Clare is also a speaker of English, it is reasonable to suppose that Clare's linguistic cognitive system is *similar* to Tom's. By contrast, Jacques, a speaker of French, has a cognitive system which is *different* in important respects to those of Tom and Clare, and different again to that of Guo, a speaker of Chinese. This proposal raises four fundamental research questions:

(1)   What is the nature of the cognitive system which we identify with knowing a language?

(2)   How do we acquire such a system?

(3)   How is this system used in our production and comprehension of speech?

(4)   How is this system represented in the brain?

Pursuit of these questions defines four areas of enquiry: linguistics itself, developmental linguistics, psycholinguistics and neurolinguistics.

At the outset, it is important to be clear that an answer to question (1) is *logically* prior to answers to questions (2), (3) and (4); unless we have a view on the nature of the relevant cognitive system, it makes no sense to enquire into its acquisition, its use in production and comprehension and its representation in the brain.

Question (1), with its reference to a *cognitive* system, looks as if it ought to fall in the domain of the cognitive psychologist. However, the Chomskian approach maintains that we can formulate and evaluate proposals about the nature of the human mind by *doing linguistics*, and much of this book is intended to establish the plausibility of this view. In order to do linguistics, we usually rely on native speakers of a language who act as informants and provide us with data; and it is with respect to such data that we test our hypotheses about native speakers' linguistic cognitive systems. Often, linguists, as native speakers of some language or other, rely on themselves as informants. Linguists (as opposed to psycholinguists, see below) do not conduct controlled experiments on large numbers of subjects under laboratory conditions. This is a major *methodological* difference between linguists and cognitive psychologists in their study of the human mind, and some critics might see it as making linguistics unscientific or subjective. However, it is important to point out that the data with which linguists work (supplied by themselves or by other native speakers) usually have such clear properties as to render controlled experimentation pointless. For instance, consider the examples in (5):

(5)   a. The dog chased the cat
        b. *Cat the dog chased the

A native speaker of English will tell us that (5a) is a possible sentence of English but (5b) is not (the * is conventionally used to indicate this latter judgement). Of course, we could design experiments with large numbers of native speakers to establish the reliability of these claims, but there is no reason to believe that such experiments would be anything other than a colossal waste of time. Native speakers have vast amounts of data readily available to them, and it would be perverse for linguists not to take advantage of this. Notice that above we said that the data supplied by native speakers *usually* have very clear properties. When this is not the case (and an example will arise in our discussion of psycholinguistics below), we proceed with more caution, trying to understand the source of difficulty.

The logical priority of question (1) should not lead to the conclusion that we must have a *complete* answer to this question before considering our other questions. Although question (2) requires *some* view on the cognitive linguistic system, there is no reason why acquisition studies of small children should not themselves lead to modifications in this view. In such a case, pursuit of question (2) will be contributing towards answering question (1), and similar possibilities exist for (3) and (4). In practice, many linguists, developmental linguists, psycholinguists and neurolinguists are familiar with each other's work, and there is a constant interchange of ideas between those working on our four questions.

Our questions foster different approaches to linguistic issues, and in this introduction we shall first take a preliminary look at these. Having done this, we shall turn to the social perspective mentioned at the outset and offer some initial remarks on how this is pursued.

Linguistics

To begin to answer question (1), Chomsky identifies knowing a language with having a mentally represented **grammar**. This grammar constitutes the native speaker's **competence** in that language, and on this view, the key to understanding what it means to know a language is to understand the nature of such a grammar. Competence is contrasted with **performance**, the perception and production of speech, the study of which falls under psycholinguistics (see below). Since this is a fundamental distinction which underlies a great deal of what we shall be discussing, it is worth trying to get a clear grasp of it as early as possible. Consider the situation of a native speaker of English who suffers a blow to the head and, as a consequence, loses the ability to speak, write, read and understand English. In fortunate cases, such a loss of ability can be short-lived, and the ability to use English in the familiar ways reappears quite rapidly. What cognitive functions are impaired during the time when there is no use of language? Obviously, the ability to use language, i.e. to perform in various ways, is not available through this period, but what about knowledge of English, i.e. linguistic competence? If we suppose that this is lost, then we would expect to see a long period corresponding to the initial acquisition of language as it is regained, rather than the rapid re-emergence which sometimes occurs. It makes more sense to suppose that knowledge of language remains intact throughout such an episode; the problem is one of accessing this knowledge and putting it to use in speaking, etc. As soon as this problem is overcome, full knowledge of English is available, and the various abilities are rapidly reinstated.

What does a grammar consist of? The traditional view is that a grammar tells us how to combine words to form phrases and sentences. For example, by combining a word like *to* with a word like *Paris* we form the phrase *to Paris*, which can be used as a reply to the question asked by speaker A in the dialogue below:

(6)   SPEAKER A: Where have you been?
       SPEAKER B: *To Paris.*

By combining the phrase *to Paris* with the word *flown* we form the larger phrase *flown to Paris,* which can serve as a reply to the question asked by speaker A in (7):

(7)   SPEAKER A: What's he done?
       SPEAKER B: *Flown to Paris.*

And by combining the phrase *flown to Paris* with words like *has* and *he,* we can form the sentence in (8):

(8)   He has flown to Paris

On this view, a grammar of a language specifies how to combine words to form phrases and sentences, and it seems entirely appropriate to suggest that native speakers of English and of other languages have access to cognitive systems which somehow specify these possibilities for combination (*exercise 1*). A very important aspect of this way of looking at things is that it enables us to make sense of how a cognitive system (necessarily *finite*, since it is represented in a brain) can somehow characterise an *infinite* set of objects (the phrases and sentences in a natural language). That natural languages are infinite in this sense is easy to see by considering examples such as those in (9):

(9)   a. Smith believes that the earth is flat
       b. Brown believes that Smith believes that the earth is flat
       c. Smith believes that Brown believes that Smith believes that the earth is flat
       d. Brown believes that Smith believes that Brown believes that Smith believes that the earth is flat

A native speaker of English will recognise that such a sequence of sentences could be indefinitely extended, and the same point can be made in connection with a variety of other constructions in English and other languages (*exercise 2*). But the infinite nature of the set of English sentences, exemplified by those in (9), does not entail that the *principles of combination* used in constructing these sentences are also infinite; and it is these principles which form part of a grammar.

The view we have introduced above implies that a grammar contains two components: (i) a **lexicon** (or dictionary) which lists all the words found in the language, and (ii) a **syntactic component** which specifies how to combine words together to form phrases and sentences. Each **lexical entry** (i.e. each item listed in the lexicon) will tell us about the linguistic properties of a word. For example, the entry for the word *man* will specify its **phonological** (= sound) properties (viz. that it is pronounced /man/ – for the significance of the slashes, see section 5), its **grammatical** properties (e.g. that it can function as a noun and that when it does, it has the irregular plural form *men*), and its **semantic** (i.e. meaning) properties (viz. that it denotes an adult male human being). The linguistic properties of words, including the nature of lexical entries, form the subject matter of part 2 of this book, while syntax (i.e. the study of how words are combined together to form phrases and sentences) provides the focus for part 3. A grammar can be said to **generate** (i.e. specify how to form) a set of phrases and sentences, and using this terminology, we can view the task of the linguist as that of developing a theory of **generative grammar** (i.e. a theory about how phrases and sentences are formed).

More careful reflection shows that a grammar must contain more than just a lexicon and a syntax. One reason for this is based on the observation that many words change their **phonetic form** (i.e. the way they are pronounced) in connected speech, such sound changes being determined by the nature of neighbouring sounds within a word, phrase or sentence. These changes are effected by native speakers in a perfectly natural and unreflective way, suggesting that whatever principles determine them must be part of the relevant system of mental representation (i.e. grammar). We can illustrate what we mean here by considering examples of changes which result from the operation of regular **phonological processes**. One such process is **elision**, whereby a sound in a particular position can be dropped and hence not pronounced. For instance, the 'f' in the word *of* (which is pronounced /v/) can be elided in colloquial speech before a word beginning with a consonant (but not before a word beginning with a vowel): hence we say 'pint o' milk' (sometimes written *pinta milk*) eliding /v/ before the /m/ of the word *milk*, but 'pint of ale' (not 'pint o' ale') where the /v/ can't be elided because the word *ale* begins with a vowel. A second regular phonological process is **assimilation**, a process by which one sound takes on some or all the characteristics of a neighbouring sound. For example, in colloquial speech styles, the final 'd' of a word like *bad* is assimilated to the initial sound of an immediately following word beginning with a consonant: hence, *bad boy* is pronounced as if it were written *bab boy* and *bad girl* as if it were written *bag girl* (*exercise 3*).

The fact that there are regular phonological processes such as those briefly described above suggests that in addition to a lexicon and a syntactic component, a grammar must also contain a **phonological component**: since this determines the phonetic form (= PF) of words in connected speech, it is also referred to as the **PF component**. **Phonology**, the study of sound systems and processes affecting the way words are pronounced, forms the subject matter of part 1 of this book.

So far, then, we have proposed that a grammar of a language contains three components, but it is easy to see that a fourth component must be added, as native speakers not only have the ability to *form* sentences, but also the ability to *interpret* (i.e. assign meaning to) them. Accordingly, a grammar of a language should also answer the question 'How are the meanings of sentences determined?' A common-sense answer would be that the meaning of a sentence is derived by combining the meanings of the words which it contains. However, there's clearly more involved than this, as we see from the fact that sentence (10) below is ambiguous (i.e. has more than one interpretation):

(10)   She loves me more than you

Specifically, (10) has the two interpretations paraphrased in (11a, b):

(11)   a. She loves me more than you love me
        b. She loves me more than she loves you

The ambiguity in (10) is not due to the meanings of the individual words in the sentence. In this respect, it contrasts with (12):

(12)   He has lost the match

In (12), the word *match* is itself ambiguous, referring either to a sporting encounter or a small piece of wood tipped with easily ignitable material, and this observation is sufficient to account for the fact that (12) also has two interpretations. But (10) contains no such ambiguous word, and to understand the ambiguity here, we need to have some way of representing the logical (i.e. meaning) relations between the words in the sentence. The ambiguity of (10) resides in the *relationship* between the words *you* and *loves*; to get the interpretation in (11a), *you* must be seen as the **logical subject** of *loves* (representing the person giving love), whereas for (11b), it must function as the **logical object** of *loves* (representing the person receiving love). On the basis of such observations, we can say that a grammar must also contain a component which determines the **logical form** (= LF) of sentences in the language. For obvious reasons, this component is referred to as the **LF component**, and this is a topic which is discussed in section 23 of this book (*exercise 4*).

Our discussion has led us to the conclusion that a grammar of a language comprises (at least) four components: a lexicon, a syntactic component, a PF component and an LF component. A major task for the linguist is to discover the nature of such grammars.

However, there is an additional concern for the linguist. Suppose grammars are produced for a variety of languages by specifying the components introduced above. Naturally, we would expect these grammars to exhibit certain *differences* (a grammar of English will be different to a grammar of Japanese), but we might also discover that they have some properties in common. If these properties appear in grammars for a wide range of languages, standard scientific practice leads us to hypothesise that they are common to the grammars of *all* natural languages, and this means that an additional goal for the linguist is the development of a theory of **Universal Grammar (UG)**. A great deal of contemporary linguistic theory can be viewed as testing hypotheses about UG on an ever wider class of languages.

As described above, UG is viewed as emerging from the linguist's study of individual grammars, but there is a different way to introduce this concept which affords it a much more important and fundamental position in the work of linguists. To appreciate this, we need to turn to the second of our questions, viz. 'How do we acquire a grammar?'

Developmental linguistics

Readers familiar with small children will know that they generally produce their first recognisable word (e.g. *Dada* or *Mama*) round about their first birthday; from then until the age of about 1;6 (one year and six months), children's speech consists largely of single words spoken in isolation (e.g. a child wanting an apple will typically say 'Apple'). At this point, children start to form elementary phrases and sentences, so that a child wanting an apple at this stage might say 'Want apple.' From then on, we see a rapid growth in children's grammatical development, so that by the age of 2;6 most children are able to produce adult-like sentences such as 'Can I have an apple, daddy?'

From this rough characterisation of development, a number of tasks emerge for the developmental linguist. Firstly, it is necessary to *describe* the child's development in terms of a sequence of grammars. After all, we know that children become adults and we are supposing that, as adults, they are native speakers who have access to a mentally represented grammar. The natural assumption is that they move towards this grammar through a sequence of 'incomplete' or 'immature' grammars. Secondly, it is important to try to *explain* how it is that after a period of a year and a half in which there is no obvious sign of children being able to form sentences, between one-and-a-half and two-and-a-half years of age there is a 'spurt' as children start to form more and more complex sentences, and a phenomenal growth in children's grammatical development in this period. This *uniformity* and (once the 'spurt' has started) *rapidity* in the pattern of children's linguistic development are central facts which a theory of language acquisition must seek to explain. But how?

Chomsky maintains that the most plausible explanation for the uniformity and rapidity of first language acquisition is to posit that the course of acquisition is determined by a biologically endowed innate **language faculty** (or *language acquisition program*, to borrow a computer software metaphor) within the human brain. This provides children with a genetically transmitted set of procedures for developing a grammar which enables them to produce and understand sentences in the language they are acquiring, on the basis of their *linguistic experience* (i.e. on the basis of the speech input they receive). The way in which Chomsky visualises the acquisition process can be represented schematically as in (13) below (where L is the language being acquired):

(13)   Experience of L

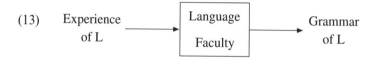

Grammar of L

Children acquiring a language will observe people around them using the language, and the set of expressions in the language which the child hears (and the contexts in which they are used) in the course of acquiring the language constitute the child's linguistic experience of the language. This experience serves as input to the child's language faculty, which provides the child with a set of procedures for analysing the experience in such a way as to devise a grammar of the language being acquired. Chomsky's hypothesis that the course of language acquisition is determined by an innate language faculty is known popularly as the **innateness hypothesis**.

Invocation of an innate language faculty becoming available to the child only at some genetically determined point may constitute a *plausible* approach to the questions of uniformity and rapidity, but there is an additional observation which suggests that some version of the innateness hypothesis *must be correct*. This is that the knowledge of a language represented by an adult grammar appears *to go beyond anything supplied by the child's linguistic experience*. A simple demonstration of this is provided by the fact that adult native speakers are not only capable of combining words and phrases in acceptable ways but also of recognising *unacceptable* combinations (see (5b) above and exercise 1). The interesting question this raises is: where does this ability come from? An obvious answer to this question is: the child's linguistic experience provides information on unacceptable combinations of words and phrases. But this is incorrect. Why do we assert this with such confidence?

Obviously, when people speak, they do make mistakes (although research has shown that language addressed to children is *almost* completely free of such mistakes). However, when this happens, there is no clear signal to the child *indicating that an adult utterance contains a mistake*, that is, as far as the child is concerned, an utterance containing a mistake is just another piece of linguistic experience to be treated on a par with error-free utterances. Furthermore, it has been shown that adults' 'corrections' of children's own speech do not take systematic account of whether children are producing syntactically acceptable or unacceptable combinations of words and phrases; parents do 'correct' their children, but when they do this, it is to ensure that children speak *truthfully*; grammatical correctness is not their target. Overall, there is compelling evidence that children do *not* receive systematic exposure to information about unacceptable sequences, and it follows that in this respect the child's linguistic experience is *not sufficient* to justify the adult grammar. From this **poverty of the stimulus** argument it follows that something must supplement linguistic experience and the innate language faculty fulfils this role (*exercise 5*).

Now, it is important to underline the fact that children have the ability to acquire *any* natural language, given appropriate experience of the language: for example, a British child born of monolingual English-speaking parents and brought up by monolingual Japanese-speaking parents in a Japanese-speaking community will acquire Japanese as a native language. From this it follows that the contents of the language faculty *must not be specific to any one human language*: if the language faculty accounts for the uniformity and rapidity of the acquisition of English, it must also account for the uniformity and rapidity of the acquisition of Japanese, Russian, Swahili, etc.; and if the language faculty makes up for the insufficiency of a child's experience of English in acquiring a grammar of English, it must also make up for the insufficiency of a child's experience of Japanese in acquiring a grammar of Japanese, for the insufficiency of a child's experience of Russian in acquiring a grammar of Russian, for the insufficiency of a child's experience of Swahili in acquiring a grammar of Swahili, etc. This entails, then, that the language faculty must incorporate a set of **UG principles** (i.e. principles of Universal Grammar) which enable the child to form and interpret sentences in any natural language. Thus, we see an important convergence of the interests of the linguist and the developmental linguist, with the former seeking to formulate UG principles on the basis of the detailed study of the grammars of adult languages and the latter aiming to uncover such principles by examining children's grammars and the conditions under which they emerge.

In the previous paragraph, we have preceded 'language' with the modifier 'human', and genetic transmission suggests that a similar modifier is appropriate for 'language faculty'. The language faculty is *species-specific* and the ability to develop a grammar of a language is *unique to human beings*. This ability distinguishes us from even our nearest primate cousins, the great apes such as chimpanzees and gorillas, and in studying it we are therefore focusing attention on one of the defining characteristics of what it means to be a human being. There have been numerous attempts to teach language to other species and success in this area would seriously challenge the assertion we have just made. Indeed, it has proved possible to teach chimpanzees a number of signs similar to those employed in the Sign Languages used as native languages by the deaf and, more recently, it has been reported that pigmy chimpanzees can understand some words of spoken English, and even follow a number of simple commands. Such research arouses strong emotions, and, of course, we are not in a position to assert that it will *never* produce dramatic results. At the moment, however, we can maintain that all attempts, however intensive, to teach grammatical knowledge to apes have been spectacular failures when the apes' accomplishments are set alongside those of a normal three-year-old child. As things stand, the evidence is firmly in favour of the species-specificity of the language faculty.

Psycholinguistics

As noted above, the psycholinguist addresses the question of how the mentally represented grammar (linguistic competence) is employed in the production and comprehension of speech (linguistic performance). The most direct way to approach this relationship is to adopt the hypothesis that a generative grammar can simply be regarded as itself providing an account of how we understand and produce sentences in real time. From the point of view of language comprehension, this gives rise to the following (highly simplified) model, where the *input* is a stretch of spoken or written language such as a particular sentence:

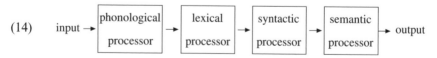

(14)   input →   phonological processor → lexical processor → syntactic processor → semantic processor → output

In terms of this rather crude model, the first step in language comprehension is to use the *phonological processor* to identify the sounds (or written symbols) occurring in the input. Then, the *lexical processor* identifies the component words. The next step is for the *syntactic processor* (also called the *parser*, and incorporating the syntactic component of the grammar) to provide a syntactic representation of the sentence (i.e. a representation of how the sentence is structured out of phrases and the phrases out of words). The last step is for the semantic processor (incorporating the LF-component of the grammar) to compute a meaning representation for the sentence, on the basis of the syntactic and lexical information supplied by earlier stages in the process. The relevant meaning representation serves as the output of the model: once this has been computed, we have understood the sentence.

An important characteristic of (14), as of all models of psycholinguistic processing, is that its various stages are to be viewed as taking place in real time, and a consequence of this is that psycholinguists can utilise their experimental techniques to try to measure the duration of specific parts of the process and link these measurements to levels of complexity as defined by the grammar itself. In fact, it is fairly easy to see that the idea that the grammar can, without any additional considerations, serve as a model of sentence comprehension is implausible. A sentence such as (15) is known as a **garden-path sentence**:

(15)   The soldiers marched across the parade ground are a disgrace

A common reaction to (15) from native speakers of English is that it is *not* an acceptable sentence. However, this reaction can usually be modified by asking native speakers to consider the sentences in (16) (recall our observation that not all linguistic data have immediately obvious properties):

(16)   a. The soldiers who were driven across the parade ground are a disgrace
        b. The soldiers driven across the parade ground are a disgrace
        c. The soldiers who were marched across the parade ground are a disgrace

Sentence (16a) should be regarded as entirely straightforward, and we can view (16b) as 'derived' from it by deleting the sequence of words *who were*. Now, if we delete *who were* from sentence (16c), which should also be recognised as an acceptable English sentence, we 'derive' (15), and at this point many readers should change their reaction to (15): it *is* an acceptable English sentence, so long as it is interpreted with the phrase *the soldiers* as the logical object of *marched* (see p. 6 above). When we read (15) for the first time, we immediately interpret *the soldiers* as the logical subject of *marched* – the soldiers are marching rather than being marched; as a consequence, the sequence *the soldiers marched across the parade ground* is interpreted as a complete sentence and the sentence processor doesn't know what to do with *are a disgrace*.

The sentence processor has been 'garden-pathed', i.e. sent down the wrong analysis route (*exercise 6*).

What is important about 'garden-path' sentences is that they show that sentence comprehension *must* involve something in addition to the grammar. As far as the grammar is concerned, (15) is an acceptable structure with only one interpretation. However, it appears that this structure and interpretation are not readily available in sentence processing, suggesting that the parser must rely (to its detriment in this case) on something beyond the principles which determine acceptable combinations of words and phrases.

There are other aspects of (14) which are controversial and have given rise to large numbers of experimental psycholinguistic studies. For instance, there is no place in (14) for *non-linguistic general knowledge about the world*; according to (14), interpretations are computed entirely on the basis of linguistic properties of expressions without taking any account of their plausibility, and an alternative would allow encyclopaedic general knowledge to 'penetrate' sentence perception and guide it to more likely interpretations. A further assumption in (14) is that the different sub-components are *serially ordered* (in that the first stage is phonological processing which does its job before handing on to lexical processing, etc.). An alternative would allow syntactic and semantic factors to influence phonological and lexical processing, for semantic factors to influence syntactic processing, etc. These issues, along with several others, will be discussed in sections 14 and 25.

Neurolinguistics

The neurolinguist addresses the fourth of our research questions: how is linguistic knowledge represented in the brain? It is easy to sympathise with the *fundamental* nature of this question, since we firmly believe that cognitive capacities are the product of structures in the brain. However, the direct study of the human brain is fraught with difficulties. Most obvious among these is the fact that ethical considerations forbid intrusive experimentation on human brains. Such considerations, are not extended to non-humans, with the consequence that the neuroanatomy and neurophysiology of non-human, primate *visual* systems, similar in their capacities to that of humans, are already understood in some detail. For language, however, we have to rely on less controlled methods of investigation, for example, by studying brain damaged patients who suffer from language disorders. In these circumstances, the extent and precise nature of the damage is not known, a factor which inevitably contributes to the tentativeness of conclusions.

The brain is an extremely complex organ, consisting of several 'layers'. The layer which has evolved most recently and is most characteristic of higher primates such as ourselves is the **cerebral cortex**, the folded surface of the **cerebral hemispheres**, which contains what is often referred to as **grey matter**. This is where the higher intellectual functions, including language, are located. There are various ways in which the cerebral cortex can be damaged. For instance, it may suffer injury from a blow to the head or through some other type of wound. Alternatively, it may suffer internal damage due to disease or a blockage in a blood vessel (an embolism or thrombosis) which results in disruption of the blood supply and the death of cortical cells. Areas of damage are generally referred to as **lesions**.

The study of patients with various types of brain damage has revealed that different parts of the brain are associated with (i.e. control) different functions. In other words, it is possible to **localise** different functions in the brain as indicated in figure 1:

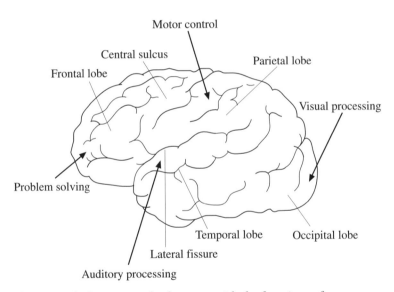

Figure 1 *The human cerebral cortex, with the functions of some areas indicated*

A language disorder resulting from brain damage is called **aphasia**, and a notable point is that this sort of brain damage almost always occurs in the left side of the brain (the left hemisphere). Damage to similar areas in the right hemisphere usually gives rise to entirely different deficits that have little to do with language. Aphasics who lose their language completely are said to suffer from **global aphasia** and while in many cases, the brain damage is extensive enough to affect other intellectual functions, sometimes patients retain a good many of the cognitive capacities they had before the injury. In particular, although these patients are unable to produce or understand language, they can often solve intellectual puzzles which don't rely on language.

As we have seen, Chomsky claims that linguistic competence is the product of a species-specific innate language faculty, and it is further maintained that this faculty is *independent* of other cognitive capacities. Of course, the **selective impairment** of language with other faculties remaining intact which we have just described is exactly what we might expect on the supposition that the language faculty is an autonomous and innate cognitive capacity.

As well as language being adversely affected while other aspects of cognitive functioning remain intact, it is possible for *specific* types of language function to be impaired, depending on where in the cortex the lesion occurs. In 1861 a French neurologist, Paul Broca, described a patient who had suffered a stroke and who could say only one word. After the patient's death, Broca studied his brain and discovered a large lesion in the frontal lobe of the left hemisphere, the area BA in figure 2:

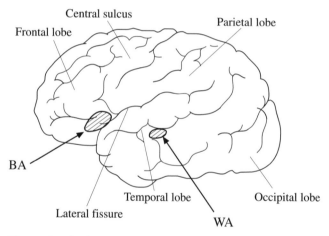

Figure 2 *The human cerebral cortex, with Broca's Area (BA) and Wernicke's Area (WA) indicated*

Broca concluded that this was the area of the brain responsible for controlling the *production* of speech, which has since come to be known as **Broca's Area**.

Later research revealed that there is a second group of aphasic patients who have considerable difficulty in *understanding* language. In many cases, such patients appear to produce language reasonably fluently, but close examination reveals that they often speak in a garbled fashion. This pattern of deficit is often referred to as Wernicke's aphasia, in acknowledgement of Carl Wernicke, a German neurologist who first described it in detail in the 1870s.

Wernicke's aphasia is associated with damage to another area of the left hemisphere known as **Wernicke's Area** (WA in figure 2) (*exercise 7*).

Unfortunately, the initial hope that by studying the linguistic problems of aphasics, we would be able to identify and isolate the language areas in the brain has turned out to be somewhat naive. As more research has been done, it has become clear that language functions cannot be easily and directly located in specific cortical regions; rather, several different areas of the brain are involved in performing linguistic tasks. This does not mean that the language faculty cannot be located in the brain, but it does entail that complex distributed representations are involved which require more sophisticated experimental procedures for their study. In recent years, new techniques have been developed for studying the activity of the brain as it performs a specific linguistic task. These so-called **imaging techniques** such as PET-scans and Event-related potentials, provide images of the brain 'at work' and we may hope that they will eventually lead to a growth in our knowledge about the physiological mechanisms underlying the knowledge of language. However, research using these techniques is still in its infancy, and in the relevant sections which follow (15 and 26) we shall restrict ourselves to discussing the linguistic characteristics of patients who have suffered brain damage and who exhibit particular syndromes.

Of course, the brain is a biological organ, and above we have noted another aspect of the biological foundations of language: the claim that the language faculty is a product of human *genetic* endowment. Species-specificity is consistent with such a claim, but we might ask how we could obtain additional empirical evidence for it. One source of such evidence may be provided by the study of genetically caused disorders of language. If the availability of the language faculty (and the consequent ability to acquire a grammar) is indeed genetically controlled, then we would expect failures of this genetic control to result in language disorders. It is, therefore, of considerable interest that there is a group of language-impaired people who suffer from **Specific Language Impairment (SLI)**, a language disorder which must be clearly distinguished from the disorders introduced above, which are *acquired* as the result of damage to the brain. This group provides us with the chance of studying the effects of what is probably a genetically determined deficit on the acquisition of language. The *specificity* of SLI is indicated by the fact that SLI subjects have normal non-verbal IQs, no hearing deficits and no obvious emotional or behavioural difficulties. Its likely *genetic source* is suggested by the fact that it occurs in families, it is more frequent in boys than in girls and it affects both members of a pair of identical twins more frequently than it affects both members of a pair of fraternal twins. The nature of the impairment displayed by SLI subjects seems to be fairly narrow in scope, affecting aspects of grammatical inflection and certain complex syntactic processes. From this it might follow that if there is a 'language gene', its effects are rather specific and much of what is customarily regarded as language is not controlled by it. More research on SLI will be necessary before we can fully evaluate its consequences for this issue, but we shall provide some additional discussion of these matters in sections 15 and 26 (*exercise 8*).

Up to now, we have focused on the four research questions raised by Chomsky's programme and tried to give some idea of how we might begin to approach them. The idea of a grammar as a cognitive (ultimately, neurological) structure is common to each of these fields, which also share an emphasis on the *individual*. At no point have we raised questions of language as a means of communication with others, or as a tool for expressing membership in a group, or as indicative of geographical origins. These are intriguing issues and the sociolinguistic perspective addresses this omission.

Sociolinguistics

Sociolinguistics is the study of the relationship between **language use** and the **structure of society**. It takes into account such factors as *the social backgrounds of both the speaker and the addressee* (i.e. their age, sex, social class, ethnic background, degree of integration into their neighbourhood, etc.), *the relationship between speaker and addressee* (good friends, employer–employee, teacher–pupil, grandmother–grandchild, etc.) and *the context and manner of the interaction* (in bed, in the supermarket, in a TV studio, in church, loudly, whispering, over the phone, by fax, etc.), maintaining that they are crucial to an understanding of both the structure and function of the language used in a situation. Because of the emphasis placed on language *use*, a sociolinguistically adequate analysis of language is typically based on (cassette or video) taped recordings of everyday interactions (for example, dinner-time conversations with friends, doctor–patient consultations, TV discussion programmes, etc.).

Recordings of language use, as described above, can be analysed in a number of different ways depending on the aims of the research. For instance, the sociolinguist may be interested in producing an analysis of **regional** or **social dialects** in order to investigate whether different social groups speak differently and to discover whether language change is in progress. Rather different is research into the form and function of **politeness** in everyday interaction, an interest which will lead to a search for markers of politeness in conversations and how these are related to social dimensions such as those enumerated above. Alternatively, the focus may be on so-called **minimal responses** (such as *mmm*, *yeah*, and *right*) or **discourse markers** (such as *well*, *you know*, and *actually*).

In addition to phenomena which arise in interactions between individuals or small groups, sociolinguistics is concerned with larger scale interactions between language and society as a whole. One such interaction is **language shift**. Here, in a multilingual setting, one language becomes increasingly dominant over the other languages, taking over more and more of the domains in which these other languages were once used. Understanding the conditions which facilitate language shift and the dynamics of the process itself is properly viewed as a sociolinguistic task. It would, of course, be possible to raise many other research topics in the study of language which share a *social* focus, but because it will play a central role in much of our subsequent discussion, we shall close this introduction by going into a little more detail on the contemporary study of **language variation and change**.

The views of lay people about language are often quite simplistic. One illustration of this concerns the relationship between the so-called **standard** languages and the **non-standard** dialects associated with those languages. Standard French and Standard English, for example, are varieties of French and English that have written grammar books, pronunciation and spelling conventions, are promoted by the media and other public institutions such as the education system and are considered by a majority of people to be the 'correct' way to speak these two languages. Non-standard varieties (sometimes called 'dialects') are often considered to be lazy, ungrammatical forms which betray a lack of both educational training and discipline in learning. Linguists strongly disagree with this view. The study of language use has shown not only that non-standard varieties exhibit grammatical regularity and consistent pronunciation patterns in the same way that standard varieties do, but also that a vast majority of people will use non-standard features *at least some of the time* in their speech. Sociolinguistic research has demonstrated that the speech of most people is, at least in some respects, **variable**, combining, for example, both standard and non-standard sounds, words or grammatical structures. The study of **language variation** involves the search for consistent patterns in such variable linguistic behaviour.

Another area where language variation plays a crucial role is in the study of **language change**. It is the principal concern of **historical linguistics** to investigate how languages change over time, and until recently, historical linguists have studied language change by relying exclusively on **diachronic** methods. These involve analysing the structure of language from a succession of dates in the past and highlighting those structural features (phonological, morphological or syntactic) that appear to have changed over that period of time. For obvious reasons, if we are considering a form of a language from many years ago, we do not have access to native speakers of the language; as a consequence, historical linguists have had to rely largely on manuscripts from the past as evidence of how languages may once have been spoken, but such evidence is of variable quality, particularly when we take account of the fact that very few people were able to write in the premodern area. In these circumstances, it is difficult to judge just how representative surviving manuscripts are of the way ordinary people actually spoke.

As an alternative to diachronic methods and aided by the invention of the tape recorder allowing the collection of a permanent record of someone's speech, William Labov has pioneered a **synchronic** approach to studying language change. Whereas diachronic techniques demand language data from different periods in time, Labov's synchronic, so-called **apparent-time**, approach requires data to be collected at only one point in time. Crucially, the data collected within the same community are from people of *different ages and social groups*. Labov reasoned that if the speech of young people within a particular social group is different from that of old people in the same group, then it is very likely that language change is taking place. This technique has a number of advantages over the traditional historical method. Firstly, the tape-recorded language data constitute a considerably more representative sample of the speech patterns of a community than do the manuscript data of traditional historical linguistics. Secondly, it allows the linguist to study language change as it is actually taking place – traditionally, historical linguists had believed this to be impossible. Finally, it allows the linguist to study how language changes spread through society, answering such questions as: which social groups tend to lead language changes? How do language changes spread from one social group to another? (***Exercises 9 and 10.***)

Labov's apparent-time model assumes that a difference between young and old with respect to a certain linguistic feature *may* be due to linguistic change. Not all variable linguistic features that are sensitive to age variation are necessarily indicative of language changes in progress, however. Slang words, for example, are often adopted by youngsters, but then abandoned when middle-age is reached. Similarly, some phonological and grammatical features, such as the use of multiple negation (e.g. *I haven't got none nowhere*), seem to be **stable** yet **age-graded**, i.e. not undergoing change, but associated with a particular age group, generation after generation.

This brief introduction to the methods and concerns of sociolinguistics may seem to suggest that these are far removed from those of other types of linguist. However, in studying variable patterns of language behaviour and the language change that this variation may reveal, the sociolinguist seeks to uncover universal properties of language, attempting to address questions such as: do all languages change in the same way? We have already met this preoccupation with universals in our earlier discussion, so we can see that at this level, sociolinguistics exhibits important affinities with other approaches to the study of language. However, a fundamental difference remains: the sociolinguist's questions about universals require answers in which the structure of society plays an integral part. In this regard, they differ from the questions with which we opened this introduction, but there is no conflict here. Taken together, the various emphases we pursue in this book present a comprehensive picture of the complex and many-faceted phenomena which the study of language engages.

Exercises

1. For the following italicised sequences of words, indicate those which are acceptable or unacceptable in English. How do you know that the unacceptable sequences are unacceptable?

    (a) John *seems asleep*
    (b) John *seems sleeping*
    (c) John *wants Bill to go*
    (d) John *wants Bill go*
    (e) John *made Bill go*
    (f) John *made Bill to go*

2. Find further examples of sets of phrases or sentences from English or other languages with the characteristics of (9) in the text. This is *very, very* easy! If we extend the sequence in (9) with the sentences becoming *longer and longer and longer* (!), we get to a point where we might be convinced that no one would ever *use* such a sentence. What reasons can you think of for use being restricted in this way? Is it possible to *specify with confidence* the point in the sequence at which there is no likelihood of a sentence being used? Do these concerns have anything to do with the theory of language?

3. Read aloud the following words or phrases first slowly and then rapidly, and comment on any differences in pronunciation which arise for sounds corresponding to the italicised letters:

    (a) *in* Kent
    (b) i*n*k
    (c) i*ss*ue
    (d) I mi*ss* you
    (e) a sell*er* of ice creams
    (f) *you* *i*diot

4. Each of the following sentences is ambiguous. Provide paraphrases for the two (or more) interpretations in each case:

(a) John bought some antique books and socks in town
(b) They are hunting dogs
(c) John and Bill agreed on the Lear Jet
(d) Who would you like to visit?
(e) Do Americans call cushions what the British call pillows?
(f) John introduced himself to everyone that Mary did

5. A further argument for an innate language faculty based on the insufficiency of children's linguistic experience to account for the characteristics of their mature grammars is provided by ambiguity. Consider again the examples in exercise 4 and, supposing that you have succeeded in identifying their ambiguous interpretations, try to conceptualise what it would mean for *your* linguistic experience to have been sufficient to account for this knowledge. What conclusions do you draw from these efforts?

6. The sentence processor is *not* 'garden-pathed' by the sentence in (16b) in the text, despite the fact that it is very similar to (15). Decide which of the following are 'garden-path' sentences:

(a) The logs floated down the river sank
(b) The logs shipped down the river sank
(c) The favourite jumped over every fence with ease won
(d) The favourite ridden over every fence with ease won
(e) The glass broken into pieces was useless
(f) The glass shattered into pieces was useless
(g) The policeman called across the street was incompetent
(h) The policeman taken across the street was incompetent

By focusing on the *verbs* which appear in sentences which do or do not produce a 'garden-path' effect, try to describe what factor might be 'misleading' the sentence processor.

7. The following example, reported by David Caplan, illustrates word finding difficulties in aphasic patients. The patient is shown a picture of an octopus and says:

Oh . . . I know what that is . . . that's an animal that lives in the sea . . . it's good to eat . . . the Japanese eat it a lot . . . its name . . . oh

. . . its name has something to do with a part of its body . . . maybe the legs . . . let's see (the patient then counted the number of tentacles) . . . eight . . . eight . . . octo . . . octopus.

Discuss how the patient dealt with his difficulties and how he finally accessed the word.

8.   Here are some utterances from an eleven-year-old SLI child describing a picture book:

(a) Once upon a time there was a man and a naughty bus
(b) The bus think he just want to scape away
(c) and he going down hill
(d) The policeman said stop and blewed whistle
(e) and he fall
(f) and when the driver found where he was he went and call telephone
(g) and can get crane pull bus out
(h) and put back on road again

Try to identify areas of linguistic difficulty for this child.

9.   Possibly the most ingenious research carried out on **phonological variation** was the American linguist William Labov's survey of the pronunciation of 'r' among the workers at three New York department stores. Labov had noticed that some people pronounced the 'r' following vowels in words such as *car* and *park* and others did not. In order to investigate the variation in the community, he visited three department stores, one middle class, expensive store (Saks), one inexpensive store (Klein) and one in between (Macy's) and asked as many assistants as he could find the whereabouts of a product he knew to be on the fourth floor of each store. The expected answer 'fourth floor' was, of course, carefully chosen, as it contains two examples of the 'r' he was looking for: in *fourth* the 'r' occurs before a consonant, and in *floor* it occurs at the end of the word. Having received the answer 'fourth floor', Labov pretended that he hadn't heard properly, asking the assistant to repeat. He thereby doubled the size of his data set and introduced a further variable into the study, as the assistants' second replies could be regarded as 'emphatic' or 'careful'. Some of Labov's results appear in figure 3:

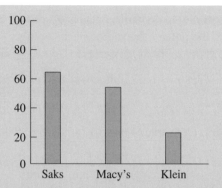

Figure 3a *Percentage of assistants using 'r' by store*

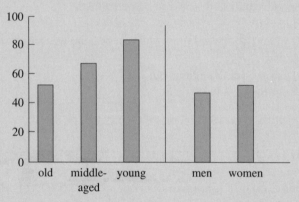

Figure 3b *Percentage of assistants using 'r' by age and by sex*

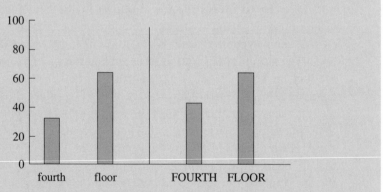

Figure 3c *Percentage of assistants using 'r' by position in the word and speech style (repetitions are capitalised)*

(a) What generalisations can you make about the way the two possible pronunciations co-exist in New York?

(b) What does the pattern of age variation suggest about the direction of language change?

(c) Which social groups appear to be leading in the use of the 'r-ful' pronunciation?

(d) Does the position of the 'r' in the word affect which pronunciation form is chosen?

(e) What do the results comparing casual and emphatic styles suggest?

10. Labov, and many others who have conducted apparent-time studies, have demonstrated the success of their techniques by returning to the communities they had earlier studied and repeating their research to see if a real-time diachronic study supported their apparent-time findings. One such follow-up study was a repeat of the New York department store survey, twenty-four years after the original research. A comparison of the results of the first and second surveys appears in figure 4. How would you interpret these findings? What do they tell you about the suitability of apparent-time methods?

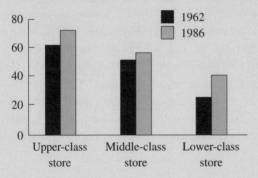

Figure 4 *Percentage of assistants using 'r' by store in 1962 and 1986*

Further reading and references

Chomsky's ideas on the nature of language and linguistic enquiry have been developed in a number of non-technical publications, since first being clearly formulated in chapter 1 of Chomsky (1965). These include Chomsky (1966, 1972, 1975, 1980, 1986a, 1988, 1995a). Despite being non-technical, all of these works are difficult for the beginner. A comprehensive and approachable account, locating Chomsky's approach within a biological framework, is Pinker (1995), and a very well-written introduction, paying particular attention to such issues as innateness and species-specificity is Aitchison (1998).

For language acquisition, a wide-ranging survey of traditional and modern studies is Ingram (1989), but introductions which are closer to the emphases we adopt in this book are Goodluck (1991) and Atkinson (1992). Garman (1990) is a good overview of psycholinguistics, and also contains a discussion of language disorders. For more detailed discussions of the topics we pursue, Harley (1995) is a good source for psycholinguistics and Caplan (1992) for language disorders and neurolinguistics. There are a number of excellent introductory sociolinguistics texts. Trudgill (1995) is a very approachable entry point to the subject, and Holmes (1992) and Wardaugh (1998) can both be recommended. More specifically on the subject of language variation and change, Aitchison (1991) is a well-written introduction, while Chambers (1995) is an excellent text, although more advanced. The department store survey is now a classic of sociolinguistics and more can be read about it in chapter 2 of Labov (1972). Details of the application of the apparent-time method to the department store situation appear in Labov (1994: 86–94).

Part 1 Sounds

1 Introduction

With the exception of the Sign Languages used by the deaf and written languages, the languages with which most of us are familiar rely on the medium of sound. Sign Languages are extremely interesting, exhibiting all the complexities of spoken languages, but their serious study requires the introduction of a considerable amount of specialised terminology for which we do not have space in an introductory book of this kind. As for written languages, they too have many fascinating features, but they are regarded as *secondary* to spoken languages for a number of reasons. For instance, children are explicitly taught to read and write sometime *after* they acquire a spoken language, and many cultures have never employed writing systems. Thus, a focus on sounds is entirely appropriate and this part of the book is devoted to discussion of the way in which the sound systems of languages are organised and the role of such systems in the acquisition and processing of languages. We will also consider the ways that sound systems differ from one dialect or variety of a given language to another and the ways in which the sound system of a given language changes over time.

Before we can discuss any aspect of the sound system of a language, we need a systematic way of describing and transcribing speech sounds, and in section 2 we introduce a standard transcription system, while at the same time explaining how the more important speech sounds are produced. It is important to be clear that the purpose of this section is to introduce *terminology* which enables us to talk about speech sounds with some precision, this being a prerequisite to our discussing any of the issues raised in our main introduction. Once our transcription system is in place, the most straightforward way to put it to use is in connection with sociolinguistic issues. Therefore, in section 3 we focus on the ways that sound systems vary across dialects, social groups, etc. We shall see that one dialect differs from another in systematic ways, i.e. that so-called 'substandard deviations' are quite regular and governed by social, contextual and linguistic principles. Section 4 examines how sound systems change over time to give rise to new dialects and ultimately new languages. Once more, we shall see that such changes are neither random nor due to 'sloppiness' on the part of speakers; rather, they are subject to coherent principles. Moreover, we shall discover that there is a close relationship between *variation* in a given language at any point in time and historical *change*.

In section 5 we begin to introduce some of the more abstract concepts which are important in understanding the phonological component of a grammar. Among these concepts is that of the phoneme, a unit of phonological analysis, and we will also touch upon the structure of the syllable, a particularly important unit in sound systems. Phonological processes have already received a brief introduction (p. 5), and in this section we shall consider some of these in more detail and introduce the important concept of **alternation**, such as we can observe in connection with the 'a' vowels in *Japan* and *Japanese*. The word *Japanese* clearly consists of *Japan* followed by the ending -*ese*, and native speakers of English will readily agree that the two 'a' vowels of *Japan* are different; the first is like the 'a' of *about* whereas the second is like the 'a' of *pan*. However, in the word *Japanese* each of the two 'a' vowels has the opposite quality and we say that they **alternate** – it seems as if the addition of -*ese* causes a change in the vowels of *Japan*. This difference is a systematic property of the language and, unlike the examples mentioned in the main introduction, it does not depend on whether we are speaking carefully or not; much of this section is devoted to such phenomena, and we will show how they can be described in terms of processes.

In the last two sections of this part of the book, we examine some of the developmental and psycholinguistic issues which arise in connection with sound systems. Section 6 discusses how phonology can throw light on the acquisition of pronunciation patterns by children learning their first language. Additionally, it illustrates the interaction between approaches alluded to in the main introduction, in that we will see that aspects of child phonology require theoretical notions which also find a role in the formulation of adult grammars. Finally, in section 7 we will consider selected aspects of speech perception along with common everyday errors in speech production (so-called slips of the tongue). This section concludes with a brief discussion of the role of phonology in understanding certain aspects of poetic systems and the way that writing systems have developed. Overall, the section seeks to establish the importance of some of the theoretical notions introduced in section 5 for the understanding of phenomena with which some readers will already be familiar.

2   Sounds and suprasegmentals

How many sounds are there in English? This seems like a reasonable enough question, but in fact it is difficult to answer, for several reasons. A major problem is that the spelling system of English (its **orthography**) is irregular and doesn't represent sounds in a completely consistent way. Sometimes one sound can be spelled in several ways as with the first sound of *Kathy* (or is it *Cathy*?), but worse, we find that some sounds just aren't given their own symbol at all. There is a difference between the first sounds of *shock* and *sock*, but the first of these sounds is represented by two symbols *s* and *h*, each of which corresponds to a sound which is different to the first sound of *shock*. Moreover, although most speakers of English will distinguish the middle sounds in *put* 'to place' and *putt* 'to strike a golf ball while it is on the green', this distinction is never made in the writing system.

We also need to be careful about what we mean by 'English', as pronunciation differs from one dialect to another. In the North of England, for instance, both *put* and *putt* are often pronounced like *put*, and dialects in the US differ as to which (if any) of the sounds in bold face in the words *merry*, *marry* and *Mary* they distinguish. These are systematic differences and not just caprice on the part of speakers, an issue which will be discussed in more detail in section 3. In the present context, however, such observations indicate a clear need for some way of writing down sounds which bypasses traditional orthography.

Moving away from English, as noted already, there are a great many languages which have never had a writing system of their own and which until recently have never been written down (hitherto undiscovered languages are still encountered in some parts of the world). For such cases, it is essential that linguists can rely on a system of writing which can be applied to any human language, even one which is completely unknown to the investigator.

For these reasons, linguists have developed systems of **phonetic transcription** in which each sound is represented by just one symbol and each symbol represents just one sound. Unfortunately, there are several such systems in use. In this book, we will use the transcription system of the International Phonetics Association, which is generally referred to as the IPA. This system, commonly used in Britain, derives from one developed in the 1920s by Daniel Jones and his colleagues at London University, one of whose aims was to provide writing systems for the unwritten languages of Africa and elsewhere.

One advantage of the IPA is that it is accompanied by a well-defined method of describing sounds in terms of the way in which they are produced. An understanding of how speech sounds are produced is a prerequisite for being able to transcribe them, so our introduction of the various symbols employed in the IPA will be accompanied by an account of the mechanisms of speech production.

Any sound is a series of vibrations moving through air, water or some other material. To create these vibrations a **sound source** is needed and these come in various types. On a guitar, for instance, the sound source is the strings which vibrate when plucked. By themselves these produce relatively little noise, but the body of the instrument is basically a wooden box which amplifies the sounds by picking up their vibrations and **resonating**, that is, vibrating in the same way, but more loudly. If you strum more than one string on a guitar, the pattern of resonance becomes very complex, with several sets of vibrations resonating at once. Speech sounds are produced in basically the same way, with bands of tissue called the **vocal cords** or **vocal folds** corresponding to the guitar strings. These are situated in the **larynx** or **voice box**, a structure in the throat (see figure 5). When air is forced out of the lungs, it causes the vocal cords to vibrate. Corresponding to the body of a guitar and functioning as a resonating chamber is the mouth and nose cavity above the larynx. Taken together, all these structures are called the **vocal tract**. The major difference

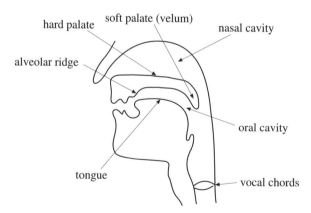

Figure 5 *Cross-section of the human vocal tract*

between a guitar and the vocal tract is that we can make different sounds by *changing the shape of the latter*, by moving the tongue, the lips and even the larynx.

Consonants

Given the apparatus described above, there are several ways of producing speech sounds. First, we can simply set the vocal cords vibrating and maintain a steady sound such as 'aaaah' or 'ooooh'. Or we can produce a very short-lived explosive sound such as 'p' or 't', and another important type of sound is illustrated by 'f' or 's', when we force air through a narrow opening to cause a hissing sound. Sounds such as 'p', 't', 'f', and 's' are called **consonants**, while those like 'aaaah' or 'ooooh' are **vowels**. The basic list (or inventory) of consonants in English is given in table 1. In all cases except for [ŋ] in *hang* and [ʒ] in *pleasure*, the consonant is at the beginning of the accompanying word – [ŋ] and [ʒ] do not occur word-initially in English. As will be apparent, in many cases the IPA symbol, written between square brackets, is identical to the ordinary printed symbol. The reasons for laying out the table in this manner will become clear from the subsequent discussion.

Table 1: IPA transcription for the English consonants			
pay	[p]	*far*	[f]
boy	[b]	*vie*	[v]
		thin	[θ]
		though	[ð]
tea	[t]	*sew*	[s]
do	[d]	*zip*	[z]
chair	[ʧ]	*show*	[ʃ]
jar	[ʤ]	*pleasure*	[ʒ]
cow	[k]		
go	[g]		
		her	[h]
me	[m]	*war*	[w]
now	[n]	*low*	[l]
		ray	[ɹ]
		you	[j]
hang	[ŋ]		

Let's first consider the sounds [p] and [f]. These differ from each other in their **manner of articulation**. The [p] sound is produced in three phases. First, we shut off the vocal tract completely by closing the lips. Then we try to force air out of the lungs. However, this air is prevented from escaping because of the closure and this causes a build up of pressure inside the mouth. Then we suddenly open the lips releasing this pressure, and the result is an explosive sound which lasts for a very short time. Such sounds are called **plosives**, and the English plosives are [p b t d k g]. The production of [f] is quite different. Here we allow a small gap between the top teeth and the bottom lip and then force air through this gap. When air at high pressure is forced through a narrow opening, it sets up friction which causes a noise. Sounds produced in this way are therefore called **fricatives**. The English fricatives are [f v θ ð s z ʃ ʒ h]. The initial consonants of *chair* and *judge* are complex sounds, which begin as plosives and end as fricatives. They are known as **affricates** and the IPA symbols [tʃ] and [dʒ] make their complex character clear.

The remaining sounds in table 1 fall into two groups. First, consider the sounds [m n ŋ]. These are produced by allowing the nasal cavity to resonate. Normally, the nasal passages are separated from the mouth and throat by a small piece of flesh, the **velum** (also sometimes called the **soft palate**), which is the backward continuation of the roof of the mouth (see figure 5). When the velum is lowered, air can pass through the nose. For instance, if we close the lips as if to produce a [b] and then lower the velum, the air from the lungs will no longer be trapped but will pass through the nose and set up vibrations there. This is how [m] is produced, and sounds such as [m n ŋ] are called **nasals**. The other remaining group of sounds is [l ɹ w j] and we shall describe how they are produced after we have looked at the other sounds in more detail.

Consonants are distinguished by more than just their manner of articulation. The sounds represented by [p t k] are all plosives, but these symbols represent different sounds. To understand the relevant distinctions here, we need to know something about the internal shape of the vocal tract, and figure 6 contains a cross-sectional view showing the way in which [m] is produced – for [p, b], the velum would be raised. The three sounds [p, b, m] are all formed by bringing the lips together and they are referred to as **bilabial** sounds. By contrast, the sounds [t d n] are made by placing the tip of the tongue against the gum ridge behind the upper teeth; this ridge is called the alveolus or the alveolar ridge and so [t d n] are called **alveolar** sounds. This articulation is illustrated for [n] in figure 7. Many languages (e.g. French, Spanish, Russian) use sounds which are slightly different to the [t d n] we find in English. Speakers of these languages place the tip of the tongue against the upper teeth themselves rather than the alveolar ridge and this produces a **dental**

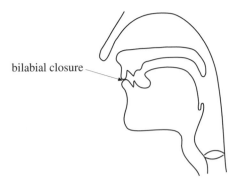

Figure 6 *Cross-section of the vocal tract, illustrating the articulation of [m]*

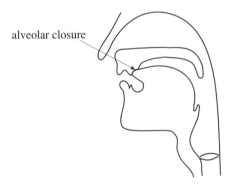

Figure 7 *Cross-section of the vocal tract, illustrating the articulation of [n]*

sound. If we need to distinguish dentals from alveolars, we can use special IPA symbols [t̪ d̪ n̪] to refer to the dentals. Different again are [k g ŋ]. To produce these, we use a different part of the tongue, the **body** or **dorsum**, which is brought against the velum as illustrated for [ŋ] in figure 8. These sounds are known as **velars** and the descriptions we have introduced here give us the **place of articulation** of the sound.

A place of articulation usually involves two types of articulator. One is a passive structure such as the alveolar ridge or the teeth; the other is the active articulator which is moved. For the alveolar, dental and velar sounds described above, the active articulator is part of the tongue. For bilabial sounds, we have an odd situation in which both lips can be regarded as simultaneously the active and passive articulators.

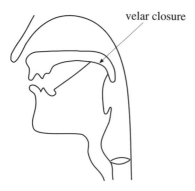

Figure 8 *Cross-section of the vocal tract, illustrating the articulation of [ŋ]*

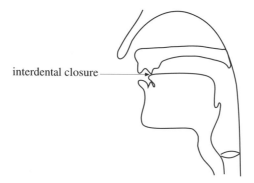

Figure 9 *Cross-section of the vocal tract, illustrating the articulation of interdental sounds*

So far, in our discussion of place of articulation, we have mentioned only plosives. Turning now to fricatives, [s z] have the same place of articulation as [t d]; thus [s] is an alveolar fricative, whereas [t] is an alveolar plosive. The sounds [θ ð] are made by bringing the blade of the tongue against the upper teeth or even between the teeth (so that the tongue tip protrudes slightly). These sounds are therefore dentals, although they are sometimes also called **interdentals** (figure 9). As already noted, the production of [f] (and [v]) involves moving the lower lip into close proximity with the upper teeth. These are therefore known as **labiodental** sounds (figure 10).

Before considering [ʃ ʒ], let's briefly look at [j], one of the sounds in the group we set aside above. The production of this sound involves raising the tongue blade towards the roof of the mouth (although not far enough to

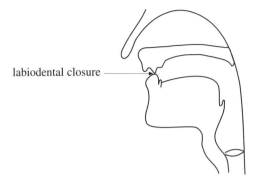

Figure 10 *Cross-section of the vocal tract, illustrating the articulation of labiodental sounds*

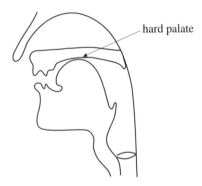

Figure 11 *Cross-section of the vocal tract, illustrating the articulation of [j]*

produce friction, see below). The roof of the mouth is called the **palate** (sometimes **hard palate**), and for this reason [j] is called a **palatal** sound (figure 11). Now, for [ʃ ʒ], we bring the tongue blade forward from the palate but not as far forward as for an alveolar sound. The place of articulation for [ʃ ʒ] is midway between the places of articulation for palatals and alveolars, and for this reason [ʃ ʒ] are referred to as **palato-alveolar** or **alveopalatal** fricatives. The affricates [ʧ ʤ] are made in the same place (figure 12).

There is one English fricative with which we have not yet dealt, [h]. Formation of this sound does not involve the tongue or lips; rather it is made simply by passing air through the vocal cords. The part of the larynx containing the vocal cords is called the **glottis**, so we often refer to [h] as a **glottal** fricative. Equally, since it is made in the larynx, we may call it a **laryngeal** fricative.

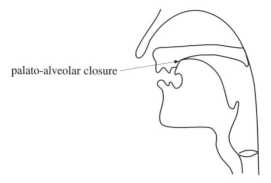

palato-alveolar closure

Figure 12 *Cross-section of the vocal tract, illustrating the articulation of palato-alveolar sounds*

We can now return to [l ɹ w j]. Above, we have noted that while [j] is palatal, its articulation does not involve moving the blade of the tongue sufficiently close to the hard palate to produce friction. Therefore, it is not a fricative, and it is necessary to recognise another manner of articulation. For each of the sounds in the set [l ɹ w j], the distance between the active and passive articulators is insufficient to cause friction, and such sounds are referred to as **approximants**. Thus, we can refer to [j] as a palatal approximant. Next, consider [w]. Production of this sound involves bringing the lips together, but again not close enough to cause complete closure or friction; it is a bilabial approximant. With the two remaining sounds, there are additional factors to take into account, although it remains convenient to continue to refer to them as approximants. Take [l] first. This is produced by placing the tongue tip against the alveolar ridge. However, unlike in the case of [t d], we do not create a *complete* obstruction; rather, we give the air an escape hatch by allowing it to pass around one side of the tongue. For this reason, [l] is called a **lateral** sound. The [ɹ] sound is produced by curling the tip of the tongue towards the alveolar ridge (or sometimes as far back as the hard palate), but again without getting close enough to cause an obstruction or create a frictional air flow. Sounds made by curling the tongue tip in this way are called **retroflex**. In fact, there is considerable variation in the way that 'r' type sounds are pronounced in English (as in many other languages). Thus, in many dialects we have a trilled 'r' [r], in which the tongue tip is brought near to the alveolar ridge and is caused to flap rapidly against it several times by air passing through the centre of the mouth. Traditionally, the sounds [l ɹ] are often referred to as **liquids** with [w j] being called **glides**. We will see an interesting connection between glides and vowels presently.

There is one final distinction we need before our description of English consonants is complete. We need to understand what distinguishes [p] from [b], [t] from [d], [s] from [z], [θ] from [ð], etc. Taking [p] and [b], we have seen that both of these are bilabial plosives, but they are different sounds. So, what is the nature of the difference between them? The answer to this question is most easily grasped for a pair of fricatives such as [s z]. Try saying these sounds one after the other and you will notice that the difference between them is that for [s] the vocal cords are not vibrating (the effect is stronger if you put your fingers in your ears). In other words, [s] doesn't seem to require any sound source. This may seem rather odd, until we realise that as a fricative [s] produces its own frictional noise. To produce [z] however, vocal cord vibration is also necessary. This gives rise to a difference in **voicing**, with sounds such as [b v ð z] being **voiced** while [p f θ s] are **unvoiced**. All the English nasals and approximants are normally voiced.

The three attributes of voicing, place of articulation and manner of articulation provide a convenient **three-term description** for many sounds. Thus, [dʒ] is a voiced palato-alveolar affricate, [f] is a voiceless labiodental fricative, [ŋ] is a voiced velar nasal and so on. However, for [l ɹ] we need a slightly more detailed description: [l] is a voiced alveolar lateral approximant and [ɹ] is a voiced alveolar non-lateral or retroflex approximant. All these sounds and a number of others are shown in the IPA chart reproduced in appendix 1. It is also convenient to use more general terms for some groupings of sounds. Thus, the bilabial and labiodental sounds all involve the lips, so these are called **labials**. The dentals, alveolars, palato-alveolars and palatals all involve the tip or the blade of the tongue (i.e. the front part of the tongue, which excludes the dorsum). These sounds are all **coronals,** while the sounds which involve the dorsum are **dorsals**. In addition, it is useful to distinguish the plosives, affricates and fricatives, which usually come in voiced/voiceless pairs from the nasals and approximants, which are intrinsically voiced. The former are called **obstruents** (because their production obstructs the airflow) and the latter are called **sonorants** (because they involve a greater degree of resonance).

While the sounds in table 1 are standardly regarded as the English consonants, there are a number of other consonantal sounds that are important in understanding the way English is pronounced. Consider the final sound of *cat* when the word is spoken in a relaxed and unemphatic manner. In many dialects, this is pronounced without any intervention of the tongue, and comes out as a 'catch' in the larynx. This is formed by bringing together the vocal cords, building up pressure behind them as for a plosive and then releasing the vocal cords. The result is, in fact, a plosive but one produced at the glottis, hence its name **glottal plosive** (or, more commonly, **glottal stop**) [ʔ]. This sound is a very common replacement for certain occurrences of [t] in many British dialects, most famously in London Cockney where *cat* and *butter* would be pronounced [kaʔ] and [bʌʔə] – we shall come to the vowel sounds appearing here shortly.

The [t] in words such as *butter* is, in fact, subject to further variation. For instance, in many varieties of American English, it is pronounced a bit like a 'd'. More precisely, the sound in question is a little shorter than [d] and is produced by very quickly flapping the tip of the tongue against the alveolar ridge (or the front of the hard palate). Such a sound is called a **flap** (or a **tap**) and its IPA symbol is [ɾ].

Finally, we must mention an important aspect of English pronunciation which is quite hard to discern. If you listen carefully to the pronunciation of 'p' in *pit* and *spit*, you should be able to hear that the 'p' of *pit* is followed by a puff of breath which is absent in *spit*. This puff of breath is called **aspiration**, and you can detect it by holding your hand in front of your mouth as you say the words. The same difference is observed in the 't' of *tar/star* and the 'k' of *car/scar*; 't' and 'k' are aspirated in *tar* and *car* but not in *star* and *scar*. We transcribe aspiration by means of a raised 'h': [pʰ tʰ kʰ]. If we wish to make it clear that a given sound is unaspirated, we use a raised 'equals' sign, as in [p= t= k=], though when there is no possibility of confusion, it is customary to omit this. Transcriptions for *pit* and *spit* including this difference in aspiration are thus [pʰɪt] and [sp=ɪt]. In transcriptions, additional symbols such as the raised 'h' or 'equals', added to a basic symbol to create another symbol for a related sound are called **diacritics**. There are a good many diacritics used by phoneticians (see the IPA chart on page 137 for additional examples).

So far, we have restricted our attention to English consonants, but of course other languages use additional consonantal sounds. In table 2, we see the English consonants from table 1 along with various other IPA symbols for sounds which occur in other languages:

Table 2: Consonantal sounds arranged by place and manner of articulation

MANNER	bilabial	labio-dental	alveolar	palato-velar	palatal	retroflex	velar	uvular	pharyngeal
plosive	p b		t d		c	ʈ ɖ	k g	q ɢ	
fricative	ɸ β	f v	s z	ʃ ʒ	ç j	ʂ ʐ	x ɣ	χ ʀ	ħ ʕ
affricate				ʧ ʤ		ʈʂ ɖʐ			
nasal	m	ɱ	n		ɲ	ɳ	ŋ	ɴ	
liquid			l r		ʎ	ɭ ɻ		ʁ	
glide	w	ʋ			j	ɥ			

As we can see, it is possible to fill a good many of the cells in table 2 with symbols representing sounds in the world's languages. Without special training, you won't be able to pronounce many of these sounds, but you should have some idea of how they are produced. For instance, a retroflex 'l' [ɭ] is made in the same place as the English retroflex [ɹ] but with the lateral manner of articulation characteristic of [l]. Retroflex sounds are found in a large number of languages of the Indian subcontinent and in Australia amongst other places. Uvular and pharyngeal sounds are made with places of articulation not found in English. Uvular sounds are like velars except that the tongue body moves further back and a little lower to articulate against the uvula. Pharyngeal sounds are common in Arabic (although they are encountered in languages throughout the world). They are made by bringing the tongue root back towards the back of the throat, often with constriction of the throat (*exercises 1 and 2*).

Vowels

Having considered consonants, we now turn to vowels. Here the description is a little more complex because the dialects of a language tend to differ most in their vowel sounds, and this is certainly true for English. Indeed, even within one country where English is spoken such as Britain, the US or Australia, there are considerable differences in vowel sounds. We will present a description of the basic system found in standard British English, making some observations about other varieties, most notably General American, as we proceed. You may find that your own pronunciation differs in interesting ways from what follows.

First, we will introduce some symbols used for transcribing English vowels, then we will ask how the vowels are produced. We'll start with the vowels appearing, with their accompanying transcriptions, in the words in (17) (the reason for the words being arranged in this way will soon become apparent):

(17)   pit   put
        [pɪt]   [pʊt]
                pet   pitta   putt
                [pɛt]   [pɪtə]   [pʌt]
                        pat   pot
                        [pæt]   [pɒt]

We will refer to these vowels as **short vowels**. The final vowel in *pitta* [ə], which is also found as the first vowel in a word like *apart*, is often called **schwa**.

How are these short vowels produced? There are two main articulators used in the production of vowel sounds, the tongue body and the lips. Of these, the tongue body is the more important. By pulling the body of the tongue *back* towards the velar region of the mouth, we get the vowels [ʊ ʌ ɒ]. These are **back vowels**. Alternatively, by raising the tongue body and pushing it *forward* to the palatal region (where we produce [j]), we get the vowels [ɪ ɛ æ]. These are **front vowels**. With the tongue body in an intermediate position on the front/back axis, we produce the **central vowel** [ə]. Another central vowel is [a], which is the usual pronunciation of the vowel in *pat* for many British speakers of English, the [æ] which appears in (17) being a feature of a conservative variety of British English, so-called Received Pronunciation (RP), and of General American. Now, as well as considering the position of the body of the tongue in terms of whether it is forward or backward in the mouth, we can also consider its *relative height*. The vowels [ɪ ʊ] are formed with the tongue body relatively high in the mouth and they are therefore called **high vowels**; for the **low vowels** [æ ɒ], the tongue body is relatively low, and for the **mid vowels** [ɛ ə ʌ] it is in an intermediate position on the high/low axis. We can represent these positions in a quadrilateral, as in figure 13:

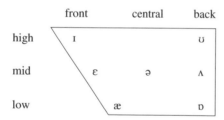

Figure 13 *The vowel quadrilateral (including only short vowels)*

Figure 13 is based entirely on the position of the body of the tongue, but there is an important difference between the sounds [ʊ ɒ] and all the others in this figure. They are accompanied by a **rounding** of the lips, whereas [ɪ ɛ æ ə ʌ] are all made without such lip rounding, and as noted above the lips are the second articulator involved in the production of vowels. In most English dialects, there are no sounds which are distinguished by lip rounding and nothing else, but there are many languages in which this is not the case. We shall return to this presently.

The next set of vowels to consider appears with accompanying transcriptions in the words in (18):

(18)   me   **moo**
        [miː]   [muː]

                mare   myrrh   more
                [mɛː]   [məː]   [mɔː]

                            mar
                            [mɑː]

One thing to immediately note about these transcriptions is that there is nothing corresponding to the 'r' in *mare*, *myrrh*, *more* and *mar*. In fact, for a good many speakers of British, Australian or New Zealand English, such occurrences of 'r' are *not* pronounced, although this is not the case for most speakers of North American English and some speakers of British English. Dialects in which the 'r' is pronounced are called **rhotic** dialects; those in which it is not are **non-rhotic**. We shall ignore this 'r'-colouring or rhoticity for now, adopting the transcriptions in (18) (but see below).

The vowels in (18) are different from those in (17) in two ways. Firstly, they are *longer*, a difference in **quantity**. Secondly, most of them differ in **quality**, with the tongue adopting a slightly different position for the vowels in, for example, *pit* and *me*. In some languages, such as Czech, Japanese or Yoruba, vowels can differ purely in length without any concomitant change in quality. In English, however, this is not always the case. The IPA symbol for 'long vowel' is ː placed after the vowel symbol, and adding the long vowels to our vowel quadrilateral we get figure 14. This figure also shows the British English [a] vowel mentioned above:

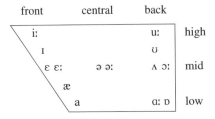

Figure 14 *The vowel quadrilateral (with long vowels)*

In figure 14 we can also see that different symbols have been used for some pairs of short and long vowels. For instance, the long 'i' vowel is written with the symbol [iː] not [ɪː] and the long 'a' vowel is written [ɑː] rather than [ɒː]. These differences correspond to differences in the sound of the vowel itself irrespective of its length – they signal differences in vowel quality. A further distinction which it is useful to make is that between short [i u] vowels (not represented in figure 14) and short [ɪ ʊ] vowels. The [i u] vowels are made with a 'tenser' articulation than are [ɪ ʊ], i.e. the position of the tongue is further from its rest or neutral position for the former pair of vowels. Because of this, we call [i u] **tense** vowels and [ɪ ʊ] **lax** vowels.

Each of the vowels we have considered up to now has a single constant quality. This is not so for the vowels in the words in (19):

(19)   bay   buy   **bough**   [rain]**bow**   **boy**
        [beɪ]   [baɪ]   [baʊ]   [bou]   [bɔɪ]

In each of these words, the vowel starts off with one quality and changes to a different quality. This is indicated in the transcriptions in (19), each of which includes two vowel symbols. Furthermore, the transcriptions for *bay* [beɪ] and *bow* [bou] include two symbols, [e o], which though familiar from English orthography, have not yet been introduced as IPA symbols. These are similar to the [ɛ ɔ] vowels but are slightly higher and tenser. We describe this difference by saying that [e o] are **mid closed** vowels while [ɛ ɔ] are **mid open** vowels. Alternatively, linguists often refer to [e o] as tense (mid) vowels and [ɛ ɔ] as lax (mid) vowels. Thus, we can contrast the set of tense vowels [i e u o] with the set of lax vowels [ɪ ʊ ɛ ɔ]. We can represent the position of these new vowels in the quadrilateral in figure 15 (note that we do not represent vowel length in this quadrilateral):

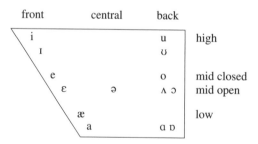

Figure 15 *The vowel quadrilateral, including mid closed vowels*

Where a vowel consists of two components like in the examples in (19), it is called a **diphthong** (from the Greek meaning 'two sounds'). The single, pure vowels in (17) and (18) are then called **monophthongs**. Some varieties of English are particularly rich in diphthongs, and diphthongs are also very common in totally unrelated languages such as Cambodian and Estonian. However, some languages lack true diphthongs altogether (e.g. Russian, Hungarian, Japanese).

Finally we come to another set of English diphthongs, mainly found in non-rhotic dialects. They are illustrated by the words in (20):

(20)   peer   poor
        [pɪə]   [pʊə]

For many speakers words such as *pear/pair* and *mare* would belong here – note that in (18) we have regarded *mare* as containing a pure vowel – and would be transcribed [peə] or [pɛə] and [meə] or [mɛə], respectively. In figure 16 we have shown the 'trajectory' involved in the formation of each of the diphthongs we have introduced (*exercise 3*):

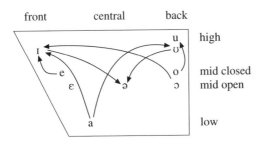

Figure 16 *The diphthongs of English*

The description of vowels we have offered so far is sufficient for many varieties of English. However, some dialects use different vowel sounds. For instance, in conservative RP you might hear *go* pronounced as [gəʊ]; and for many US speakers some of these diphthongs are long monophthongs (e.g. *day* [deː]). It should be noted that lip rounding, which was observed above as a feature of the English vowels [ʊ ɒ], is also a characteristic of [u o ɔ]. The vowel quadrilaterals we have examined do *not* explicitly indicate whether a vowel is accompanied by rounding or not.

There is one final feature of the transcription of English vowel sounds worth mentioning here. As already observed, unlike many varieties of British English, most dialects of American English have vowels with an 'r'-colouring to them, as in *bird, fear, card, more, air, murder*. It is produced by retracting the tongue as if to produce the sound [ɹ] as in *run* during the production of the vowel sound. Where greater accuracy isn't essential, it is often transcribed by just adding [r] after the vowel, e.g. *murder* [mərdər]. However, where we need more precise transcriptions, we use special symbols such as [ɚ ɛ˞]. Thus, we can transcribe *murder* as [mɚdɚ] and *air* as [ɛ˞ː]. The little hook on [ɚ] and [ɛ˞] can be thought of as a diacritic.

We conclude this survey of basic sounds by briefly looking at vowel sounds which do not occur in standard varieties of English. Focusing on lip-rounding, there is a strong tendency in the world's languages for back vowels which are not low to be rounded and for front vowels and low vowels to be unrounded. However, we do find vowels which are exceptions to this tendency, and some of the more common correspondences are shown in (21):

(21)

	front		back	
unrounded	rounded	rounded	unrounded
i	y	u	ɯ
ɪ	ʏ		
e	ø	o	ɣ
ɛ	œ	ɔ	ʌ
		ɒ	ɑ

Thus, [y ʏ ø œ] sound like [i ɪ e ɛ] except that in producing them, the lips are rounded. On the other hand, the sounds [ɯ ɣ] correspond to [u o] but are produced with spread lips.

With two exceptions, all the vowels discussed so far have been placed close to the right or left edge of the vowel quadrilateral, and generally with a little practice, we can feel confident about locating such vowels. However, we observed that the sound schwa [ə] and the vowel [a] occupy a central position on the front/back axis, and vowels such as these are generally less easy to be sure about. From this, it does not follow that such vowels do not exist, and a number of central vowels are shown in figure 17 along with the rounded and unrounded vowels from (21):

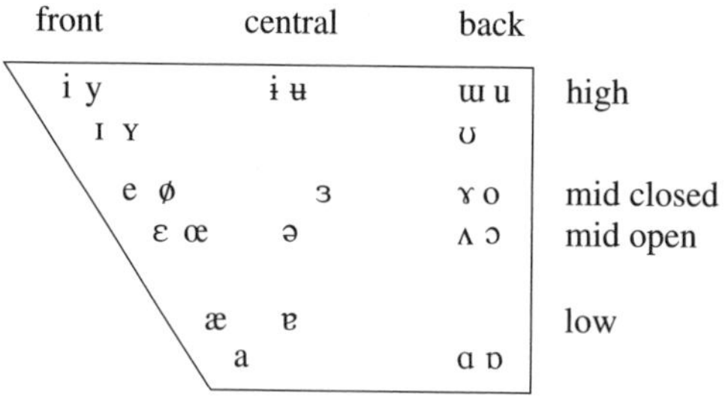

Figure 17 *The vowel quadrilateral, including central vowels*

The four new vowels in figure 17 [ɨ ʉ ɜ ɐ], are all unrounded except for [ʉ], a central high rounded vowel.

Finally, it should be noted that the 'r'-colouring of American vowels mentioned above is not the only sort of colouring which vowels can undergo. Another colouring which vowels often receive is **nasalisation**. This is the result of allowing air to pass through the nasal passage, as though for a nasal consonant such as [n], while still letting the air flow through the mouth. A nasal vowel is indicated by a diacritic symbol placed over the vowel, e.g. [õ, ɛ̃, ã]. In languages such as French, Polish, Yoruba (one of the main languages of Nigeria) and many others, nasal vowels play an important role. Here are some words of Yoruba in transcription:

(22)   oral vowels   nasal vowels

    [ka] 'to be placed on'   [kã] 'to touch'
    [ku] 'to remain'   [kũ] 'to apply paint'
    [si] 'and'   [sĩ] 'to accompany'

Nasal vowels are also heard in many varieties of English. A typical pronunciation of the word *can't*, in American English especially, is, in fact, [kæ̃ːt], with the sequence [æn] being replaced by a long nasalised vowel (*exercises 4, 5 and 6*).

Suprasegmentals

So far in this section we have examined **segments**, that is, individual sounds and their pronunciations. However, pronunciation involves far more than just stringing together individual sounds. We shall now examine the level of organisation which exists above the level of the segment, the **suprasegmental level**.

All words can be divided into one or more **syllables**. Although most of us can easily recognise syllables (including small children, see section 6), it is rather difficult to give a strict definition of the term. One way of determining the number of syllables in a word is to try singing it; each syllable is sung on a separate note (though not necessarily on a different pitch, of course). We shall be considering the structure of syllables in detail in section 5; here we will just consider their basic shape.

A syllable typically contains a consonant or set of consonants followed by a vowel followed by another consonant or set of consonants, e.g. *cat* [kæt] or *springs* [spɹɪŋz]. A string of more than one consonant such as [spr] or [ŋz] is called a **cluster** (or more precisely a **consonant cluster**). However, either set of consonants may be missing from a syllable as, for example, in *spray* [spɹeɪ] (no final consonant), *imps* [ɪmps] (no initial consonants) or *eye* [aɪ] (no consonants at all). Words with one syllable (*springs, cat*) are **monosyllabic**, while words with more than one syllable are **polysyllabic**. From this, we might conclude that the only obligatory part of a syllable is the vowel, but this is not quite correct. What a syllable must have is a **nucleus** or **peak**, and characteristically this is a vowel. However, in restricted cases, it is possible for the nucleus of a syllable to be a consonant. For instance, the word *table* is disyllabic (has two syllables), containing the syllables [teɪ] and [bl̩]. There is no vowel in the second syllable, and its nucleus is the consonant [l̩], a **syllabic consonant**. In transcription we represent a syllabic consonant by a mark placed beneath it: [l̩]. In English [m n] can also be syllabic, as in *bottom* [bɒtm̩] and *button* [bʌtn̩]. It is sometimes useful to mark the division between syllables in transcription. This is done by placing a dot between syllables, e.g. *polysyllabic* [pɒ.lɪ.sɪ.la.bɪk]

Next we consider the devices involving changes in loudness or the pitch of sounds that languages use to convey meaning. These are stress, tone and intonation, which collectively are called **prosodic** phenomena. We begin with stress.

If we compare the words *transport* in *means of transport* and *to transport goods* we can hear an important difference in pronunciation. In *means of transport* the first syllable, *tran-*, gets greater emphasis than the second, *-sport*, while in *to transport goods* it's the second which gets the greater emphasis. This emphasis is called **stress**, and we say that in *means of TRANsport* the first syllable bears stress, while in *to tranSPORT* the second syllable is stressed. The other syllable remains unstressed. Physically, a stressed syllable tends to be louder and often a little longer than an unstressed one. In the official IPA system stress is indicated by means of the sign ' placed before the stressed syllable: ['transpɔːt] TRANsport (noun) vs. [tran'spɔːt] tranSPORT (verb). However, many linguists prefer to indicate main stress by means of an acute accent over the stressed vowel: [tránspɔːt] (noun) vs. [transpɔ́ːt] (verb).

Some syllables have a degree of stress intermediate between full stress and no stress. Consider the word *photographic*. The main stress falls on the third syllable in [fou.tə.gra.fɪk]. The second and fourth syllables are unstressed. However, the first syllable has some stress, though not as much as the third. This is called **secondary stress**. In IPA it is transcribed with the mark ˌ : [ˌfoutə'grafɪk]. An alternative is to indicate secondary stress by a grave accent placed over the vowel: [fòutəgráfɪk].

The type of stress which distinguishes words such as ['transpɔːt] from [trans'pɔːt] is known as **lexical stress** or **word stress**. There is another type of stress in which certain words within phrases are given more emphasis than others. Consider (23):

(23)   Tom builds houses.

In a neutral pronunciation each word receives an even amount of emphasis, though slightly more falls on the stressed syllable of *houses*: *Tom builds HOUSes*. This is a natural answer to a question such as 'What does Tom do?' or 'What does Tom build?' However, if we put more emphasis on *builds* to get *Tom BUILDS houses*, then this can only be a natural answer to a question like 'What does Tom do with houses?', or more likely a correction to someone who thinks that Tom repairs houses or sells them. Finally, in *TOM builds houses* we have a reply to the question 'Who builds houses?' This type of stress is often called **phrasal stress**. (Many linguists also refer to it as **accent**, though this mustn't be confused with the term 'accent' meaning the particular type of pronunciation associated with a given dialect.) It can often be important in disambiguating sentences which are ambiguous in the purely written form (*exercise 7*).

Turning to our second prosodic phenomenon, the pitch of the voice is very important in language, and all languages make use of it for some purpose. In some languages different words are distinguished from each other by means of pitch. Here are some more Yoruba words:

(24)   high tone   mid tone   low tone

        tí   'that, which'   ti   'property of'   tì   'to push'
        ʃé   'isn't it?' etc. ʃe   'to do'   ʃè   'to offend'
        ɔkɔ́ 'hoe'   ɔkɔ 'husband'   ɔkɔ̀ 'canoe'

The word *tí* with the mark ′ over the vowel is pronounced at a higher pitch than the word *ti*, which in turn is pronounced at a higher pitch than *tì*. These different pitches are called **tones**. We say that *tí* has **high tone**, *ti* has **mid tone** and *tì* has **low tone**. Notice that one of the systems for transcribing stress uses the same symbols for primary and secondary stress as are used here for high and low tone. In most cases this doesn't cause any confusion, though languages do exist which have both independent tone and independent stress. In such cases, we can use the IPA symbols for stress and use the grave and acute accents for tone.

Some languages distinguish only two levels of tone, while others distinguish up to four levels. When a language distinguishes words from each other using pitch in this way we say that it has **lexical tone**.

The words *stvari* 'things' and *stvari* '(in) a thing' in Serbo-Croatian are distinguished by tone, though in a different way from the Yoruba examples we have just described. In the word meaning 'things' the pitch falls from high to low during the course of the vowel [a], while in the word meaning '(in) a thing' the pitch rises from low to high on that vowel. Tones of this sort, where the pitch changes during the course of the syllable are called **contour tones**, as opposed to the tones of Yoruba which are called **level tones**. In some languages we get more complex contour tones in which the tone first rises then falls or vice versa. The classic example is Mandarin Chinese. In (25) we see four words which are distinguished solely by their tones, with the broken lines indicating pitch and the unbroken lines being reference pitches (the words appear in the standard Pinyin transcription, the official romanisation of the language in the People's Republic of China, and correspond to IPA [ji]):

(25)   word   meaning   tone

        yī   'one'   high level

        yí   'lose'   rising

        yǐ   'already'   falling-rising

        yì   'idea'   falling

Both level tones and contour tones qualify a language as having lexical tone, i.e. as being a **tone language**. English is not a tone language, but, like all spoken languages, it uses pitch extensively. The uses of pitch with which we are familiar in English are uses of our final prosodic phenomenon, intonation. Consider the instances of the word *me* in (26), where the pitch is represented graphically:

(26)   a.   b.   c.   d.   e.
        me   me?   me!   me   me?!

The pitches applied to these words are very similar to the contour tones of languages like Chinese. However, in English such changes do not produce completely different meanings; each of (26a) to (26e) involves a reference to the speaker, but by changing the 'tone' over the word the speaker changes the *attitude* he or she is expressing. Thus, we move from a simple statement (26a) to a question (26b), to a strong assertion (26c), to a matter of fact assertion (26d) and in (26e) to an expression of disbelief. Unlike in Chinese, however, these tones cannot be regarded as an inherent part of a single word. If the utterance consists of more than one syllable, as in (27), then we find the tone is spread over the whole of that utterance, and gives rise to the same range of attitudes as we saw in (26):

(27)   a.   b.   c.   d.   e.

eat peas   eat peas?   eat peas!   eat peas   eat peas?!

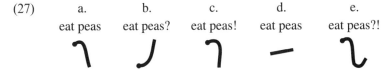

As observed already, all spoken languages make use of **intonation** (including those like Chinese, Serbo-Croatian or Yoruba that have lexical tone), though the exact use differs greatly from one language to another and from one dialect to another. Knowing intonation patterns is an important though often neglected part of speaking a foreign language and many intonation patterns which sound polite in one language or dialect sound rude or funny in another. It is said that the British regard Americans as rude and pushy in part because neutral, polite American intonation sounds peremptory to a British speaker, while Americans often feel that Britons are overweening or fawning because what is neutral for British intonation sounds over the top to the American ear.

This section has provided a basic description of the sounds of language. In the next section we'll see how different varieties of one and the same language can be distinguished by the types of sounds they use and the ways in which they use them.

Exercises

1.   Using the IPA chart give a description of the following sounds:

ɣ ɮ ɸ ʐ χ ɳ ç tɕ ɦ

For instance for [p] we would say 'voiceless bilabial plosive'.

2.   Give the IPA symbol for each of the following consonants:

(a) voiced uvular nasal stop
(b) alveolar implosive stop
(c) voiced retroflex lateral approximant
(d) voiceless palatal affricate
(e) voiced labiodental nasal stop

3.   This is a text in IPA transcription of a short passage as it would be spoken by a speaker with a British accent. Rewrite this in ordinary orthography.

ðə nɔ:θ wind ənd ðə sʌn wə dɪspjuːtɪŋ wɪtʃ wəz ðə stɹɒŋɡə, wɛn ə tɹavlə keim əlɒŋ ɹapt ɪn ə wɔːm klouk. ðeɪ əɡɹiːd ðət ðə wɒn huː fəːst səksiːdəd ɪn meɪkɪŋ ðə travlə teɪk hɪz klouk ɒf ʃʊd bɪ kənsɪdəd stɹɒŋɡə ðən ðɪ ʌðə. ðɛn ðə nɔ:θ wind bluː əz haːd əz hiː kʊd, bʌt ðə mɔː hɪ bluː ðə mɔː klouslɪ dɪd ðə travlə fould hɪz klouk əɹaund hɪm; ənd ət laːst ðə nɔːθ wind ɡeɪv ʌp ðɪ ətɛmpt. ðɛn ðə sʌn ʃɒn aut wɔːmlɪ, ənd ɪmiːdjətlɪ ðə tɹavlə tʊk ɒf hɪz klouk. ənd sou ðə nɔ:θ wind wəz əblaɪdʒd tə kənfɛs ðət ðə sʌn wɛz ðə stɹɒŋɡəɹ əv ðə tuː.

4.   Using the IPA chart give a description of the following vowels:

œ ɯ ʌ ə ɐ a y ʉ ɜ œ ɨ

For instance, for [e] we would say 'mid closed front unrounded' or 'tense mid front unrounded'.

5.   Give the IPA symbol for each of the following vowels:

(a) high tense back rounded
(b) open (lax) mid front rounded
(c) central mid unrounded
(d) central low unrounded
(e) high tense front rounded
(f) high lax back rounded

6.   The following is a text transcribed as it might be read by a British speaker and an American speaker. Rewrite the text in orthography and then comment on the differences in the two accents.

British version

jouhan səbastɪən baːk sɪkstiːn eɪtɪ faɪv tʊ sɛvntiːn fɪftɪ keɪm frəm ə famlɪ wɪtʃ pɹədʒuːst ouvə naɪntɪ pɹəfɛʃnl mjuːzɪʃnz baːks autpʊt wez ɪmens kʌvɹɪŋ nɪəlɪ ɔːl ðə meɪdʒə mjuːzɪkl ʒɒnɹəz əv hɪz ɪəɹə tʃeɪmbə wəːks ɔːkestɹəl swiːts n kntʃeːtouz piːsəz fə haːpsɪkɔːd nd ɔːɡən ənd ən ɪnɔːməs əmaunt əv kɔːɹəl mjuːzɪk fə ðə tʃəːtʃ ðiːounlɪ taɪp əv wəːk hiː dɪdnt kəmpouz wəz ɒpɹə ðou sʌm wʊd seɪ ðət hɪz mədʒɛstɪk sɛtɪŋ əv ðə snt maθjuː paʃn ɪz ɪn fakt wɒn əv ðə ɡreɪtɪst maːstəpiːsəz əv ɔːl ɑpəɹatɪk lɪtɹətʃə

American version

jouhæn səbæstɪən bɑːk sɪkstiːn eɪɾɪ faɪv tə sevntiːn fɪfɾɪ keɪm frəm ə fæmlɪ wɪʧ pɹəduːst ouvɚ naɪnɾɪ pɹəfeʃnl mjuːzɪʃnz bɑːks aʊtpʊt wəz ɪmens kʌvɹɪŋ nɪɛˑlɪ ɔːl ðə meɪʤɚ mjuːzɪkl ʒanɹəz əv hɪz ɛɹə ʧeɪmbɚ wɚks, ɚkestɹəl swiːts n knʧɛˑɾouz piːsəz fɚ hɑˑpsɪkɚd nd ɚgən ənd ən ɪnɚməs əmaunɾ əv kɔɹəl mjuːzɪk fɚ ðə ʧɚʧ ðɪ ounlɪ taɪp əv wɚk hɪ dɪdnt kampouz wəz apɹə, ðou sʌm wʊd seɪ ðət hɪz məʤestɪk sɛɾɪŋ əv ðə snt mæθjuː pæʃn ɪz ɪn fækt wan əv ðə greɪɾəst mæstɚpiːsəz əv ɔːl apəɹæɾɪk lɪɾɹəʧə

7.   Transcribe the text below into IPA following your native accent as closely as you can, indicating lexical stress on polysyllabic items. Note that in some cases there might be several alternative ways of pronouncing a given sound or sound sequence.

For some, Britain and the United States are two countries divided by a common language, and the same could be said of other places where English is spoken, such as Canada, Australia, New Zealand or South Africa. Nonetheless, on the whole English speakers tend to communicate with each other somehow. Nor should we jump to the conclusion that it's just across national boundaries that accent and dialect differences occur. The differences in the speech of Americans from New England and those from the Deep South can be at least as great as the differences between New Englanders and British speakers, or between Australians and New Zealanders.

3   Sound variation

In our main introduction we observed that language varies across both time and space. If we compare the English spoken in the cities of Perth, Pittsburgh, Port Elizabeth and Plymouth, we can point not only to differences between these four cities, but also to historical differences which distinguish these varieties today from those spoken in these locations 150 years ago. This important study of historical and geographical variation has been a preoccupation of linguists for well over a century now, and continues to be a strong focus of research in dialectology and historical linguistics. It is only in recent times, however, that linguists have begun to investigate linguistic variation *within* communities. The French spoken in Marseilles may be different from that spoken in Montréal, but what about the use of language *within* these cities? Does everyone in Montréal speak an identical variety of French? Clearly not, we might suppose, but it was not until the 1960s that linguists began to take this view seriously and study variation within villages, towns and cities.

In this section we will examine **phonological variation** – the variability in language which affects those features which have been introduced in the previous section: sounds, syllables, stress and intonation. Because of the nature of existing research, our discussion will be concerned exclusively with sounds.

Linguistic variables and sociological variables

So what is phonological variation? A reasonable definition might be that it is the existence within the speech of a single community of more than one possible realisation (or **variant**) of a particular sound. A simple introductory example is the variable loss of the glottal fricative [h] in the northern English city of Bradford, with words like *hammer* being pronounced [hamə] or [amə]. Table 3 shows how often different social class groups in Bradford use the two different possibilities [h] or Ø (i.e. nothing):

Table 3: The omission of [h] in Bradford	
Social class	Percentage of the number of occurrences of [h] that were omitted, i.e. Ø
lower working class	93
middle working class	89
upper working class	67
lower middle class	28
middle middle class	12

We can see clearly in this table that there are class differences in the use of [h] – the higher someone's social class, the more likely they are to use [h]. This class difference is interesting, but more important is the fact that everybody in this Bradford research used *both* forms at least some of the time. Even the lower working class speakers occasionally used [h] and the middle middle class speakers sometimes omitted it. The variation within this community, then, is relative. Different groups use different *proportions* of the two variants, and this is typical of variation. *Absolute* differences, situations where one group within the community uses a particular form *all of the time* in contrast with other groups which *never* use that form, occur less frequently (***exercise 1***).

In order to describe this quantitative variation, linguists have devised the notion of the **linguistic variable**, an analytical construct which enables them to contrast people's use of different variants. A variable is a linguistic unit which has two or more variants that are used in different proportions either by different sections of the community or in different linguistic or contextual circumstances. Variables can be concerned with phonological factors, the topic of this section, and also with word structure, word meaning and syntax. For the example above, we say that the variable (h) – variables are normally put in round brackets – has two variants [h] and Ø, the use of which relates to a person's social class.

The procedure for analysing the use of a variable in a particular community is as follows:

(i)   recordings are made of conversational speech from people belonging to different groups in the community;

(ii)   researchers listen to these recordings, noting down the pronunciation of a representative number of instances of each variable. Normally, they analyse at least thirty examples of each variable for each person they record;

(iii) each person's relative use of the different variants is calculated. The results of this are often presented as percentages, showing that a particular speaker used x% of one variant and y% of the other;

(iv)   it is then possible to amalgamate these results to produce group scores. So, for example, the researcher may calculate an average of the scores of all the working class speakers and compare this figure with the averaged scores of middle class speakers.

We have seen for the example of (h) in Bradford that there appears to be a relationship between **social class** and language use. Such a relationship has been found in many westernised speech communities around the world – from Chicago to Copenhagen, from Brisbane to Berlin. Outside western societies, however, the notion of social class is less easy to apply. Most research of this type in non-western societies has used **education level** as a means to measure socio-economic divisions when correlating language use to social structure. An example is provided by the occurrence of *vowel assimilation* by Farsi (Persian) speakers in Teheran. Assimilation was briefly mentioned in the introduction (p. 5), and we can illustrate its role in Teheran Farsi using the Farsi verb meaning 'do'. The standard pronunciation of this verb is [bekon], but the vowel in the first syllable may assimilate to the second vowel, giving the variant [bokon]. Figure 18 shows that the *higher* the educational achievement of speakers, the *less* likely they are to assimilate vowels.

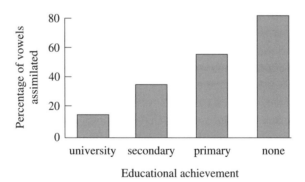

Figure 18 *Sound variation and speaker educational achievement: vowel assimilation in Teheran Farsi*

Whether we rely on social class or education, what appears common to all societies is that *social structure is reflected in linguistic structure* in some way. We should expect therefore that, besides the socio-economic characteristics of speakers, other social factors will also affect and structure linguistic variability.

This certainly appears to be the case if we consider the **gender** of the speaker.

The relationship between language variation and speaker gender is probably the most well studied in sociolinguistic research. One of the most consistent findings is that, all other things being equal, women use proportionately more standard variants than men. Again, examples can be found from many very different societies around the world and an illustration appears in figure 19, where we can see that women are using more of the standard variants: the General American standard [θ] as opposed to non-standard variants [f] or [t] or Ø (*exercise 2*).

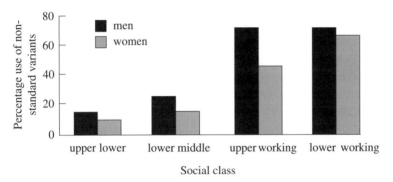

Figure 19 *Sound variation and speaker gender: the use of non-standard variants of (θ) in Detroit*

The **ethnic group** to which a speaker belongs has also been found to have an effect on language variation. In the data from Sydney presented in figure 20, the ethnic (Italian, Greek or 'Anglo', i.e. British-Irish) identity of Australians is seen to be relevant to the use of a non-standard [f] pronunciation of (θ) in words such as *think*, *thumb*, etc.

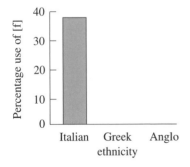

Figure 20 *Sound variation and speaker ethnicity: the use of [f] for (θ) among Italian, Greek and Anglo lower working class teenage boys in Sydney*

As is clear, whilst the Italian teenagers pronounce over a third of all their examples of (θ) as [f], the Greek and Anglo teenagers never did this. In Sydney at least, it seems that the use of [f] as a variant of (θ) is a marker of Italian ethnicity.

A final example of how social structure has been shown to determine a person's linguistic behaviour is of a different nature from the speaker-defined categories mentioned above. Linguists have established that the quantity and nature of a person's **social network links** within their community may be an important factor in such behaviour. Lesley and James Milroy, who carried out sociolinguistic research in the Northern Irish city of Belfast, measured network strength along two dimensions: firstly they assessed the extent to which people had close social ties with family, friends and work-mates in the neighbourhood, and secondly they looked at the extent to which these ties were multi-functional, e.g. if a tie to another network member was based on *both* friendship *and* employment, or *both* employment *and* kinship, as opposed to just one of these. People who had many multi-functional social ties were considered to have strong social networks and people who didn't were labelled as having weak networks. It was hypothesised that strong social networks would act as norm-enforcing mechanisms, subtly enforcing pressure on their members to conform to normal local behaviour, including linguistic behaviour. A number of variables which showed an intimate connection between a person's network strength and their use of local Belfast variants were discovered, and a small sample of the results of this research appear in table 4.

Table 4: (th) and (ʌ) in the speech of two Belfast residents		
	Percentage use of local Belfast variant of (th)	**Percentage use of local Belfast variant of (ʌ)**
Hannah	0	0
Paula	58	70
(th) – deletion of [ð] between vowels as in e.g. mother		
(ʌ) – use of [ʌ] in words such as *pull, took, foot*		

This table compares the use of two salient linguistic variables (th) and (ʌ) by Paula and Hannah, two residents of Belfast. They are both in unskilled jobs, have husbands with unskilled jobs and have a limited educational achievement. Yet their linguistic behaviour is radically different and the explanation for this appears to come from the differing strengths of their social networks. Paula is a member of a strong social network in Belfast – she has a large family living locally, she frequently visits her neighbours, many of whom she works with, and she belongs to a local bingo-playing club. Hannah, however, has fewer local ties. She has no family members in the locality, isn't a member of any local groups and works with people who do not live in her neighbourhood.

In summary, we have painted a picture of an intimate relationship between a number of **sociological variables** – social class, educational achievement, gender, ethnicity and social network – and a range of linguistic variables. It seems quite clear that our position in society can shape certain aspects of our linguistic behaviour. Linguistic variability is not divorced from social conditioning. We now turn to a different type of variation.

Stylistic variation

We are all probably conscious that we speak differently to a teacher than to our friends over a coffee. We tend on the whole to speak using a more standard dialect with the teacher, and use more non-standard or informal language when having a chat. Similarly, we may find that we speak in a more standard way when discussing some topics – say, politics or linguistics – than when discussing others – yesterday's baseball game, or your neighbour's latest antics. Linguistic variability which is dependent on the social context we find ourselves in or the topic of the conversation is usually termed **stylistic variation**. Allan Bell, a linguist from New Zealand, developed a model for the analysis of stylistic variation known as **audience design**. He claimed that in designing our style of speech at any particular time, we assess the sociolinguistic characteristics of our addressees and adapt the way we speak to conform to these characteristics.

Let's look at an example. Nik Coupland investigated the extent to which an assistant in a travel agency in Cardiff, Wales shifted her speech to match that of the social class of her clients. One of the variables he studied was the glottalisation of (t) – i.e. the use of [bʌʔə] instead of [bʌtə], and the results of this part of his study appear in figure 21. These results show how the assistant altered her use of this variable quite radically when speaking to clients of different social classes (*exercises 3 and 4*).

The model of audience design helps to explain why people seem, to a non-native ear, to 'pick up' the accent of places they stay in. A British or North American English speaker spending a couple of years in Australia would have a predominantly Australian English speaking audience, and would accommodate to that variety so often when conversing that, to non-Australians, they may 'sound like an Aussie'. What this indicates, then, is that variation in language is constrained not only by the social characteristics of the speaker, but

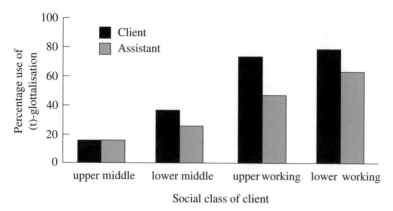

Figure 21 *Travel agency assistant's style shifting to clients: (t) glottalisation*

also those of the *addressee* in any conversation; variation is also **interactionally** determined.

Linguistically determined variation

We would be wrong to go on from the above to claim that it is *only* social factors which determine the structure of variation within a speech community. Linguistic factors, too, play a considerable role in determining the relative use of different variants of a variable. One variable which appears to behave in the same way across the English speaking world is so-called **consonant cluster deletion** or more specifically **-t/-d deletion**. This involves the variable deletion of word-final [t] or [d] when it follows another consonant. So we find examples such as those in (28), where the candidate for deletion appears in bold and the phonetic transcriptions give variant pronunciations depending on whether [t] or [d] delete:

(28)   **Data Set 1:**
    best friend   → [bɛst frɛnd] – [bɛs frɛnd]
    cold weather   → [koʊld wɛðə] – [koʊl wɛðə]

    Data Set 2:
    he stuffed the turkey → [hiː stʌft ðə tɜːkiː] – [hiː stʒʌf ðə tɜːkiː]
    she seemed funny   → [ʃiː siːmd fʌniː] – [ʃiː siːm fʌniː]

    Data Set 3:
    most of the time   → [moʊst əv ðə taɪm] – [moʊs ə ðə taɪm]
    ground attack   → [graʊnd ətæk] – [graʊn ətæk]

Data Set 4:

| *he seemed odd* | → | [hiː siːmd ɒd] – [hiː siːm ɒd] |
| *she passed a test* | → | [ʃiː pɑːst ə tɛst] – [ʃiː pɑːs ə tɛst] |

(Note that in these examples, we transcribe 'r' sounds as [r], a common practice unless more precision is needed.)

As you read this set of data, you will probably feel that the further you go down the sets, the less likely you would be to hear the *second* example in each phonetically transcribed pair, that is the example in which [t] or [d] is deleted. This is because in each set of data the word final [t] and [d] are in different *linguistic* contexts, and it is these contexts which are affecting whether or not deletion of [t] or [d] seems likely. In data sets 1 and 2, the [t] and [d] are followed by consonants, whereas in sets 3 and 4 they are followed by vowels. Research has shown that deletion is less likely before vowels than before consonants. In data sets 2 and 4, the [t] and [d] are the realisation of the past tense ending -*ed*, whereas they don't have this function in sets 1 and 3. We would expect, based on evidence from many English speaking communities around the world, to find less deletion in this context, since *phonetically* the [t] and [d] are the only indication of the tense of the verb. This means that linguistic factors (whether the candidate for deletion precedes a vowel or a consonant and whether it encodes past tense or not) predict most deletion in Data Set 1 and least in Data Set 4. Below is a table which provides evidence from a number of dialects of English to support this prediction.

Table 5: Deletion of [t] and [d] in English

	Followed by a consonant		Followed by a vowel	
Language Variety	Percentage deletion in non -*ed* clusters	Percentage deletion in -*ed* clusters	Percentage deletion in non -*ed* clusters	Percentage deletion in -*ed* clusters
Standard American English	66	36	12	3
White Working Class American English	67	23	19	3
Black Working Class American English	97	76	72	34
Puerto Rican Working Class English	93	78	63	23

In table 5 it is important to note that the ordering predicted on the basis of the linguistic factors is the same in each of the dialects investigated, despite the fact that there are quite considerable differences in the actual figures with the Puerto Rican speakers generally deleting final [t] and [d] much more frequently than speakers of Standard American English. What these differences show, of course, is that social factors as well as linguistic factors are playing a part in this variation.

The pattern that we see in table 5 illustrates what is known as an **implicational scale**. This notion is exemplified in a hypothetical case in table 6:

Table 6: A hypothetical implicational scale			
	easy to delete ←——————————————————————→ hard to delete		
Language Variety	**non -ed clusters followed by a consonant**	**-ed clusters followed by a consonant**	**non -ed clusters followed by a vowel**	**-ed clusters followed by a vowel**
Dialect A	+	+	+	+
Dialect B	+	+	+	−
Dialect C	+	+	−	−
Dialect D	+	−	−	−

Here '+' signifies that a particular deletion always takes place and '−' that it never takes place. Thus, in Dialect A, final [t] and [d] are always deleted, irrespective of linguistic context and in Dialect D they are always deleted when followed by a consonant so long as they do not encode tense – otherwise they are never deleted in Dialect D. Dialects B and C are intermediate between A and D. Now, we can look at table 6 and formulate the implicational statement in (29):

(29)   If a particular dialect deletes final [t] and [d] in a specific linguistic environment, then the same dialect will delete [t] and [d] in all environments that more readily allow for deletion.

In Dialect B, for instance, the most unlikely environment which allows consonant deletion is in non -ed clusters followed by a vowel. This implies that it is possible to delete consonants in *all environments to the left* of this one on the grid. In the actual study reported above, we do not find deletion occurring always or never in a particular environment; rather we see different frequencies of deletion. For such a case, then, it is necessary to replace (29) with the implicational statement in (30):

(30)   If a particular dialect deletes final [t] and [d] with a certain frequency in a specific linguistic environment, then it will delete final [t] and [d]

with a greater frequency in all environments that more readily allow for deletion.

The statement in (30) is true of table 5 because in each row the figures increase as we move from right to left (*exercise 5*).

To summarise, we can see that variability in language is not free and random, but is characterised by what William Labov has called 'structured heterogeneity' – a set of social, interactional and linguistic factors which have complex effects on the linguistic forms found within a speech community.

Variation and language change

Finally, here, we introduce the vital role that variation plays in language change, the subject of the next section. If a sound *changes* in a particular community, this implies the existence of *sound variation* as an intervening stage in the process of change. A change from an old form to a new one *necessarily involves a stage where both the old and new forms co-exist*, not only in the speech of the community as a whole, but also in the speech of individuals. You do not go to bed one night with an old sound and wake up the next morning with a new sound having completely replaced the old one! The co-existence of old and new forms leads, of course, to language variation.

In the introduction, we have already met aspects of William Labov's research into the use of (r) among the workers of three New York department stores. As noted in exercise 9 (pp. 21f.), Labov had observed that some New Yorkers were using [r] following vowels in words such as *car* and *park*. So *car* was changing from [kɑː] to [kɑr] and *park* from [pɑːk] to [pɑrk], etc. He proposed that the New York speech community was changing from being 'r'-less (or non-rhotic, see p. 41) to being 'r'-ful (rhotic), and in order to investigate how this change was spreading throughout the community, he followed the procedure described in exercise 9. Having posed his question, which required the answer 'fourth floor' to over 250 assistants, he was able to compare the use of (r) across a number of speaker characteristics, contextual styles and linguistic environments. These are set out in table 7.

As might be expected from our earlier discussion, Labov found that the different social, contextual and linguistic factors had varying effects on the use of (r). He found, for example, that assistants in Saks were more likely to use [r] than those in the other stores; [r] was more likely to be used in the emphatic second reply; and [r] was more likely in the word *floor* than in *fourth* (see introduction, figure 3, p. 22). Particularly important for our discussion of the role

Table 7: Social, contextual and linguistic variables from Labov's study of (r) in New York department stores

characteristics of the shop assistants

store (upper middle class, lower middle class, working class)

job within store (floorwalker, till operator, shelf filler, etc.)

floor within store (higher floors sell more expensive products)

sex

ethnicity

age

contextual characteristics

first reply given versus emphatic reply given after Labov had pretended not to hear

linguistic environment

(r) before a consonant versus (r) in word-final position

of variation in language change, however, is the fact that every stage in the advancing change to [r] could be found in the speech of some of the assistants. Some used virtually no [r] at all, others – who were obviously further ahead in the change – used [r] all the time, but most used it some of the time but not on every occasion. The study thus provided Labov with a convenient snap-shot of the progress of this change through the speech of individuals, particular groups and the whole New York speech community (*exercises 6 and 7*).

Exercises

1. If we are able to shift our speech so readily, why do you think that people continue to speak dialects with a low prestige?

2. Why do you think that, all other things being equal, women use more standard variants of variables than men?

3. In order to demonstrate the effects of audience design, Allan Bell collected data from a team of news readers who appear on two New Zealand radio stations, YA, a prestige, high-status channel, covering current affairs and political debate, and ZB, a lower-status, commercial, light entertainment station. YA had an audience largely made up of older, professional, well-educated listeners, whereas the audi-

ence of ZB was relatively younger, less well educated and had lower status jobs. He was interested in whether a particular news reader would speak differently on YA than on ZB. He investigated the amount of non-standard (t)-flapping used by the news readers on the two stations – for example, [bʌɾə] instead of [bʌtə] (*butter*). Figure 22 contains his findings for four news readers:

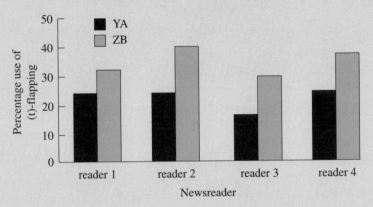

Figure 22 *(t)-flapping among news readers on two New Zealand radio stations.*

How would you explain Bell's findings? Are they what you would expect?

4.   In southern British English (as well as in almost all of the English-speaking world) there is variation in the use of (ing) in words such as *morning*, and *laughing*. The variants are [ɪŋ] – the standard variant – and [ɪn], a non-standard variant. In table 8 are the results of a study which investigated whether the *sex of the addressee* had an effect on which variant was used by one male informant.

Table 8: Percentage use of standard and non-standard variants of (ing) according to the sex of the addressee		
variant	male addressee	female addressee
[ɪŋ]	26%	72%
[ɪn]	74%	28%

How would you account for these findings?

5.   Construct an implicational scale for the following three dialects and their acceptance or rejection of (t)-glottalling in different linguistic environments. The asterisk marks an *unacceptable* form in a particular variety.

Dialect 1:

He went	[hiː wɛn?]
I built four	[aɪ bɪl? fɔː]
She hit Eddie	*[ʃiː hɪ? ɛdɪ]
Debbie likes butter	*[dɛbɪ laɪks bʌ?ə]

Dialect 2:

A letter came	*[ə lɛ?ə kæɪm]
They met Sue	[ðæɪmɛ? suː]
I sold my coat	[aɪ sɒuld maɪ kʌu?]
Get off!	[gɛ? ɒf]

Dialect 3:

The cat jumped	*[ðə kæ? dʒʌmpt]
I called Pat	[aɪ kɔːld pæ?]
You'd better come!	*[juːd bɛ?ə kʌm]
Matt and Dee	*[mæ? ən diː]

6.   Design a small linguistic survey appropriate for your own town or city similar to William Labov's department store research. Which variable would you study and why? What question(s) could you ask to ensure that you got a reply that contained your variable? Which groups in your local speech community would you study?

7.   Jack Chambers, a Canadian linguist, investigated the ability of Canadian children to acquire an English accent after their parents had moved to southern England. He studied the children's use of features which were markedly different in the two varieties of English, including:

(a) the pronunciation of [t] between vowels: In Canadian English intervocalic [t] (as in *butter*, *petal*) is pronounced as a flap [ɾ], whereas in southern British English it is either [t] or [?];

(b) whether or not the vowel in *Don* and *hot* is the same as in *Dawn* and *water*: In Canada, the vowels are the same [ɑ], in southern England they are not – *Don* has [ɒ] whereas *Dawn* has [ɔː].

Tables 9a and 9b below indicate the success of three children, aged nine, thirteen and fifteen, at 'losing' their Canadian forms and acquiring the southern British ones. How would you account for the age variation in their success?

Table 9a: Canadian children's acquisition of southern British English variants of (t)	
Age	Percentage acquisition of southern British variants of (t):
9	100
13	79
15	19

Table 9b: Canadian children's acquisition of the southern British contrast between *Don* and *Dawn*	
Age	Percentage acquisition of southern British *Don-Dawn* distinction
9	89
13	79
15	9

4   Sound change

Linguistic change is a process which appears to pervade all human languages. The extent of this change can be so radical that the intelligibility of former states of the language can be jeopardised. The language of Shakespeare causes some problems for the late twentieth-century reader, but these are not insurmountable. However, if we go further back to the writings of Chaucer, we are faced with a much more alien, less easily recognised form of English. If we observe language change on a much smaller time-scale, say, that of the average life span of a human being, comprehension difficulties such as those confronting the reader of Chaucer do not arise. Languages actually change quite slowly, and hence the ability to communicate successfully with all generations of speakers of our own language variety is maintained. In this section we will look at how the *sounds* of languages can change over time, both from a diachronic and synchronic perspective. Diachronic research on sound change has enabled us to chart changes which have taken place in earlier historical periods, while synchronic approaches allow us to observe language changes in progress today. In addition, we will examine sound change from the perspective of one of the principal problems of language change, namely, the *transition problem* – what is the route by which sounds change?

Consonant change

In section 2 we saw that *consonants* can be largely classified according to a simple *three-term description*:

(a)   voicing: do the vocal cords vibrate?
(b)   place of articulation: where is the flow of air obstructed?
(c)   manner of articulation: how is the flow of air obstructed?

Consonant changes often involve a shift in one or more of these terms. One example of a consonant changing from voiceless to voiced is the so-called **flapping** mentioned in section 2 (p. 38) as common in the English spoken in North America – it also occurs frequently in Australasia. It will be recalled that a flap involves tapping the tip of the tongue quickly against the alveolar ridge and it occurs when the 't' sound is surrounded by two vowels. From our point of view, the important thing is that a flap is voiced, whereas [t] is unvoiced, so here we have an instance where a voiceless sound has changed into a voiced sound, i.e. a change with respect to (a) above. Some examples from Australian English appear in (31):

(31) *litter*: [litɐ]   →   [liɾɐ]
      bitter: [bitɐ]   →   [biɾɐ]
      get off: [getɒf]   →   [geɾɒf]

(Note: [ɐ] is an unrounded central low vowel, somewhat lower than [ə], see figure 17.)

There are a number of place of articulation changes currently underway in southern British English. Each of these is a change with respect to (b). One well-known example is the change from [t] to [ʔ], as illustrated in (32):

(32) *butter*: [bʌtə]   →   [bʌʔə]
      plot: [plɒt]   →   [plɒʔ]

In this example, both the old and the new sounds are voiceless and have the same manner of articulation (they are both plosives). The place of articulation, however, has changed from being alveolar to glottal.

A second example is affecting [ɹ] when it occurs prevocalically. In these contexts, we often hear [ʋ] as in the examples in (33):

(33) *rob*:   [ɹɒb]   →   [ʋɒb]
      brown: [bɹaʊn]   →   [bʋaʊn].

Here, both the old and new sounds are voiced approximants. They differ in that the older [ɹ] is retroflex whereas the newer [ʋ] is labio-dental; that is, the new form has the same *place* of articulation as [v], but the *manner* of articulation of [w].

A final example illustrating a change in place of articulation concerns the loss, in certain environments, of the interdental fricatives /θ/ and /ð/, which are merging with the labio-dental fricatives /f/ and /v/ respectively. Examples illustrating these changes appear in (34) and (35). The change in (35) applies only to non-initial [ð]:

(34) *thumb*:   [θʌm]   →   [fʌm]
      nothing: [nʌθɪŋ]   →   [nʌfɪŋ]

(35) *bother*:   [bɒðə]   →   [bɒvə]
      breathe: [briːð]   →   [briːv]

Again, there is no change in voicing – [θ] and [f] are both voiceless, while [ð] and [v] are both voiced – and no change in manner of articulation – old and new sounds are fricatives. What has changed is the place of articulation, from interdental to labio-dental.

It is also possible to identify changes in manner of articulation. Included in this category is the process of **spirantisation** – a change from plosive to fricative ('spirant' was the nineteenth-century term for 'fricative', which today survives only in the form 'spirantisation', showing that even linguistic jargon undergoes historical change!). A classic example of spirantisation can be found in the accent of the English city of Liverpool, where the voiceless stops [p t k] have become the voiceless fricatives [ɸ s x] respectively, and the voiced stops [b d g] have become the voiced fricatives [β z ɣ] respectively, in non-word initial positions. In each case, the new sound retains its original place of articulation and its voicing characteristics, but by turning from a stop into a fricative, it has undergone a change in manner of articulation, i.e. it illustrates a change in (c) in our three-term description of consonants. Table 10 includes examples of each of the six changes:

Table 10: Spirantisation in Liverpool			
	bilabial	**alveolar**	**velar**
voiceless	*pepper*	*better*	*locker*
	[pɛpə] → [pɛɸə]	[bɛtə] → [bɛsə]	[lɒkə] → [lɒxə]
voiced	*baby*	*steady*	*haggle*
	[bɛɪbi] → [bɛɪβi]	[stedi] → [stezi]	[hagl] → [haɣl]

Notice that most of the consonant changes discussed above do not result in the language having fewer or more sounds. However, the change exemplified in (34) does have this consequence, since [θ] is being replaced by [f] in all linguistic contexts – word initial (*three*, *think*), word medial (*ether*) and word final (*moth*, *pith*) – the conclusion of this process will be a variety of English which lacks [θ] entirely.

Sometimes changes can involve consonants being completely lost rather than replaced by others. We can point to examples such as the loss of [h] in words such as those in (36):

(36) *hand*: [hand] → [and]
      house: [haʊs] → [aʊs]
      Harry: [haɹɪ] → [aɹɪ]

This change is spreading in Britain, receding in Australasia, and not known in North America.

Another example is the loss of the glide [j] before [uː] in words such as *tune, duke, new, enthusiasm, resume, solution*, etc., a change commonly known as **yod-dropping**. So, in some varieties of American English we find changes such as those in (37):

(37) *New Zealand*: [njuːziːlənd] → [nuːziːlənd]
      student: [stjuːdənt]   → [stuːdənt]
      avenue: [ævənjuː]   → [ævənuː]

Some dialects have gone further than others in this change, dropping the [j] in words such as *beautiful* [buːtəfəl] and *cute* [kuːt].

It is also possible for a consonant to be *inserted* where one previously didn't exist. A well-known example of this is provided by the dialects which have inserted [p] in the emphatic forms of the words *yes* and *no*:

(38) *yeah*: [je]   → [jep] 'yep'
      no: [nʌʊ] → [nʌʊp] 'nope'

Also familiar from some British and Australasian accents is the insertion of [k] after *-ing* in the words *nothing* and *something*:

(39) *nothing*:   [nʌfɪŋ] → [nʌfɪŋk]
      something: [sʌmfɪŋ] → [sʌmfɪŋk]

A final example from the history of English involves the insertion of the bilabial stops [p b] in such Middle English words as *shamle* and Old English *bremel* resulting in their contemporary forms [ʃæmbl] *shamble* and [bræmbl] *bramble* (***exercise 1***).

Vowel change

What about *vowel* changes? Section 2 showed that vowels are usually classified with respect to (a) height; (b) front/backness; (c) lip rounding or spreading. As with consonants, changes can affect vowels along each of these dimensions. Some examples appear in table 11.

Table 11: Vowel changes in contemporary varieties of English				
change in	change from	change to	example	which dialect of English?
height (raising)	[æ]	[ɛ]	*bad* [bæd] → [bɛd]	London, Southern Hemisphere
front/back (backing)	[ɛ]	[ʌ]	*bell* [bɛl] → [bʌl]	Norwich, England
lip position (rounding)	[ɜː]	[øː]	*nurse* [nɜːs] → [nøːs]	New Zealand

In addition, it is possible for monophthongs to become diphthongs. An example from Australian English appears in (40):

(40)   [iː] → [əɪ]: *eat the peanuts* is pronounced [əɪtðəpəɪnɐts]

Or, in Philadelphia, USA, we find the change in (41):

(41)   [æ] → [eːə]: *mad, bad* and *glad* are respectively pronounced as [meːəd], [beːəd] and [gleːəd]

The converse process of diphthongs (and **triphthongs** – complex vowels which exhibit three distinct qualities) becoming monophthongs is also attested. The examples in (42) are from East Anglian English, with the last three involving triphthongs:

(42)   *sure*:   [ʃʊə]   →   [ʃɛː]
         player: [pleiə]   →   [plæː]
         fire: [faiə]   →   [faː]
         tower: [tauə]   →   [taː]

We saw above that for consonants it is possible for a sound change to result in the loss of a particular sound when it is systematically replaced by another which already exists in the language. Similar situations can be identified for vowels (**vowel mergers**), along with the opposite process where a vowel splits into two distinct sounds (**vowel splits**). Figure 23 illustrates an example of the latter taking place in London round about 1550 and its consequences for the speech of contemporary Londoners.

What we see here is a situation where the high back vowel [ʊ] split. In 1400 all the words *put, bush, pull, cup, luck* and *mud* included the vowel [ʊ]. By about 1550, the vowel in *cup, luck* and *mud* had lowered to [ɣ], but *put, bush* and *pull* retained [ʊ]. Later, in some dialects (most notably in South East England and

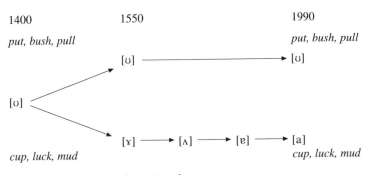

Figure 23 *A vowel split in London*

Australasia), the lowered vowel in *cup*, *luck*, and *mud* moved through a number of stages to the front, so as to become [a] in contemporary dialects. This split occurred both in southern England and Scotland and is found in all the English varieties of North America and the Southern Hemisphere. It did *not* occur in Northern England, which retains [ʊ] in such words as *cup*, *luck* and *mud*. There is evidence that some of the present day [ʊ]-class words are unrounding in Southern British varieties, so *book* is being pronounced by some as [bɯk], [ɯ] being an unrounded [ʊ].

Mergers are far more common than splits and examples are easy to find from around the English speaking world. One instance which was noted in section 2 is the identical pronunciation (as [meriː]) of the words *merry, marry* and *Mary* in parts of the western and central USA. Similar examples are the merger in some dialects, of [ʊə] and [ɔː], so both *sure* and *shore* become [ʃɔː], and the merger in a few rural Eastern English dialects of [au] and [ɛə] with the result that *cow* and *care* are pronounced identically as [kɛː].

A slightly more complex case can be identified in New Zealand, the Caribbean and Norfolk, where the diphthongs [iə] and [ɛə] have merged. Interestingly, however, whereas in Norfolk the merger has resulted in [ɛə] taking over in words where [iə] was previously found, in both New Zealand and the Caribbean, a *new* diphthong [eə] has replaced both of the original sounds. Thus, whereas both *bear* and *beer* have come to be pronounced like *bear* in Norfolk, they have both come to be pronounced as [beə] in the other two locations.

Finally, we can note an example of the rural dialect of Norfolk *not* undergoing a merger which has affected most other English varieties. This is the merger of the diphthongs in *toe* and *tow*, which were distinct in Middle English. They began to merge in the seventeenth century, but as the examples from Norfolk English in (43) show, this dialect has not been affected by this process:

(43)   *toe* [tʊu]   *tow* [tʌu]
         rose [ɹʊuz]   *rows* [ɹʌuz]
         moan [mʊun]   *mown* [mʌun]

So far we have looked at a number of essentially *independent* sound changes. In the case of many vowels, however, linguists have noticed that a change to one vowel can have a knock-on effect for others in the neighbouring area of phonetic space, where we understand this notion in terms of the vowel quadrilaterals from section 2. Sometimes cases arise in which one vowel will change and leave a 'space' into which a second vowel moves. It is not uncommon for several vowels to be linked together in this way in a series of changes known as a **chain shift**.

As we saw briefly in the main introduction, while our knowledge of the linguistic changes which have occurred over time is largely based on *diachronic* research – a detailed analysis of the gradual historical development of a particular linguistic feature – methods which can accurately chart language changes *as they take place within a community of speakers* have recently been introduced. These so-called apparent-time methods involve the simulation of a historical dimension within a synchronic study, and apparent-time researchers collect tape recordings of the language varieties used within a particular community and compare the speech of people *born* at different times. By comparing the speech of those born in 1920 with that of those born in 1970, it is claimed, we are comparing the language acquired by children at two distinct points in the history of the language. The language of the older speakers should therefore reflect an earlier stage in the development of the language than the varieties spoken by the younger age groups (see introduction, exercise 10).

Apparent-time studies have enabled linguists to observe some quite complex examples of chain shifting in progress. For example, William Labov and his colleagues have carried out extensive research on a series of vowel shifts, known as the Northern Cities Chain Shift, which is underway in American cities such as Chicago, Detroit and Buffalo. Some shifts in the chain are almost complete and others are in their infancy, but overall the chain forms a complete 'loop' in phonetic space. The oldest change in the chain is the raising of [æ] in words such as *hat*, *pack*, *last*, *bath* and *man*. In these words, the vowel is shifting from [æ] to [eə] or [ɪə] (the raised [ə] indicates a very weak second component to a diphthong). The space left by [æ], a low front vowel, has been filled by a fronting of [ɑ] (in words such as *got*, *not* and *pop*) to [æ]. Similarly, the space vacated by [ɑ], a low back vowel, has been filled by the lowering of [ɔ] to [ɑ] in words such as *caught, talk* and *taught*. We thus see a sequence of changes with vowels taking over the 'space' vacated by other vowels. Furthermore, something like the converse of what we have just described has also occurred as part of the Northern Cities Chain Shift. Specifically, the change of [æ] to [eə] or [ɪə] produced a 'congested' area of mid closed/high front vowels. As a result, these have also begun to move. In particular, [ɪ] (in words such as *pip, tin* and *sit*) is moving from [ɪ] to [e], and [e] (in words such as *pet, lend* and *spell*) is moving back to the position of [ʌ]. Finally, [ʌ] – in *cup, butter, luck,* etc. – is moving slightly further back and rounding, to fill the position vacated earlier in the process by /ɔ/.

From the above description and figure 24, it should be clear that the chain involves a series of changes which constitute a closed 'loop' in phonetic space.

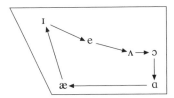

Figure 24 *The Northern Cities Chain Shift*

Now notice that some of the changes in this chain have been caused by one vowel moving and *pulling* other vowels behind it. This is the case with the [æ] – [ɑ] – [ɔ] chain: [æ] moved first and the others 'followed'. Such chain shifts are called **drag-chains**. Sometimes, however, a vowel may move *towards* the position of another vowel, causing that vowel to move itself. This is the case with the [ɪ] – [e] – [ʌ] part of the chain: [ɪ] lowered to the position of [e], which backed into the position of [ʌ] which, consequently, had to move back itself. This sort of shift is called a **push-chain** (*exercises 2 and 3*).

The transition problem: regular sound change versus lexical diffusion

Having observed a number of different types of sound change, we can turn to the question of how, more precisely, these changes affect the words in which they occur. Does a sound change affect every word which contains that sound at the same time or are some words affected before others? Are vowel changes phonetically gradual, taking small steps in phonetic space on their route to the new vowel, or are they abrupt, 'jumping' from one vowel to another without going through intermediate phonetic stages?

Two hypotheses have been put forward to account for the way sounds change. The first was initially proposed in the nineteenth century by the Neogrammarian group of historical linguists and it regards sound change as *regular*. Two important principles underlie this hypothesis. The first of these is that if a sound change takes place, it will take place in *all* words with similar environments *at the same time*. There will be no exceptions. The outcome of this is that sound changes must be *phonetically gradual*, but *lexically abrupt*. A vowel shift, adhering to this principle, would move through phonetic space towards its new destination in small steps, rather than in one step, and the change would apply to every word in which that vowel occurred. If, for instance, we take the change from [ɛ] to [e] in the Southern Hemisphere varieties of English of Australia, New Zealand and South Africa, we would expect to find: (a) small phonetic changes to gradually shift [ɛ] to [e]; and (b) *every* word which contained [ɛ] to move to [e]. In the case of South African English, this appears to be correct with all words with [ɛ] passing through a stage where they had a vowel intermediate between [ɛ] and [e].

The second Neogrammarian principle elaborates on the notion of 'similar environment' which appears in the first principle. Specifically, it states that if a sound change takes place, the *only* factors which can affect that change in any way are *phonetic* ones, such as the phonetic characteristics of the segments which surround the feature undergoing change. These changes, then, may be phonetically conditioned: the changing sound in some of the words may shift faster than in others because it is surrounded by a phonetic environment which particularly favours the change. Conversely, in some words the phonetic environment may hinder and slow down the change. However, according to the Neogrammarians, it is impossible for a sound change to operate, say, in nouns but not in verbs, since this would be an example of a change being subject to non-phonetic conditioning (i.e. grammatical category membership). An example which appears to be consistent with this emphasis on phonetic environment appears in Labov's studies of the Northern Cities Chain Shift which we have just described. He found that the change from [æ] to [ɪə] was most favoured when the vowel preceded a nasal consonant, as in *aunt*, *dance* and *hand*, but hindered when the vowel preceded a velar consonant, such as in *black* and *track*.

Despite the predictive success of Neogrammarian principles in some cases, a number of historical linguists, particularly those working on dialects of Chinese, became unhappy with the hypothesis that sound change always displayed regularity. This was because they discovered examples of changes which did not conform to the expected neat and regular patterns. Instead, they found instances of what has come to be known as **lexical diffusion**. Taking its name from such instances, the lexical diffusion hypothesis also depends on two principles, which are directly opposed to the principles of the Neogrammarians. This hypothesis maintains that: (a) rather than being phonetically gradual, sound changes are phonetically discrete, 'jumping' from the old sound to the new one without passing through any intermediate phonetic stages; (b) rather than the whole lexicon undergoing the sound change at the same time, individual words change from the old form to the new one in a manner which is not phonetically predictable in a neat way.

One often cited example of lexical diffusion in English is a sound split which took place in southern British English and is sometimes known as the TRAP-BATH split. In the latter part of the seventeenth century, the [æ] in some but not all words which contained it began to *lengthen*, and then *move back*, ultimately to [ɑ:]. Currently, in Standard British English we have the pattern in table 12 (remember that RP is Received Pronunciation, a rather conservative variety of British English):

Table 12: [ɑ:] and [æ] in Standard British English (RP)		
following phonetic environment	RP [ɑ:]	RP [æ]
__f#	*laugh, staff, half*	*gaffe, faffe, naff*
__fC	*craft, after, shaft, daft*	*faffed*
__θ	*path, bath*	*math(s), Cathie*
__st	*last, past, nasty*	*enthusiast, aster*
__sp	*clasp, grasp*	*asp*
__sk	*ask, flask, basket*	*gasket, mascot*
__sl	*castle*	*tassel, hassle*
__ns	*dance, chance, France*	*romance, cancer, fancy*
__nt	*aunt, grant, slant*	*rant, ant, canter*
__n(t)ʃ	*branch, blanch*	*mansion, expansion*
__mpl	*example, sample*	*ample, trample*
__nd	*demand, remand*	*stand, grand, panda*

(# indicates a word boundary and C any consonant in the top two entries of the left-hand column in this table; the crucial vowel is in bold throughout)

Notice that the change charted in table 12 is *not* altogether phonetically regular. There are some tendencies: most words with following /f/ have undergone the change – there are only a few rarely occurring exceptions. Overall, however, from a phonetic perspective, we have a picture of a rather messy and irregular change. Since it has not taken place in a phonetically regular way, but has seen individual words change independently of any precise phonetic conditioning, it provides an example of lexical diffusion.

The change from [æ] to [ɑː] appears to be most advanced in Standard British English and other southern British English dialects, but has most notably *not* taken place in northern England. Between the north and the south we have a mixed picture, and we can search for more evidence of the lexical nature of the shift by looking at a dialect which has not yet advanced quite as far as Standard British English in the reallocation of words from [æ] to [ɑː]. Such a dialect is that of the small urban centre of Wisbech situated near the northern area of England which has not undergone the shift.

There are two findings about the Wisbech dialect which are notable here. Firstly, younger residents of the town are more likely to have acquired or almost acquired the Standard British English system than the older ones – a good, though not totally accurate indication that change is still underway. Secondly, there does not seem to be a 'common route' through the change that all speakers in the community follow. In other words, while some speakers will have, for example, [læst], [plænts] and [kæsl], but [glɑːsəz] and [pɑːθ], others, with very similar social backgrounds, will have [glæsəz] and [plænt], but [lɑːst], [kɑːsl] and [pɑːθ] (*exercises 4, 5 and 6*).

Research by William Labov comparing examples of regular sound change with lexical diffusion suggests that regular sound change is most common in vowel shifts (fronting, raising, backing, etc.) and lexical diffusion most widespread in cases of vowel lengthening (such as the TRAP-BATH split) and shortening. It appears to be the case, then, that rather than one of our hypotheses being the universally correct one, each seems to apply to different sorts of change.

Suprasegmental change

As well as affecting vowels and consonants, change may also occur among suprasegmental phenomena such as stress and intonation. An example of such a suprasegmental change is the shifting of *stress* in disyllabic words from the second to the first syllable. Particularly interesting are some noun–verb pairs in which the verb is becoming indistinguishable from the noun because of this process. It will be recalled from section 2 (p. 46) that the standard pattern in Modern English is for disyllabic verbs to be stressed on the second syllable, whereas corresponding nouns are stressed on the first syllable. Thus, we have such pairs as (44) and (45):

(44)   a. They won the ['kɑntest] easily (noun)
       b. She wanted to [kən'test] the case in court (verb)

(45)   a. She hired an ['ɛskɔːt] (noun)
       b. The bouncer needed to [əs'kɔːt] the drunkard from the club (verb)

An exception to this pattern is provided by *address* in most varieties of British English, which is stressed on its final syllable, irrespective of whether it is a noun or a verb:

(46)   a. Give me your [əd'rɛs] (UK, noun)
       b. She demanded the right to [əd'rɛs] the audience (UK, verb)

Now, at the beginning of the seventeenth century, many words which could function as either nouns or verbs behaved like *address*. So, for example, *increase*, *protest* and *record* carried stress on their final syllables even when they functioned as nouns. We thus see that there has been a process of shifting stress from the final to the initial syllable in such words when they are used as nouns, a process which has not taken place in the case of *address*.

Interestingly, *address* has undergone this stress shift in American English:

(47)   a. Give me your ['ædrɛs] (USA, noun)
       b. She demanded the right to [əd'rɛs] the audience (USA, verb)

Furthermore, there is evidence that the stress shift is extending to the *verbal* use of some words in varieties of British English, as illustrated by the examples in (48) and (49):

(48)   a. There was a steep ['ɪŋkriːs] in inflation last month (noun)
       b. The government was forced to ['ɪŋkriːs]/[ɪŋ'kriːs] interest rates yesterday (verb)

(49)   a. Bob's ['transfɜː] to the personnel department was proving difficult (noun)
       b. She went to the bank to ['transfɜː]/[trans'fɜː] some money (verb)

What we have, therefore, is a situation where some 400 years ago there was generally no stress-based distinction between our pairs of nouns and verbs. Such a distinction has been introduced in the intervening period, with *address* exceptionally maintaining its original properties in British English. And now, under a general tendency for stress to shift forward from the final syllable, the distinction is beginning to be lost again, even though the pronunciations of both nouns and verbs are different to what they were 400 years ago. The word *envy* offers a final perspective on this process. In 1600, it already exhibited the 'modern' stress-based contrast between its uses as a noun and a verb. However, stress-shift has applied to the verb in the intervening period with the result that today we have only the single pronunciation ['ɛnvɪ]. The examples in (48) and (49) suggest that *increase* and *transfer* are embarking on the route which *envy* has already completed (*exercise 7*).

We conclude this section with an example of intonational change which is affecting the varieties of English spoken in Australia, New Zealand and North America. In these countries, some people are acquiring a rising, question-like intonation contour in *declarative* (i.e. non-questioning) utterances.

Consider the small dialogue in (50), which involves a young New Zealander recounting an experience on a Pacific cruise – italics mark the clauses with rising intonation.

(50)   FRANK: These guys I met were in a fairly cheap sort of cabin – all
                they had was a porthole and I looked out of this porthole
                and it was black. And a fish swam past. [laughs]
        HUGH: [laughs]
        FRANK: *They were actually that low down.*

Research has shown that these patterns of rising intonation are found most frequently, as in the example above, when telling stories, and giving explanations and descriptions, and are found rarely in the expressing of opinions. The change appears to have begun in Australasia just after the Second World War, and, it is said, is now being heard in parts of the UK (*exercises 8 and 9*).

Exercises

1.   The data in table 13 show the variable use of (t)-glottalisation in the speech of children of different ages from the English city of Milton Keynes. Comment on the data, paying particular attention to:

(a) differences between boys and girls
(b) differences between children of different ages
(c) differences between conversational style and reading style

Table 13: (t)-glottalisation in the speech of Milton Keynes children				
Age 8	**girls**		**boys**	
	[t]	[ʔ]	[t]	[ʔ]
reading	80%	20%	44%	56%
conversation	20%	80%	12%	88%
Age 12	**girls**		**boys**	
	[t]	[ʔ]	[t]	[ʔ]
reading	100%	0%	74%	26%
conversation	90%	10%	60%	40%

2. Consider the data in table 14. Can you suggest what is happening in South African, Australian and New Zealand English, relative to the other dialects?

Table 14: Pronunciations of some simple words in a number of varieties of English					
Word	Northern British English	Standard British English	New Zealand English	Australian English	South African English
kit	[kɪt]	[kɪt]	[kət]	[kit]	[kɪt]
pin	[pɪn]	[pɪn]	[pən]	[pin]	[pin]
dress	[dɹɛs]	[dɹes]	[dɹes]	[dɹes]	[dɹes]
net	[nɛt]	[net]	[net]	[net]	[net]
trap	[tɹap]	[tɹæp]	[tɹɛp]	[tɹɛp]	[tɹɛp]
back	[bak]	[bæk]	[bɛk]	[bɛk]	[bɛk]
luck	[lʊk]	[lʌk]	[lɐk]	[lak]	[lɑk]
cup	[kʊp]	[kʌp]	[kɐp]	[kap]	[kɑp]

(Note that the vowels in the Standard British English column are not always the same as the vowels we have described in section 2 for this variety, a reflection of the fact that there is some flexibility in what the phrase 'Standard British English' refers to.)

3. Consider the data in table 15 from a dialect of English. The table shows the pronunciations of a number of changing vowels, and provides representative examples of words in which these vowels occur.

What can you conclude about the initial stages of the changes that took place? How are they related to each other? What happened subsequently? You may need to look at a vowel chart to help you answer these questions.

Table 15: Vowel changes in an English dialect

Word	Pronunciation of the vowel before the change	Pronunciation of the vowel during the change	Pronunciation of the vowel today
time	[iː]	[əɪ]	[aɪ]
sweet	[eː]	[iː]	[iː]
clean	[ɛː]	[eː]	[iː]
name	[aː]	[ɛː]	[ɛɪ]
hope	[ɔː]	[oː]	[ou]
goose	[oː]	[uː]	[uː]
south	[uː]	[əu]	[au]

4. The data below comes from a social dialect survey carried out in Texas. Table 16 displays the loss of [j] before [uː] and after alveolar consonants, e.g. *tuna*: [tjuːnə] → [tuːnə], and table 17 the merger of [uː] and [ʊ] before [l], e.g. *school*: [skuːl] → [skʊl]

Is sound change in progress? How can you tell? How would you confirm your intuitions?

Table 16: Percentage retention of /j/ in Texas English

Age of Speakers	Percentage retention of the /j/ before /uː/ and after alveolar consonants
18–29	41
30–44	45
45–60	56
61 +	65

Table 17: Percentage of vowel mergers in Texas English	
Age of speakers	Percentage of merged vowels
18–29	60
30–44	61
45–60	29
61 +	17

5. In many varieties of English spoken in North America, Ireland, Scotland and New Zealand, the words *whine* and *wine* are pronounced differently, whereas elsewhere they are usually pronounced the same. A study has been conducted in the New Zealand city of Dunedin which investigated the extent to which this contrast between *whine* [ʍaɪn] and *wine* [waɪn] was being maintained, and some results from this study appear in table 18. Comment on this change and consider the reasons for the direction of the change.

Table 18: The use of [ʍ] and [w] in Dunedin, New Zealand		
Age	Percentage use of [ʍ]	Percentage use of [w]
12–19	0	100
20–29	9	91
30–39	23	77
40–49	53	47
50–59	88	12
60–69	91	9

6. One change currently underway in southern British English (as well as in the Australasian and some North American varieties) involves the vocalisation of [ɫ] to [ʊ] (for the purposes of this exercise, you can treat [ɫ] as [l], but you might like to find out about the difference between these two sounds). Hence, *bottle* typically has changed from [bɒʔɫ] to [bɒʔʊ]. This change in Britain is spreading northwards from London into East Anglia and the Midlands. The two maps below show the extent to which the change to [ʊ] is affecting a predominantly rural area 100 miles north of London. Map 1 shows how the change has affected forty-five- to sixty-five-year-olds in the area, and map 2 shows the extent to which fifteen- to thirty-year-olds use

the new form. The main urban centres are marked on the maps. Consider how the change has advanced both in historical and geographical terms. Why do you think some of the urban centres seem to be more advanced in the change than are their rural surroundings?

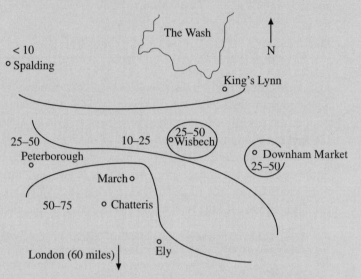

Map 1 *Percentage use of [ɫ]-vocalisation among forty-five- to sixty-five-year-olds living in an area of Eastern England*

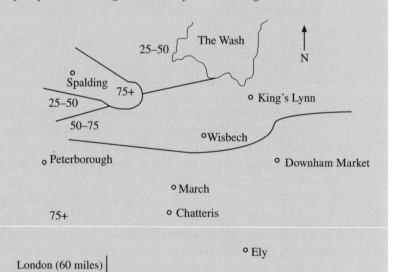

Map 2 *Percentage use of [ɫ]-vocalisation among fifteen- to thirty-year-olds living in an area of Eastern England*

7.   Are the following examples of sound changes, discussed in this section, cases of 'regular sound change' or of 'lexical diffusion'? How do you know?

(a) the ʊ/ʌ split?
(b) the shift to syllable initial stress?

8.   Do you think that the new rising intonation form used in North America and Australasia has a particular meaning? Does an utterance with this intonation mean something different from an utterance with a falling intonation?

9.   Collecting data on variation and change in language involves understanding the way the speech community is structured socially as well as linguistically. If you were to conduct research in your own neighbourhood, what sociological factors do you think you would need to take into account and why?

5   Phonemes, syllables and phonological processes

We began section 2 by asking how many sounds there are in English, but we found there were various practical difficulties in responding to this question and we never arrived at an answer. There is a further reason why the question can't be answered straightforwardly, and understanding this is our first concern in this section. In fact, speech sounds can differ from each other in a non-discrete, continuous fashion. We can see this particularly easily in the vowel system. One of the main differences between the [iː] of *read* [ɹiːd] and the [ɪ] of *rid* [ɹɪd] is length. But just how long is a long vowel? An emphatic pronunciation of *read*, say in a plaintive 'Leave me alone – I'm trying to READ' has a much longer vowel than a non-emphatic pronunciation. The precise length of any vowel will depend on the rate of speaking, degree of emphasis and so on. A similar case is presented by the aspirated plosives. In any dialect, a [pʰ] sound, as in the word *pit* will be aspirated to a greater or lesser extent depending on the degree of emphasis. We see, therefore, that there is a sense in which sounds form a continuum; from this perspective, there is an *infinite* number of speech sounds in any language.

Phonemes

Fortunately, there is another perspective from which sounds are discrete units or **segments**, and we can come to terms with this by asking the question: what is the difference between the words *pit* and *bit*? From section 2, we can say that *pit* starts with a voiceless bilabial plosive and *bit* starts with a voiced bilabial plosive. Otherwise, the words are identical. A pair of this kind, in which everything except the portion under consideration is identical, is called a **minimal pair**. This pair shows that voicing can distinguish one word from another, and that the pair of sounds [p b] can *distinguish words*. However, when we consider different types of [p], with different degrees of aspiration or no aspiration at all, we get a different picture. There are no words in English which differ solely in whether they contain an unaspirated or an aspirated plosive. That is, English does not have distinct words like, say, [pʰɪt] and [pɪt]. In fact, [pɪt], with totally unaspirated [p], is unpronounceable without explicit training for most English speakers. Conversely, we could never find pairs such as [spɪt] and [spʰɪt] in English – following initial [s] the *only* 'p' sound we find is the unaspirated [p]. The same is true of [t tʰ] and [k kʰ], as in the pairs of words *star*, *tar* and *scar*, *car*. In other words, the **distribution** of the sounds [p pʰ] is governed by a rule or principle according to which we never find [p] in the positions reserved for [pʰ] and we never find [pʰ] in the positions reserved for [p]. This type of patterning is called **complementary distribution** (the positions in which we find the two sounds complement each other).

Things needn't be this way. There are languages in which [p] and [pʰ] can be used to distinguish words, that is, in some languages [p/pʰ t/tʰ k/kʰ] and similar pairs are **contrastive** sounds. In (51) we show examples from Bengali (or Bangla), spoken in Bangladesh, in which [p] and [pʰ], [t] and [tʰ], and [k] and [kʰ] contrast (and there is also a contrast between [ʧ] and [ʧʰ]):

(51) **aspirated**   **unaspirated**

    [kʰal]   'canal'   [kal]   'time'

    [ʧʰai]   'ashes'   [ʧai]   'I want'

    [tʰaka]   'to remain'   [taka]   'to stare'

    [matʰa]   'head'   [mata]   'to be enthusiastic'

    [pʰul]   'flower'   [pul]   'bridge'

Returning to English, we can simplify our description of the sound inventory by thinking of [p t k] and [pʰ tʰ kʰ] as variants of the 'p', 't' and 'k' sounds. Thus, we can say that there are just the three voiceless plosives, but they have slightly different pronunciations depending on their position in the word. Ignoring other positions, initially we get the aspirated variant and after [s] we get the unaspirated variety. Thus, we could transcribe the words *pit/spit*, *tar/star*, *car/scar* as [pit/spit], [tɑː/stɑː], [kɑː/skɑː] on the understanding that a general rule will tell us exactly how to pronounce the plosive. It is no accident, then, that this distinction between aspirated and unaspirated sounds is never marked in ordinary English orthography (though it is marked in the spelling system of Bangla). In fact, native speakers of English who have not had some kind of phonetic or linguistic training are usually completely unaware of the distinction.

From the above, it follows that we need to be able to talk about sounds at *two levels*. At one level we must be able to describe the fact that English has aspirated as well as unaspirated plosives. This is necessary simply to capture an important difference between the plosive system of English and those of languages such as French, Spanish, Russian, Samoan, Inuit and many others in which plosives are never aspirated. On the other hand, we also need to be able to capture the idea that in English [p] and [pʰ] are variants of 'the same sound'. But what sound?

To answer this question, we need another, less concrete, concept of 'sound'. We will call these more abstract sounds **phonemes** and write them between slashes: /p t k/. A transcription into such phonemic symbols is called a **broad transcription**. However, when we want to talk about the precise, concrete sounds which can be detected by phonetic analysis we will speak about **phones**. These are written between square brackets. Thus, [p pʰ t tʰ k kʰ] represent six phones but in English they correspond to only three phonemes, /p t k/. A transcription which includes phonetic detail about the pronunciation of individual phones, and written in square brackets, is referred to as a **narrow transcription**. There is always some choice as to exactly how much phonetic detail an analyst might include, so the notion of 'narrow transcription' is a relative one.

We will also say that the two variants [p pʰ] of the phoneme /p/ are **allophones** of that phoneme. The term 'allophone' is based on a Greek expression meaning 'different sound'. The phenomenon of variation in the pronunciation of phonemes in different positions is called **allophony** or **allophonic variation**, and we can illustrate this diagrammatically for our English voiceless plosives as in (52):

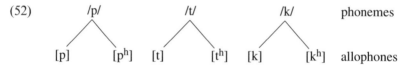

(52)   /p/   /t/   /k/   phonemes

    [p]   [pʰ]   [t]   [tʰ]   [k]   [kʰ]   allophones

Note that the transcription at the level of allophones has to be rather approximate, given that we can have different degrees of aspiration – in principle, there is an infinite number of distinctions at this level. However, there is only a fixed number (three) of voiceless plosive phonemes in the language.

If we turn to the vowel system, we have noted that length is a continuous quality, permitting any number of distinctions. Obviously, this is also the case for the front/back and high/low axes introduced in section 2 as playing a major role in the categorisation of vowels. However, we can simplify this complexity by taking some decisions as to what features of the pronunciation are crucial, and hence can be said to belong to the phoneme, and which are less crucial. Different accounts tend to do this in different ways, and we shall do no more than illustrate the issues that arise here. Consider, the pairs of vowels [iː uː] and [ɪ ʊ]. Members of the first pair are *longer* than members of the second pair, but there is also a difference in *quality*: [iː uː] are *tense* vowels, whereas [ɪ ʊ] are *lax*. Furthermore, the distinction between the pairs is crucial, since we have such minimal pairs as *beat/bit* and *pool/pull*. We will assume that vowel length is the important factor in these distinctions. Thus, we can say that [iː uː] are the long vowels corresponding to [ɪ ʊ]. This means that the more lax pronunciation of the short vowels [ɪ ʊ] is secondary to the length distinction. In a broad, phonemic transcription we could thus use just one symbol for each, say /i u/, with an additional indication of length. Thus, the long phoneme /iː/ would be pronounced [iː] and the short phoneme /i/ would be pronounced [ɪ], and similarly for /uː/ (pronounced as [uː]) and /u/ (pronounced as [ʊ]). Likewise, we might want to say that [a ɒ] are short equivalents of [ɑː ɔː]. There is some controversy as to whether this gives a satisfactory answer for English, however (for reasons which go well beyond the scope of an introduction such as this). In addition, it is helpful to get used to the more accurate narrow transcriptional system for vowel sounds, since vowels differ so much from one variety to another. Therefore, we will continue to make more distinctions than may be strictly necessary.

We can now recast our original question as 'How many phonemes are there in English?', and we get the answer given in table 19, where in some cases we continue to use distinct symbols for the long and short vowels in acknowledgement of the uncertainty to which we have just alluded:

Table 19: The English phoneme inventory

Consonants:

	Labials		Coronals				Dorsals	Gutturals
	Bilabial	Labio-dental	Dental	Alveolar	Palato-alveolar	Palatal	Velar	Glottal
Plosives	p b			t d	ʧ ʤ		k g	
Fricatives		f v	θ ð	s z	ʃ ʒ			h
Nasals	m			n			ŋ	
Approximants	w			l ɹ		j		

(Note that the term *gutturals* is used to refer to the class of uvular, pharyngeal and glottal consonants. English has only /h/ in this class.)

Vowels:

Short:

ɪ			ʊ
	ɛ	ə	ʌ
		a	ɒ

Long:

iː			uː
	ɛː	əː	ɔː
			ɑː

Diphthongs: eɪ aɪ aʊ ɔɪ oʊ ɪə ʊə

This is our first experience of the importance of distinct **levels of analysis** in linguistics, an extremely important notion. In the current context, we have a relatively concrete level, more closely linked to *physical* sound and a more abstract level, related to the organisation of *patterns* of sounds in the grammar of the language (and ultimately in the minds of speakers). Specifically, what we can suggest is that the phonological representation, which appears in the lexicon as part of the lexical entry for a word, is a *phonemic* and not a *phonetic* representation. The manner in which a phonemic representation is converted to a phonetic representation is part of the PF-component of the grammar (see the introduction, p. 5) and we shall be saying more about this presently (***exercise 1***).

Syllables

When the Japanese borrowed the monosyllabic sporting term *sprint* it came out as *supurinto* with four syllables. When an English speaker tries to pronounce the Russian name *Mstislav* (two syllables in Russian!) it generally acquires an extra initial syllable to become [əmstɪslav] or [mɪstɪslav]. Speakers of Cantonese Chinese tend to pronounce the words *walk, walks* and *walked* identically, as [wɔʔ]. Why is this? The answer is that different languages permit different kinds of syllables, and native speakers of languages bring their knowledge of syllables and syllable structure to their attempts to produce words from other languages. To see what kinds of syllables we find, we need to look at syllable structure more carefully.

Words like *bat, cat, rat, flat, spat,* and *sprat,* are said to rhyme. This is because they have identical pronunciations after the first consonant or consonant cluster. We can divide a syllable therefore into two halves, the **Rhyme** (or **Rime**) and the **Onset**. We have already referred (p. 46) to the vowel in the middle of the syllable as the **Nucleus** (or **Peak**). The consonant or consonant cluster after the Nucleus will be called the **Coda**. These terms are illustrated in (53) for the word *quilt*:

(53)

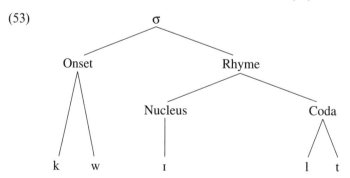

The symbol σ (= Greek letter 'sigma') is often used to represent a syllable.

The order of the consonants in the onset and the coda is interesting here, because some consonant orders yield impossible words. Thus, compare the consonant clusters at the beginnings and ends of the 'words' in (54) and (55). In each case, the illicit sequence (marked with *) is intended to be pronounced as a single syllable:

(54)   nelp   */nɛpl/
        lump   */lʌpm/
        hard   */hadr/

(55)   play   */lpeɪ/
        pray   */rpeɪ/
        quick   */wkɪk/
        cue   */jkuː/

Returning to (53), a form such as *quilt* /kwɪlt/ is fine but */wkɪtl/ is an impossible form in English. There is a systematic reason for this. We distinguished in section 2 between obstruents (plosives, affricates and fricatives) and sonorants (nasals and approximants). The reason /wkɪtl/ makes a bad syllable perhaps has something to do with the fact that we have a sequence of sonorant (/w/) + obstruent (/k/) in the onset and of obstruent (/t/) + sonorant (/l/) in the coda. The reverse order in each position is, of course, well formed. Why might this be the case? The answer to this question requires us to recognise that *sonority* is not an all-or-nothing property. Thus, while the notion was introduced in section 2 in connection with consonants, it is easy to see that a vowel is more sonorant than any consonant. We can give the following approximate values of the *degree of sonority* of different classes of sound, starting with the least sonorant: plosives – 1, fricatives – 2, nasals – 3, approximants – 4, vowels – 5. In a word such as *quilt* the sonority of each sound gradually rises to a peak at the nucleus and then falls at the coda, as shown in (56):

(56)

However, if we look at the sonority profile we obtain from the non-syllable */wkɪtl/, we get the shape shown in (57):

(57)

This has three separate peaks, and we would normally expect this pattern to yield three syllables.

This type of sonority profile helps explain why certain types of consonant cluster are impossible in onsets or codas. Such restrictions on sound combinations are called **phonotactic constraints**. The notion of the syllable (and its constituents, onset and coda) helps us explain why the sequence -*lp* is possible in *help* but not at the beginning of a word, and why, conversely, the sequence *br*- is fine in *brush* but not at the end of a word: given the **sonority principle** (that the sonority profile of a legitimate syllable must rise continuously to a peak and fall continuously after that peak), -*lp* is a possible coda, but not a possible onset, while *br*- is a possible onset but not a possible coda.

Other phonotactic constraints are more subtle. Thus, in English we cannot have an onset consisting of a plosive + a nasal. Hence, *kn-, pn-, gm-*, and so on are excluded. However, plosives are less sonorous than nasals, so we might expect these clusters to be possible, as they are in many languages (check this by sketching a sonority profile for a word like *bnick* /bnɪk/ in the way we did for *quilt*). The grammar of English, it seems, regards the sonority of a nasal as being *too similar* to that of a plosive, however, and so excludes these as possible onsets. The only sounds that combine happily with obstruents to form an onset cluster are the approximants /l r w j/. On the other hand, the reverse order of nasal + plosive is perfectly good as a coda (e.g. *imp, ink*).

That the sonority principle, refined as outlined above, is part of the grammar of native speakers of English provides us with a ready interpretation of the fact that such speakers can clearly distinguish the non-occurring *blick* on the one hand from *bnick* and *nbick* on the other; the form /blɪk/ is consistent with the sonority principle as it applies to English, and so is a *possible*, though non-occurring, form. Put differently, it is an *accident* that *blick* is not in the English lexicon, whereas the absence of *bnick* and *nbick* is determined by the grammar.

Normally, only two consonants are allowed in an onset. However, the phoneme /s/ behaves in an unusual fashion. It can combine with almost any onset to form a cluster of up to three consonants. Thus, we get *spl-, str-, skw-* and so on. We don't find **sbr-, *sdw-*, or *sgl-* however, because there is a mismatch between the voicelessness of the first segment and the voiced second segment in these cases. As a result, we can have only an unvoiced obstruent immediately after /s/. However, we can have a voiced sonorant, i.e. nasal or approximant, in this position: *sn-, sm-, sl-, sj-, sw-*.

As we might imagine, the difficulty that Japanese or Cantonese speakers have with some types of English word is attributable to the phonotactic principles operating in their native grammars. Japanese disallows almost any type of cluster, especially in an onset, and so a Japanese speaker speaking English resorts to the same strategy as an English speaker confronted with Russian – the insertion of additional syllables. In Cantonese only nasals and the glottal stop are possible codas. Therefore, it is impossible to distinguish codas such as *-k, -ks* and *-kt* (**exercise 2**).

Syllabification and the Maximal Onset Principle

So far we've considered only words of one syllable. When we break a polysyllabic word such as *central* /sɛntrəl/ into syllables, we have a problem with the consonant cluster *-ntr-*. We can't split it as *sɛ . ntrəl* or *sɛntr . əl* because **ntrəl* and **sɛntr* are not permissible syllables in English. However, do we split it as *sɛnt . rəl* or *sɛn . trəl*? Either solution would provide two possible syllables in English.

A clue as to how to answer this question comes from looking at the syllable structures found in the languages of the world. In many languages, codas are highly restricted or even impossible (as in Hawaiian). In many other languages, all syllables must have an onset. This is true, for instance, of the Yawelmani dialect of the Yokuts language of California; and in languages such as German, Czech or Arabic, while it might appear that we can have words beginning with vowels, in fact these are always pronounced with an initial glottal stop. Thus, all syllables in these languages have an onset. Finally, in the Senufo language of Guinea all syllables consist of exactly an onset and a vowel: onsets are obligatory and codas are excluded. All this demonstrates that onsets have priority over codas cross-linguistically. For this reason we will assume that where there is indeterminacy, we make sure that a consonant is placed in an onset rather than a coda. In fact, there is evidence from the structure of English syllables that this is the correct solution to the syllabification problem we are considering. Thus, in the dialect of the authors the 't' at the end of a syllable can be glottalised, so that a phrase such as *mint rock* can be pronounced: [mɪnʔrɒk]. This glottalisation is impossible if the 't' comes at the beginning of the syllable. For instance, the 't' of *man trap* can't be glottalised.

Now, in this dialect, the 't' of *central* can't be glottalised (i.e. *central* cannot be pronounced [sɛnʔrəl] by the authors), showing that it must be in the onset position. This means that *central* should be syllabified as in (58) rather than as in (59) (where O is Onset, R is Rhyme, N is Nucleus and Co is Coda):

(58)

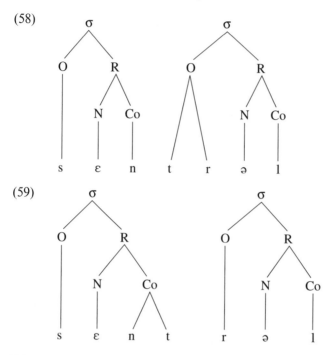

(59)

We can ensure that we get this result by appealing to the **Maximal Onset Principle**. This simply states that when there is a choice as to where to place a consonant, we put it into the onset rather than the coda (*exercises 3 and 4*).

Phonological processes

When we combine words with affixes and other words to form larger words and phrases, we often find that the phonemes of the word taken in isolation undergo changes due to the influence of surrounding phonemes (see the example of *Japan* and *Japanese* in section 1). One such set of changes is illustrated in (60) (transcribing standard British pronunciation):

(60)   a. *photograph*   [foutəgrɑːf]
        b. *photography*   [fətɒgrəfɪ]
        c. *photographic* [foutəgrafɪk]

When we look at the transcriptions (or listen carefully to the pronunciations) of the words in (60), we find that there is a complex *alternation* between the vowels /ou ɑː ɒ a/ on the one hand and schwa /ə/ on the other, though, of course, this is obscured by the orthographic representations (spelling). What is happening is easy to see when we consider the stress patterns. When a syllable has either main or secondary stress, then we get one of /ou ɑː ɒ a/, but when it receives no stress, then we have /ə/ instead.

The pattern illustrated in (60) is a very regular one which speakers of English will readily impose on new words, words borrowed from other languages and so on. Moreover, speakers do this unconsciously. However, it doesn't happen in all languages. Indeed, many languages do not even have the schwa vowel. English speakers, when learning languages such as Spanish, Polish, Navajo or any of the large number of languages which don't show this pattern, tend to impose it anyway, and have to learn to suppress it in order to acquire a good accent in those languages. All this means that the distribution of schwa and the other vowels is governed by a **phonological rule**, part of the grammar of someone who has acquired English as a native language.

A simple way to represent such a rule is as a **phonological process**, in which one sound is changed into another sound under certain circumstances. For our example there are two straightforward possibilities (we'll ignore the unstraightforward ones!). We could say that /ou/, /ɑː/, /ɒ/, /a/ get turned into /ə/ when they have no stress at all, or we could say that /ə/ gets turned into /ou/, /ɑː/, /ɒ/, or /a/ when it bears some degree of stress. We represent the process by means of an arrow, and the two possibilities appear in (61) and (62):

(61)   /ou ɑː ɒ a/   (when unstressed)   →   [ə]

(62)   /ə/   (when stressed)   →   [ou ɑː ɒ a]

Which of these is correct? It is easy to see that (62) at best offers an incomplete account of the phenomena. If we start out with /ə/ as in (62), then we have to replace it with one of four vowels, *but we don't know which*, and we would need an additional rule or rules to deal with this. However, if we start out with /ou/, /ɒ/, /ɑː/ or /a/ as in (61), then we replace any of these with [ə] just provided they are unstressed, and there is nothing more to say. Adopting this second option, then, we can say that the words *photograph, photography* and *photographic* have a basic or **underlying form** (also called an **underlying representation** or **UR**), shown in (63):

(63)   a. *photograph*   /foutɒɡrɑːf/
          b. *photography*   /foutɒɡrɑːfɪ/
          c. *photographic*   /foutɒɡrafɪk/

Rule (61) will now apply to derive the representations in (60). These representations, which show the way the word is actually pronounced, are called **surface forms** or **surface representations (SRs)**.

It is interesting to consider the analysis we have proposed above in the light of the orthographic representations of our three words. Given that the 'o' can represent the two sounds /oʊ/ and /ɒ/ (and given that 'ph' can represent /f/), we see that the spelling is closer to the UR than to the SR. This is quite common in English and other languages with a long history of literacy. In earlier forms of the language there would have been no vowel reduction (or at least much less) and all the vowels now pronounced as schwas would have been pronounced as full vowels. Then, the language changed, and unstressed vowels started getting reduced. However, writing systems are generally very conservative and often don't respond to such changes. Therefore, the spelling system of English often fairly closely represents the pronunciations of about five hundred years ago (coinciding with the introduction of printing into England by Caxton).

An important point to be clear about here is that rule (61) works *in conjunction with* the underlying representations that we have proposed for the word *photograph*, etc. If we didn't get the right URs, then we wouldn't be able to figure out the right rule. This means that when writing phonological rules (i.e. when writing the PF-component of a grammar), there is no simple way of computing the correct forms and the correct rules. The procedure we must follow is one of formulating a hypothesis about what the forms might be, trying to construct a set of rules which will give us the appropriate surface representations and then modifying the URs if necessary in order to obtain the correct rule system. This means that grammar writing (and the whole of linguistics) is a *hypothesis testing activity*: we set up a hypothesis, test that hypothesis against whatever data we have collected and then, if necessary, modify the hypothesis and retest it.

The phonological process we have just been discussing is called **vowel reduction** and it is very common in the world's languages. The term derives from the intuition that the schwa vowel is not really a 'proper' vowel. In most dialects of English there is some justification for this, in that a short schwa can never be found in a stressed position. More generally, however, schwa can behave like a fully fledged vowel in other languages, and can be stressed (e.g. in Bulgarian).

Vowel reduction is not found universally, so that in each language in which it is found it must be stated as a rule, and children acquiring the language must figure out whether their language does or doesn't have it. We have represented what must be learned as a phonological process in which one sound in the underlying representation is transformed into another. The operation of this process is illustrated in (64):

(64)   //foutɒgrɑːfɪ//   UR
   ↓ ↓
   ə ə   Vowel Reduction
  [fətɒgrəfɪ] SR

Here, we have put the UR between double slashes //...// to distinguish it from a broad IPA transcription between single slashes /.../. However, you will often see URs between single slashes, too, and we ourselves adopted this convention in (63).

In (64) we have a simple example of a phonological **derivation**. We say that the SR is **derived** from the UR by the rule of Vowel Reduction. In a full grammar a good many rules might apply to one UR to derive the final form. In section 6, we shall apply this type of analysis to children's speech, and exercise 2 in that section shows that where there are several rules applying to one form, we may need to apply them in a set order. Later in this section we will see other examples of phonological processes. Next, however, we need to look more carefully at the internal structure of individual speech sounds (*exercise 5*).

Phonological features

As we have seen, the IPA system for describing speech sounds divides them up into classes on the basis of a number of properties (place of articulation for consonants, frontness/backness for vowels, etc.). One of these properties is voicing, which serves a particularly important function in distinguishing English obstruents. The voiced sounds /b d g v ð z ʒ ʤ/ are paired with the voiceless sounds /p t k f θ s ʃ ʧ/ on this basis. Where we have classes of this sort in linguistics, we often describe the situation by means of **features**. The crucial feature here is that of voicing and the sounds in question are either voiced or not voiced. For classes of this sort that split into two groups we need a **binary feature**, which has one of two **values** or **specifications** denoted by '+' and '−'. The feature name itself is written inside square brackets: [voiced]. Voiced sounds are therefore marked [+voiced], while unvoiced sounds are marked [−voiced]. Sometimes, when we wish to name a binary feature such as this we refer to it as [±voiced] (the symbol '±' is read 'plus or minus') to emphasise that we are speaking about a binary feature.

Voicing is a **distinctive feature** for English obstruents, in that it serves to distinguish one phoneme from another. Sonorants (including vowels) are also voiced sounds, but they don't have any voiceless counterparts in English. This means that sounds such as /l w n ɪ ou/ are all [+voiced]. However, once we know that these sounds are sonorants, we also know they are voiced. Hence, the feature [voiced] is **redundant** for these sounds. When a feature is redundant for a group of sounds in a given language, then by definition it can't form the basis for a phonemic contrast.

We can continue to divide up the sounds of English using such features. The features most commonly used correspond roughly, but not exactly, to the classification in the IPA. Thus, nasals have the specification [+nasal] and all other sounds are [−nasal]. Other binary features are given in appendix 2 at the end of part 1 of the book (pp. 138ff.). One feature appearing there is worth further comment: [continuant]. The continuant sounds are those in which air can pass through the oral tract (i.e. the mouth). This includes the fricatives, the approximants and the vowels. These sounds are all [+continuant]. However, in nasals and plosives the air is prevented from escaping through the mouth; in the case of plosives it is bottled up until the plosive is released, and in the case of nasals it escapes through the nose. These sounds are collectively called **stops** and they bear the specification [−continuant]. Affricates are an intriguing case, because in their articulation they start out as plosives and then turn into fricatives. A convenient way of notating this is to use both specifications for [continuant] and to label them [−/+continuant]. It is important not to confuse the notations [±continuant] and [(−/+continuant]: [±continuant] is the *name of the feature*, with an informal indication that the feature has one of two values '+' or '−' (usually!); [−/+continuant] is a special type of *feature value* for an affricate indicating that the sound, in a sense, has both specifications, one after the other.

For place of articulation, the picture in contemporary phonology is a little different. Consonants don't divide up into pairs of classes; rather a sound is either labial, or coronal, or dorsal, or guttural (see table 19). This means that we need to distinguish a feature of Place of Articulation (or [PLACE]) and give it *four* values: [PLACE: Labial], [PLACE: Coronal], [PLACE: Dorsal], [PLACE: Guttural]. Since the names 'Labial', 'Coronal' etc. unambiguously refer to Place features, we often omit specific reference to PLACE. However, we must bear in mind that when we see a sound marked [Labial], this is really a shorthand for [PLACE: Labial].

By using features in this fashion, we can represent all the consonants of English in a distinctive way. For instance, on the basis of what we have considered so far, both /s/ and /ʃ/ are characterised as [− voiced], [− nasal], [+continuant] and [PLACE: Coronal]. However, the feature system in appendix 2 enables us to distinguish /s/ from /ʃ/ by appealing to the fact that /s/ is made slightly more forward (more **anterior**) in the mouth than is /ʃ/, that is, /s/ is [+anterior], whereas /ʃ/ is [− anterior]; more generally, alveolar and dental sounds are [+anterior], while palato-alveolar, palatal and strongly retroflexed sounds are [−anterior].

The feature values for an inventory of sounds is usually represented as a **feature matrix**. We have given such a matrix for the English consonants as appendix 3 (p. 141) (*exercise 6*).

Features and processes

Our discussion so far has got us to the point where each of the segments in an underlying representation consists of a set of features with appropriate values, and we have also seen that we need to specify how URs are converted to SRs. In (64), we regarded this latter as the replacement of a phoneme by a different segment (various stressed vowels were replaced by [ə]), but if we no longer have phonemes in URs, but rather a sequence of sets of features, we must ask how phonological processes can be formulated. We shall do this by discussing aspiration in English voiceless plosives.

We saw earlier that the sounds /p t k/ have two pronunciations. In words like *par, tar, car* they are aspirated, while in *spar, star, scar* they are unaspirated. However, we also know that there are no pairs of phonemes in English distinguished solely by aspiration, i.e. aspiration is not distinctive in English. How are we to represent the difference between unaspirated and aspirated sounds? The simplest way is to appeal to another feature, which we can call [aspirated]. Even though this feature is not a distinctive feature in English, it is necessary to assume such a feature in Universal Grammar (UG). This is because, aspiration *is* a distinctive feature in some languages (e.g. Bengali, see 51, p. 85). However, it is also important in describing the Phonetic Form (PF) of English words.

The pattern of aspiration of /p t k/ is part of the phonological system of Standard English. This implies that there is a phonological rule which governs the distribution of aspiration. We will present a simplified version of this rule to illustrate how features can be used in formulating rules. We want to account for two things: first, the fact that it is precisely the voiceless plosives which have aspirated allophones and second, the fact that the unaspirated allophone is found after *s*- ([sp=ɪt]) and the aspirated one is found at the beginning of a word ([pʰɪt]) – in what follows, in the interests of simplicity, we shall assume that aspiration occurs in other contexts too.

The way we will proceed is to assume (adopt the hypothesis) that the underlying representations for words like *pit* and *spit* do *not* specify whether the plosive is aspirated or not. After all, we don't need this information in order to distinguish the two types of word, since aspiration is not a distinctive feature in English. Put differently, aspiration is a completely redundant feature because its distribution can always be predicted, unlike voicing, which serves to distinguish words like *pit* and *bit*. The way we indicate that a feature is redundant is to give it the specification '0': [0aspirated]. We often say that such a sound is **underspecified** for the feature (for the use of a similar notion of underspecification in connection with children's syntax, see section 24, p. 391). However, we can't pronounce an underspecified sound (because we won't know whether to aspirate the sound or not), so ultimately we will need a rule which will specify various occurrences of /p t k/ as [+aspirated] or [−aspirated]. The idea that some features are specified in underlying representations while other features are underspecified is very important, because this is the main way of formalising the idea that some feature specifications are contrastive in the language.

The aspiration rule is stated informally (i.e. in ordinary prose) in (65):

(65) a. In /p t k/, [0aspirated] is given the specification [−aspirated] after
         s-
      b. In /p t k/, [0aspirated] is given the specification [+aspirated] in
         other positions

'Specification' is a process which we can symbolise using an arrow → (as we did in the case of vowel reduction). The notion 'in a given position' is symbolised by a slash which represents the **environment** or **context** in which the process occurs. Incorporating these two pieces of notation into (65) gives us (66):

(66) a. In /p t k/, [0aspirated]   →   [−aspirated]/*s*____
      b. In /p t k/, [0aspirated]   →   [+aspirated]/other positions

The part of the rule in (66a) says that the phonemes /p t k/ are realised as the unaspirated allophones immediately after /s/, and (66b) says that they are realised as the aspirated allophones elsewhere. The line ____ in (66a) is called the **focus bar**. If the plosives had been aspirated whenever they preceded *s* (in the clusters -*ps*, -*ts*, -*ks*), then the focus bar would have come to the left of the *s* in the statement of the appropriate rule. Recalling that we can use the IPA diacritic '=' to indicate that a sound is unaspirated, we can say that the two rules in (66) are interpreted as in (67):

(67) The phonemes /p t k/ are realised (pronounced) as
      a. the allophones [p= t= k=] after *s*
      b. the allophones [pʰ tʰ kʰ] elsewhere

Now, we can improve on the formulation in (66) in an important way by making use of distinctive features. Notice that the aspiration affects a specific group of sounds, the voiceless plosives. It isn't an accident that aspiration affects these sounds and not others. For instance, the English aspiration process is a natural process, of a kind we might expect to see in other languages. But we can imagine dozens of other entirely unnatural processes affecting different hypothetical groupings of consonants, such as /p l n/ or /v g s/. However, it is only well-defined groups such as 'voiceless plosives' which undergo phonological processes. Such well-defined groups are called **natural classes**, and one of the most important functions of distinctive features is that they present us with a means of distinguishing natural from unnatural classes.

The set /p t k/ is *exactly* that set of sounds which simultaneously bear the specifications [−voiced, −continuant]. All the other [−continuant] sounds (i.e. stops such as /b/ or /n/) are voiced and all the other voiceless sounds are either continuants (the voiceless fricatives) or affricates (and hence [−/+continuant]). On the other hand, a non-natural class such as /p l n/ can't be represented in such simple terms. Thus, /p l n/ are all consonants, hence, [+consonantal] (see appendix 2 for this feature), but the [+consonantal] class includes all the other consonants too. The feature [−voiced] doesn't apply to the whole set because /l n/ are voiced, but neither does [+voiced] because /p/ is [−voiced]. If you check against the feature matrix in appendix 3, you will see that there are no other features which members of this class have in common. This means that a characterisation of this set in terms of features will be very cumbersome and will have to take the form of (68):

(68)   Feature characterisation of /p l n/:

> [−voiced, −continuant, Labial]   (/p/)
>
> OR
>
> [+lateral]   (/l/)
>
> OR
>
> [+nasal, Coronal]   (/n/)

This crucially involves the use of the word 'or', which means that we have to resort to effectively *listing* the separate phonemes of the set. The set /p l n/ is thus like a set {milk, elephant, violin}: apart from the fact that they are all physical objects they have nothing in common. However, the set /p t k/ is more like the set {violin, viola, cello}, which is a natural grouping characterisable as 'set of instruments used in forming a string quartet'.

It might be objected that we've weighted the scales by selecting an obviously unnatural grouping like /p l n/. But the same will be true of, say, /p t g/, which is at least a set of plosives, with only one member different to our natural class.

This, too, however, can't be described using features without resort to 'or', but this time it's simply because /g/ is [+voiced] while the other two sounds are [−voiced]. Thus, a small change (in this case of one feature specification for one sound) can make all the difference between a natural class and a non-natural class. In a language like English we wouldn't expect /p t g/ to be involved in a phonological process to the exclusion of, say, /b d k/. Neither of these is itself a natural class, but /p b t d k g/ is, being *exactly* characterised as [−continuant, −nasal].

To return to aspiration, using the distinctive feature notation we can rewrite (66) as (69), where we have abbreviated the names of the features in standard ways:

(69)   a. [−voiced, −cont, 0asp] → [−voiced, −cont, −asp] /s_____
         b. [−voiced, −cont, 0asp] → [−voiced, −cont, +asp] /other positions

In practice, these rules can be further simplified by virtue of a notational convention which says that we don't need to mention feature specifications on the right-hand side of the arrow if they don't undergo a change via application of the rule. This means that we don't need to mention [−voiced, −cont]. Thus, we have (70):

(70)   a. [−voiced, −cont, 0asp] → [−asp] /s_____
         b. [−voiced, −cont, 0asp] → [+asp] / other positions

Finally, we now employ a further notational convention which allows us to collapse the left-hand sides of the two subparts of (70). There are only two possible values for the feature [aspirated], so there are two subrules telling us how a voiceless plosive is pronounced, as shown in (71):

(71)   a. [−voiced, −cont, 0asp] → $\begin{cases} [-\text{asp}]/s\_\_\_\_ \\ [+\text{asp}] \end{cases}$
         b.

These two subrules are interpreted as follows: when we encounter a voiceless plosive which has no specification for [aspiration], we first look to see if it is preceded by /s/. If it is, then it is marked [−asp]. Under any other circumstances, it is marked [+asp]. This means that we *must* apply subrule (71a) before subrule (71b), because if (71b) applied first, it would incorrectly aspirate the voiceless plosive in a word like *spit*. However, there is a very important principle in linguistics which means that we don't have to stipulate that (71b) follows (71a). This is known as the **Elsewhere Condition** and it states that where two rules could apply to the same input and produce different outputs, then the rule which applies in the *more specific* set of contexts applies first, thereby preventing application of the second rule. In the present case, (71a) applies only when the plosive is preceded by /s/, whereas (71b) is written to apply anywhere. Thus, (71a) is obviously the more specific rule and will apply in preference to (71b) wherever its conditions are met. Subrule (71b) is called the 'Elsewhere case', or more generally the **default** case. It states that the default specification of [aspiration] for voiceless plosives is [+aspiration] so that a voiceless plosive will be aspirated by default (i.e. other things being equal). The Elsewhere Condition with its associated notion of a default is an important component of UG, and its consequence in this case is that a child acquiring English does not have to learn that (71a) must be applied before (71b) (*exercises 7 and 8*).

Exercises

1. The sounds [ç h s] are in complementary distribution in native words in the Olsk dialect of Even, a Tungusic language spoken in Yakutia, Siberia. By examining the following Even words, decide what governs this distribution. ([ie] and [iæ] are diphthongs consisting of [i] + [e]/[æ])

bead	nısɑ	*blows*	huːn	*bottom*	hɛr	*cave*	hor
foundation	hat	*his skill*	hɔːn	*hot*	hoːksi	*knife*	çırqan
knows	hɑːn	*pocket*	çiep	*poplar*	hʊl	*rotted*	çiævʊs
sad	bʊlʊs	*sole*	hɛssə	*soup*	çilʲ	*Soviet*	hɔvʲɛːt
spectacles	bʊsqʲı	*star*	ɔsıqam	*vein*	hula	*weapon*	us

2. List all the theoretically possible combinations of two consonants in English, then investigate how many of these could be onsets. Which of the impossible combinations can be explained in terms of their sonority profile?

3. Recall that the symbol = means an unaspirated consonant and the symbol ʰ means aspiration. Show how the pattern of data below can be explained by the Maximal Onset Principle. Assume that separate words are syllabified separately. (Note that it will be necessary for you to generalise the text discussion of aspiration so as to take account of the position of plosives in *syllables.*)

   1a. stub   [st=ʌb]
   b. this tub   [ðɪs tʰʌb]
   c. disturb   [dɪst=əːb]

2a. spare   [sp=ɛː]
  b. this pear [ðɪs pʰɛː]
  c. despair   [dɪsp=ɛː]

3a. scar   [sk=ɑː]
  b. this car   [ðɪs kʰɑː]
  c. discard   [dɪsk=ɑːd]

4. Break the following words into syllables, and, applying the Maximal Onset Principle, identify the onsets, nuclei and codas by providing a diagram such as that in (58). Some of these words may have more than one acceptable pronunciation, usually depending on rate of speech, so there may be more than one correct answer for a given item.

    (a) *comfortable*; (b) *confessional*; (c) *secretary*; (d) *cooperative*; (e) *existentialism*.

5. In General American English *photograph, photography* would be pronounced [ˈfouɹə,græːf], [fəˈtɑgɹə,fiː] where [ɾ] represents the 'flap' or 'tap'. Here we see that the sound written 't' represents two sounds [t ɾ]. Assume that one of the two is the basic, underlying form. Then, using the data below, formulate a rule which will account for the distribution of these two sounds. Justify your choice of the underlying form for [t ɾ].

sit	[sɪt]
sitting	[sɪɾɪŋ]
sitter	[sɪɾɚ]
satire	[sætaɹɪ]
satirical	[sətɪɹɪkl]
tone	[toun]
atone	[ətoun]
teatime	[tiːtaɪm]

6. We can describe vowels using distinctive features, too, relying on the following correspondences (for simple vowel systems):

Back	[+back]	Front	[−back]
Low	[+low]	Mid or High	[−low]
High	[+high]	Mid or Low	[−high]
Rounded	[+round]	Unrounded	[−round]

Notice that a mid vowel is defined as one which is neither high (i.e. it is [−high]) nor low (i.e. it is [−low]). This allows us to characterise a reasonably large set of vowels using the feature matrix in table 20 below (this is essentially the vowel system of Finnish):

Table 20: A distinctive feature matrix for vowels							
	i	y	e	ø	a	ɑ	o	u
high	+	+	−	−	−	−	−	+
back	−	−	−	−	−	+	+	+
low	−	−	−	−	+	+	−	−
round	−	+	−	+	−	−	+	+

Enumerate all the vowels with the following feature characterisations:

(i)   [+high, −round]
(ii) [−high, +back, −low, +round]
(iii) [+back, +low, +round]
(iv) [+high, −back, +low, −round]
(v)   [−back, −round]
(vi) [+back, −low, −round]
(vii) [+back, −low]
(viii) [+back, +round]

In certain cases there may be no vowels corresponding to the particular feature set. When is this an accident of the language and when is there a principled reason for it?

7. Using the vowel matrix in table 20 identify which of the following sets constitute natural classes and give a feature characterisation for those that are natural classes. Be careful to ensure that your feature characterisation includes all the vowels in the given set and, especially, that it excludes any sounds not in the set:

(i)   i e æ
(ii) ø o u
(iii) i y e ø
(iv) æ ɑ o u
(v)   i y e ø æ ɑ o

8.   The following examples illustrate a common phonological process in English. First, write as accurate a phonetic transcription of these phrases as you can. Try to transcribe the way they would be pronounced in ordinary casual conversation, rather than in carefully enunciated speech. Then, identify what the phonological process consists of and determine what conditions the change. (Pay particular attention to the end of the first word of each phrase. Not all the examples illustrate a change as such – some are included in order to help you figure out the basic form of the first word.)

in April
in May
in September
in November
in December
in Britain
in Paris
in Europe
in July
on course
on paper
on beta-blockers
on trust
on average
thin cakes
thin girls
thin boys
thin material
thin dress
thin excuse

6   Child phonology

One of the tasks of a child learning his or her language is to figure out the sound system. This involves learning how to distinguish all the linguistically important differences, and also how to produce them. It's rather easier to record what small children say than to determine what they understand, so most systematic research has examined production. At the same time, it is widely believed that children's phonological perception runs ahead of their productive abilities, and this mismatch between perception and production will take on considerable significance as our discussion proceeds. Because most of the relevant research has been conducted on English-speaking children, we shall restrict ourselves to the acquisition of English.

Early achievements

It is remarkable that children seem to be *innately* disposed to perceive the sounds of language. In an ingenious series of experiments, Peter Eimas and his colleagues have shown that very young babies can hear the sorts of distinctions that are often used in languages and to which we have given some attention in the previous section. The techniques revolve around one idea: a baby quickly gets bored unless *something different* happens in its environment. Experimenters therefore play a series of identical sounds to a baby, say the syllable [pa]. At first the baby is interested and turns its head to the sound. As the sounds are repeated, it loses interest and stops turning its head. But when a slightly different sound, say [ba] or [pʰa], is presented, the baby notices this difference and turns its head to the sound. In other experiments the baby's heart rate is measured, or the baby starts sucking on a dummy (pacifier). In each case, perceptual sensitivity to what are phonemic distinctions in many languages has been established for children as young as four days old.

Children are also innately disposed towards producing speech sounds. In the early months babies babble, that is, they produce a whole series of speech-like noises. These often contain a host of sounds which are not part of the language surrounding the baby. Moreover, it is clear that the child isn't learning to produce these sounds from the speaking population surrounding it. Babies born profoundly deaf *also go through a normal period of babbling*.

A little later, usually towards the end of the first year of life, a child will start to try to use sounds meaningfully. Often the child will apparently invent its own little 'language' at this stage. The British linguist Michael Halliday has described in detail how between the ages of nine and fifteen months his son Nigel used quite specific vocalisations in particular contexts with identifiable communicative intents. These vocalisations were not related in any obvious way to the adult language spoken around the child. However, this was quickly superseded by attempts to produce adult words. In the case of Nigel, this seems to have started very abruptly during the course of just one day, in which a whole host of adult-like utterances were recorded. It's very hard to generalise about exactly when a child will start trying to produce the adult system, but a typical picture would be for a child's first words to appear any time between ten and fifteen months (if the child is learning more than one language this onset may be later). Sometimes there is a great deal of variation in the pronunciation of these early words, though on occasions the child may pronounce words very accurately. A famous case of the latter from the research literature is that of Hildegard Leopold, who was studied by her linguist father as she learnt English and German. Her first English word was *pretty*, pronounced more or less as in adult English.

Phonological processes in acquisition

After the child has acquired about fifty or so words, a sudden change often takes place. Children *simplify* their pronunciations and at the same time start acquiring a great many new words extremely quickly. Words which may have been pronounced correctly at first suffer this simplification: Hildegard's *pretty* is again an appropriate illustration. During this period her near adult form gave way to [pɪtɪ] and then [bɪdɪ]. By the age of about four or five, however, children have mastered all but the trickiest articulations in their language (such as English [θ]). The interesting questions are: what route do children take towards this mastery? and how do they navigate their route?

As already noted, it appears that children generally *know more than they can say*. Thus, one little boy, Amahl Smith, whose development between the ages of two and four was studied by his father, at one stage pronounced both *mouth* and *mouse* as [maʊs]. However, in perception he didn't confuse the two words, as indicated by the fact that he reliably identified pictures of a mouth or a mouse when asked to do so by his father. In fact, Amahl provided more subtle *production* evidence for this claim: at an earlier stage he couldn't pronounce [θ ð s z] and these came out as [t d]. Thus, he pronounced *mouth* and *mouse* as [maʊt]. At this stage he was also learning how to pluralise nouns. Given his phonological system, a word like *cats* was pronounced as [kæt] – the plural /s/ became [t] and the resulting sequence [tt] in [kætt] was simplified to [t]. However, his plural for *mouse* was [maʊtɪd], not [maʊt]. This is understandable if we assume that he knew that *mouse* really ended in /s/ and not /t/ and that words ending in /s/ normally form their plural by the addition of [ɪz] (see *bus/buses*, *kiss/kisses*, etc.). Interestingly, this sort of example (which is far from unique) also shows that the child can't have been just imitating plural forms: the child will not have heard a form *mouses* to imitate. We shall return to this mismatch between perception and production below.

An influential theory about the way children learn articulation is based on the **generative theory of phonology** introduced in section 5. There we saw that phonologists relate underlying representations (URs) to surface representations (SRs) by means of phonological rules, which are a way of referring to phonological processes. We can use this idea to account for aspects of child phonology by assuming that the child perceives and stores the adult forms of words more or less correctly (the evidence cited in the previous paragraph is consistent with this in the case of Amahl) and then imposes a set of phonological rules to simplify those pronunciations. The forms actually pronounced by the child are therefore equivalent to surface representations. This is an appealing model because a good many of the distortions introduced into children's speech seem to be regular and in many cases can be regarded as the consequence of phonological processes which are rather similar to those observed in adult languages (see below for illustration). As the child develops, the simplifying processes will be altered, to permit a greater variety of output forms, or lost altogether (so that the child's form is the same as the adult's).

For instance, to account for Hildegard Leopold's form /pɪtɪ/ for *pretty* on this model we can assume that she imposed a process of *consonant cluster simplification* onto adult forms, the effect of which is to transform the sequence /pr/ into /p/. This process is shown schematically in (72), where C stands for any consonant:

(72)   C C → C

The schematic picture emerging from this way of looking at things is represented in figure 25:

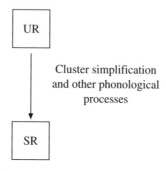

Figure 25 *Preliminary model of child phonology*

Other common types of phonological process for which children present evidence are illustrated in the speech of Amahl Smith. At the age of two, he simplified almost all consonant clusters to a single consonant, e.g. *stamp* → [dap], *drink* → [gɪk], *socks* → [gɔk], *scales* → [geil], *crumb* → [gʌm], *bring* → [bɪŋ], *spoon* → [buːn]. The only clusters he produced were in words such as *camera* → [gæmdə], *bandage* → [bændɪt], *cheque-book* → [gɛkbʊk], but this is easy to understand once we recognise that the most complex type of syllable Amahl was able to pronounce was of the form *consonant + vowel + consonant* (CVC). If a word (for him) had two syllables, such as *bandage*, then this would give rise to a cluster in the middle of the word, provided the two syllables were individually pronounceable, hence [gɛk] + [bʊk] to give [gɛk.bʊk] and so on.

Notice that in the examples we have cited here, at the beginning of a word the consonant is voiced, even if the adult word has a voiceless consonant or consonants in this position. Thus voiceless /s/ gives rise to voiced [g] in *sock,* voiceless /st/ becomes voiced [d] in *stamp,* etc. Voiceless sounds immediately followed by a vowel are very frequently voiced in early child speech, a phenomenon known as **Prevocalic Voicing**. It is not very common to find Prevocalic Voicing in adult phonologies, though there is a rather similar phenomenon in a large number of languages in which a voiceless sound is voiced if it occurs between two vowels.

Also illustrated in some of the above words is a very common process in child phonology, often know as **Stopping**, in which a fricative such as [f z ʃ] or an affricate [ʧ, ʤ] is simplified to the corresponding stop consonant, i.e. [p d t] or [t d]. This kind of process could not be found in this form in adult phonologies, because it takes *all* fricatives and affricates and turns them into stops.

Thus, if it were to occur in an adult phonology we would never know, because we would never see any fricatives or affricates in the language in the first place. Prevocalic Voicing is a process which occurs in a specific environment or context, and such a process is called **context-sensitive**. Most of the phonological rules of adult phonologies (including that determining whether a plosive is aspirated or not discussed in the previous section) are of this kind. On the other hand, Stopping is a process which occurs in all contexts or environments and therefore is called **context-free**.

Still another process apparent from Amahl's forms is one in which a velar sound [k g ŋ] *at the end of a word* appears to influence a coronal sound, such as [s t d tʃ], *at the beginning of that word*. Thus, the /d/ of *drink* becomes [g] in the context of the following /k/. Now this phenomenon is rather reminiscent of phonological processes found in a variety of languages, and which are termed **harmony** processes. The process just illustrated is therefore often called **Velar Harmony**. In adult languages, harmony processes tend to affect vowels rather than consonants, i.e. **vowel harmony** is more widely attested than is **consonant harmony**. Thus, in Finnish, Hungarian, Turkish and a variety of other languages, essentially all the vowels of a word have to be either front vowels (such as [i e œ y]) or back (such as [u o ɔ ɑ]). If an ending is added to a word which has front vowels, then the vowels of the ending will be [−back], but if the same ending is added to a word with back vowels, then the vowels of the ending will be [+back]. For instance, the plural ending in Turkish is *-ler* (with a front vowel) when added to the words *ev* 'house', or *ip* 'rope' (which contain front vowels), so we get *evler* 'houses', *ipler* 'ropes'. However, it is *-lar* (with a back vowel) when added to the words *oda* 'room', or *pul* 'stamp' (which contain back vowels), giving *odalar* 'rooms', *pullar* 'stamps'.

Vowel and consonant harmony are themselves examples of **assimilation** processes (see introduction, p. 5). In such a process one set of sounds, the **target** of the assimilation, becomes more similar to another set of sounds, the **trigger** for the assimilation, by acquiring a specification for some feature or set of features from the trigger. Thus, in the vowel harmony of Turkish, endings acquire the specification [−back] from words with [−back] vowels and the specification [+back] from words with [+back] vowels. In general, the target of an assimilation process only acquires *some* of its features from the trigger, giving **partial assimilation**. Thus, the Turkish plural ending only alternates with respect to the feature [back], it doesn't become *-lir* after *ip* or *-lur* after *pul*, which would be the case if it were also taking on the height and rounding characteristics of the preceding vowel. There are cases of assimilation in other languages, though, in which the trigger does become identical to the target, in which case we speak of **total assimilation**.

We can also see instances in Amahl's speech where more than one process applies. Thus, in *socks*, pronounced as [gɔk], the initial /s/ is stopped to [t] and it also harmonises with the following /k/ to give [k]. In addition it is voiced to [g]. Sometimes a sequence of processes acting in this way can give rise to sounds or sound sequences which are not found in English. Thus, Amahl's pronunciation of the word *snake* was [ŋeɪk], and we have already observed that [ŋ] never occurs initially in an English word. Work out which two processes of those mentioned above give rise to this form (*exercises 1, 2 and 3*).

Perception, production and a dual lexicon model

While the simple model in figure 25 can account for a wide range of data and also acknowledges the discrepancy between child perception and production (URs correspond to what is perceived, whereas SRs correspond to what is produced), there are acquisition phenomena which suggest that it must be elaborated. We shall now consider one such phenomenon in some detail.

A very frequent production problem for children is the pronunciation of the approximants [w l r j] (because of its familiarity, throughout this discussion, we will use [r] for the English 'r' sound, although, as observed in section 2, it would be more accurate to use [ɹ]). Amahl Smith, for instance, couldn't pronounce [r j] if there was an [l] elsewhere in the word. Thus, *yoyo* was pronounced [joujou] but *yellow* and *lorry* were pronounced [lɛlou] and [lɒlɪ] and there was no distinction between his pronunciations of *lorry* and *lolly* – both were pronounced [lɒlɪ]. However, he could distinguish *red* and *led* in his production even at a time when he pronounced *lorry* and *lolly* identically. How can we account for this set of observations?

From section 2 we know that the sounds involved can all be described as coronal approximants. We also know that a characteristic distinguishing [l] from [r j] is that it is produced by passing air round the side of the tongue, i.e. it is a lateral sound, a distinction which is captured by the feature [±lat] in the feature system of appendix 2. Thus, [l] is [+lat] while [r j] are [−lat]. What happens in Amahl's pronunciation is that the non-lateral sounds come to share the same feature specification for the lateral feature as the neighbouring /l/ sound. Of course, this is just another example of harmony, so we can call Amahl's process **lateral harmony**.

A consequence of the existence of lateral harmony is that there can be no contrast between /l/ and either /r/ or /j/ when there is already an occurrence of /l/ in the word. This means that the feature [±lat] cannot be *distinctive* in such a word. In section 5 we said that when a feature is never distinctive, as in the case of the feature [aspirated] in English, we give that feature a specification of zero in the UR. This means that we ought to give the feature lateral a zero specification ([0lat]) in words like *lorry* for Amahl. Indeed, this is a common way of handling such harmony processes in adult grammars. However, we must also acknowledge that both the /l/ and the /r/ of adult *lorry* are pronounced by the child as [l]. Hence, while we wish to maintain that these segments are [0lat] in the child's UR, we must somehow also ensure that they are [+lat] in the SR.

At first sight, it might appear that the obvious way to approach this problem is to treat it like the cases of velar harmony mentioned above. There we suggested that initial coronals harmonise with final velars, and it is easy to see how this could be expressed as a rule along the lines of (73):

(73)   [Coronal] → [Dorsal]/ # _____ V [Dorsal]#

      (Here, the symbol # indicates a word boundary)

Recall that what appears after the slash is a specification of the context in which the rule applies, so (73) says that the place feature [Coronal] is changed to [Dorsal] when it occurs initially and precedes an arbitrary vowel (V) and a final sound with the place feature [Dorsal]. In order to be effective, (73) requires the presence of the place feature value [Dorsal] in a word's UR, and we can immediately see an important difference between this situation and the case of lateral harmony we are considering. For the latter, we are supposing that *both* crucial segments are [0lat] in the relevant representation of *lorry*, i.e. there is *no* lateral segment in this representation to trigger the harmony, since [lat] is not distinctive in such words for Amahl at this stage in his development.

A way of dealing with this is to say that the UR of *lorry* has a 'floating' feature [+lat], which in a sense *is a property of the whole word*. This [+lat] feature is then anchored to specific segments, namely those which correspond to non-labial approximants, /r j l/ in the adult words. This is achieved by **spreading** the [+lateral] feature to those segments, as illustrated for *yellow* and *lorry* in figure 26. Note that underspecified segments don't, strictly speaking, correspond to a single phoneme, so we'll represent them using capital letters R, J and L. The dotted boxes here are simply to indicate that while [+lat] is not attached to anything on the left-hand side of the arrows, it is nonetheless an integral part of the representations.

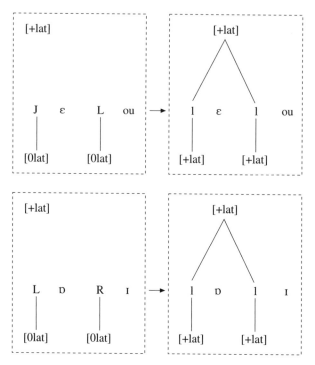

Figure 26 *Lateral harmony as feature spreading*

Now, an intriguing aspect of this analysis is that it doesn't fit the simple model of figure 25 in which the child is assumed to have representations which correspond to the adult URs. In these latter, *distinctive* features including [±lat] are fully specified and there is no place for [0lat] or other underspecified values ([0asp] is, of course, a different case, as [asp] is not distinctive in *adult* English). The reason for assuming full specification was that children appear to *perceive* sound distinctions in an adult-like manner from a very early age, and there is good reason to believe that this perceptual accuracy extends to words which include /l r j/. This means that the representations which reflect the child's perceptions are fully specified. However, children's production of words is much less accurate than their perception at this age. We can therefore think of the underspecification of the lateral feature in words like *lorry* or *lolly* as the way in which the theoretical model reflects this inaccuracy in pronunciation. On the perceptual side, Amahl knows that *lorry* has an /r/. However, he doesn't know how to pronounce that /r/ in a word of that shape. We can propose, therefore, that the initial set of representations in figure 26 (those on the left-hand side of the arrows) are representations of the child's production ability, an indication that the child doesn't know how to articulate the /j/ in *yellow* or /r/ in *lorry*. If this is correct, there are *three* representations we must consider: (a) what the child actually says (the SRs in figure 25, the right-hand side of figure 26); (b) the adult forms (the URs of figure 25), to which the child appears to have access via perception; (c) forms which are relevant to the child for production (the left-hand side of figure 26).

What the above discussion suggests is that it is plausible to maintain that there are *two* phonological representations stored in the child's mind, one for perception (b immediately above) and one for production (c). We call these **input representations** and **output representations** and there clearly has to be some relationship between them. In general, the output representations are similar to the input representations but with certain aspects of the representation missing or simplified. For instance, suppose we maintain that the child's input representation (based on perception) for *lorry* corresponds to the adult representation /lɒlɪ/. In order to 'derive' an appropriate output representation (what we have on the left-hand side of figure 26), we have to assume two processes. First, the [−lateral] feature representation of /r/ is replaced by [0lateral]. This is called **despecification**. Then, the [+lateral] feature is 'floated' or **delinked** from the /l/, so that the /l/ segment itself is also [0lateral]. This is illustrated in fig. 27, where for clarity we have separated delinking (indicated by breaking the line between /l/ and [+lat]) and 'floating'.

The output representation in figure 27 can now serve as the UR for the process of lateral harmony illustrated in figure 26 and this UR can be referred to the child's **output UR**, i.e. the underlying representation, which is subject to phonological processes that determine the form of the child's utterances. Thus, we are now proposing *two* types of processes. The type of process represented by figure 27 is called a **selection rule**, and, taking the adult form as input, it gives rise to an output UR which contains a number of unspecified features and other aspects of representation which need to be filled in. This filling in is achieved by other processes, which we call **pronunciation rules**. The spreading of the floating [+lateral] feature to give lateral harmony is an example of such a rule.

In the model that results from this type of analysis children are credited with two types of phonological representation, one corresponding to their perception of the word and the other determined by the set of distinctive features, syllable templates and so on over which they have mastery in production. Because there are two distinct sets of lexical representations, we will call such a model a **dual lexicon model**. The overall structure of the model is illustrated in figure 28.

It is possible to see how the model in figure 28 can account for other processes

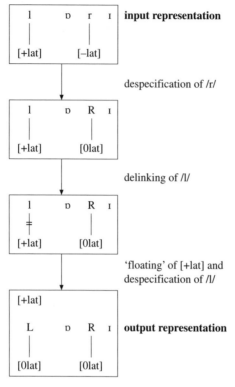

Figure 27 *Lateral harmony: constructing the output UR*

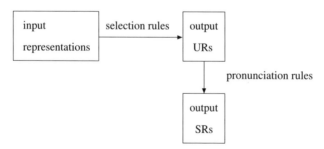

Figure 28 *A dual lexicon model of child phonology*

which we have so far assumed to be accommodated in the simpler model of figure 25. For instance, we noted above that Amahl Smith's most complex syllables were of the form CVC, that is they included at most one onset consonant and at most one coda consonant. Obviously, this can be accommodated to the model of figure 25 by relying on a rule such as (72) linking URs and SRs, but our dual-lexicon approach now provides us with an alternative way of dealing with this phenomenon, provided we take English syllable structure into account (as discussed in section 5 (pp. 89ff.)). Specifically, we can propose that Amahl operates with a **syllable template** over the input representations governed by the Sonority Hierarchy. Children in general find it easier to pronounce sounds and combinations which differ from each other maximally, so they tend to choose the least sonorous elements as onsets and codas and the most sonorous elements as nuclei. At early stages, only one consonant is allowed in the onset or the coda and so this has to be the least sonorant of the cluster. We know from section 5 (pp. 90f.) that /s/ in clusters such as *stay* or *string* is exceptional in English, so this will not enter into early child templates even in clusters such as *sm-* or *sl-*, in which it is the less sonorant (though children tend to differ in the precise way they treat these clusters).

In the case of codas, there is rather more variability between children; in part which item from a cluster is pronounced by a child depends on the language being learned. However, Amahl treated the voiceless plosive in a coda cluster such as the *-mp* of *stamp* as we would predict from the Sonority Hierarchy. How this works is illustrated in figure 29 for *stamp*, which at this stage Amahl pronounced as [dap]:

input representation

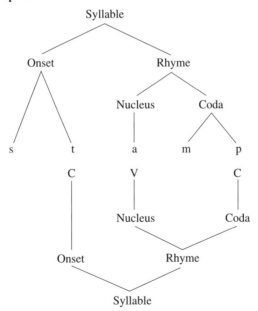

Syllable template (=a constraint on syllable structure determining a selection rule)

Figure 29 *Matching input representation to syllable structure template*

This template, operating as a selection rule, produces the syllable [tap] along with an unattached [s] and an unattached [m]. What happens to these items which are not integrated into the child's syllable via the matching process? The answer is that they are deleted by a general process which phonologists refer to as **Stray Deletion** or **Stray Erasure**. In terms of the model in figure 28, this is a pronunciation rule. In general, any material which is left over because it has not been associated with some part of the template or has not been incorporated into the word by means of some pronunciation rule is deleted by this process. In the case of lateral harmony discussed above, the floating [+lat] feature in the output representation in figure 27 is saved from extinction by the pronunciation process of lateral spreading. There are no comparable processes which will save the unassociated /s/ or /m/ of *stamp* in Amahl's system. Thus, the only segments which survive to the level of the output SR for *stamp* are [tap]. Additionally, along the way the [t] is voiced to [d] by Prevocalic Voicing, another pronunciation rule, giving us the attested form [dap].

This concludes our brief survey of the nature of child phonology. We have, of course, only scratched the surface of this developing and fascinating field. However, consideration of what goes on when children acquire sound systems has enabled us to draw attention to some important notions in theoretical phonology, notions which are regularly applied in the analysis of adult phonological systems. Of particular importance is *underspecification*, especially as a way of formalising harmony processes, and another useful notion is that of the *floating feature*. We have also seen the fundamental importance of syllable structure, in understanding the nature of children's forms, and the idea of associating segments to a template to filter out combinations which are not allowed in the phonological system is used widely. However, perhaps most important of all is the idea of *distinct levels of representation*, and especially the idea that there is at least a distinction between an underlying level and a surface level. Although the model of child phonology we have introduced here raises additional complications (because unlike adults, children can't pronounce most of the words they can recognise), if we look at the output (right-hand) side of the model in figure 28, we see there the two-level system introduced in figure 25. The distinction between underlying and surface levels is one of the key ideas in phonology and indeed in linguistics generally, and even in widely different theoretical approaches it tends to reappear in some guise or other (*exercises 4 and 5*).

Exercises

1.   Below is a sample of words from the first stages of development of
      Amahl Smith. Assuming that the child's underlying representations
      are identical to the adult surface representations, what **neutralisation
      processes** (processes which ensure that Amahl does *not* make a dis-
      tinction which is made in the adult system) affect Amahl's speech at
      this time? (The transcriptions have been simplified slightly.)

word	adult pronunciation	child's pronunciation
apple	/apl/	/ɛbu/
bath	/bɑːθ/	/bɑːt/
brush	/bɹʌʃ/	/bʌt/
bus	/bʌs/	/bʌt/
caravan	/kaɹavan/	/gawəwan/
church	/tʃəːtʃ/	/dəːt/
dark	/dɑːk/	/gɑːk/
feet	/fiːt/	/wiːt/
finger	/fɪŋgə/	/wɪŋə/
flower	/flaʊə/	/wawə/
John	/dʒɒn/	/dɒn/
knife	/naɪf/	/maɪp/
leg	/lɛg/	/gɛk/
light	/laɪt/	/daɪt/
nipple	/nɪpl/	/mɪbu/
other	/ʌðə/	/ʌdə/
sing	/sɪŋ/	/gɪŋ/
snake	/sneɪk/	/ŋeːk/
sock	/sɒk/	/gɒk/
stop	/stɒp/	/bɒp/
table	/teɪbl/	/beːbu/
taxi	/taksɪ/	/gɛkiː/
uncle	/ʌŋkl/	/ʌgu/
write	/ɹaɪt/	/daɪt/
yes	/jɛs/	/dɛt/
zoo	/zuː/	/duː/

2.   Neil Smith, Amahl's father, uses the following data to argue that his
      son's phonological processes must apply in a strictly defined order.

State the processes in as general a form as possible. Then show why, when so stated, they must apply in a set order (assume that the child's underlying forms are identical to the adult surface forms):

bottle	/bɒkəl/	colour	/kʌlə/	gentle	/dɛŋkəl/
kennel	/kɛŋəl/	kettle	/kɛkəl/	metal	/mɛkəl/
muzzle	/mʌdəl/	nice	/naɪt/	nose	/noːd/
nozzle	/nɒdəl/	pedal	/pɛgəl/	pencil	/pɛntəl/
pickle	/pɪkəl/	puddle	/pʌgəl/	sew	/təu/
shoe	/tuː/	tassel	/tatəl/	television	/tɛlɪwɪdən/
whistle	/wɪtəl/	zoo	/duː/		

3. Marlys Macken has argued that Amahl Smith has actually *misstored* the pronunciation of a word such as *puddle*, and represented it not with the adult pronunciation but as /pʌgəl/. If this were the case, how would it affect your conclusions in exercise 2?

4. Here are two sets of words from an early and a later stage of Amahl Smith's development. Formulate two syllable templates, one for each of the two sets of data. Comment on the differences between the templates. How do the templates account for the child's data?

word	adult pronunciation	early stage	later stage
ant	/ant/	ɛt	ant
black	/blak/	pak	blak
break	/bɹeɪk/	peːk	bɹeɪk
child	/tʃaɪld/	taɪl	taɪld
clean	/kliːn/	kiːn	kliːn
count	/kaʊnt/	kaʊt	kaʊnt
drink	/dɹɪŋk/	kɪk	dɹɪŋk
friend	/fɹɛnd/	wɛn	fɹɛnd
hand	/hand/	ɛn	and
hold	/hould/	uːd	uːld
jump	/dʒʌmp/	tʌp	dʌmp
lunch	/lʌnʃ/	lʌt	lʌnt
mend	/mɛnd/	mɛn	mɛnd
monkey	/mʌŋkiː/	mʌgiː	mʌŋkiː
pencil	/pɛnsɪl/	pɛtəl	pɛntəl
Smith	/smɪθ/	mɪt	mɪt

snake	/sneɪk/	ŋeːk	neɪk
spider	/spaɪdə/	paɪdə	paɪdə
spring	/spɹɪŋ/	pɪŋ	plɪŋ
stamp	/stamp/	tap	tʰamp
stroke	/stɹouk/	koːk	tɹoːk
swing	/swɪŋ/	wɪŋ	wɪŋ
think	/θɪŋk/	kɪk	tʰɪŋk

5.   Here are two sets of words from different stages in Amahl Smith's development.

(a) Describe the syllable template for the child at each stage.

(b) The words at Stage A show two phonological processes that affect consonants, one of which only affects final consonants at Stage A in particular circumstances. Describe these processes in words.

(c) What crucial difference between the Stage A and Stage B pronunciations might account for the change in the pronunciation of the final consonants between the two stages?

	Stage A	**Stage B**
quick	kɪp	kwɪk
queen	kiːm	kwiːn
squeeze	kiːb	kwiːz
quite	kaɪp	kwaɪt
twice	daɪp	twaɪs
win	wɪn	wɪn
sweet	wiːt	swiːt
spoon	puːn	spuːn

7　Processing sounds

There are two aspects to the real-time processing of language in which we all indulge on a day-to-day basis. One is hearing what others say to us, or in the case of written language and sign languages, seeing what others are saying to us. This is the problem of **speech perception**, and a fundamental part of it for spoken languages is the recognition of speech sounds. The other is producing language ourselves, **speech production**. For spoken varieties of language this includes the problem of control of the muscles of the vocal tract (lungs, throat, tongue, lips) responsible for making the sounds. For sign languages, it is the problem of control of movements of the hands and face. In psychology, the organisation of movement is referred to as **motor control**.

Speech perception

Suppose you are singing a note on a certain pitch. If you wish to sing a different note, one option you have is to shift to the new note gradually and continuously (you can also jump straight to it, but this option doesn't concern us here). This indicates that the pitch of the human voice, determined by the rate at which the vocal cords vibrate, admits of any number of gradations. Now contrast this with someone playing two notes on a piano. A piano has a finite number of *discrete* notes, and as a consequence it isn't possible to play a note *between* C and C#; it is, however, perfectly feasible to sing such a note.

What are speech sounds like? Do they gradually shade into one another like the notes we sing, or are they discrete like the notes of a piano? If we recall our descriptions of the way speech sounds are produced in section 2, we should be immediately attracted by the former possibility. Take place of articulation and the difference between, say a dental and an alveolar sound. The former requires contact between the tip of the tongue and the upper teeth, whereas the latter requires contact between the tip of the tongue and the alveolar ridge. But the space between the bottom of the upper teeth and the back of the alveolar ridge is a continuous space and the tip of the tongue can make contact at any of the infinite number of points in this space. This suggests that the shift from [ṭ] to [t] or from [ṣ] to [s] will be gradual and continuous rather than discrete. Or consider vowel sounds and the front/back and high/low axes, which are fundamental in categorising these sounds. Given any two points on either of these axes, there will always be another point between them, suggesting that the shift from a high to a mid to a low vowel or from a front to a central to a back vowel will again be gradual and continuous.

An alternative perspective is, however, presented by our discussion in section 5, where we saw that *as far as the structure of the language is concerned*, this infinity of speech sounds is reduced to a finite inventory of functioning units, the phonemes of the language.

Let's approach this topic by changing our question. Rather than being concerned with what speech sounds are like, let's ask: what is our *perception* of speech sounds like? Obviously, it could be the case that we perceive all the infinite gradations which the continuous nature of such notions of place of articulation, front/back and high/low make available, or it might be that our perceptual systems are 'tuned' to the phonological structure of our native language, so that we simply do not hear differences in speech sounds which are not linguistically significant. The answer to our revised question is surprisingly complex, and it is likely that a complete understanding of this matter lies some way in the future. Part of the answer, however, seems to depend on what sort of speech sound we are considering.

In order to systematically investigate the issue which concerns us, it is important to be able to control the characteristics of the speech sounds we test. Native speakers cannot vary their speech sounds with the required degree of control, but it is possible to produce speech sounds synthetically using a speech synthesiser. For example, reasonably accurate tokens of syllables such as /ba/ or /pe/ can be produced in this way, and it is then possible to introduce slight, carefully controlled changes into the acoustic form of the synthesised syllables and words, changes which correspond to a gradual shift in place of articulation of a consonant or the height or frontness of a vowel, etc.

One set of experiments we can perform is on vowel sounds. We can synthesise tokens of, say, the words *pit* and *pet*. Then, starting with our token of *pit*, we change its acoustic characteristics in a number of discrete steps until we get to our token of *pet*. The outcome of this process is referred to as an [ɪ – ɛ]-series, i.e. a set of synthesised stimuli with something which is unambiguously *pit* at one end, something which is unambiguously *pet* at the other and a number of acoustically intermediate forms. Such a series can then be used in a variety of experiments with native speakers.

One commonly performed experiment is an **identification experiment**. In this, members of the series are simply presented to native speakers in random order, and they have to say whether they hear *pit* or *pet* – note that we do not allow them to say that a stimulus is neither *pit* nor *pet*, i.e. we employ what is called a 'forced choice paradigm'. A typical (idealised) result from such an experiment appears in figure 30:

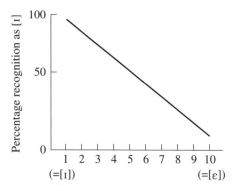

Figure 30 *Results of an identification experiment for an [ɪ – ɛ]-series*

Here along the y-axis we have the number of times subjects report that they have heard *pit* as opposed to *pet* and along the x-axis the items in the series of synthesised stimuli, with 1 corresponding to the original *pit*, 10 to the original *pet* and 2–9 labelling the intermediate stimuli. What results such as this seem to show is that the perception of vowels is *continuous*, with each vowel appearing to shade gradually into the next. For items such as 4, 5 and 6, intermediate between *pit* and *pet*, subjects appear to have recourse to guessing.

A rather different experimental procedure which leads to the same conclusion is a **discrimination experiment**. Such an experiment typically presents native speakers with pairs of adjacent stimuli from a synthesised series followed by a third stimulus which is identical to one of the first two. The subjects' task is to say whether the third stimulus is identical to the first or the second. Obviously, we would expect such a task to be difficult for subjects if their perception is continuous and this turns out to be the case for a vowel series such as that we have considered above. Results of a typical experiment are presented in figure 31 (again these are idealised – empirical enquiry never yields lines as straight as this – but this does not affect the point under discussion):

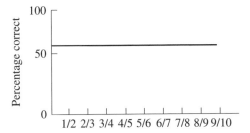

Figure 31 *Results of a discrimination experiment for an [ɪ – ɛ]-series*

Here, on the x-axis, we have pairs of synthesised stimuli which are presented for discrimination and what the straight line indicates is that subjects did only slightly better across the whole series than they would if they were guessing, i.e. discrimination of adjacent pairs was uniformly poor in this case.

What we have described so far is perhaps not very surprising, but when we turn to the perception of consonants a very different picture emerges. A contrast which has been extensively studied is the voiced-voiceless contrast in [b/p], [d/t] and so on. As we know from section 2, voicing occurs when the state of the larynx permits the vocal cords to vibrate. In our earlier discussion, we talked as if voicing occurs *during* the production of voiced consonants, but for plosives this is not quite correct. In fact, if the syllable [ba] is produced in English, the vocal cords do not begin to vibrate until a short time *after* the release of the bilabial closure. By contrast, if [pa] is produced, there is a relatively long time between the release of the closure at the lips and the onset of vocal cord vibration for the vowel, and if the consonant is heavily aspirated, this time becomes even longer. Thus, the *acoustic correlate* of the distinction between voiced, voiceless and aspirated voiceless plosives lies in the time interval between the release of the closure and the beginning of the voicing associated with the following vowel sound. This interval is called **Voice Onset Time** or VOT. Now, of course, time is a continuous variable, and using synthetic stimuli, it is possible to create a set of syllables, comprising a [b – p]-series in which VOT is systematically varied. Obviously, with a short VOT, we expect subjects to perceive [b], whereas with a long VOT, we predict that they will perceive [p]. The interesting question is: what happens with intermediate values?

In figure 32 we see the results of an identification experiment on the perception of [b] and [p], with VOT varying along the x-axis.

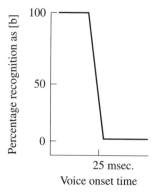

Figure 32 *Results of an identification experiment for a [p – b]-series*

What is significant here is what happens when the VOT value is about 25 msecs. Subjects shift suddenly from reporting [b] to reporting [p]. However, any VOT value less than about 20 msec. is heard as [b], while any VOT greater than about 30 msec. is reported as [p].

Of course, on the basis of this identification experiment, we cannot conclude anything about the subjects' abilities to perceive distinctions *within* categories, but the discrimination experiment enables us to investigate this. What we find here is that if test stimuli fall on opposite sides of the boundary indicated in figure 32, subjects are very accurate in their identifications. If, however, the stimuli fall on the same side of the boundary, then subjects' responses indicate that they are guessing, i.e. they cannot perceive the difference between a stimulus with a VOT of, say, 40 msec. and another with a VOT of, say, 60 msec. Typical results from such an experiment appear in figure 33, where on the x-axis, we have the mean VOTs for the stimuli being presented for discrimination (e.g. 25 msec. gives the result for discrimination of stimuli with 20msec. and 30msec. VOT).

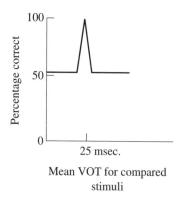

Figure 33 *Results of a discrimination experiment for a [b – p]-series*

What figure 33 indicates is that hearers can discriminate the phonetic categories, voiced vs. voiceless, very well but they cannot hear differences *within* these
categories. This type of perception is known as **categorical perception**, because
the hearer perceives in terms of categories (voiced or voiceless) rather than in
terms of minute gradations of sound. It is of considerable interest that categorical perception appears to be rather unusual and it may well be an aspect
of the special capacities which humans have for language mentioned in our
main introduction. A further observation which supports this possibility
comes from the behaviour of infants. As we mentioned in the last section, it is
possible to perform experiments with very young babies, and to use such measures as head turning, sucking or heart rate as indicators that they do or do not
perceive a difference between two sounds. When this is done with babies that
have been exposed to some form of language, it is discovered that they too perceive VOT categorically, many months before they start trying to pronounce
adult plosive sounds themselves.

Speech production

At some stage in the production of speech the speaker has to formulate plans for moving the articulators in such a way as to produce the required
sounds in the required order. This is far and away the most complex motor
control problem faced by human beings. The number of different muscles
involved is enormous and the fine tuning required to get even an approxima-
tion to human speech is extremely delicate. The complexity of the process is
seen to be even greater when we realise that we can and do introduce extremely
subtle changes into our normal speech, by altering its rhythm and loudness
and especially our tone of voice (intonation) so as to achieve different nuances
of meaning. We can even play with our speech, by imitating other accents or
modes of speaking. When we speak to someone with a different accent, we
unconsciously accommodate to that accent in a fashion that is only really
apparent to a person who is trained in phonetics (see section 4 for sociolinguistic perspectives on this phenomenon).

Given the complexity of the problem, it is all the more remarkable that we
speak with relatively few errors. However, errors are made in normal speech
and these throw considerable light on the nature of the speech production
process. Later in the book, we shall be looking at speech errors made by people
which involve whole words, and how these might be used to investigate the
nature of the mental lexicon. Here, we shall focus on errors which indicate the
importance of individual sound segments and syllable structure with a view to
understanding the process of speech production. In most cases the errors we

cite have been collected by linguists or psycholinguists listening to conversations, lectures, or TV and radio programmes.

One of the types of speech error that we all make, and which everyone is aware of, is in the context of the tongue twister. In every language there are certain sequences of sounds or syllables which, for some reason, are particularly hard to pronounce. Some of these can be remarkably innocent-looking. For instance, you can get friends to try saying the name *Peggy Babcock* three times very quickly. Make a note of what they actually say, using phonetic transcription (you will probably find it necessary to tape record their attempts), and see what types of error are made.

The problem posed by tongue-twisters is one of vocal gymnastics, something akin to patting your head and rubbing your tummy at the same time. However, there are different sorts of errors which, in many ways, are more interesting, because they don't have such obvious correlates in non-speech motor control. One of the most famous types of speech error is illustrated in (74):

(74)　　a. You have hissed all my mystery lectures [missed all my history lectures]
　　　　b. You have tasted the whole worm [wasted the whole term]
　　　　c. our queer old dean [our dear old Queen]

These are examples of Spoonerisms, allegedly uttered by the Reverend William Spooner, a lecturer at Oxford University in the last century. ('Allegedly' because undergraduates were in the habit of making up such things and attributing them to their notorious mentor.) What is happening here is that two sets of sounds are being exchanged, as shown for (74b) in (75):

(75)　　(w)asted the whole (t)erm　　⇒　　(t)asted the whole (w)orm

Example (74a) is similar in that single whole segments are exchanged, but (74c) is different, as we can see if we refer to phonetic transcription, as in (76):

(76)　　[(d) ɪə ould (kw) iːn]　　⇒　　[kwɪə ould diːn]

In terms of segments, we are exchanging *two sounds for one* here, however our discussion of syllable structure in section 5 has shown us how we can construe this as an exchange of one unit for another. The cluster *kw-* in *queer/queen* is the *onset* of the syllable which comprises this word, and it is this onset which is being exchanged with the onset of the syllable [diːn]. Indeed, it turns out that syllable structure is important in analysing speech, since it is only onsets that get exchanged for onsets, or codas for codas. We don't find constituents of the syllable getting confused with each other in exchanges. In other words, we don't find the onset of one word being exchanged with the coda of a later word, i.e. we don't observe errors of the form shown in (77):

(77)   a (d)og and a ca(t)   ⇒   a tog and a cad (unattested error type)

Simple as this observation is, it provides a very direct indication of the involve-ment of syllable structure in speech production. If the speech production mechanisms did not have access to this structure, there would be no reason to expect that such errors would not occur – logically, they are just as plausible as those involving the switching of onsets or codas.

Exchanges are not the only kind of speech error involving individual sounds. In (78–82) we see a number of other, reasonably common types (in each case collected by researchers from ordinary conversations):

(78)   a. it's a meal mystery [real mystery]
         b. fonal phonology [tonal phonology]

(79)   a. give the goy [give the boy]
         b. Michael Malliday [Michael Halliday]

(80)   his retters [letters]

(81)   country presents [peasants]

(82)   the Britch [British]

The examples in (78) are *anticipations*, in which a sound is anticipated from a following word, whereas those in (79) are *perseverations* in which a sound is repeated from an earlier word. Example (80) is a *substitution* of one phoneme by another, while (81) is the *addition* of a phoneme (producing incidentally a real word). Finally, in (82) we see a case of *omission* of a phoneme (*exercise 1*).

Exchanges are a relatively commonplace type of error, so it may not be immediately apparent that they pose an important theoretical problem for the modelling of action. In fact, they indicate very clearly that we formulate a *plan* of what we are about to say before we actually get round to saying it. As early as 1951 the psychologist Karl Lashley used this as an argument against Behaviourism, a psychological position which maintains that all our actions are governed by habitual responses to stimuli. Lashley pointed out that errors of *serial order* of the kind illustrated by exchanges demonstrate that we must plan ahead, and that we don't simply respond to whatever stimulus has just impinged on us.

The idea of forward planning is enshrined in an influential model of speech production called the **scan-copier model**. According to this model, we first form an abstract representation of the next phrase we are about to utter. Then we copy that representation into a 'buffer'. This then gets translated into movements of the articulators. As we saw from example (74b), syllable structure is very important, so it is appropriate to assume that the scan-copier is sensitive to syllable structure. This model is shown schematically in figure 34:

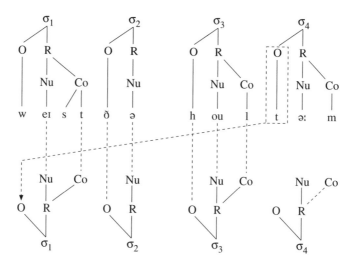

Figure 34 *A simplified version of the scan-copier model of speech production*

In figure 34 we see the stage at which the phrase *waste the whole term* has been put into the buffer (we omit the past tense *-ed* on *wasted* for simplicity). This is an 'abstract' representation of what the speaker intends to say. However, we now need to copy this to the next level of representation, that at which we specify the instructions to the articulators of the vocal tract. For the sake of argument, we'll assume that the syllabic structure of the phrase has been copied. This forms the skeleton for the set of instructions to the articulators and is illustrated in the bottom half of figure 34. We now need to fill in the appropriate slots in the copied syllable structure. The system scans the contents of the buffer from left to right and copies onsets to onset slots, codas to coda slots and so on. As it does so, it monitors its progress by checking off each of the segments it copies. A checked-off segment will not normally be eligible for further copying, of course. In figure 34 the system has made an error by running ahead of itself, and has selected as onset of its first syllable the onset of the final syllable (it is probably no coincidence that this final syllable is the most emphasised word in the phrase). The scanner continues, this time from the correct syllable, and copies the nucleus then the coda of *waste* and moves on to the next syllable. When it reaches the fourth syllable it encounters a problem. The onset here, inside the dotted rectangle, has already been copied. It seems that the copier has two options at this point. First, it can ignore the fact that the onset 't' has already been copied, and copy it again, giving the phrase *tasted a whole term*. This is an anticipation error. However, if, as we have suggested above, a checked-off item is not available for further copying, this route will not be available; arguably, then, the only course open to the copier is to recognise that the /w/ onset of the first syllable has yet to be copied and to use this stray /w/ to fill in the stray onset slot in the final syllable; this will also result in the stray consonant being finally checked off by the monitor. This gives us our spoonerism.

There is one further point to make about phonology and speech errors. Section 14 will examine cases where whole words (or meaningful parts of words) are exchanged, but examples of this of particular relevance here appear in (83):

(83)   a.   ministers in the church $\Rightarrow$ ministers in the church-[əz]
       b.   take the steaks out of the freezer $\Rightarrow$ take the freezer-[z] out of
                                                            the steak-er

In (83a) the plural ending of *ministers* is perseverated on the word *church*. In (83b) we have an exchange between *steak* and *freezer*. In both cases the plural ending accommodates its pronunciation: on *ministers* in (83a) it is /z/ but when it gets added onto *church* it is pronounced as /əz/, in accordance with the phonological rules of English. In (83b), when the plural ending finds itself attached to the wrong word, it again accommodates from the /s/ form in *steaks* to the /z/ form of *freezers*. More generally, we find that speech errors *never* give rise to phonological combinations that would be disallowed by the language. That is, we don't find violations of phonological rules or of the phonotactic constraints of the language. This means that a speech error is nonetheless always a pronounceable word in the language. This shows that the forward planning mechanism operates at a level before the final phonological adjustments take place, such as the pronunciation of the plural ending (*exercises 2, 3 and 4*).

Other aspects of phonological processing

When linguists study the form and function of the linguistic expressions found in their native language, and write grammars to account for them, their primary source of data is provided by their own intuitions regarding how a word is pronounced, whether a sequence of words is a legitimate sentence, etc. If they work on a language which is not their own, such data may be provided by an informant who is a native speaker (see introduction, p. 2). Obviously, if we study the utterances produced by small children or the results of psycholinguistic experiments, we are dealing with different kinds of data, and insofar as such data are used to test and modify theories of grammar they can be regarded as providing an indirect source of evidence on the nature of linguistic competence. Other sources of indirect evidence, of particular relevance to sound systems, are language games, poetic devices, and writing systems, and we will close this part of the book by looking briefly at the last two of these (for a language game, see exercise 5).

One aspect of phonological structure which seems to be easily identifiable even by non-linguists is the syllable. For instance, it is relatively easy to get people to identify the number of syllables in a word, and even very small children (as young as three) can be trained to tap out the number of syllables of polysyllabic words like *elephant*. Many poetic systems work on a syllabic principle. Particularly famous are Japanese verse forms such as the haiku, in which each line has to have a set number of syllables.

Rhyme constituents, too, are very salient. Rhyme, of course, is the basis of classical European versification, but very small children are aware of rhymes and often play rhyming games with themselves in which they make up nonsense words to rhyme with words they know. Perhaps less obviously, onsets can also be important in poetic systems. Before rhyming became the organising principle of English verse, around the time of Chaucer, English poetry operated with a system of alliteration. For instance, in the mystical poem *The Vision of Piers Ploughman* by William Langland (a contemporary of Chaucer), there are no rhymes. However, every line generally has at least three accented words whose stressed syllables begin with the same onset. Sometimes, if there is a consonant cluster, it is just the first member that governs the alliteration, as in the last line of the opening of the Prologue reproduced in (84) (the alliterated onsets are in bold):

(84)   Prologue

>   In a **s**omer **s**esoun whan **s**ofte was the **s**onne,
>   I **sh**oop me into **sh**roudes as I a **sh**eep were,

> In habite as an heremite unholy of werkes,
> Wente wide in this world wonderes to here.
> Ac on a May morwenynge on Malverne hilles
> Me befel a ferly, of Fairye me thoghte.
> I was wery forwandred and wente me to reste
> Under a brood bank by a bourne syde;
> And as I lay and lenede and loked on the watres,
> I slombred into a slepynge, it sweyed so murye.

Translation:

> In a summer season, when mild was the sun,
> I dressed myself in clothes as if I were a sheep,
> In habit as a hermit untrue to his holy vows,
> I went wide in this world to hear wonders.
> But on a May morning on Malvern hills
> A strange experience befell me, from Fairyland it seemed.
> I was weary from wandering and went to rest
> under a broad bank by the side of a stream;
> And as I lay and leaned and looked at the water,
> I fell into a sleep, it [=the stream] made such a sweet sound.

There is one important phonological unit which ordinary language users tend not to be consciously aware of. This is the phonemic segment. This is not to say that the segment-sized unit plays no role in the phonological system of the language, of course. It would be impossible to state a good many phonological rules without reference to segmental structure. Moreover, there is ample evidence that segment-sized units are important in speech production. As we have seen above, speech errors at the phonological level tend to involve constituents of syllables, down to the level of the segment. However, segment-sized units have a far less important role in poetry or writing systems than do, say, syllables or even rhymes.

It might seem bizarre to say that the segment plays little role in writing systems, since very many languages have alphabetic writing systems and such systems are clearly based on segments. However, when we look at the history of writing it turns out that the alphabet derives from a writing system devised by Phoenician merchants about 4,000 years ago. This itself was developed from a hieroglyphic system in which whole words were represented by pictures. Phoenician was a Semitic language (like Arabic and Hebrew), in which consonants play a particularly salient role, and presumably because of this the system gradually came to represent individual consonant phonemes (though not vowels – to this day, the written forms of Semitic languages tend not to represent vowels directly). The Phoenician alphabet was taken over by the Greeks (who modified the symbols for consonants not appearing in Greek and used them as vowels). It is also thought to be the precursor of the

Armenian and Georgian alphabets. The Greek system gave rise to a number of others, including the Latin alphabet. This then formed the basis of a good many other writing systems throughout the world. The upshot is that, as far as we can tell, all alphabetic writing systems derive from the Phoenician system. In other words a phoneme-based writing system seems to have been 'invented' (or rather, gradually evolved) just *once* in the history of human literacy.

Now, many cultures have evolved their own writing systems independently, and in all other cases they are either based on pictures representing whole words (like Ancient Egyptian hieroglyphs or modern Chinese ideograms) or they are based on the syllable. Syllabic systems include those of Japanese, Inuit, later forms of Egyptian and Sumerian cuneiform and the Linear B script with which Greek was written on Mycenaean Crete. An intriguing case is that of the Cherokee writing system, adopted in 1821. This was devised single-handedly (and in the face of opposition from some of his fellow Cherokees) by a man named Sequoyah, who decided that his people needed a script in which to write their language. Though he could speak only Cherokee, and though Cherokee was not written at that time, he adapted written symbols he had seen in printed books. This meant that he had to spend about thirty years trying to figure out the phonological system of the language. What he produced was effectively an exhaustive analysis of the syllable structure of Cherokee, one of the most remarkable feats of linguistic analysis ever recorded. What is interesting about Sequoyah's writing system is that even this extremely gifted intellectual was not led to analysing the structure of his language in terms of phonemes, but rather in terms of syllables (*exercise 5*).

This concludes our discussion of some of the major issues which arise when we begin to systematically examine the way sounds are used in human languages. As far as the notion of a *grammar*, introduced in our main introduction is concerned, the core section of this part of the book is section 5. There we saw that as soon as we begin to describe what native speakers know about their language, it is necessary to postulate a variety of theoretical constructs, e.g. *phonemes, syllables* and *distinctive features* which belong to a complex system of representation. This latter comprises a number of *levels* and these levels are linked by what we have referred to as *phonological processes*. Together, these representations and the processes linking them constitute the *PF-component* of a grammar, and in sections 6 and 7, we have discussed a small sample of the evidence available from studies of language acquisition and of language processing pointing to the involvement of these abstract constructs in the developing child's and in the adult's *use* of language.

More basically, we have seen the necessity of having available notation (the

IPA system of section 2) which enables us to be precise and unambiguous in our discussions of sounds, and the usefulness of IPA notation was amply demonstrated in sections 3 and 4, where we put it to use in illustrating the systematic nature of sound variation and historical sound change. We now turn our attention to words.

Exercises

1. Collect a corpus of speech errors. This will entail carrying a notebook with you everywhere for two or three weeks! Analyse the phonological errors as: 'exchanges', 'anticipations', 'perserverations', 'additions' and 'others'. What are the main difficulties in collecting such a corpus?

2. Analyse the following errors in terms of the scan-copier model:

   a. spack rice   [spice rack]
   b. fart very hide   [fight very hard]
   c. face spood   [space food]
   d. do a one stetch swip [step switch]
   e. flay the piola   [play the viola]
   f. blake fruid   [brake fluid]
   g. week at workends   [work at weekends]

   What is special about the error in (e)? How does the error in (f) relate to syllable structure? How many possible analyses are there for (g)?

3. The following examples in broad IPA transcription contain errors. Discuss the relevance of these for the role of phonology in processing:

   a. /gɪv ðə nɪpl ən ɪnfənt/ for 'give the infant a nipple'
   b. /ən æŋgwɪʤ lækwɪziʃn prɒbləm/ for 'a language acquisition problem'
   c. /ɪt sɔːtənlɪ ɹʌn auts fæst/ for 'it certainly runs out fast'
   d. /sɛvɹəl ɹæbɪts houl/ for 'several rabbit holes'

4. Analyse the following sample of typing errors, where the target word appears on the right in each case. Identify the exchanges, perseverations, and anticipations. Do these obey the same sorts of constraints

as those of errors in spoken language? What other types of error are illustrated here?

carerr	*career*
exercieses	*exercises*
fromal	*formal*
godd	*good*
hooly	*holly*
imemediately	*immediately*
incidentalyy	*incidentally*
lingiustics	*linguistics*
matirial	*material*
spychology	*psychology*
teh	*the*
whtether	*whether*
substition	*substitution*
langauge	*language*
studnet	*student*

5. An interesting systematic way of distorting words is seen in 'secret languages'. These seem to abound in all cultures. Here is a passage in Pig Latin, transcribed into IPA. What is the system behind this secret language? What phonological units does it refer to?

igpeɪ atinleɪ ekstteɪ ɪtʃweɪ æzheɪ ɔːleɪ əðeɪ ɛtəzleɪ əveɪ ɪðeɪ ælfəbɛteɪ:

əðeɪ ɪkkweɪ aunbreɪ ɒksfeɪ ʌmpsʤeɪ ɔuvəreɪ əðeɪ eɪzɪleɪ ɒgdeɪ.

Further reading and references

A good introduction to basic phonetics which extends the content of Section 2 can be found in Ladefoged (1993). Laver (1994) gives a much more detailed survey of modern phonetics.

Sound variation and its relationship to social, linguistic and interactional factors are discussed in more detail in a number of texts, including Chambers (1995), Chambers and Trudgill (1980) and Wolfram and Schilling-Estes (1998). Other books tend to concentrate on specific social factors. For instance, Milroy (1987a) is the classic introduction to variation and social networks and Bell (1984) has been particularly influential in the study of stylistic variation. Milroy (1987b) is an excellent introduction to the methods of data collection and analysis in variation studies. The Bradford study mentioned in section 3 is reported in Petyt (1985), and the work on (θ) and -t/-d deletion is by Wolfram (1991). The research on Farsi vowel assimilation is outlined in greater detail in Hudson (1996), and the work on (θ) in Australian English comes from Horvath (1985). The second dialect acquisition research was carried out by Chambers (1992).

Good introductions to sound change (approached exclusively from the historical linguistic perspective) can be found in Trask (1996) and McMahon (1994). Chambers (1995) and Milroy (1992) offer a sociolinguistic approach to sound change. An introductory account of the Northern Cities Vowel Shift is presented by Wolfram and Schilling-Estes (1998), and much more detailed discussions of chain shifts, mergers, splits and the Neogrammarian-Lexical Diffusion argument can be found in Labov (1994). The research on intonation change referred to in section 4 is from Britain (1998). Variation in the use of (t) in Milton Keynes is outlined in Kerswill, P. and A. Williams (forthcoming), 'Creating a new town Koine: children and language change in Milton Keynes', *Language and Society*, and the study of Texan English can be found in Bailey, Wikle, Tillery and Sand (1991). The New Zealand research on (wh) is published in Bayard (1995).

The topics introduced in section 5 are dealt with in more detail in Spencer (1996) and Gussenhoven and Jacobs (1998). For a more advanced summary of these questions see Roca (1994).

The most influential study in the generative study of child phonology (section 6) is Smith's (1973) diary study of his son, Amahl, from the age of two to four. The technical analysis is written in a framework which is now somewhat out of date (that of Chomsky and Halle 1968) but Smith provides a useful overview of his work in a less technical form at the beginning of the book, and it is still well worth reading. There is no up-to-date, linguistically based introduction to child phonology. Vihman (1994) provides a more psychologically oriented overview of the topic. Chapter 2 of Goodluck (1991) gives a brief summary of some of the issues, including the use of features in child phonology, and Ingram (1989) gives a useful discussion of the nature of children's phonological representations. Ferguson, Menn and Stoel-Gammon (1992) is an interesting collection of articles giving an overview of a good many issues.

The linguistic justification for the dual lexicon model presented here is given in Spencer (1986), though this is rather too technical for beginners. A gentler introduction to the model can be found in Spencer (1988). A very readable, non-technical introduction to much of the material covered here is provided by Smith (1989, chapters 4 and 8).

Further information about speech perception and production (section 7) can be found in almost any introduction to psycholinguistics. More advanced information can be found in texts such as Borden and Harris (1984). For further discussion of what speech errors can tell us about speech production see Levelt (1989, chapter 9). There are several interesting collections of articles on speech errors, including Fromkin (1973, 1980).

Appendix 1

The International Phonetic Alphabet (revised to 1993, updated 1996)

THE INTERNATIONAL PHONETIC ALPHABET (revised to 1993, updated 1996)

CONSONANTS (PULMONIC)

	Bilabial	Labiodental	Dental	Alveolar	Postalveolar	Retroflex	Palatal	Velar	Uvular	Pharyngeal	Glottal
Plosive	p b			t d		ʈ ɖ	c ɟ	k ɡ	q ɢ		ʔ
Nasal	m	ɱ		n		ɳ	ɲ	ŋ	N		
Trill	B			r					R		
Tap or Flap				ɾ		ɽ					
Fricative	ɸ β	f v	θ ð	s z	ʃ ʒ	ʂ ʐ	ç ʝ	x ɣ	χ ʁ	ħ ʕ	h ɦ
Lateral fricative				ɬ ɮ							
Approximant		ʋ		ɹ		ɻ	j	ɰ			
Lateral approximant				l		ɭ	ʎ	L			

Where symbols appear in pairs, the one to the right represents a voiced consonant. Shaded areas denote articulations judged impossible.

CONSONANTS (NON-PULMONIC)

Clicks		Voiced implosives		Ejectives	
ʘ	Bilabial	ɓ	Bilabial	ʼ	Examples:
ǀ	Dental	ɗ	Dental/alveolar	pʼ	Bilabial
ǃ	(Post)alveolar	ʄ	Palatal	tʼ	Dental/alveolar
ǂ	Palatoalveolar	ɠ	Velar	kʼ	Velar
ǁ	Alveolar lateral	ʛ	Uvular	sʼ	Alveolar fricative

OTHER SYMBOLS

ʍ Voiceless labial-velar fricative
w Voiced labial-velar approximant
ɥ Voiced labial-palatal approximant
ʜ Voiceless epiglottal fricative
ʢ Voiced epiglottal fricative
ʡ Epiglottal plosive

ɕ ʑ Alveolo-palatal fricatives
ɺ Alveolar lateral flap
ɧ Simultaneous ʃ and x

Affricates and double articulations can be represented by two symbols joined by a tie bar if necessary.

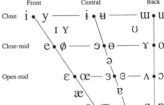

DIACRITICS   Diacritics may be placed above a symbol with a descender, e.g. ŋ̊

̥	Voiceless	n̥ d̥	̤	Breathy voiced	b̤ a̤	̪	Dental	t̪ d̪
̬	Voiced	s̬ t̬	̰	Creaky voiced	b̰ a̰	̺	Apical	t̺ d̺
ʰ	Aspirated	tʰ dʰ	̼	Linguolabial	t̼ d̼	̻	Laminal	t̻ d̻
̹	More rounded	ɔ̹	ʷ	Labialized	tʷ dʷ	̃	Nasalized	ẽ
̜	Less rounded	ɔ̜	ʲ	Palatalized	tʲ dʲ	ⁿ	Nasal release	dⁿ
̟	Advanced	u̟	ˠ	Velarized	tˠ dˠ	ˡ	Lateral release	dˡ
̠	Retracted	e̠	ˤ	Pharyngealized	tˤ dˤ	̚	No audible release	d̚
̈	Centralized	ë	̴	Velarized or pharyngealized	ɫ			
̽	Mid-centralized	e̽	̝	Raised	e̝	(ɹ̝ = voiced alveolar fricative)		
̩	Syllabic	n̩	̞	Lowered	e̞	(β̞ = voiced bilabial approximant)		
̯	Non-syllabic	e̯	̘	Advanced Tongue Root	e̘			
˞	Rhoticity	ɚ a˞	̙	Retracted Tongue Root	e̙			

VOWELS

Front   Central   Back
Close   i y ——— ɨ ʉ ——— ɯ u
        ɪ ʏ   ʊ
Close-mid e ø ——— ɘ ɵ ——— ɤ o
                    ə
Open-mid   ɛ œ — ɜ ɞ — ʌ ɔ
            æ   ɐ
Open   a ɶ ——————— ɑ ɒ

Where symbols appear in pairs, the one to the right represents a rounded vowel.

SUPRASEGMENTALS

ˈ   Primary stress
ˌ   Secondary stress   ˌfoʊnəˈtɪʃən
ː   Long   eː
ˑ   Half-long   eˑ
˘   Extra-short   ĕ
| Minor (foot) group
‖   Major (intonation) group
.   Syllable break   ɹi.ækt
‿   Linking (absence of a break)

TONES AND WORD ACCENTS

LEVEL			CONTOUR		
e̋ or ˥	Extra high		ě or ˩˥	Rising	
é ˦	High		ê ˥˩	Falling	
ē ˧	Mid		e᷄ ˧˥	High rising	
è ˨	Low		e᷅ ˩˧	Low rising	
ȅ ˩	Extra low		e᷈ ˧˦˨	Rising-falling	
↓	Downstep		↗	Global rise	
↑	Upstep		↘	Global fall	

137

Appendix 2

The information that is contained in appendix 2 and 3 is a slightly modified version of material appearing in Andrew Spencer's *Phonology* (Blackwell, Oxford, 1996). The authors are grateful to Blackwell for their permission to use this material.

List of distinctive features

This list includes definitions of the binary features used in this book as well as a number of others in common use which you will come across in wider reading.

consonantal   [±cons]   The [+cons] sounds are the obstruents, nasals and liquids, in which there is a relatively tight constriction in the vocal tract, compared with the [−cons] sounds, the glides and vowels.

approximant   [±approx]   In [+approx] sounds the constriction is not very great; the class includes liquids as well as glides and vowels. Fricatives and stops (including nasal stops) are [−approx].

sonorant   [±son]   The [+son] sounds are the [+approx] sounds (vowels, glides and liquids) together with the nasals. The [−son] sounds are called obstruents (plosives, affricates and fricatives).

continuant   [±cont]   A non-continuant sound or a *stop* ([−cont]) is one in which there is a constriction in the *oral* tract which prevents the air from passing through. The plosives are [−cont] as are the nasals, in which the air passes through the nose and not the mouth. All other sounds (including fricatives) are continuants. (Affricates begin as [−cont] and then become [+cont].)

strident   [±strid]   Stridency is only relevant for fricatives and affricates. A strident sound is relatively noisy when compared to a non-strident one. Labiodentals, sibilants and uvulars (fricatives/affricates) are [+strid]; all other fricatives/affricates are [−strid].

nasal   [±nas]   Nasal sounds are produced by lowering the velum and allowing air to pass through the nasal passages. Nasal stops and nasalized vowels are [+nas]. Sounds made by raising the velum and thus preventing air from passing through the nasal cavity are called 'oral' sounds and have the feature specification [−nas].

lateral   [±lat]   In a [+lat] sound such as [l] the air is made to pass round the sides of the tongue instead of flowing over the top of the tongue as with all other sounds.

anterior   [±ant]   This feature is relevant only for Coronal sounds. An anterior ([+ant]) sound is made by bringing the tongue towards or onto the alveolar ridge or the teeth. If a sound is produced with the tongue placed further back than the alveolar ridge then it will be a posterior sound, [−ant]. The anteriors are the dentals and alveolars, the posterior sounds are the retroflex, palato-alveolar and palatal sounds.

voiced   [±voiced]   In voiced sounds the vocal folds can vibrate during the articulation of the sound; in voiceless sounds the configuration of the larynx doesn't permit this. In English the only sounds which are phonemically voiceless are the voiceless obstruents (plosives, fricatives and affricates) [p t k f s ʃ h ʧ]. Sonorants, including vowels, in English are all voiced.

aspiration   [±asp]   This feature doesn't distinguish phonemes in English. Aspirated consonants are those which are followed by a slight puff of breath (due to a relatively long VOT). The [−asp] sounds lack this puff of breath.

Vowel features: some of the following features are also applied to consonants, but for the purposes of this introduction we will regard them as applying just to vowels and glides.

high   [±high]   The [+high] vowels include [i y ɨ u j w]; vowels such as [e, o, a, ɑ] are [−high]. The body of the tongue (dorsum) is raised close to the roof of the mouth in high sounds, whereas it occupies a more mid or low position for [−high] sounds. NB: just because a sound is [−high] doesn't mean to say that it's also [+low] (see below).

back   [±back]   The [+back] vowels and glides include [u ɔ ɑ ɒ ʌ w], while the front ([−back]) sounds include [i, y, e, œ, ø, æ, j]. To make a [−back] sound the tongue body (dorsum) is brought forward, whereas it is retracted for the back sounds, such as [u, o, ɔ, ʌ, ɑ, ɒ, w]. The central vowels such as [ɨ, ə, a] are generally taken to be [+back].

low   [±low]   The low vowels include [æ a ɑ ɒ]. To produce these the tongue body is brought close to the floor of the mouth. This means that mid vowels such as [e, o, ɛ, ɔ] are [−low]. (See also [±high] above.)

rounded   [±rounded]   Rounded sounds are produced by contracting the lips as for the sound [u]. Vowels and glides such as [u y œ ɒ ɔ o w] are all [+rounded].

Appendix 3

Distinctive feature matrix for English consonant phonemes

	p	b	t	d	k	g	f	v	θ	ð	s	z	ʃ	ʒ	h	m	n	ŋ	w	l	r	j	tʃ	dʒ
cons	+	+	+	+	+	+	+	+	+	+	+	+	+	+	+	+	+	+	−	+	+	−	+	+
approx	−	−	−	−	−	−	−	−	−	−	−	−	−	−	−	−	−	−	+	+	+	+	−	−
son	−	−	−	−	−	−	−	−	−	−	−	−	−	−	−	+	+	+	+	+	+	+	−	−
cont	−	−	−	−	−	−	+	+	+	+	+	+	+	+	+	−	−	−	+	+	+	+	-/+	-/+
strid							+	+	−	−	+	+	+	+	−								+	+
nas	−	−	−	−	−	−	−	−	−	−	−	−	−	−	−	+	+	+	−	−	−	−	−	−
lat	−	−	−	−	−	−	−	−	−	−	−	−	−	−	−	−	−	−	−	+	−	−	−	−
voiced	−	+	−	+	−	+	−	+	−	+	−	+	−	+	−	+	+	+	+	+	+	+	−	+
[PLACE]	L	L	C	C	D	D	L	L	C	C	C	C	C	C	G	L	C	D	L	C	C	C	C	C
ant			+	+					+	+	+	+	−	−			+			+	+	−	−	−

Note: L = LABIAL, C = CORONAL, D = DORSAL, G = GUTTURAL

Part 2 Words

8 Introduction

All languages have words, and words are probably the most accessible linguistic units to the layman. As part 1 has amply demonstrated, in order to get a sense of the sounds which are used in an utterance, a good deal of analysis is required, and most speakers of a language cannot easily identify these sounds. Similarly, sentences do not have the same intuitive immediacy as words, an observation that probably owes much to the fact that when we speak, we often employ sequences of words which do not comprise complete sentences. The following mundane dialogue illustrates this perfectly:

(85) SPEAKER A: Where are you going?
      SPEAKER B: Shopping.
      SPEAKER A: What for?
      SPEAKER B: To buy some socks.

Of the utterances in (85), only the first corresponds to a complete sentence, the others being elliptical and not including information which A and B can readily supply from the context of their conversation.

Now, while it is not true to suggest that we always fully articulate the sequence of sounds which go to make up a word (see examples of elision and assimilation cited in the main introduction), it is also not true that we systematically get by with 'word fragments'. Just imagine the difficulties we would confront if in either spoken or written text we did indulge in such an activity: we might be faced (along with A and B) with trying to interpret (86):

(86) SPEAKER A: Whareying?
      SPEAKER B: Shing
      SPEAKER A: Whor?
      SPEAKER B: Tymsos

Despite this comfortable familiarity of the word based on our everyday experience with language, it should come as no surprise that serious consideration of words leads to intriguing problems and sometimes, when we're lucky, solutions. Of all linguistic constructs, the word is probably closest to familiar physical objects, but, as the history of physical science has shown, beneath these everyday objects lies a world that we cannot perceive without expensive equipment and which is organised in ways which few of us can readily understand. It would be misleading to suggest that our understanding of words (or, indeed, any aspect of language) is as developed as natural scientists' understanding of the physical world; but we should be ready to be surprised and to have challenged those preconceptions which emanate from our practised acquaintance with words in our native language.

The next four sections of this part of the book develop some of the issues which are important in understanding the nature of words from the theoretical perspective introduced in our main introduction. It will be recalled that we proposed there that a grammar of a language must contain a *lexicon,* i.e. a listing of the words occurring in the language along with their linguistic properties. In part 1, particularly section 5, we developed some ideas on the nature of the phonological information which appears in a lexical entry, one aspect of the *form* of a word. This focus on form will continue in sections 9, 10 and 11, where we will examine in some detail aspects of the morphological and syntactic information which must appear in lexical entries. Additionally, (most) words have one or more *meanings*, and section 12 raises some of the issues which arise when we consider how the semantic properties of a word might be represented in its lexical entry and what implications considerations of word meaning have for the overall organisation of the lexicon. Having introduced a set of notions for dealing with the cognitive representation of words in the lexicon, we move to the other perspectives from the introduction. The quite remarkable acquisition of words by small children is the topic of section 13 and the ways in which experimental studies might throw light on how we store words in our memory and perceive and produce them in our everyday linguistic interaction are dealt with in section 14. Some language disorders give rise to problems which are rather specifically to do with words, and we shall introduce these difficulties and discuss their implications in section 15. Finally, adopting the sociolinguistic perspective, in section 16 we examine some of the issues which affect words when languages or varieties of a single language are in contact.

9   Word classes

A natural first step in a scientific approach to words is to seek to establish the different types of words which appear in languages. That such information is readily available to native speakers and, furthermore, is predictively useful for them is easy to demonstrate. Suppose, for instance, that you hear the sentence in (87):

(87)   A plingle has arrived

Of course, you don't know what *plingle* means, but you can immediately infer that *plingle* is the sort of expression which occurs in the constructions *the plingle, two plingles, every plingle which has ever existed*, etc. In short, (87) enables you to assign *plingle* to a particular class of words, and once you know what class of words it belongs to, you know a great deal about its potential for occurrence within the language. It is reasonable, then, to suppose that the word class to which a word belongs is specified in that word's lexical entry. The immediate task facing us in this section is that of developing criteria for assigning words to classes.

Lexical categories

A familiar distinction is that between **nouns** (N) and **verbs** (V), and there are several ways in which we can justify this for English. For instance, nouns often refer to types of concrete objects in the world (e.g. *cake, engine, moon, waiter*, and, we might now suppose, *plingle!*), while verbs typically refer to activities (*collide, steal, applaud, snore*). Furthermore, verbs and nouns exhibit a different range of forms: most nouns have a special form for the plural (*engine ~ engines*), while verbs have a larger number of forms, as shown by the sentences in (88):

147

(88)   a. Harriet *applauds* my suggestion
        b. Tom and Harriet *applaud* my suggestion
        c. The children are *applauding* the clown
        d. The children *applauded* the clown

Third, nouns and verbs combine with other words to form phrases in distinct ways. For example, a noun will often be found preceded by a **definite** (*the*) or **indefinite article** (*a/an*) (*the moon, an engine*). A verb cannot be preceded by these articles (**the applauds,* *an applauded). If we form a phrase consisting of an article and a noun, this can often follow a verb to form a larger phrase (*steal an engine, applaud the waiter*) – we say that *an engine* and *the waiter* function as **complements** of the verbs *steal* and *applaud* in these constructions. However, verbs themselves cannot generally function as complements of other verbs (**steal applauding,* *applaud collides). Alternatively, an article–noun sequence may combine with a verb to form a whole sentence (*the waiter snores*) – here *the waiter* functions as the **subject** of the sentence (see section 17 for further discussion of subject and complement). Again, verbs themselves cannot generally fulfil this role (**stole collides,* *collides snores). Generally, we say that subjects and complements are **arguments** of verbs and a typical simple sentence, such as that in (89) consists of a verb (*stole*) and its arguments (*the waiter, a cake*):

(89)   The waiter stole a cake

A third major word class recognised in traditional grammar is **adjectives** (A). These typically refer to properties which people or things possess and they are used to modify nouns, e.g. ***happy*** man, ***noisy*** engine. Although they share with articles the property of appearing in front of a noun, if an article and an adjective both combine with a noun, they do so in a fixed order (*a happy man,* **happy a man, the noisy engine,* *noisy the engine). We can also ascribe a property by putting the adjective after a form of the verb *be* to form a sentence (*the man is happy, the engine was noisy*). Like nouns and verbs, many adjectives have special forms indicating the extent to which a property is true of something, the **comparative** form, *happier*, 'happy to a greater degree than', and the **superlative** form, *happiest*, 'happy to the greatest degree'.

A fourth class of word is **adverbs** (ADV). While an adjective modifies a noun, an adverb typically modifies a verb, adjective or another adverb, indicating how, when or why something happened or the degree to which a property characterises an individual or event. Examples illustrating these three uses appear in (90) – the modifying adverbs are in italics and the modified item is in bold:

(90)   a. The waiter *carelessly* **dropped** the plate
        b. The engine is *really* **noisy**
        c. The audience applauded the clown *very* **enthusiastically**

(note that in 90c, the adverb *enthusiastically*, itself modified by *very*, modifies the verb *applauded*).

Adverbs can readily be formed from a majority of adjectives by the addition of *-ly*: *happily*, *slowly*, *reluctantly*, etc. However, adverbs which do not fit this characterisation are far from uncommon: *very*, *well*, *yesterday*.

Another important word class is illustrated in (91):

(91)   a. Harriet was sitting *under* a tree
        b. They're due to arrive *before* noon
        c. That is the end *of* the news
        d. There was a debate *about* economic policy

The italicised words in (91) precede nouns (or phrases centred around nouns, such as *a tree* or *economic policy*). They typically serve to relate objects, people or events in space or time (*under*/*before*), though often the relationship is more abstract as in (91c, d). Words of this type are called **prepositions** (P), and they do not have the capacity to appear in a range of different forms (**unders, *abouted, *ofest, *beforely*).

Up to now, we have distinguished five word classes or **lexical categories**. In doing this, we have appealed to three types of criteria for establishing a category: semantic (relying on meaning), morphological (relying on word forms) and syntactic (taking account of behaviour in phrases). Taken together, these criteria identify our separate classes quite well. However, it is important to be clear that there are plenty of cases where one or other type of criterion fails to work. For instance, some nouns refer to abstract ideas rather than concrete objects (*justice, idea, quantity*); worse still, there are nouns such as *game* and *speech* which refer to types of activities, the semantic criterion we introduced for recognising verbs. For some nouns the pluralisation criterion does not work in a straightforward fashion, either because their plural forms are irregular (*men, women, children*) or because they lack a plural form entirely (**furnitures, *sakes*). Likewise, there are verbs which refer to states rather than activities (*fear, border (on)*), and other difficulties with applying these criteria too rigidly will become apparent as we proceed. Despite these problems, it is uncontroversial to suppose that lexical entries in the lexicon must contain an indication of word class membership (***exercises 1, 2 and 3***).

A particularly interesting illustration of the semantic correlations breaking down arises from observing that English provides many ways of forming new words from old ones. For example, we can form a noun *happiness* from the adjective *happy*. That *happiness* is a noun is indicated by the fact that it can be preceded by the definite article (*the happiness John felt*), and that it is not an adjective by the fact that it does not have comparative and superlative forms (**happinesser, *happinessest*). Thus, *happiness* is a noun denoting the *property* of being happy. So, both the adjective and the noun seem in this case to denote a property; in this case semantic criteria for establishing class membership are not useful. Of course, the example we have chosen here is not exceptional and it illustrates the pervasive process of **word formation**. The word *happiness* is formed by adding an ending, *-ness*, to *happy* (the spelling change is irrelevant here, and has no effect on the pronunciation). Such a process is referred to as **derivational morphology** (because we derive a new word from the old one). Derivational processes typically apply to nouns, verbs and adjectives, allowing us to change the category of the word, and we shall return to a more systematic discussion of such processes in the next section.

Functional categories

Nouns, verbs, adjectives, adverbs and prepositions are the major word classes of English, and they are the sorts of words we find in dictionaries with meanings attached to them (see section 12). However, not all words are straightforwardly meaningful in this way, and this observation paves the way for extending the word classes which must be recognised in grammars for languages. Consider the italicised words in the following example:

(92)   Bill thinks *that* Tom *and* Dick *have been* visiting Harriet *to* ask for help with one *of the* assignments *which have to be* finished for *the* next morphology class

It is difficult to begin to ascribe a simple meaning to such words in the way that we often can for words in our major classes. For instance, imagine being asked by someone who doesn't know English well what *think* or *assignment* means in (92). Since major class words normally denote objects, ideas, events, states, properties and so on, native-speakers of English can usually formulate answers of some kind to such questions. However, suppose that instead you are asked what *that* or *of* or *to* mean in (92), and it is unlikely that you will have an answer. A better way of thinking of these words is as fulfilling a particular *function* in the sentence. For instance, *that* (in this usage) is traditionally regarded as a subordinating conjunction. It is attached to the beginning of the sentence *Tom and Dick have been visiting Harriet . . .* to indicate that the clause it introduces is a statement rather than a question. The word *to* in *to ask* signals that this was the purpose of Tom and Dick's visits, while the *to* in *to be finished* is there simply because it appears to be part of English grammar that the verb *have* in its meaning of 'obligation' must be followed by *to* and the base form of a verb (notice that *must*, a synonym of this type of *have*, does not require this *to*; indeed, it would be ungrammatical to add it: *the assignments which must be finished/*must to be finished*). From a quite different perspective, *which* appears to be somehow dependent on *the assignments* (they have to be finished) and to be devoid of any meaning in its own right. The reader is invited to reflect on the remaining italicised words in (92).

Words such as the above, which do not denote objects, ideas, etc., are known as **function words** and they belong to classes known as **functional categories**. They are distinguished from nouns, verbs, adjectives, adverbs and prepositions, which are often called **content words**. The distinction has proved important not only in the description of individual languages but also in the study of the acquisition of language and the study of language disorders (see sections 13, 24 and 26).

There is an important relationship between function words and content words, in that very often the syntactic criteria for assigning words to lexical categories rely on specific types of function words. For example, above it was pointed out that nouns can be preceded by a definite or indefinite article (*the* or *a(n)*). The function of the article is (very roughly) to make what the noun refers to either more or less specific. If you say *I bought a car* this simply refers to a car-buying event on your part, without implying anything about the car concerned, but if you say *I bought the car*, then you must be assuming that your addressee already knows which car you are talking about (for example, because you have described it earlier). We can be even more specific with **demonstratives**, *this* or *that*. The articles *the/a* and the demonstratives belong to a class of function words called **determiners** (D). These are often found before nouns, though the determiner may be separated from the noun by one or more adjectives, e.g. *a bright, shiny, new car*.

Verbs can also be preceded by a type of function word, the **auxiliary verbs** (AUX) such as *can, will, must, have, be*:

(93)   a. You *can* go to the ball
         b. Linguistics *is* developing rapidly
         c. Sam *has* lost the plot again

That auxiliary verbs behave quite differently from **lexical verbs** (V) can be seen by examining their role in forming questions:

(94)   a. Harriet *is* studying linguistics
     b. *Is* Harriet studying linguistics?

(95)   a. Tom *can* speak Urdu
     b. *Can* Tom speak Urdu?

Here we see that the formation of a question involves 'moving' an auxiliary verb to the initial position in the structure. Lexical verbs do not 'move' in this way in Modern English (see sections 21 and 22 for much more extended discussion):

(96)   a. Harriet *studies* linguistics
     b *Studies* Harriet linguistics?

Furthermore, a sentence is negated by placing *not* (or *n't*) after an auxiliary:

(97)   a. Harriet *is* studying linguistics
     b. Harriet *is*n't studying linguistics

Again, this is not possible with lexical verbs:

(98)   *Harriet *studies*n't/*studies* not linguistics

We can immediately see, then, that not only are auxiliary verbs useful in enabling us to assign lexical verbs to the appropriate class, but that they also have distinctive properties which justify the recognition of the separate functional category AUX.

    Another important type of function word is the **pronoun** (PRN). This is a group of words the members of which (roughly speaking) stand for a noun expression (like *John, the president, a book of mine*, etc.). The commonest pronouns are the **personal pronouns**, which can be (partially) described in terms of number (singular/plural) and person (first person when the speaker is included, second person for the addressee when the speaker is excluded and third person in other cases):

Table 21: Personal pronouns in English		
number **person**	**singular**	**plural**
first	I/me	we/us
second	thou/thee/you	you
third	he/him, she/her, it	they/them

(The second person singular pronoun *thou/thee* is obsolete in standard dialects of Modern English, though it survives in other varieties.)

This table shows that *we/us* is a first person plural pronoun, that *he/him* is a third person singular pronoun, etc. Nouns such as *Tom*, or *apples* can also be regarded as third person forms (singular and plural respectively) because they can be replaced by the corresponding personal pronouns *he* and *them*.

Another type of function word is illustrated in (92) by *and*. Such words are called **co-ordinating conjunctions** (CONJ) and further examples are shown in (99):

(99)   a. naughty *but* nice
         b. your money *or* your life
         c. Harriet is English *but* she speaks Russian

These conjunctions serve to join words or phrases together to form larger phrases of the same type (99a, b), or join whole sentences together to form new sentences (99c).

The subordinating conjunction *that* has already been mentioned in connection with (92). In modern linguistics, words like this are known as **complementisers** (C) because one of their most important uses is to introduce complement clauses, Additional examples of this type are shown in (100):

(100)   a. Tom wonders *if* it will rain
         b. Tom arranged *for* Dick to leave early

Up to this point, then, we have seen that it is necessary to recognise at least five lexical categories (N, V, A, ADV, P) in the grammar of English along with a number of functional categories (D, AUX, PRN, CONJ, C). We have also suggested that category membership will be specified as part of a word's lexical representation in the lexicon. Without wishing to suggest that our set of categories is exhaustive, we shall now focus on verbs and on some of the complexities which arise in consideration of their morphological properties.

The morphological properties of English verbs

Verbs in English have a simple form, such as *read, write, format,* called the **base** form. However, consider the verbs in sentences such as *Tom reads comics, Dick writes poems, Harriet formats disks.* These are in a special form, consisting of the base form plus an ending *-s*. This form is used whenever the word or phrase referring to the person doing the reading, writing or formatting (i.e. the subject), is third person singular and the verb is in the present tense. The *-s* form is not used for any other person (*I, we, you*) or for third person plural subjects: *I/we/you read/*reads novels, the girls write/*writes* *letters*. Because of these different verb forms, we say that the verb **agrees** with its subject. In English, the agreement system has almost entirely disappeared (in some dialects it has completely withered away, see section 16), and the third person singular agreement form in the present tense is its last vestige.

The special agreement forms for third person singular subjects are characteristic of verbs as a class. Other special forms of this class are shown in (101):

(101)　　a. Harriet *took* a picture of Dick
　　　　　b. Harriet is *taking* a picture of Dick
　　　　　c. Harriet has *taken* a picture of Dick
　　　　　d. A picture of Dick was *taken* by Harriet

It is a characteristic of English verb forms that they signal the time when an action or event occurs. In (101a) the picture taking event is presented as taking place in the past, whereas in (101b) it is presented as unfolding at present. In (101c) the event took place in the past, but because of the use of the auxiliary *have*, the action is perceived as retaining relevance for the present (so that 101c might be taken as implying that the picture of Dick is available and could be viewed). The use of the special form *took* in (101a) signals **Tense**, which is primarily used to indicate the time at which an event took place (but also has secondary uses, as in *I wish I **took** you seriously*). In this case we have the past tense, indicating that the event occurred before the moment at which (101a) is uttered. The form *took* is, in fact, an irregular past tense form, and regular verbs in English form their past tense by adding the (orthographic) suffix *-(e)d*. Because of this, it is customary to refer to this form as the *-d* form of a verb. The verbs in (101b, c) are in special forms used with the auxiliaries *be* in (101b) and *have* in (101c). These forms are called the **present participle** (or **progressive** form) and the **perfect participle**, respectively. The former of these is often referred to as the *-ing* form of the verb, for the obvious reason that it involves adding the ending *-ing* to the base form. Similarly, we can characterise the perfect participle as the *-n* form, although a little caution is necessary here as the perfect participles of all regular verbs involve the addition not of *-en* but of *-ed* (e.g. *he has walk**ed** a long way, she has jump**ed** over the stream*). Even in these circumstances, however, a perfect participle ending in *-ed* is referred to as the *-n* form of the verb! Some justification for this apparent perversity will be given in the next section (*exercise 4*).

When a word appears in a variety of forms depending on its grammatical role in the sentence we say that it **inflects** or undergoes **inflection**. A category such as Tense is therefore called an **inflectional category**. The category of Tense has two forms, past and non-past, in English, signalled in the case under discussion by *took* (past) versus *take/takes* (non-past). Specific values of an inflectional category of this sort are called **inflectional properties**, and we shall have more to say about these in the next section.

Earlier, we noted that the phrase referring to whatever is performing the action denoted by the verb is referred to as the subject of the sentence. Additionally, the phrase referring to whatever is affected by the action denoted by the verb, one type of complement, is referred to as the verb's **object**. Now, there are many verbs such as *sleep* and *hop* which refer to states or activities which are not directed towards another entity; as a consequence, such verbs cannot occur with objects and they are called **intransitive verbs**. By contrast, verbs which do take objects are called **transitive**.

The simple picture we have just described is complicated somewhat by example (101d). Here, Harriet is still the one taking the picture, and it is still the picture that is being affected by the action of being taken (in that it is being created). However, grammatically speaking, *a picture of Dick* is the subject in (101d). This is clear if we consider agreement in (101d) in contrast to (102):

(102)   Pictures of Dick were taken by Harriet

Here the form *were* is the appropriate form for a third person plural subject (**pictures of Dick was taken by Harriet*), indicating this reversal of grammatical roles, which is a systematic phenomenon affecting transitive verbs. When it occurs, the verb appears in another special inflectional form (identical to the perfect participle) and is accompanied by the auxiliary *be*, the old object becomes the subject of the new verb form while the old subject is either introduced by the preposition *by*, as in (101d), or is omitted altogether. The traditional term used to distinguish sentences in which the relations of subject and object are changed is **voice**. Thus, we say that (101a) is in the **active** (voice), while (101d) is in the **passive** (voice). The verb form *taken* in (101d) is the **passive participle**, and it is usual to refer to it, like the formally identical perfect participle, as the -*n* form of the verb (see section 21, pp. 333f. for further discussion of passive constructions).

English has little inflection. Nouns have only two forms, singular and plural, and verbs have relatively few forms. Subject agreement takes place only with third person singular subjects, and then not in the past tense (with the exception of forms of *be* as in *I was, you were*, etc.). Not all words inflect in exactly the same way, of course. Languages have irregularities in morphology. For instance, as we have noted, the regular past tense form consists of adding -*ed* to a verb (*walk → walked*), though *take* has an irregular form *took*. English has about two hundred verbs with inflectional irregularities. The implications of these observations for the structure of the lexicon are straightforward. As the lexicon is a repository for the *idiosyncratic* linguistic properties of words, if a word is regular inflectionally, there will be no need to specify its inflectional forms in the lexicon. Thus, the lexical entry for the noun *train* will not contain any indication that the plural form of this word is *trains*; and the lexical entry for the verb *jump* will not include the information that this verb has a third person singular present form *jumps*, a past tense form *jumped*, etc. These facts are entirely predictable, so do not need to be specified. However, the fact that *women* is the plural form of *woman* will be listed in the lexical entry for *woman*, as will the fact that *gave* is the past tense form of *give* in the latter's lexical entry, etc.

Inflectional classes in Italian and Russian

Focusing on English up to now, we have seen that the only type of inflectional information which needs to appear in a word's lexical entry is that which exhibits irregularity. However, differences in inflection are not always the result of irregularity and in some languages, we find that *regular* words may fall into distinct inflectional classes, which cannot be predicted from any other property of the word. We shall close this section by briefly considering some examples of this type.

In table 22 we see examples of the Italian verb meaning 'speak'. In Italian the verb agrees with the subject, and we can immediately see that this system of agreement is much 'richer' than the English system we have described above. Additionally, Italian verbs have a number of **moods**, or verb forms which express speakers' attitudes to what they are saying. One is for ordinary statements, the **indicative mood**, and another is used to express doubt, possibility and so on, the **subjunctive mood**. Italian also has a number of tense forms, including past tense forms, which again (unlike English) signal agreement systematically. Each verb also has an **infinitive** form, corresponding to the English verb preceded by *to,* as in *to speak*, etc.

Table 22: *parlare* 'to speak': first conjugation

number	person	present indicative	present subjunctive	past indicative
sing.	1	parlo	parli	parlai
	2	parli	parli	parlasti
	3	parla	parli	parlò
plural	1	parliamo	parliamo	parlammo
	2	parlate	parliate	parlaste
	3	parlano	parlino	parlarono

However, these are not the observations on which we wish to concentrate here. The point of current interest arises if we contrast table 22 with tables 23 and 24.

Table 23: *credere* 'to believe': second conjugation

number	person	present indicative	present subjunctive	past indicative
sing.	1	credo	creda	credei
	2	credi	creda	credesti
	3	crede	creda	credè
plural	1	crediamo	crediamo	credemmo
	2	credete	crediate	credeste
	3	credono	credano	crederono

Table 24: *finire* 'to finish': third conjugation

number	person	present indicative	present subjunctive	past indicative
sing.	1	finisco	finisca	finii
	2	finisci	finisca	finisti
	3	finisce	finisca	finì
plural	1	finiamo	finiamo	finimmo
	2	finite	finiate	finiste
	3	finiscono	finiscano	finirono

All Italian *regular* verbs have the inflectional properties illustrated in one of these three tables. Thus, on the basis of these properties, we can divide all such verbs into three inflectional classes, traditionally called **conjugation classes**. Membership of a particular conjugation class is a purely morphological property of the verb. There is no reason, for instance, why *parlare* could not have been conjugated like *finire*. Given our developing view of the lexicon, the consequence of the existence of conjugations is that information about the conjugation of a verb must be included in the verb's lexical entry. Thus, the lexical entry for *parlare* in a grammar of Italian must include an indication that it is a first conjugation verb. Note carefully that this does not require that all the inflectional information included in table 22 be listed in the verb's lexical entry; as a first conjugation verb, *parlare* is entirely regular, and the full range of inflectional forms can be derived by general rule.

Nouns too can occur in much more elaborate inflectional systems than the singular/plural contrast we have noted for English. In tables 25 to 28, we see some Russian noun forms in broad transcription (the words are all stressed on the first syllable except for the various forms of *sonata*, which are stressed on the second syllable, and the diacritic ′ indicates **palatalisation**, whereby the standard articulation for [t], [l], etc. is accompanied by the body of the tongue being raised towards the hard palate – in IPA this diacritic appears as ʲ). Russian nouns inflect for number, like English nouns, but they also inflect for **case**. A case is a special form of the noun which frequently corresponds to a combination of preposition and noun in English. In addition, the Nominative case is used for nouns functioning as subjects and the Accusative for object nouns.

Table 25: *kod* 'code': Class I

	singular	plural
Number		
Case		
Nominative (subj.)	kod	kodi
Accusative (obj.)	kod	kodi
Genitive ('of . . .')	koda	kodov
Dative ('to . . .')	kodu	kodam
Instrumental ('with . . .')	kodom	kodami
Prepositional ('about . . .')	kode	kodax

Table 26: *sonata* 'sonata': Class II

	singular	plural
Number		
Case		
Nominative (subj.)	sonata	sonati
Accusative (obj.)	sonatu	sonati
Genitive ('of . . .')	sonati	sonat
Dative ('to . . .')	sonate	sonatam
Instrumental ('with . . .')	sonatoj	sonatami
Prepositional ('about . . .')	sonate	sonatax

Table 27: *kost'* 'bone': Class III	singular	plural
Number		
Case		
Nominative (subj.)	kost'	kost'i
Accusative (obj.)	kost'	kost'i
Genitive ('of . . .')	kost'i	kost'ej
Dative ('to . . .')	kost'i	kost'am
Instrumental ('with . . .')	kost'ju	kost'ami
Prepositional ('about . . .')	kost'i	kost'ax

Table 28: *bl'udo* 'dish': Class IV	singular	plural
Number		
Case		
Nominative (subj.)	bl'udo	bl'uda
Accusative (obj.)	bl'udo	bl'uda
Genitive ('of . . .')	bl'uda	bl'uda
Dative ('to . . .')	bl'udu	bl'udam
Instrumental ('with . . .')	bl'udom	bl'udami
Prepositional ('about . . .')	bl'ude	bl'udax

Again, we have a case of words falling into *arbitrary* inflectional classes (although *within* these classes, inflection is entirely regular) and Noun classes of this sort are called **declensions**. Russian also has a system of **gender**: all nouns are either masculine, feminine or neuter. In general, the correspondence is Class I = masculine, Class II, III = feminine, Class IV = neuter. However, this correspondence is not perfect. For instance, the word *muzcina* ([muʒtʃina]) declines like a Class II noun and should be feminine, but in fact it is masculine. This is perhaps not surprising given that the word means 'man'!

Exercises

1. The following words have unusual plurals. Identify as many other words as you can which show similar behaviour in the plural.

   man   change vowel of singular form
   sheep   no change at all
   phenomenon   replace -*on* with -*a*
   wife   replace voiceless fricative with voiced fricative then add /z/

2. The following words do not have plurals, or undergo an interesting shift in meaning when pluralised. Describe the nature of these meaning changes. How would you account for this behaviour?

butter	coffee	darkness	flour	intelligibility
justice	milk	sugar	tea	wine

3. Consider the adjectives below. Some form a comparative and superlative in -*er*/-*est* and others do not, in which case the comparative/superlative meaning is conveyed by *more*/*most*, e.g. *more*/*most sarcastic* and not **sarcasticer*/**sarcasticest*. What might account for this difference in behaviour?

big	burnt	complex	cooked	curious	dark	fiendish
fond	frantic	friendly	frightened	grand	happy	honest
hopeful	hot	intelligent	kind	lazy	lonely	pleased
porous	pretty	remarkable	round	scared	sceptical	scratched
silly	small	stupid	trenchant	usual	weird	wise

4. Assign *all* the words in the following examples to word classes by means of a **labelled bracketing**. This involves placing the word between square brackets [. . .] and labelling the left-hand bracket with the word category using the abbreviations we have introduced in the text. For instance, *John has left* would come out as [$_N$ John] [$_{AUX}$ has] [$_V$ left]:

   (a) The gerbils will probably want feeding again before we can go out to the cinema.

(b) Why did you call that nice policeman an offensive and irrespon-
     sible pig?
(c) Will speaking fluent Martian help us to learn linguistics?

(Hint: if you get stuck, note that the technique of labelled bracketing is introduced with discussion in section 19.)

10 Building words

In the previous section, we have referred to both *derivational* and *inflectional* processes which enable us to form words from other words. The field of linguistics which examines the internal structure of words and processes of word formation is known as **morphology**, and in this section we shall introduce some of the important ideas in this domain by illustrating their application to English word structure.

Morphemes

Many words in English can easily be split into smaller components. Consider words like *reader, printer* and *formatter*. These are all nouns related to the verbs *read, print* and *format*, and they all mean roughly 'person or instrument that *Verb*-s'. Clearly, it is the ending *-er* (spelt *-or* in certain words, e.g. *actor, supervisor, governor*) which conveys this new aspect of meaning and we can say that *-er/-or* creates a new noun from a verb. We can also create new verbs from verbs, as illustrated by pairs such as *read ~ re-read, print ~ re-print* and *format ~ re-format*. Here, the new verb begins with *re-* and means 'to *Verb* something again'. In both these cases, the complex word consists of a number of components, each with its own meaning. We call such components **morphemes**, and to make them easier to identify we can separate them by means of a dash (e.g. *read-er*). You will often see the morpheme described as the **minimal linguistic sign.** What this means is that the morpheme is the smallest component of a word which contributes to its meaning. We will see that if we are to subscribe to this, we have to understand 'meaning' rather broadly.

In *reader* we have a morpheme *-er* attached to a word *read*. However, we cannot split *read* itself into smaller morphemes. This means that we can say that the word *read* is itself a single morpheme. A morpheme which can also stand as a word is called a **free morpheme**. By contrast, *-er/-or* and *re-* are unable to function as free standing words and these are called **bound mor-**

phemes. The verbs *read, print* and *format* are the starting point for the derivation of *reader, printer* and *formatter* in the sense that these verbs specify the activity undertaken by the person to whom *reader* etc. refers. We therefore assume that *-er* and *re-* are attached to the morphemes *read, print* and *format* to form the derived words. The ultimate starting point for deriving a word, that is, the most basic morpheme in a word, is its **root**. A morpheme such as *-er/-or* added to the right of a root is a **suffix**. One added to the left of the root, such as *re-*, is a **prefix**. The general term covering suffixes and prefixes is **affix**.

We often find more than one affix added to a word. Consider *indecipherability*. The root is the noun *cipher*. From this, we form a verb *de-cipher* from which the adjective *de-cipher-able* is formed. This is then negated by the prefix *in-* to give *in-de-cipher-able*, and finally we create a noun from the adjective by adding *-ity* (and making a change to *-able-*, of which more later, pp. 175ff.): *in-de-cipher-abil-ity*. The structures of the items in this sequence can be represented by **labelled bracketings** as in (103) (see section 9, exercise 4):

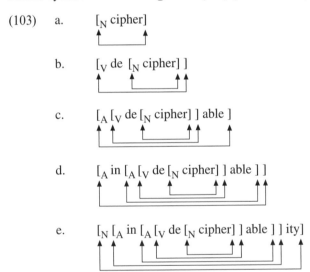

(103)   a.   [$_N$ cipher]

b.   [$_V$ de [$_N$ cipher]]

c.   [$_A$ [$_V$ de [$_N$ cipher]] able]

d.   [$_A$ in [$_A$ [$_V$ de [$_N$ cipher]] able]]

e.   [$_N$ [$_A$ in [$_A$ [$_V$ de [$_N$ cipher]] able]] ity]

In (103), we have explicitly indicated paired brackets using double-headed arrows, although it should be noted that such arrows are *not* part of the conventional labelled bracketing notation. Taking (103c) for illustration, we have [$_A$ marking the beginning of the adjective *decipherable* and its paired unlabelled bracket marks the end of this word; [$_V$ marks the beginning of the verb *decipher* and the paired unlabelled bracket marks the end of this word; and [$_N$ marks the beginning of the noun *cipher* the end of which is indicated by the paired unlabelled bracket.

Alternatively, we can represent the same information using the **tree diagrams** in (104):

(104)   a.

N
|
cipher

b.

V
de   cipher
N
cipher

c.

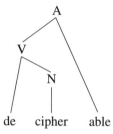

A
V
de   cipher   able
N

d.

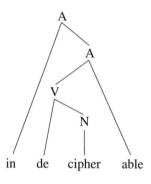

A
A
V
N
in   de   cipher   able

e.

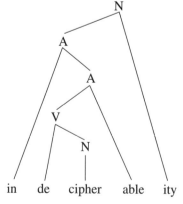

N
A
A
V
N
in   de   cipher   able   ity

To illustrate the interpretation of such trees, take (104c). This tells us that *cipher* is a noun (N), that *decipher* is a verb (V) formed by adding the prefix *de-* to the noun *cipher* and that *decipherable* is an adjective (A) formed by adding the suffix *-able* to the verb *decipher*.

Although English has a fair number of affixes, it also makes use of a morphological process whereby, *without any affixation*, a word of one syntactic category is used as though it belonged to a different category. This commonly happens when we treat nouns as verbs, as in the examples in (105):

(105)   a. Smith *motored* along for three hours
        b. Mary *codes* her messages skilfully
        c. The tourists are *fishing* near the bridge

Furthermore, we are equally likely to find examples of verbs being used as nouns in such phrases as *a splendid **catch**, a dangerous **run**, a fitful **sleep***. This process is known as **conversion**, and in some cases it is difficult to tell which is the original category. For example, is *rain* basically a verb (106a) or a noun (106b), or is it more appropriate to regard it as having dual category status, with neither the noun nor the verb being derived from the other?

(106)   a. It *rained* everyday on our holidays
        b. This *rain* is good news for the farmers

Morphological processes – derivation and inflection

One of the key concepts in morphology is that of 'word'. Up to now, we have taken this concept for granted, but now we are going to have to be a little more careful. Note first that the term 'word' as it is used in ordinary language hides an important ambiguity, which we must understand before we can proceed. Consider the following examples:

(107)   a. cat
        b. cats

(108)   a. cat
        b. dog

How many words are illustrated in (107) and (108)? The answer seems clear: two in each example. However, while it is obvious that this is the only answer for (108), there is a sense in which only *one* word appears in (107). This is the word CAT, with (107a) being its singular form and (107b) the plural. This second sense of 'word' is the one we intend to convey when we say 'this dictionary contains 50,000 words' or 'I know 5,000 words of Greek.' The term we use for this more abstract notion of 'word' is **lexeme**, and when we wish to make it clear that we are discussing a lexeme, the convention is to write it with capital letters. Thus, (107) illustrates only the lexeme CAT, while (108) illustrates the two lexemes CAT and DOG. What, then, of *cat* and *cats* in (107)? These are the singular and plural forms of the lexeme CAT, and we say that (107) illustrates two **word forms** of one lexeme. The singular and plural forms of a lexeme are examples of **inflections**, and we say that CAT inflects for the plural by taking the suffix *-s*. In (108) we again have two word forms (*cat, dog*), but these are the singular forms of two lexemes, CAT and DOG. From the point of view of meaning, different lexemes refer to distinct concepts, whereas this is not so for word forms. Up to this point, then, we have replaced the problematic 'word' with two distinct notions: lexeme and word form.

Returning now to the processes with which we introduced this section, we can ask about the status of *read* and *reader* with respect to the lexeme/word form distinction. Clearly, both *read* and *reader* are word forms, but in addition they refer to rather different (though related) concepts, one a process and the other a physical object taking part in that process. Thus, adding *-er* to a verb creates a new lexeme and READER and READ are distinct lexemes. Of course, each of them has a number of word forms: *reader* and *readers* in the case of READER, and *read* (/riːd/), *read* (/rɛd/), *reads, reading* in the case of READ. Moreover, the new lexeme is of a different syntactic category from that of the original lexeme (a verb has become a noun). The creation of new lexemes is the province of **derivational morphology** (or 'derivation'). Of the major lexical categories from section 9, prepositions (P) do not participate in derivation in English (or most other languages for that matter), while adverbs (ADV) are often derived from adjectives by the suffixiation of *-ly* (*bad* ~ *bad-ly*, *noisy* ~ *noisi-ly,* etc.). The other three categories (N, V and A) can, however, readily be derived from each other.

We have already seen that verbs can give rise to nouns via *-er/-or* suffixation, and to other verbs via *re-* prefixation. The third possibility for verbs is illustrated by the suffix *-able*. Suffixed to verbs, this gives words such as *read-able, print-able, format-able*, etc. which are adjectives with the meaning 'such that can be *Verb*-ed'. This suffix is also spelt *-ible* in cases such as *convert-ible*. Starting with adjectives, in *happi-ness, sad-ness, disinterested-ness*, etc. we create nouns by suffixation of *-ness*. We also find cases in which an adjective is turned into a verb, e.g. by suffixation of *-en* as in *short-en, weak-en, wid-en*, etc.; and the negative prefix *un-* creates a complex adjective from another adjective as in *un-happy*. Finally, if we take noun roots, we can create adjectives such as *boy-ish* and *child-ish* using the suffix *-ish*, verbs such as *motor-ise* and *demon-ise* with the suffix *-ise,* and complex nouns such as *boy-hood, child-hood* and *nation-hood* by means of the suffix *-hood*. These options are summarised in table 29 (***exercise 1***):

Table 29: Examples of derivational morphology in English.			
	Derived Form		
	Noun	**Verb**	**Adjective**
Basic Form			
Noun	boy-*hood*	motor-*ise*	child-*ish*
Verb	print-*er*	*re*-write	read-*able*
Adjective	sad-*ness*	short-*en*	*un*-happy

To date, we have seen various examples of derivations enabling us to form new lexemes in English. Derivation is not the only function of morphology, however. In the previous section, we considered examples such as *Tom reads comics*, pointing out that the verb *reads* consists of the base form *read* and a suffix *-s*. However, this suffix doesn't create a new lexeme; rather it signals agreement with a third person singular subject of the sentence (as well as the fact that the verb is present rather than past tense). Realising agreement is an important function of **inflectional morphology**, and as the Italian examples in the previous section showed, it is much more widespread in some languages than in English.

The *-s* ending which signals agreement in English is often thought of as a morpheme. However, such a morpheme does not have a meaning in the way that *re-* or *-er/-or* have meanings. Rather, it is an inflection which expresses an inflectional category (of agreement) and the purpose of this category is to signal a syntactic relationship, that of the verb to its subject. It is in this sense that we have to interpret rather broadly the notion of a morpheme as a minimal sign *having a single meaning*. Indeed, it is often thought appropriate to resort to a more neutral terminology in such cases. Instead of regarding the English agreement suffix *-s* as a morpheme, we can refer to it as an **inflectional formative** or **inflectional piece**, (or simply an 'inflection'), and instead of saying that an inflection means, say, 'third person singular' we say that it is the **exponent** of the property 'third person singular'. As we will see in the next section, there is much more than just terminology at stake here.

A further important concept can now be introduced if we return to (107). We have already noted that (107a, b) illustrate two word forms of the lexeme CAT. However, both of these word forms 'contain' the word form *cat* – (107a) just is *cat*, whereas (107b) is *cat-s*. Thus, we need to observe that the word form *cat* is found in two distinct *functions* in (107). In (107a) it is simply the singular form of the noun, but in (107b) it is the form of the noun to which the plural suffix is added. The form obtained when we remove inflections is called the **stem**. In regular nouns in English the stem is always the same as the singular word form. However, in a plural form such as *knives* the stem is pronounced with a voiced final fricative [naɪv], while the singular ends in an unvoiced fricative [naɪf]. In other words, the plural form of the lexeme KNIFE has a special stem form. Note that the notion of stem is distinct from that of root. The root is the smallest morphological form associated with a lexeme, while a stem is that form to which inflections are added. Thus, the root of the word form *printers* is *print*, but the stem (of the plural form) is *printer-*, which itself consists of a root and a derivational suffix *print-er-*.

The important distinction between lexemes and word forms enables us to explain a widely observed phenomenon in morphology: inflectional affixes tend to appear outside derivational affixes. Thus, in English we have *painter* 'one who paints', a form of a derived noun lexeme (PAINTER) formed from a form of the verb lexeme PAINT by suffixation of *-er*. The plural form of this new lexeme is *paint-er-s* and not **paint-s-er*. This makes sense if we regard plural formation as something which happens to the lexeme. The morphological rule of plural formation is to add *-s* to the end of the stem of the lexeme: *cat-s, painter-s*, and this rule doesn't need to worry about whether the lexeme itself is derived or not. Clearly, we can't form the plural of a derived lexeme such as *painter* until we have created that new lexeme, so we do not see forms such as **paint-s-er*.

A further complication concerning the notion of 'word' can be appreciated if we return to the inflectional categories of English verbs discussed in section 9. If we take a regular verb lexeme such as CROSS it has the word forms *cross, crosses, crossing* and *crossed*. Setting the base form *cross* and third person singular present form *crosses* aside, let's focus attention on *crossed*. As we have observed, one function of this form, illustrated in (109) is to express past tense:

(109)   The dog crossed the road safely

Additionally, *crossed* helps to form a special verb construction called the **perfect aspect** together with the auxiliary verb *have* as in (110):

(110)   I have crossed this road before

We have referred to the word form *crossed* in this construction as the *perfect participle* (p. 154), and the same form is found with the passive voice combined with the auxiliary verb *be*:

(111)   This river is crossed by three bridges

In (111) *crossed* is referred to as the *passive participle*. But now note that the terminology we have introduced to date for replacing the unclear concept 'word' does not enable us to come to terms with these distinctions. Focusing entirely on the lexical verb, there is only one lexeme in (109)–(111), viz. CROSS. Furthermore, there is only one word form of this lexeme in these examples, viz. *crossed*. It is necessary, then, to introduce a third sense of 'word' which is distinct from both lexeme and word form.

For many verbs, the past tense and the participle forms are distinct e.g. *sang* (past) and *sung* (perfect/passive participle). Therefore, we can say that the single word form *crossed* corresponds to *two* distinct inflected forms, the past tense form of CROSS and the perfect/passive participle form of CROSS. We will call a description such as 'the past tense form of CROSS' a **grammatical word** or **morphosyntactic word**. This means that *crossed* corresponds to *two* grammatical words, though it is a *single* word form of a *single* lexeme. At this point, it is useful to recall that in the previous section, we insisted that perfect/passive participle forms should be referred to as the -*n* forms of verbs even when they were suffixed with -*ed*. It should now be clear that the distinction between the -*d* and -*n* forms of verbs which we introduced there is a distinction between two *grammatical words*. In many cases, this distinction corresponds to a distinction between two word forms (*ate* ~ *eaten*, *sang* ~ *sung*, *gave* ~ *given*); in the case of regular verbs, however, only one word form corresponds to these two grammatical words (*crossed* ~ *crossed*, *walked* ~ *walked*, *jumped* ~ *jumped*, etc. (**exercise 2**).

The -*ing* suffix is also rather complex. Suffixed to a verb form which is combined with the auxiliary *be* it forms the present participle in a **progressive aspect** construction, as in (112):

(112)   Harriet is formatting a disk

It is also used to create from a verb a form which has some of the characteristics of nouns, as (113) illustrates:

(113)   Formatting disks is fun

In this example, the phrase *formatting disks* behaves rather like an ordinary noun such as *history* in *history is fun* (or indeed the phrase *the history of Switzerland* in *the history of Switzerland is fun*). However, in a phrase such as *the person formatting my disks* the word seems to behave more like an adjective, in that it forms a phrase, *formatting my disks*, which serves to describe *person*, rather like the adjective *responsible* in *the person responsible for my disks.* The use of a participle form as an adjective-like modifier is even clearer in an expression such as *running water.*

At this point, it is appropriate to assess the implications of our discussion so far for the lexical entries which form a fundamental component of a grammar. We can now see that it is lexemes which appear in the mental lexicon. When we say that speakers of English know the word *walk* we are saying that their lexicon contains a lexical entry WALK which provides several kinds of information. Firstly, there is information about the meaning of the lexeme (see section 12). Secondly, there is the syntactic information that it is a V and is intransitive. Thirdly, there is information about how to pronounce all the word forms associated with the lexeme. Now, the lexeme itself doesn't have a pronunciation; rather, it can be realised by one or more word forms and it is they which have a pronunciation. In regular cases the lexical entry just contains the pronunciation of the base form. For instance, the lexeme WALK has the base form *walk* which is pronounced /wɔːk/. Sometimes things are more complex and the lexical entry will contain the pronunciation of certain of the stem forms of a lexeme, as in the case of KNIFE, with its irregular plural stem. In other cases, it is necessary to include the pronunciation of a whole word form as in the case of the irregular verb BRING with the past tense form, /brɔːt/.

In (114), we see highly simplified lexical entries for WALK, KNIFE and BRING:

(114)   a. Lexical entry for WALK
             Phonology: /wɔːk/   base
             Syntax: V, intransitive
             Semantics: 'move on foot with alternate steps'
         b. Lexical entry for KNIFE
             Phonology: /naɪf/   base
                               /naɪv/   plural stem
             Syntax: N
             Semantics: 'instrument for cutting'
         c. Lexical entry for BRING
             Phonology: /brɪŋ/   base
                               /brɔːt/   [past tense]
             Syntax: V, transitive
             Semantics: 'carry something towards the speaker'

Other types of information (e.g. the fact that the third person singular present forms of WALK and BRING end in -*s*) are predictable from the principles of English morphology and therefore don't need to be included in the lexical entries. More subtly, we haven't mentioned the perfect/passive participle form (such as occurs in *has brought* and *was brought*) in (114c), even though this is also irregular. This is because, in the general case, the perfect/passive participle form is identical to the past tense form, and this principle of English morphology allows us to predict the perfect participle form of most verbs in the language. There are some exceptions. For example, *sang* is the past tense form of *sing* but *sung* is the perfect participle (*has sung*). In such cases, the lexical entry will have to contain the perfect participle form as well as the past tense form.

Having urged caution with respect to the concept of 'word' in the above discussion and introduced terminology which obviates confusion when precision is called for, we shall continue to use the word 'word' from here on, unless it is necessary to be circumspect.

Compounds

English shares with many languages the ability to create new words by combining old words. For instance, *blackbird* is clearly formed from the adjective *black* and the noun *bird*. However, a blackbird is a different thing from a black bird. First, *blackbird* denotes a particular bird species, not just any old bird which happens to be black; and second, female blackbirds are brown, but a black bird has to be black. The expression *blackbird* is a type of word, just like *thrush* or *crow*, but it happens to consist of two words. It is therefore called a **compound word**.

A blackbird is a type of bird, a windmill a type of mill, a coffee table a type of table and so on. We say that *bird, mill* and *table* are **heads** of the compounds *blackbird, windmill* and *coffee table*. The other part of the compound is a **modifier**. It is possible to form compounds out of compounds. For instance, we can have *finance committee, finance committee secretary, finance committee secretary election, finance committee secretary election scandal,* and so on. Now, the way these are written makes them look rather like phrases, but they behave in sentences just like single words. The above list consists of compound nouns and determiners such as *the* and adjectives such as *efficient* have to precede these compounds just as they would a single non-compound noun: *the highly efficient finance committee secretary*. The fact that they are written with spaces between the elements of the compound is a fact about English orthography and an arbitrary one at that. There are no principled criteria that would tell us whether *windmill* has to be written as one word, as two words (*wind mill*) or as a hyphenated word (*wind-mill*).

There is no theoretical limit to the lengths of compounds because the process of forming compounds can feed itself ad infinitum: a compound noun is itself a noun and can be subject to further compounding. This property is called **recursion** and we say that compounding in English is **recursive**. This is an important property which makes compounding resemble the syntactic processes of phrase- and sentence-formation (see p. 4 and section 19).

Another respect in which compounding is reminiscent of syntactic processes is in the types of ambiguities it permits. Consider a compound such as *toy car crusher*. This can refer to either a device for crushing toy cars (say, in a recycling factory) or a child's toy modelled after a car crusher. The ambiguity can be represented in terms of labelled brackets and tree diagrams as in (115):

(115)   a.   toy car crusher   'crusher for toy cars'

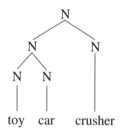

[$_N$ [$_N$ [$_N$ toy] [$_N$ car]] [$_N$ crusher]]

b.   toy car crusher   'car crusher which is a toy'

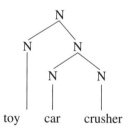

[$_N$ [$_N$ toy] [$_N$[$_N$ car] [$_N$ crusher]]]

An ambiguity of this sort, which results from the way the words are bracketed together, is called a **structural ambiguity**. It is an important type of phenomenon, because it is very difficult to see how we could explain such ambiguities without resorting to something like the structures in (115) (***exercise 3***).

English permits a variety of compounds. We can combine adjectives with nouns (*sweetcorn, lowlife*), or nouns with nouns (*windmill, coffee table*). In these cases it is the first element (*sweet-, low-, wind-, coffee*) which receives the most stress in the compound. We can also combine two adjectives (*dark blue, icy cold*) or nouns with adjectives (*canary yellow, iron hard*), but in these cases the stress usually falls on the last element. However, in English it is rare for a verb to participate in compounding. Examples such as *swearword* (verb + noun) and *babysit* (noun + verb) are exceptional.

We observed earlier that inflection generally appears outside derivation, a fact that we put down to derivation giving rise to new lexemes and regular inflectional processes such as pluralisation applying to lexemes. Now derivation can appear inside compounding in the sense that a derived word can be compounded with another word. Thus, in the compound *printer cable*, the first element, *printer*, consists of the verb *print* suffixed with *-er*, giving the overall structure [$_N$[$_N$[$_V$print]-er] [$_N$cable]]. We clearly don't first form a (non-existent) compound of the verb *print* and the noun *cable* (*print cable*) and then add *-er* to the *print* component. (Apart from other considerations, as we have just noted, it is virtually impossible in English to form a compound by adding a noun to a verb.)

The situation with regard to inflection is more revealing. Thus, with noun + noun compounds we seldom find morphology on the first noun. A dog catcher is presumably someone who catches more than one dog, yet we don't say *dogs catcher*, and even if we had a cable for use with several printers we wouldn't call it a *printers cable*. The lack of plurals in this position even extends to words which only ever occur in the plural, so that although there is no word *trouser* we do have *trouser leg* and *trouser press*. There are a few cases of plurals inside compounds, e.g. *systems analyst, arms control*, but usually the plural form is more than just a simple plural, and involves some change of meaning suggesting that we have a different lexeme from that linked to the singular form. On the other hand, we do have *dog catchers* and *printer cables*. Here, the plural formation rule pluralises the whole compound (*exercise 4*).

Clitics

Another puzzle about words can be illustrated by the examples in (116), How many words are there in each of these examples?

(116)　a. it's
　　　　b. they've
　　　　c. she'll
　　　　d. wasn't

It will come as no surprise that there are *two* correct answers. In one sense *it's* is a single word (indeed, it's just a single syllable), homophonous with (that is, being pronounced identically to) *its*. However, while *its* means 'pertaining or belonging to it' (*its name, its function*), *it's* means the same as *it is* or *it has*. Thus, there is a sense in which it combines two distinct words. The *-s, -ve, -ll* and *-n't* components of the words in (116) correspond to the full words *is/has, have, will/shall* and *not* and can be thought of as words. However, they can't stand alone in a sentence and they can't be stressed – to be pronounced they have to be attached to some other word (much like an affix). For this reason they are referred to as **bound words**.

A similar phenomenon is represented by the possessive *-'s* of *Harriet's hat*. It is often thought that *Harriet's* is a suffixed form of *Harriet*, just as the plural form, *hats*, is a suffixed form of *hat*. However, this is misleading, because we can have expressions such as *the man who Harriet met's hat* or *the girl I'm speaking to's hat*. Here, the *-'s* ends up attached to a verb form (*met*) or a preposition (*to*). This is not the normal behaviour of a suffix. What is happening here is that *-'s* is added to the last word of a whole phrase, *the man who Harriet met* or *the girl I'm speaking to*. Unlike the bound word, this type of element never corresponds to a full word and hence it is called a **phrasal affix**.

Bound words and phrasal affixes are examples of **clitics** (from a Greek word meaning 'to lean') and the word that a clitic 'leans' on is its **host**. Clitics such as *-'s* and *-'ve* appear to the right of their hosts, like suffixes. Such clitics are called **enclitics**. In other languages we find clitics which attach to the left side of the host, as though they were prefixes, called **proclitics**. Pronouns in Romance languages behave like this. Thus, in Spanish the unstressed pronouns *me* 'me' and *las* 'them' appear immediately before the verb in (117):

(117)   Me las enseña
         me them (he) shows
         'He shows them to me'

When the verb is in the imperative form however, the clitics follow the verb (they are enclitics):

(118)   ¡Enséñamelas!
         show.me.them
         'Show them to me!'

Notice that in Spanish orthography the proclitics are written separately, while the enclitics are written as one word with the verb. However, once more this is merely an orthographic convention, which does not bear at all on the status of these items as clitics.

Allomorphy

We noted earlier that when -*ity* is suffixed to *indecipherable*, a change occurs in the suffix -*able*. Specifically, there is a change in its pronunciation from [əbl̩] to [əbɪl], a change which is reflected by a change in spelling to -*abil*-. To look at what is going on here in a little more detail, we will consider a similar, but more regular case involving the pronunciation of the suffix -*al*. This creates adjectives from nouns, and its pronunciation also changes when such an adjective is converted to another noun by the suffixing of -*ity*. So consider the sets of examples in (119):

(119)   a. nation, nation-al, nation-al-ity
         b. music, music-al, music-al-ity
         c. tone, ton-al, ton-al-ity
         d. origin, origin-al, origin-al-ity.

In each case, -*al* is pronounced as a syllabic /l̩/ at the end of the word and as /al/ before -*ity*. What is happening here is that -*ity* causes the word stress to move to the immediately preceding syllable. When -*al* is unstressed it is pronounced as /l̩/ but when stressed it is pronounced with a vowel /a/. This is a regular phonological alternation. Thus, we can say that the morpheme -*al* occurs in two shapes /l̩/ and /al/ depending on stress. The shapes of morphemes as they are actually pronounced in a word are referred to as **morphs**, and where two morphs are variants of one morpheme we say they are **allomorphs** of that morpheme. The terminology here mirrors that of the phoneme, phone and allophone discussed in section 5.

We have said that the /al/ ~ /l̩/ alternation depends on stress. Since stress is an aspect of the phonology of a word, we can therefore say that the alternation is **phonologically conditioned**. This means that we can describe the difference between the two in purely phonological terms. However, this is not true of all allomorphy. In some cases, a word form will be idiosyncratic in that it contains unusual inflections. Thus, the plural form of the lexeme OX is *oxen*. This is simply a peculiar property of this particular lexeme, and so we say that the plural allomorph -*en* is **lexically conditioned** here (*exercise 5*).

A well-known irregular verb in English is GO. This has a base form /gou/ and a past tense form /wɛnt/, which is completely different. This change in form illustrates the phenomenon of **suppletion**. Since there is no overlap at all in form between *go* and *went*, this is a case of **total suppletion**. The example of *bring* ~ *brought* to which we have already referred (114c) is also a case of suppletion, but as the form /brɔːt/ bears a partial resemblance to the base form /brɪŋ/ (they have the same syllable onset), we say that it is **partial suppletion**. In these cases we can't say that the allomorphy is triggered by some phonological factor such as stress. Again, we have idiosyncratic properties of the lexemes concerned and so further instances of lexically conditioned allomorphy. Of course, it is precisely such lexically conditioned allomorphs which must appear in lexical entries (*exercises 6 and 7*).

The concept of allomorphy pertains to morphemes, and it encourages the view that complex word forms consist of strings of morphemes with the form of these morphemes (their allomorphs) being determined by either phonological or lexical factors. However, while this view is attractive in some cases, in others it proves difficult to sustain. We can illustrate the type of problem it confronts by considering again the exponents of the property 'perfect participle'. These include the endings -*ed* (*walked*) and -*en* (*taken*), and perhaps in these cases, it is appropriate to suppose that there is a morpheme PERF(ect) which enables us to analyse *walked* as *walk* + PERF and *taken* as *take* + PERF, with -*ed* and -*en* being treated as lexically conditioned allomorphs of this morpheme PERF. However, we also find forms such as *sing* ~ *sung* where the perfect participle differs from the base form by virtue of a vowel change. Should we regard *sung* as analysable as *sing* + PERF, with something (what exactly?) being a distinct allomorph of PERF in *sung*? It doesn't make much sense to say this, but it's a question of a type that recurs continually with inflection. An alternative is to say that there is a **morphological process** of perfect participle formation and this can be **realised** in a variety of ways, including affixation (-*ed* suffixation and -*en* suffixation) and a vowel change. We therefore speak of the affixes -*ed*/-*en* or the vowel change to /ʌ/ in *sung* as **realisations** of the morphological process. Morphologists sometimes also use **exponents**, a term we have already met, for referring to realisations. Adopting this perspective, it is common to represent morphological properties as *features*, similarly to the way we treated phonological properties in section 5, and so we can say that a perfect participle form of a verb has the feature [+perfect participle]. Thus, selecting a verb from the lexicon with this feature is a signal to trigger whatever phonological operation realises that function, whether regular affixation of -*ed*, the irregular -*en* suffixation, vowel change, or the choice of a suppletive form like *brought*.

One upshot of this reasoning is that we don't now have to say that complex words consist of morphemes, neatly strung out in a row each with its own meaning. Instead, we regard the operations of affixation (if they are what the morphology requires) as separate from the morphological process which is realised by each affixal morpheme. The morphological function itself is then represented by the set of features the word bears. The idea that affixes don't necessarily have a fixed meaning in the way that words do is known as the

Separation Hypothesis. For simple cases, of course, such as regular plurals or past tenses in English, it does no real harm to simplify the description and treat the affixes as things which have their own form and their own meaning. Thus, for many purposes in syntax it is sufficient to think of the past tense form *walked* as WALK + PAST TENSE, just as *coffee table* is COFFEE + TABLE. However, when we come to look at more complex inflectional systems in the next section we will see that the notion of Separationism is an important idea.

Exercises

1. This is an exercise in English derivational morphology. Analyse the following words into root and derivational affix. Identify the function of each affix, the grammatical category of the root and that of the derived word:

absorbent	arrival	childish	counterexample
defamation	employee	employment	encircle
freedom	generative	grammarian	greenish
lady-like	lioness	manhood	Marxist
mishear	motorise	Owenite	Protestant
purify	resentful	Roman	Stalinism
unaware	undo	vaccinate	Vietnamese

2. Take the Italian verbs in tables 22 to 24 and the Russian nouns in tables 25 to 28 in section 9. How many (a) lexemes (b) word forms (c) grammatical (morphosyntactic) words are there altogether in those tables?

3. Draw trees diagrams for the following compounds. Note that they all have more than one meaning and therefore require more than one tree. How does the tree structure relate to the difference in meaning?

   (a) student film society
   (b) New York taxi driver
   (c) child psychology graduate

4. Analyse the following words into morphemes and explain their structure in terms of derivation, inflection, compounding, affixation and conversion. Give a brief explanation of the meaning or function of each bound morpheme.

inoperability   disloyalty   unhappier
desalinated   counterintuitively   depilification
brickbatted   rowing boats

5a.   English regular plural allomorphy:

Regular nouns in English form their plural by 'adding an -*s* (or some-times -*es*)': *cats, dogs, cows, horses, ostriches, flamingos*, etc. However, this -*(e)s* suffix undergoes phonologically conditioned allomorphy, appearing as [s], [z] or [əz]/[ɪz]. Use the following examples, to iden-tify the phonological conditions of this allomorphy. (Hint: you will need to pay particular attention to the phonological nature of the final segment of the singular form):

antelopes   cats   chaffs   coelacanths
cows   dabs   dogs   doves
ducks   eels   fishes   flamingos
gnus   horses   iguanas   lambs
ostriches   squids

b.   English third person singular and possessive -'*s* allomorphy.

Collect together as many examples of uses of the third person singu-lar ending and the possessive -'*s* phrasal affix, using 5a as a model. Both of these morphemes undergo allomorphy. Describe this allo-morphy and identify the conditioning factors. Compare your results with your answer to 5a. (Hint: don't forget the possessive forms of regular and irregular plural nouns.)

c.   English regular past tense allomorphy

Regular verbs in English form their past tense by 'adding a -*d* (or sometimes -*ed*)': *walked, played, waited,* etc. However, this -*(e)d* suffix undergoes phonologically conditioned allomorphy, appearing as [t], [d] or [əd]/[ɪd]. Use the following examples to identify the phonological conditions of this allomorphy. Comment on the rela-tionship between this allomorphy and the allomorphy you have described in 5a and 5b.

aged   exploded   filled   fished
kissed   laughed   played   proved
raided   rubbed   sagged   screamed
sinned   sipped   suited   waited
walked   watched

6.   The perfect/passive participle of *bring* is *brought*. However, children (and some adults) sometimes use the form *brung*. On the other hand, it is very rare for a child to coin a form such as **rought* for the past tense or perfect/passive participle of *ring* (although *ringed* is common in children's speech, see section 13). Why might this be so?

7.   Take the verbs BE, HAVE, DO and MAKE. Enumerate all their inflectional forms and transcribe them phonetically. Then segment each word form into morphemes. How many distinct stems do we need for each verb? How many forms show partial suppletion and how many show total suppletion? How many stems are used for more than one word form in each verb?

11 Morphology across languages

The previous section has concentrated almost entirely on English morphological phenomena. In fact, languages differ considerably in the extent and nature of the morphological processes employed in their grammars. Vietnamese, for example, has no bound morphemes, so that the only morphology in the language is compounding. By contrast, there are languages in which morphology is extremely intricate and accounts for much of the grammar's complexity. In this section we will look at some examples of the types of morphological system that are found in the languages of the world, and the kinds of functions realised by that morphology. A range of the examples we consider will be seen to provide further support for the Separation Hypothesis introduced at the end of the previous section.

The agglutinative ideal

In the last century linguists introduced a classification of morphological systems which is still often referred to today. This classification distinguished **isolating, agglutinating** and **inflectional** languages. We start with isolating languages. These, exemplified by Vietnamese, Chinese and a number of other Far Eastern languages, as well as a number of West African languages have few, if any, bound morphemes. Thus, in Vietnamese, there is no morpheme corresponding to English -*er* in *driver*, this concept being conveyed by a compound with roughly the structure '*drive + person*'.

At the other extreme are languages such as Turkish, Finnish, Hungarian, the Bantu languages of Africa, many languages of the Americas and Australasia and most of the languages of Russia. Here, words of great complexity, consisting of many morphemes, are formed. A (fairly typical) word from the classic example of an agglutinating language, Turkish, appears in (120) (note that this example uses the orthographic system of Turkish):

(120)   çalıştırılmamalıymış
          'apparently, (they say) he ought not to be made to work'

The segmentation of this word into its component morphemes is indicated in (121):

(121)   çalış – tır – ıl – ma – malıy – mış
          work   cause   passive   negation obligation inference

The root, the verb *çalış* 'work' comes at the beginning and the suffixes each add their own component of meaning.

Languages such as Turkish give the impression that every morpheme has just one meaning and every meaning in the language is assigned its own unique morpheme. This is often thought of as a kind of morphological ideal, with the characterisation of such languages as agglutinating conveying the idea that morphemes are glued together one by one.

It is indeed the case that a 'perfect' isolating or agglutinating language would have the property that every morpheme would have just one meaning and every individual component of meaning expressible in the language would correspond to just one morpheme. The difference between the two types would be that in an agglutinating language some of the morphemes would be bound, giving the possibility of the construction of complex words like that in (120), whereas in an isolating language they would all be free. In practice, however, there are innumerable deviations from such ideals, and it's unlikely that any language has ever met the ideal. Moreover, there are many languages which show, say, agglutinating tendencies in some areas of grammar and isolating tendencies in others. For this reason it is much more interesting to ask whether *specific morphological processes* are isolating, agglutinating or something else. Whether a language can be so categorised is something of a non-question. With this background, we can now ask what sorts of departures from agglutination are found in morphological processes.

The most important deviations are found in languages which are traditionally regarded as inflectional. We can use inflectional systems such as those of Italian or Russian, illustrated in section 9, to introduce the appropriate concepts. Let's start with the Russian nouns. First, notice that each word form in tables 25 to 28 consists of a stem and a *single* inflectional formative. For instance, in *kod-ov* 'of codes', we have the stem *kod* followed by the inflection *-ov*, which simultaneously carries three distinct types of morphological information: morphological class, number and case. This type of deviation is called **cumulation** and we say that an ending like *-ov* in *kod-ov* **cumulates** the properties class I, genitive and plural.

In addition, some inflectional formatives correspond to more than one set of morphological functions. Thus, -a can indicate class I or class IV genitive singular (kod-a 'of a code'/bl'ud-a 'of a dish'), class II nominative singular (sonat-a 'sonata') or class IV nominative and accusative plural (bl'ud-a 'dishes'). This means that bl'uda realises several different grammatical words (just as walked realises two distinct grammatical words in English, see p. 169). When a single form systematically realises more than one inflectional form, we say it is an example of **syncretism**.

The Russian examples in section 9 all use regular nouns. However, many nouns show various types of irregularity. For instance, the noun oblako 'cloud' declines just like class IV bl'udo 'dish' in all forms, except that in the genitive plural it declines like class I kod 'code' to give oblakov 'of clouds'. For this word, then, (and a handful of similar cases) the ending -ov serves as a special class IV genitive plural marker. This is basically a form of **inflectional allomorphy**, and represents our third main deviation from ideal agglutination.

The Italian verbs in section 9 also illustrate cumulation, syncretism and inflectional allomorphy (though you will only be able to detect examples of cumulation and syncretism). However, unlike what happens with the Russian nouns, it is clear that the endings on these verbs can be separated into several distinct inflectional pieces. For instance, each conjugation tends to be marked by a particular vowel in the present indicative and past tense, -a for first conjugation, -e for second conjugation and -i for third conjugation. Thus, the third person plural past tense forms can be split up as parl-a-rono 'they spoke', cred-e-rono 'they believed', and fin-i-rono 'they finished'. But the finire class is rather odd, in that in the present forms (indicative or subjunctive) we get an additional piece, -sc-, appearing in some forms, namely all the singular forms and the third person plural. This means that the difference between the singular and third person plural forms on the one hand, and the first and second person plural forms on the other is marked twice, once by -sc- and again by the particular agreement endings.

The -sc- formative is a **partial exponent** (along with the agreement inflections) of the properties first/second person singular and third person (singular or plural). This means that in, say, the second person singular present indicative fin-i-sc-i 'you finish', we can say that -sc- and the final -i both contribute to the meaning, and both help to distinguish the word from the first person singular past form finii (which is identical to finisci except it lacks the -sc- formative). At the same time, it is only the class III verbs which exhibit this behaviour, so the -sc- formative also helps to identify the morphological class. In other words, the signalling of one morphological property is spread across more than one inflectional formative, and one inflectional formative is an exponent of more than one morphological property. This complex situation is illustrated for *finisci* and *finii* in (122):

(122) a.

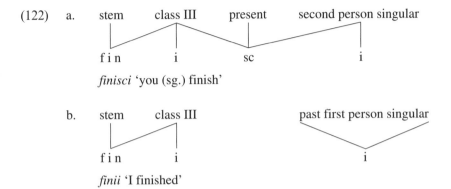

finisci 'you (sg.) finish'

b.

finii 'I finished'

This is an example of **extended exponence**, in that properties such as class III and second person singular are extended over more than one inflectional piece. However, it is worth pointing out that, by and large, even where we have cumulation, extended exponence and other deviations from perfect agglutination, we usually find that one of the affixes is the **principal exponent** of a given morphological category or property. Thus, in the verb form *fin-i-re* 'to finish', *-i-* is the principal exponent of class III and realising this property is the principal function of this suffix. Likewise, *-re* is the principle (in fact the only) exponent of the property 'infinitive' and *-re* has no other function (***exercises 1 and 2***).

An interesting fact about English is that a single base form such as *walk* or *book* is in most cases a perfectly good word. Therefore, we are tempted to think that we take the base form of a word and then add inflections to it (e.g. *walking, book-s*), or conversely that we can get to the base form by stripping off the inflections. This makes sense for English and a number of other languages including German, Hungarian, and Turkish, but for many inflecting languages stripping off all the inflections often produces something which cannot function as a word. Thus, Italian verbs (and nouns) need some sort of inflectional ending to form a proper word. The bare stem can't be used on its own: **parl*, **cred* or **fin* are not possible words in Italian. The same is true broadly speaking of Russian, Spanish, Greek, Latin, Japanese, Swahili, Chukchee, Navajo (for verbs at least) and many others. Moreover, we sometimes get a different form depending on which set of inflections we strip off. For instance, there are many verbs in Italian which have irregular past forms and an irregular first person singular form in the present. Thus, *valere* 'to be worth' has a first person singular past form *valsi* ('I was worth') and a first person singular present indicative form *valgo* 'I am worth'. When we strip off the endings, we get the form *vals-* for the past form and *valg-* for the first person singular present indicative form. Both of these are different from the form *val-* obtained by stripping off the infinitive ending *-re* and the conjugation class marker *-e-* from *valere*. This leads to the conclusion, then that the verb *valere* has three stems, *val-*, a distinct first person past tense stem, *vals-*, and a distinct first person singular present indicative stem, *valg-*.

While English has small numbers of examples justifying more than one stem appearing in the representation of a lexeme (see the discussion of KNIFE in the previous section), we can generally think of its inflection (or that of German, Hungarian, etc.) as being **word-based**, while Italian (or Spanish or Russian, etc.) inflection is **stem-based**. The distinction has implications for psycholinguistic theories of the way that words are processed by the mind/brain and the way that language processing develops in children or is disturbed by brain damage (see sections 15 and 26).

A fourth class of language, often added to the traditional typology, is the class of **polysynthetic** languages. This class is illustrated by Chukchee, a language spoken in NE Siberia. In (123b) we see a *word* which corresponds to the *phrase* in (123a):

(123)   a. nəteŋqin   ŋelgən
           good   hide
           'a good skin, hide'
        b. teŋŋelgən
           'a good skin, hide'

In (123a) *teŋ* is the adjective root and *nə-* . . . *-qin* combines with this to form an adjective *nəteŋqin* 'good'. In (123b) the adjective root has formed a compound with the noun *ŋelgən* 'hide' to make a single word. There are various ways in which we can show that this is a single word and not just a closely knit phrase, one of which is the fact that adjective roots like *teŋ* never appear without their prefix *nə-* and suffix *-qin* except in compounds.

In (124) we see a similar phenomenon:

(124)   a. tə-lʔu-gʔen   ŋelgən
           I-saw-it   hide
           'I saw a/the hide'
        b. tə-ŋelgə-lʔu-k
           I-hide-saw-I
           'I saw a/the hide'

In (124a) the verb form *təlʔugʔen* has a prefix *tə-* marking a first person singular subject ('I') and a suffix *-gʔen* marking a third person singular object, agreeing with the direct object *ŋelgən* 'hide'. In (124b) three things have happened. First, the object has now joined the verb and formed a compound verb stem *ŋelgə-lʔu* 'hide-saw'. Second, in so doing it has lost the *-n*, which in fact is a case suffix. Third, the verb now ends in a suffix referring again to the first person singular subject. This suffix occurs with *intransitive* verbs in Chukchee, but this is explicable, as the verb in (124b) is intransitive because its original object has actually formed a compound with it (to have this compound appear with an object would produce a structure equivalent to the English *I saw the hide the tent* with too many complements).

Compounding of this kind, functioning as an alternative to a syntactically formed phrase, is known as **incorporation**. The noun incorporates its adjective in (123b) and the verb incorporates its object in (124b). Adjective incorporation is not very widespread (though in Chukchee itself it is extremely common), but object incorporation or noun incorporation is very frequently found in the world's languages. In fact, in Chukchee, object incorporation can apply to the result of adjective incorporation:

(125) a. tə-lʔu-gʔen   nəteŋqin   ŋelgən
          I-saw-it   good   hide
          'I saw a/the good hide'

       b. tə-lʔu-gʔen   teŋ-ŋelgən
          I-saw-it   good-hide
          'I saw a/the good hide'

       c. tə-teŋ-ŋelgə-lʔu-k
          I-good-hide-saw-I
          'I saw a/the good hide'

Here, we first incorporate the adjective into the noun in (125b). Then, this compound noun, which functions as an object in (125b), is incorporated into the verb in (125c). Words like *təteŋŋelgəlʔuk* are not especially uncommon or exotic in Chukchee.

Incorporation is found in a large number of language groups; many languages of the Americas, such as the Iroquoian languages, the Mayan languages, Nahuatl (the language of the Aztecs), large numbers of languages of the Pacific including Maori, Samoan, and Tongan, a number of Australian languages, certain of the languages of India and a host of others exhibit incorporation.

What are referred to as polysynthetic languages are those that make use of incorporation in their morphology, though they may also have agglutinating or inflectional processes or even show isolating tendencies. Chukchee, for instance, is typical in having a large number of very regular derivational processes, which are relatively agglutinating, just like Turkish. However, it also has a rich inflectional system showing cumulation, multiple exponence, syncretism and so on (*exercise 3*).

Incorporation processes like those described above strike us as 'exotic'. It is noteworthy, then, that a similar phenomenon is found with a very common type of compound in English. This is illustrated in (126):

(126)　　a. Tom drives taxis
　　　　　b. Tom is a taxi-driver

The compound in (126b) includes the object of the verb *drive* from which the deverbal noun *driver* is derived. Similar examples are *taxi-driving*, *insect repellent* and *motorcycle maintenance*. In these compounds the head is derived from a verb (*drive, repel, maintain*). The non-head of the compound functions effectively as the object of the verb (see *drive taxis, repel insects, maintain motorcycles*). This is referred to as **synthetic compounding**. If it were possible to form a verb from these, as in (127), we would have proper noun incorporation in English:

(127)　　a. *Tom taxidrove yesterday
　　　　　b. *Agent Orange insectrepels very effectively
　　　　　c. *Bikers should motorcyclemaintain regularly

Even where it looks as though we have such a case, as in *Dick babysat for Tom and Harriet*, we generally find that there is no syntactic equivalent: **Dick sat the baby for Tom and Harriet*. The verb *babysit* is just an idiosyncratic form, not a regular compound, and we are justified in concluding that English does not exhibit proper incorporation.

Types of morphological operations

We have already seen numerous examples of prefixation and suffixation, and the examples of vowel changes and suppletions, as in English past tense forms *sang* and *brought* have indicated that there are additional ways in which the morphological structure of a word can be modified. The Chukchee example in (123) provides another case, where the root *teŋ* in the word *nə-teŋ-*

qin is *simultaneously* prefixed and suffixed to form the adjective. A similar phenomenon is seen in German. In regular verbs the perfect/passive participle is formed by simultaneously adding a prefix *ge-* and a suffix *-t* to the verb stem. Thus, from the stem *hab* 'have' we get *ge-hab-t* 'had'. Since the prefix and suffix are added together, we can think of *nə-*... *-qin*, or *ge-*... *-t* as a composite, discontinuous morpheme. Such a morpheme is called a **confix** or **circumfix**.

The languages of the Philippines illustrate another type of affixation. Here are some verb forms in the major language of those islands, Tagalog:

(128)	verb stem	infinitive	meaning
a.	aral	umaral	'teach'
b.	sulat	sumulat	'write'
c.	basa	bumasa	'read'
d.	gradwet	grumadwet	'graduate'

The crucial thing about these examples is that *aral, sulat, basa* and *gradwet* are single, undecomposable morphemes. In (128a) we see the prefix *um-* added to a vowel-initial stem. However, (128b, c, d) do not have the infinitive forms **umsulat, *umbasa, *umgradwet.* Rather, when the stem begins with a consonant, the affix goes *inside* the stem morpheme, after the onset of the first syllable. This is a regular and pervasive process in Tagalog and several hundred related languages, as can be seen from the fact that it applies to the recent English loan word from *graduate*. An affix which is inserted strictly inside another affix or stem like this is known as an **infix**.

Prefixes and suffixes (and circumfixes) behave like things which are added to stems. This is like compounding in that we simply concatenate two entities, and, indeed, such affixation often develops historically from compounding. Morphology of this type is called **concatenative**, and it encourages the view, briefly discussed in the previous section, that complex word forms consist simply of strings of morphemes. However, very often a morphological process seems to be realised by a *phonological operation* performed on the stem itself, as in the case of the vowel changes in *sing ~ sung ~ sang*. Indeed, infixation can be construed in this way as involving first affixation, then a phonological operation which moves the affix to a position inside the stem. It should also be clear that infixation represents another type of deviation from agglutination.

Tagalog illustrates a further way in which affixation looks more like a process than a straightforward concatenation of morphemes. Here are some more verb forms in this language:

(129)	verb stem	future	meaning
a.	sulat	susulat	'write'
b.	basa	babasa	'read'
c.	trabaho	tatrabaho	'work'

From (129) we can see that the future tense form of the verb involves taking the first syllable and copying the first consonant from its onset and its vowel to create a new syllable which appears as a prefix. This type of process is known as **reduplication**, and it provides a rather vivid demonstration of the inappropriateness of suggesting that Tagalog has a morpheme FUTURE with various lexically conditioned allomorphs. Obviously, the list of such allomorphs would be rather long and such a list would fail to make explicit the fundamental fact about Tagalog future formation. This fact is acknowledged by suggesting that there is a morphological feature, say [+future], which can attach to verb lexemes. When this happens, a phonological process is triggered which produces the correct future form of the verb by consulting the syllable structure of the stem form and performing the appropriate operations (*exercise 4*).

On several occasions, in this and the previous section, we have invoked examples of vowel changes in English verb forms as another type of phonological operation which subserves a morphological purpose. Alongside *sing ~ sang ~ sung*, we find *ring ~ rang ~ rung, hang ~ hung, fling ~ flung*, etc., and it is now time to introduce the technical term for this sort of process. It is known as **Ablaut** (sometimes called **Apophony**). A larger number of English verbs combine a vowel change with suffixation, especially in the participle, so we find such sets of forms as the following: *write ~ wrote ~ written, give ~ gave ~ given, take ~ took ~ taken, do ~ did ~ done*. Each of these simply involves a vowel change in forming the past tense form (the second member of each set); for the participles (the third member of each set), however, there is suffixation of *-en* with or without a vowel change. A specific kind of Ablaut, which is particularly common in Germanic languages (and some other language groups), occurs when a back vowel is replaced by a front vowel. A number of German plurals are formed this way: /apfl ~ epfl/ 'apple', /fogl ~ føgl/ 'bird', /brudr ~ brydr/ 'brother'. This type of vowel fronting is known as **Umlaut**, and there are vestiges of this in English irregular plurals such as *men, teeth* and *geese*.

The last morphological process we shall consider here is represented marginally by some English verbs which are derived from nouns. The difference between *a mouth* and *to mouth* or *a house* and *to house* is that the final consonant is voiced in the verb: /mauθ ~ mauð/, /haus ~ hauz/. In the Nilotic language DhoLuo, spoken in Western Kenya, much more systematic use is made of this process in the formation of plurals. Here are some singular and plural forms of nouns in this language:

(130)   DhoLuo plurals

	singular		plural	
a.	kede	'twig'	kete	'twigs'
b.	got	'hill'	gode	'hills'
c.	luθ	'stick'	luðe	'sticks'
d.	puoðo	'garden'	puoθe	'gardens'
e.	buk	'book'	buge	'books'
f.	tʃogo	'bone'	tʃoke	'bones'
g.	apwojo	'rabbit'	apwotʃe	'rabbits'
h.	kwatʃ	'leopard'	kwaje	'leopards'

One way of forming a plural involves adding a suffix *-e* as in these examples. In general when this occurs, the voicing of the final consonant of the stem changes from voiced to voiceless or vice versa (with the palatal glide /j/ being treated as the voiced correlate of the voiceless palato-alveolar affricate /tʃ/).

The above phenomenon exemplifies what is often called **consonant mutation**, and this is even more obvious and varied in its effects in Celtic languages. Look at the way adjectives behave in Literary Welsh when modifying masculine nouns and feminine nouns (adjectives come after nouns in Welsh):

(131)   Welsh consonant mutation

	masculine nouns		feminine nouns	
a.	dur klir	'clear water'	nos glir	'clear night'
b.	gwint poeθ	'hot wind'	teisen boeθ	'hot cake'
c.	hogin tal	'tall lad'	geneθ dal	'tall girl'
d.	ti glan	'clean house'	calon lan	'clean heart'
e.	ɬivr bax	'little book'	ferm vax	'little farm'

[/ɬ/ is a voiceless /l/]

Operations such as reduplication, Ablaut and consonant mutation are rather different from the concatenative types of morphological operation discussed earlier because they do not involve adding anything (such as an affix) to a stem or base in any obvious sense. This type of morphology is often referred to as **non-concatenative morphology**, and, as we have observed, it is very difficult to interpret in terms of the morpheme concept. For instance, in the past tense form *sang*, what is the past tense morpheme? Or in the plural form *men*, what is the plural morpheme? We don't want to say that it is the /a/ or the /ɛ/ because this would imply that the non-past form was */sng/ and the singular form */mn/, which is clearly not the case. Earlier, we pointed out that a single morph may realise several different functions at once. Thus, the *-sc-* of the Italian verb form *finisci* in (122a) realises class III, present tense and second person singular, while the inflectional suffix of a Russian noun realises simultaneously noun declension, number and case. Equally, we have found that a single function may be realised by several different morphs. Thus, in *finisci* class III is realised by the first *-i-* suffix and by *-sc-* as well as by the stem itself, and in the perfect participle form *driven* (/drɪvn/), 'perfect participle' is realised by the *-en* suffix and by the Ablaut /aɪ/ ⇒ /ɪ/ (see *drive* (/draɪv/). These phenomena are more intelligible if we appeal to Separationism, and distinguish the abstract morphological processes of tense formation, agreement, perfect participle formation, plural formation and so on, from the concrete operations of suffixation, Ablaut and so on (*exercises 5 and 6*).

Exercises

1. Segment the Italian verb forms in tables 22 to 24 in section 9 into their components. Identify the basic meanings of each inflectional piece. What cases can you find of cumulation and syncretism?

2. Analyse the following English verb forms to show how they illustrate cumulation, syncretism, inflectional allomorphy and extended exponence. (Hint: you may find it useful to transcribe the verb forms into IPA):

    (she) walk**s**
    (they have) d**ri**v**en**
    (we) walk
    (he) walk**ed**
    (you have) sp**oken**

3. Below are some Chukchee words, slightly simplified. Segment them into their component morphemes and provide a rough meaning for each morpheme. Comment on the types of affixation found and on any allomorphy you observe.

ekwetək	to set off
eretək	to fall
nəwilək	to come to a halt
rəgelək	to go in
rənwiletək	to stop someone
rərgeletək	to introduce

rərgelewək	to lure in
rərultetək	to move something away
rətejŋetək	to feed (something to someone)
rətenmawək	to prepare (something)
rekwetewək	to send someone off (on a journey)
reretək	to drop
rultək	to step aside
runtəmewetək	to calm someone
tejŋetək	to eat (something)
tenmawək	to get oneself ready
untəmewək	to calm oneself down

4. In the data below we see examples of reduplication in the Palan dialect of Koryak (a language closely related to Chukchee). What is the rule for forming a noun of this kind in Koryak?

tʃajtʃaj	'tea'	həlwehəl	'wild reindeer'
jiŋejiŋ	'mist'	jilhejil	'gopher'
kalikal	'book'	liŋliŋ	'heart'
mətqmət	'fat'	milgmil	'fire'
nutenut	'tundra'	tərgtər	'meat'
wətwət	'leaf'	wiruwir	'seal'
ʔawtaʔaw	'flint'		

5. Some plural forms in Arabic are very difficult to predict from the singular form. However, there are patterns. What is the common, invariant component of the following Arabic nouns (the forms are slightly simplified in some cases)? How can the plural be constructed from the singular form in each case? (A doubled vowel, e.g. *aa*, represents a long vowel, e.g. [aː]; representing long vowels in this way may make it easier to see the principles that underlie this system. Note that the nouns come in two groups depending on the form of the singular.)

singular	plural	meaning
qidħ	qidaaħ	arrow
dʒamal	dʒimaal	camel
ħukm	ħakaam	judgement
ʔasad	ʔusuud	lion
jundub	janaadib	locust

radʒul	ridʒaal	man
ʕinab	ʕanaab	grape
nafs	nufuus	soul

saħaabat	saħaaʔib	cloud
ʔumθulat	ʔamaaθil	example
dʒaziirat	dʒazaarʔir	island
ħaluubat	ħalaaʔib	milch-camel
kariimat	karaaʔim	noble
marħalat	maraaħil	stage

6.   What deviations from agglutination are exhibited by the Swahili verb
forms shown below? (The data are slightly simplified.)

(i)a.

nilitaka	I wanted	tulitaka	we wanted
ulitaka	you (sg.) wanted	mlitaka	you (pl.) wanted
alitaka	he/she wanted	walitaka	they wanted

b.

nitataka	I shall want	tutataka	we shall want
utataka	you (sg.) shall want	mtataka	you (pl.) shall want
atataka	he/she shall want	watataka	they shall want

c.

ninataka	I want	tunataka	we want
unataka	you (sg.) want	mnataka	you (pl.) want
anataka	he/she wants	wanataka	they want

(ii)a.

sikutaka	I did not want	hatukutaka	we did not want
haukutaka	you (sg.) did not want	hamkutaka	you (pl.) did not want
haakutaka	he/she did not want	hawakutaka	they did not want

b.

sitataka	I shall not want	hatutataka	we shall not want
hautataka	you (sg.) shall not want	hamtataka	you (pl.) shall not want
haatataka	he/she/it shall not want	hawatataka	they shall not want

c.

sitaka	I do not want	hatutaka	we do not want
hautaka	you (sg.) do not want	hamtaka	you (pl.) do not want
haataka	he/she/it does not want	hawataka	they do not want

12 Word meaning

So far, we have not attempted to develop any analytic account of the semantic representations which appear in lexical entries. Indeed, in the examples in (114) (section 10), what we see under the heading 'semantics' is taken directly from an ordinary dictionary. Whether such dictionary definitions can be regarded as supplying the meanings of words for the purposes of linguistic analysis is something we shall briefly consider later in this section after we have introduced some basic ideas.

As well as being concerned with the contents of lexical entries, a further matter which will arise in this section is that of the overall *structure* of the lexicon. In the introduction (pp. 4f.), we talked about the lexicon as a *list* of lexical entries, but it is at least conceivable that it has a more interesting structure than this. To say that the lexicon is no more than a list is to accept that there is no reason why items which are similar to each other in some linguistically relevant way are 'close' to each other in the mental lexicon. As we shall see, similarity of meaning is a rather rich notion, and as subsequent sections of this part of the book will show, it seems to play an important role in human cognitive processing. In such circumstances, it is important for our model of the lexicon to properly represent this notion.

A difficulty we immediately encounter when we turn to the meanings of words is that native speakers do not provide the rich source of data we have been relying on in our discussions of phonology and morphology. The contrast between *TRANSport* (Noun) and *transPORT* (Verb) is one native speakers will readily confirm, as is the fact that *singed* is not the Past Tense form of *sing*, etc. These are judgements of *form* with which native speakers are comfortable, but meanings seem much less tangible and correspondingly less open to study by the methods we have used up to now. We, therefore, have to resort to less direct methods for probing the semantic aspect of the lexicon and of lexical entries.

Entailment and hyponymy

Consider the sentences in (132):

(132)   a. Max managed to finish *Infinite Jest*
         b. Max finished *Infinite Jest*

Suppose that the sentence in (132a) is *true*. Then, the sentence in (132b) is also true. There is no possible state of affairs in which (132a) is true while (132b) is false. In these circumstances, we say that (132a) **entails** (132b), and a general definition of entailment appears in (133):

(133)   A sentence (S_1) entails a sentence (S_2) if and only if whenever S_1 is true, S_2 is also true

Before going further, it is important to be clear that this relation of entailment does not obtain between sentences which just happen to be true in the current or any other state of affairs. Take, for instance, the sentences in (134):

(134)   a. The dodo is extinct
         b. Berlin is the capital of Germany

Both these sentences are true at the time of writing this book, but it is not the case that (134a) entails (134b). The definition in (133) contains the word 'whenever', and while (134a) was true in 1980, (134b) was not – indeed, in 1980 there was no unified Germany for Berlin to be the capital of. Intuitively, this lack of an entailment relationship between (134a) and (134b) is linked to the fact that there is no meaning relationship between the sentences: knowing that (134b) is true does not help at all in understanding (134a). However, the case of (132) is different: knowing that (132b) is true *whenever* (132a) is tells us something about the meaning of the lexeme MANAGE, and it would be reasonable to conclude of someone who maintained that (132b) could be false while (132a) was true that they did not know the meaning of this lexeme.

Now consider the sentences in (135):

(135)   a. Max failed to finish *Infinite Jest*
         b. Max didn't finish *Infinite Jest*

Again, we note that (135a) entails (135b), but in this case the entailed sentence contains the negative clitic *n't*. The entailed sentences (132b and 135b) are semantic 'opposites' and this coincides with the fact that the two lexemes MANAGE and FAIL, while having a good deal in common semantically (they both concern relations between someone trying to do something and whatever they are trying to do) are themselves 'opposites' (***exercise 1***).

Let's now consider some simpler examples of entailment relations, which will help us to build up a picture of how the lexicon might be structured. That the (a) examples in (136 – 8) entail the (b) examples is uncontroversial:

(136)   a. The thing in the cage is a lion
        b. The thing in the cage is an animal

(137)   a. The thing in the grass is a snake
        b. The thing in the grass is a reptile

(138)   a. The thing in the tree is a sparrow
        b. The thing in the tree is a bird

In each case, what we have is a relationship of entailment between pairs of sentences which is due to the presence of particular pairs of words: *lion* and *animal* in (136), *snake* and *reptile* in (137) and *sparrow* and *bird* in (138). Focusing on (136), we have the general schema in (139) where X is an expression which identifies an individual, *the thing in the cage*, *Simba*, etc.:

(139)   'X is a lion' entails 'X is an animal'

When we find this situation, we say that *lion* is a **hyponym** of *animal* (equivalently *lion* and *animal* are in the semantic relationship of **hyponymy**, sometimes referred to as **meaning inclusion**). On the basis of (137) and (138), we can also assert that *snake* is a hyponym of *reptile* and *sparrow* is a hyponym of *bird*. Looking at the semantic relation from the converse perspective, we say that *animal*, *reptile* and *bird* are **superordinates** of *lion*, *snake* and *sparrow* respectively. A very straightforward test for many examples of hyponymy is to use (140):

(140)   An X is a kind/type of Y

Thus, a lion is a type of animal, a snake is a type of reptile, etc.

An important property of hyponymy is that it is a 'one-way' relation. Thus, while (136a) entails (136b), it is not the case that (136b) also entails (136a). There are possible states of affairs in which a designated creature is an animal without it being a lion, and, relying on (140), this corresponds to the fact that an animal is not a type of lion. To put this another way, being an animal is a *necessary condition* for being a lion; it is not, however, a *sufficient* condition.

Recognition of hyponymy as a semantic relation which holds between some words raises a number of issues. First, we must recognise that as well as *animal* being a superordinate of *lion*, it is also itself a hyponym of *creature*. As well as (139), we have (141):

(141)   'X is an animal' entails 'X is a creature'

This means that for this part of the English lexicon, the **taxonomy** (a structure in which we meet more *general* terms as we ascend to higher levels) defined by the semantic relation of hyponymy is multiply layered. Part of this taxonomy is illustrated in (142):

(142)

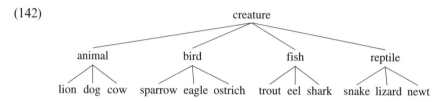

In (142), *lion, dog, cow,* etc. are **co-hyponyms** of the superordinate *animal,* which is a co-hyponym of *creature* along with *bird, fish* and *reptile.*

It is readily apparent that this taxonomy can be further extended at certain points to include another level. For instance, *dog* has *spaniel, corgi, rottweiler,* etc. and *snake* has *cobra, viper, anaconda,* etc. as co-hyponyms. However, this is not the case for all the items at the lowest level of (142) (e.g. *ostrich*), and for other cases, extension of the taxonomy involves a resort to morphologically complex forms (*white shark, blue shark, basking shark,* etc.). This is an issue to which we shall return in sections 13 and 15. Examples of taxonomies from other parts of the vocabulary of English are not difficult to find (*exercise 2*).

All the words appearing in the taxonomy in (142) are nouns. Do members of other word classes enter into hyponymy relations? For verbs, there are some clear instances. Consider the pairs of examples in (143) and (144):

(143)   a. X borrowed/stole/found/bought Y
          b. X got Y

(144)   a. X walked/ran/staggered/crawled to Z
          b. X moved to Z

In both of these cases, the various sentences in (a) entail the sentence in (b): there is no possible state of affairs in which someone can borrow something and not get it, etc., so we can justify the partial taxonomies in (145) and (146):

(145)

(146)

Note that we cannot straightforwardly extend (140) to apply to examples such as these. However, if we manipulate the syntax appropriately, it is easy enough to come up with a formulation which produces a simple test for whether a verb X is a hyponym of another verb Y. The sentence in (147) will serve this purpose:

(147)   X-ing is a sort of/type of Y-ing

The semantic relation of hyponymy must be distinguished from another semantic relation which is illustrated by pairs such as those in (148):

(148)   a. body, arm
          b. arm, elbow
          c. house, roof
          d. engine, carburettor

It is easy to see that the one-way entailment that we have seen to be character-istic of hyponymy does not obtain for cases such as these. Thus, neither (149a) nor (149b) obtains:

(149)   a. 'X is a body' entails 'X is an arm'
          b. 'X is an arm' entails 'X is a body'

The relationship between *arm* and *body* is one whereby the objects to which they refer are in a part–whole relation, and the term used for this relationship is **meronymy**. We also say that *arm* is a **meronym** of *body* and that *arm*, *leg*, etc. are **co-meronyms**. As (148a, b) show, it is also possible to have meronymic structures with more than one level, as in (150):

(150)

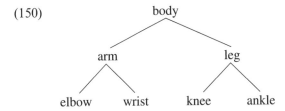

Note, however, that structures such as this are not to be confused with taxono-mies – as we move up such a structure, we encounter 'larger' entities, not more general categories (*exercise 3*).

While large sections of the vocabulary of a language can be analysed in terms of relations such as hyponymy and meronymy, such analysis is not always straightforward. For instance, consider the set of verbs in (151):

(151)   think, believe, hope, wish, know, realise

These verbs (and the set could be extended) are known as *propositional attitude verbs*, i.e. they are all used to express something about the nature of the attitude of someone to a particular proposition, and the fact that they are labelled in this way indicates that they are perceived as having something in common semantically. However, there is no verb in English which qualifies as a superordinate for members of this class. In these circumstances, there is a **lexical gap**, and if we wished to represent the fact that the verbs in (151) do form a natural set, we could do so using (152), where φ indicates the position of the gap (*exercise 4*):

(152)

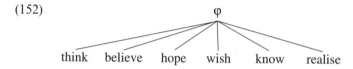

Synonymy or **identity of meaning** is a semantic relation with which most readers will be familiar. However, it is doubtful whether there are lexemes in a language which can be regarded as completely identical in meaning. As a consequence, linguists often distinguish different types of synonymy, and among these **cognitive synonymy** can be defined in terms of entailment, as in (153) where S(L) means that L occurs in a sentential context S:

(153)   Lexemes L_1 and L_2 are cognitive synonyms if and only if $S(L_1)$ entails $S(L_2)$ and $S(L_2)$ entails $S(L_1)$

(Note that strictly speaking it is not lexemes which occur in specific contexts but the appropriate word forms.)

To illustrate, consider the pair of lexemes HORSE and STEED. These are cognitive synonyms because if we consider a sentential context such as *Sir Lancelot rode a white . . .* both entailments in (154) obtain:

(154)   a. 'Sir Lancelot rode a white horse' entails 'Sir Lancelot rode a white steed'
         b. 'Sir Lancelot rode a white steed' entails 'Sir Lancelot rode a white horse'

Why can we not simply drop the modifier 'cognitive' and say that these two lexemes are synonyms? Because there are sentential contexts where their appearance, while not affecting the truth value of the containing sentence, certainly affects its acceptability. For the case at hand, we feel that (155b), while just as true as (155a), is rather odd (*exercise 5*):

(155)   a. Horses eat hay
       b. Steeds eat hay

Obviously, synonymous lexemes exhibit considerable overlap of meaning. Interestingly, the same is true of pairs of words opposite in meaning to which we now turn.

Meaning opposites

We have already noted properties of *manage* and *fail* which led us to regard these items as 'opposites'. Oppositeness of meaning is a pervasive semantic relation in the lexicons of human languages and it comes in several varieties. Here we shall introduce two particularly important types.

Consider the pairs of *dimensional adjectives* in (156):

(156)   tall-short; high-low, wide-narrow, fat-thin, old-young, old-new

We can readily agree that each of these pairs illustrates oppositeness of meaning, but it is worthwhile to use our entailment relation to pursue the properties of such pairs in a little more detail. Thus, taking just *tall* and *short* (the other pairs behave identically), we have the entailments in (157) which make explicit that these are indeed semantic opposites:

(157)   a. 'X is tall' entails 'X is not short'
       b. 'X is short' entails 'X is not tall'

Now, we might expect that these entailments could be *reversed*, but this is not the case. The entailments in (158) do *not* obtain:

(158)   a. 'X is not short' entails 'X is tall'
       b. 'X is not tall' entails 'X is short'

The reason for this is easy to see. If we imagine all of those objects which can be described using *tall* and *short*, they fall into not two but three categories: there are tall things, there are short things and there are things in between which are neither tall nor short (*exercise 6*). It follows that if X in (158a) designates one of these things, then 'X is not short' will be true, but 'X is tall' will not be true, i.e. the entailment does not hold. Pairs of opposites which behave like *tall* and *short* with respect to entailments are known as **antonyms** and they exhibit the semantic relation of **antonymy**.

Remaining with adjectives, opposite pairs such as those in (159) behave rather differently to antonyms:

(159)   open-closed (of a store); married-single; dead-alive; broken-unbroken

Here we find analogous entailments to those in (157):

(160)   a. 'The store is open' entails 'The store is not closed'
       b. 'The store is closed' entails 'The store is not open'

For this case, however, the converse entailments *do* obtain:

(161)   a. 'The store is not closed' entails 'The store is open'
       b. 'The store is not open' entails 'The store is closed'

This reflects the fact that for a store, there is no state of being neither open nor closed but somewhere in between the two. Opposites like those in (159) are referred to as **complementaries** and the corresponding semantic relation is **complementarity** (*exercise 7*).

Semantic features

The semantic relations we have introduced above, are clearly important in suggesting that there may well be *links* of different kinds *between* lexical entries, i.e. the lexicon in a grammar is more than just a *list* of lexical entries. However, we have not yet sought to look inside a lexical entry and see how semantic information is represented there. We shall now see whether we can make any headway with this problem.

A proposal which many linguists have found attractive over the years is that the meaning of a lexeme should be *decomposable* into a set of **semantic features**. The best way to illustrate what this involves is to immediately consider the triples of words in (162):

(162)   a. ram, ewe, lamb
       b. bull, cow, calf
       c. stallion, mare, foal

In these triples, the first two words are opposites, and for concreteness we can regard them as complementaries. However, they are not merely opposites: for each pair, it appears that the same fundamental distinction underlies their oppositeness. This is the distinction of gender, so we might propose a two–valued gender feature with values [male] and [female]. Such a feature can then function as part of the meaning of a word, and our intuition that *ram* differs in meaning from *ewe* in the same way as does *bull* from *cow* and *stallion* from *mare* is now explicated: the distinction in each case comes down to the presence of [male] or [female] in the representation of the words' meanings.

Next, consider the relationship between *ram* and *ewe*, on the one hand, and *lamb* on the other. We haven't offered a name for this semantic relationship, but this doesn't matter, since all we need to recognise is that it is the same relationship as that obtaining between the pair *bull* and *cow* and the single word *calf*, and of course this observation can be extended to the items in (162c). Again, then, we can propose a two–valued 'maturity' feature with values [adult] and [non-adult], with the former being part of the meaning of *ram*, *ewe*, *bull*, *cow*, *stallion* and *mare* and the latter part of the meaning of *lamb*, *calf* and *foal*. Proceeding in this fashion, then, we can begin to build up representations of the meanings of our lexical items, as indicated for the ovine members of (162) in (163):

(163) a. ram – [male, adult . . .]
       b. ewe – [female, adult . . .]
       c. lamb – [non-adult . . .]

In (163c), *lamb* does not of course have either [male] or [female] in its semantic representation, as it is not gender specific. There are a number of reasons why this general programme might be attractive.

First, it establishes important correspondences between the semantic representations of words and the phonological representations of sounds. It will be recalled from section 5 that distinctive phonological features have the role of distinguishing the sounds in a language and that the *same* feature distinguishes distinct pairs of sounds. Thus, the feature [± voiced] underlies the distinction between /p/ and /b/, /t/ and /d/, /k/ and /g/, /s/ and /z/, etc. Here, we are considering something entirely analogous in the domain of word meaning: the feature [male]/[female] underlies the distinction between the meanings of *lamb* and *ewe*, *bull* and *cow*, *stallion* and *mare*, etc.

A second attraction is that we appear to be provided with an *understanding* of semantic relations such as antonymy, complementarity and hyponymy. Taking the two types of opposites, it is not unreasonable to suppose that feature analysis will uncover a small number of binary features which can be regarded as underlying *all* opposites. Consider again dimensional adjectives. Obviously, we will need some way of distinguishing *tall* and *short* as a pair from *wide* and *narrow* as a pair, but within each pair all we need to note is that one member ascribes more than average extent along a dimension, whereas the other ascribes less than average extent along that same dimension; a tall child is taller than the average child (of that age), a *narrow* road is narrower than the average road (of that type), etc. We can code this as a feature, say, [±Average] and offer the partial analyses in (164):

(164)   a. tall – [+Average . . .]
         b. short – [−Average . . .]
         c. wide – [+Average . . .]
         d. narrow – [−Average . . .]

Pairs of complementaries will employ other oppositely valued features and the logical properties of antonyms which distinguish them from complementaries (recall the contrast between 158 and 161) will be ultimately explained in terms of the difference between these features and [±Average].

As for hyponymy, the label 'meaning inclusion' gives an immediate clue as to how this should be handled. If we consider a pair such as *snake* and *reptile*, we might suppose that we have the analysis in (165) for the latter:

(165)   reptile – $[F_1, F_2, \ldots F_n]$

Obviously, we have not done the analysis, but it is easy enough to think of candidates such as [animate] and [cold-blooded] for the sorts of features we might need. With (165) in place, then, *snake* will have an analysis along the lines of (166):

(166)   snake – $[F_1, F_2 \ldots F_n, F_{n+1}, \ldots F_m]$

In (166), we see the features $F_1, F_2 \ldots F_n$ corresponding to the meaning of *reptile* – the meaning of *reptile* is actually included in the meaning of *snake*. Additionally, however, we have the features $F_{n+1} \ldots F_m$ and these features will serve to distinguish the meaning of *snake* from the meanings of other words denoting reptiles.

Finally, there is something inherently appealing about the idea that meanings can be decomposed into more basic parts. If something along these lines is *not* correct, it is very unclear what a theory of word-meaning might look like (***exercise 8***).

Despite the positive views we have just sketched, there are a number of difficulties which the supporter of semantic features must face. We can raise one of these in the context of the *partial* analyses we have presented in (163) and (164). Take (163) first. What we have there is sufficient to distinguish the meanings of *ram*, *ewe* and *lamb* from each other. However, we have done nothing to distinguish this set of items from the sets in (162b, c). In terms of the semantic features we introduced above, the three items in (162b) will receive exactly the same analysis as we have in (163) and the same goes for the three items in (162c). Of course, this incompleteness is acknowledged by the dots in (163), but this ought not to disguise the fact that in a complete account something must replace the dots. What might that be?

We can observe that the semantic relationship between *lamb* and *calf* is identical to both the semantic relationship between *ram* and *bull* and that between *ewe* and *cow*. Using the methodology we adopted above, we can propose a feature with values [ovine] and [bovine] as underlying this relationship. Consideration of the set of words in (162c) requires that this feature also takes the value [equine], and then we can offer an analysis like that in (167) which could be extended to our full set of items in an obvious way:

(167)   ram – [male, adult, ovine]

There is nothing to object to here from a formal perspective, but we are unlikely to feel as comfortable with [ovine], [bovine] and [equine] as we are with our earlier features, which brought with them an air of 'basicness' and the belief that they would find wide employment in the analysis of word meanings in any language. By contrast, our new feature will find no role outside the very restricted domain which led to its introduction. Furthermore, consideration of additional species is just going to lead to a proliferation of feature values, and we might begin to suspect that our feature vocabulary is going to end up not much smaller than the set of words which we set out to account for.

This pessimism is reinforced by considering (164) in a similar way. Again, our analysis is incomplete, and in order to complete it, we will have to introduce features which distinguish *tall* and *short* from *wide* and *narrow*. In itself, this may seem easy; after all, *tall* and *short* are concerned with vertical extent, whereas *wide* and *narrow* refer to extent in horizontal dimensions. So, we could introduce a feature with values [vertical] and [horizontal] and add these values to (164) to yield a complete analysis – note that this makes explicit that *tall* and *short* are indeed similar in meaning. Now, [vertical] and [horizontal] don't have the uncomfortable specificity of [ovine], but a little more reflection suggests that something equally worrying is not too far away if we pursue an analysis of dimensional adjectives along these lines. For instance, consider the antonymic pair *high* and *low*. Like *tall* and *short,* they refer to extent along the vertical dimension, so at least one additional feature is going to be necessary to distinguish these pairs. But it is not at all clear what this feature might be (see exercise 6).

Furthermore, the worry we are pursuing here also arises in connection with our brief account of how a theory of semantic features might enable us to deal with hyponymy. We noted that additional features would appear in the meaning of *snake* when comparing it to the meaning of *reptile*, but we did not offer any clues as to what these features might be. Obviously, something like [having the characteristics of a snake] would do the job, but this is hardly enlightening.

An analysis such as that in (167) can be seen as providing a **definition** of the meaning of *ram* with the features providing *necessary and sufficient conditions* for something being a ram. That is, if anything is a ram, then it is male, it is adult and it is ovine (the features are individually necessary), and if anything is male, adult and ovine, then it is a ram (the features are jointly sufficient). However, we have noted that some of the features emerging from this analysis (e.g. [ovine]) have unattractive properties. Of course, we are all familiar with the idea that dictionaries contain definitions of word meanings, so we shall close this section by looking briefly at familiar monolingual dictionary entries to see whether they provide any additional perspectives on the semantic components of lexical entries.

Dictionaries and prototypes

Consider a typical dictionary entry for *octagon* as in (168):

(168)   octagon – a plane figure of eight sides and eight angles

This has all the characteristics of a definition, with the expression following the dash providing necessary and sufficient conditions for something being an octagon. We confirm this by noting that the entailments in (169) hold, indicating that the conditions are individually necessary:

(169)   a. 'X is an octagon' entails 'X is a plane figure'
         b. 'X is an octagon' entails 'X has eight sides'
         c. 'X is an octagon' entails 'X has eight angles'

Furthermore, (170) holds, showing that the conditions are jointly sufficient:

(170)   'X is a plane figure and X has eight sides and X has eight angles' entails 'X is an octagon'

For the case of *octagon*, then, we can conclude that (168) provides a good definition and that it is plausible to regard the expressions which appear in the definition (*eight*, *side*, *angle*, etc.) as being unlike [ovine], in that they are conceptually more 'primitive' than the item they are being used to define.

It is no accident, perhaps, that *octagon* is an expression used in plane geometry, a branch of mathematics. When we move outside this highly formal and precise domain, we soon begin to encounter difficulties. Consider the example of *spaniel* in (171):

(171)   spaniel – a kind of dog, usually liver-and-white or black-and-white, with long pendent ears

An immediate observation on (171) is that the phrase introduced by *usually* does not even introduce a necessary condition: if spaniels are *usually* coloured in one of these ways, it presumably is the case that the occasional spaniel comes differently turned out. Such an occasional spaniel will be sufficient to falsify the entailment in (172):

(172)   'X is a spaniel' entails 'X is liver-and-white or black-and-white'

If it is definitions we are after, we may as well remove this condition, leaving (173):

(173)   spaniel – a kind of dog, with long pendent ears

It seems uncontroversial to say that if anything is a spaniel it is a dog, so being a dog looks like a good necessary condition for being a spaniel; what now of long pendent ears?

It is not inconceivable (indeed, it seems highly likely) that sometime in the history of spaniels there have been examples lacking the relevant attributes. This *spaniel* has short ears because it was born like this, or because its ears have been bitten in a fight, or because its ears have been surgically shortened for cosmetic purposes. Such a spaniel remains a spaniel, thereby demonstrating that possessing long pendent ears is not a necessary condition for spanielhood. Accordingly, we must remove this condition from the definition, leaving us with (174):

(174)   spaniel – a kind of dog

But (174), consisting of a single necessary condition, does not approach sufficiency. If it were sufficient, (175) would hold:

(175)   'X is a kind of dog' entails 'X is a spaniel'

Any whippet suffices to show that (175) does not obtain.

What we have found for *spaniel* is that there is at least one condition, that of being a dog, which counts as a necessary condition, and again without further argument here, it is usually possible to locate conditions which are individually necessary in this sense (see the relation of hyponymy discussed above); it is the provision of a set of conditions which are jointly sufficient which gives rise to the difficulties we have encountered.

So much for spaniels. The position we have arrived at is that whereas for some nouns dictionaries do indeed provide definitions, for others they do not, and this raises the question as to what the status of (171) is. In fact, the appearance of the word 'usually' is revealing, as it suggests that what (171) does is provide a description of a *typical* or *normal* spaniel, and this might lead us to wonder whether the semantic representations of at least some lexemes have similar characteristics.

We shall see in sections 14 and 15 that there is a range of psycholinguistic evidence which suggests that lexical semantic representations are **prototypical** in that they supply descriptions of typical members of categories. For our purposes here, we can simply note that there is some linguistic evidence which points in the same direction. Consider the appropriateness of the adverbial expressions such as *strictly speaking* or *technically* in the following examples:

(176)   a. Strictly speaking, an ostrich is a bird
         b. Strictly speaking, a robin is a bird
         c. Technically, a whale is a mammal
         d. Technically, a trout is a fish

In our view, all of these sentences are true and syntactically well formed, but, whereas (176a, c) are entirely appropriate, there is something odd about (176b, d). We can account for this oddness, if we propose that the appropriate use of expressions like *strictly speaking* and *technically* is partly determined by prototypicality or 'goodness' of category membership. We have already noted that both *ostrich* and *robin* are hyponyms of *bird*, but in the taxonomy (142), there is no indication that robins are somehow more representative of the class of birds than are ostriches. We are now suggesting that the taxonomic structure requires elaboration if it is to adequately represent the structure of the mental lexicon. For instance, we might suppose that our lexical entry for BIRD, rather than containing a set of features which provide necessary and sufficient conditions for something being a bird, consists of a description (perhaps in the form of a set of features) of a prototypical bird. This description will approximate a description of a robin but not an ostrich, with the consequence that BIRD and ROBIN will be 'closer' to each other than will BIRD and OSTRICH. Evidence suggesting that this is not entirely fanciful will be introduced in section 14 (*exercise 9*).

Exercises

1.   Consider the sets of sentences below and decide for each set whether (a), (b) or both entail (c):

(i) a.   Smith knows that trupids are a type of kontel
     b.   Smith doesn't know that trupids are a type of kontel
     c.   Trupids are a type of kontel
(ii) a.   Brown believes that prons grow on fargets
     b.   Brown doesn't believe that prons grow on fargets
     c.   Prons grow on fargets
(iii) a.   Green maintains that byfters eat mung
      b.   Green doesn't maintain that byfters eat mung
      c.   Byfters eat mung
(iv) a.   Jones recognises that pogballs make you greep
     b.   Jones doesn't recognise that pogballs make you greep
     c.   Pogballs make you greep

By considering other verbs which can be followed by the complementiser *that* and an embedded sentence, try to develop an informal hypothesis which will account for your data.

2.   Which of the following statements are true?

(a) *tennis* is a hyponym of *sport*
(b) *pea* and *vegetable* are co-hyponyms
(c) *plant* is a superordinate of *tree*
(d) *lamb* is a hyponym of *creature*
(e) *lemon* and *tomato* are co-hyponyms
(f) *poker* is a hyponym of *game*
(g) *game* is a hyponym of *sport*
(h) *poker* is a hyponym of *sport*
(i) *bread* is a co-hyponym of *butter*
(j) *disease* is a superordinate of *influenza*
(k) *swing* and *toy* are co-hyponyms

Use your answers to construct partial taxonomies for the relevant sections of vocabulary. For each taxonomy, try 'extending' it upwards and downwards beyond the levels which the words in (a) to (k) require and comment on any difficulties or points of interest which arise.

3.   The relation of hyponymy is *transitive*. What this means is that if A is a hyponym of B and B is a hyponym of C, then A is a hyponym of C. Identifying the meronymy relation with that of part–whole, we have (i):

(i) A is a meronym of B if and only if an A is a part of a B

Thus, *arm* is a meronym of *body* as an arm is a part of a body. Use the following sets of expressions to investigate whether meronymy is transitive:

(a) knuckle, finger, hand, arm, body
(b) handle, door, room, house, street, city, country (= nation)

4.   The examples of verbs of movement which appear in (146) could be extended to include such examples as *swim, fly, fall, ascend, descend, cross*, etc. Suppose we regard the instances in (146) as all types of deliberate movement on land with no inherent direction. This characterisation would exclude the items in the above list and would lead to the construction of a more complex taxonomy for verbs of movement. Starting from the above items, try to identify what factors might be important in constructing such a taxonomy. Present your taxonomy, clearly indicating lexical gaps where they occur.

5.   The following sets of lexemes are cognitive synonyms. For each member of each set, think of a sentential context in which it is more acceptable than other members of its set.

(a) HORSE, NAG
(b) SUP, DRINK
(c) BUY, PURCHASE
(d) FIDDLE, VIOLIN
(e) MUM, MOTHER, MA

6.   It is interesting to try to ascertain which types of objects can be both tall and short. Obviously, people can, but 'short' buildings are low buildings (as opposed to high, that is tall, buildings!) and 'short' trees are just small trees. List further examples of types of object which are typically regarded as having vertical extent and see which dimensional adjectives are used for referring to this extent. Repeat the exercise for types of object which are typically regarded as having

horizontal extent, starting from *wide road*, *narrow road*, *wide ocean*, *narrow ocean (here the asterisk means that the phrase is odd *in some way* – there is nothing wrong with it syntactically).

7. The comparative forms of adjectives *(bigger, older,* etc.) have been introduced in section 9. Many adjectives do not occur with this *-er* suffix, but form their comparative using *more* (e.g. *more suspicious*, *more intelligent*, *suspiciouser, *intelligenter). For the purposes of this exercise, both the *-er* form and the *more* form are simply referred to as the comparative. Starting from the examples given in the text and adding as many of your own examples as you can, investigate the status of the comparatives of antonymic and complementary adjectives. In your investigation, you should comment on the *interpretation* of sentences such as the following:

(a) Smith is more married than Brown
(b) Green is more alive than Jones

8. Consider the subset of English kinship vocabulary including *father*, *mother*, *son*, *daughter*, *grandfather*, *grandmother*, *grandson*, *granddaughter*. By considering sets of lexemes which exhibit the same semantic relationships, devise a set of semantic features according to which each of these items receives a distinct semantic representation. Next, extend the analysis so that it includes *uncle*, *aunt*, *nephew*, *niece* and *cousin*.

9. You are to investigate directly the proposal that semantic representations of lexemes may exhibit prototype structure. Begin by constructing sets of items from a small number of superordinate categories (e.g. sport, fruit, vegetable). Then ask native speakers to rate each of the items on a scale of 1 to 7 for their 'goodness' of category membership. The instructions you should use are:

> I am going to read out the names of a number of items each of which is an X (sport, fruit, vegetable, etc.). Using a number between 1 and 7, you must indicate how good a member of X you consider each item to be. For example, suppose X is *sport* and the item I read is *tennis*. If you think that tennis is a particularly good member of this category, you should give it 7, if you think it is a particularly bad member, you should give it 1, if you think that it

is intermediate, you should give it 4, and so on. Are there any questions?

Summarise your results in a systematic way and, where possible, pool them with those of others in a class so that the total sample is as large as possible. Discuss the significance of your results.

13   Children and words

In the previous sections of this part of the book, we have introduced a large number of the tools used by linguists when they examine words and their structure in a range of languages. From now on, we seek to apply some of these tools, beginning with the child's acquisition of words. Like most aspects of first language acquisition, this process, once started, is something that parents and other adults take very much for granted. The very first strings of sounds produced by the child which are recognised as words are greeted with great acclaim, but from then on sight is often lost of the child's massive achievement.

In considerations of first language acquisition, it is customary to be concerned with questions of *order*. For example, if we suppose that part of what is involved in acquiring a language is the establishment of appropriate word classes and assigning specific words to those classes, we can immediately ask whether there is evidence that children acquire word classes in a particular order. Assuming a positive answer to this question immediately gives rise to a second, more difficult question: why? Pursuit of the first question is a largely *descriptive* enterprise, which could be viewed as a prerequisite to seriously posing the second; answers to the second question will, if adequate, provide us with an *explanatory* account of some aspect of acquisition. In this section, we shall see that there is considerable evidence for small children controlling remarkably sophisticated systems of linguistic representation from a very early age. Of course, in a general sense, this is what we might expect if the child comes to acquisition innately equipped to achieve linguistic competence.

Early words – a few facts

It has been estimated that small children acquire on average about ten new words each day. While they sometimes make what adults regard as errors in their use of words, some of which we shall discuss below, in many respects children's early words are used with remarkable linguistic accuracy.

The linguistic concepts which have been introduced earlier enable us to raise a number of questions about order of acquisition. As far as major lexical categories go, children's early production vocabularies exhibit a preponderance of nouns, typically used to refer to objects in the child's immediate environment (e.g. *mummy, daddy, dolly, car*). Alongside these, children are often quick to develop a small number of 'general purpose' verbs. The sort of thing we have in mind will be familiar to parents, and is illustrated by the following interaction:

(177)   PARENT: (puts hat on doll)
         CHILD: (removes hat, gives it to parent) Do it
         PARENT: (puts hat on doll)
         CHILD: (removes hat, gives it to parent) Do it
         PARENT: (hides hat behind back)
         CHILD: (finds hat, gives it to parent) Do it
         PARENT: (indicates behind back) Put it here?
         CHILD: (nods) Do it

Here we see the verb *do* (or possibly the sequence *do it*, if this is the only context in which *it* appears) being used to cover a range of actions, and reliance on one or more verbs of this type is characteristic of the early stages.

Small numbers of adjectives (e.g. *nice, big*) and prepositions (e.g. *up, down*) also occur in transcripts of early child speech. Now, it is important to be clear that in making this sort of claim, we are viewing things from the perspective of adults. At the earliest stages, children do not string words together into phrases and sentences, nor do they systematically inflect words, so the morphosyntactic criteria for recognising lexical classes, which were introduced in section 9, cannot be applied to the very beginnings of language production. However, when these criteria do become applicable, evidence for lexical categories is readily available (see section 24).

A different, and in many ways more interesting, question arises if we contrast the acquisition of lexical categories with that of functional categories (see section 9). While the evidence that lexical categories are present from a very early stage is overwhelming, the same cannot be said for functional categories. A typical utterance from a two-year old is (178):

(178)   Car go innere (as child places car in toy garage)

Setting aside the phonological characteristics of the phrase *innere*, there are two observations to make about this utterance. First, *car*, a singular count noun, requires a determiner in English (*a car, the car, this car,* etc.); second, since *car* is a third person singular subject, the agreement inflection *-s* should appear on the verb (*car goes innere*). Both of these items are missing from the child's utterance and such apparent omission of members of functional categories (in this case a member of D) along with certain inflections is a characteristic of early child English. Indeed, the extent of such omissions and their implications for theories of the child's morphosyntactic development have been major research questions during the last decade. We shall return to these matters in detail in section 24.

Suppose, for present purposes, that members of functional categories are indeed absent in the English-speaking child's early language. Various possibilities might account for this including a lack of perceptual salience (typically, functional category items do not carry stress) and semantic opaqueness – coming to terms with the semantics of determiners (*the, a, this, that*) or complementisers (*that, if, for*) looks like a rather forbidding task, and while nouns which refer to concrete objects and verbs which denote activities bear *some* relation to the child's non-linguistic experience, it is not clear that this is true of *for* in *I'm anxious for you to eat this*. We can surely understand a child systematically ignoring such items. More intriguingly, it has been suggested that the early absence of functional categories (if, indeed, they are absent) may be explicable in terms of an unfolding genetic programme. After all, to say that language is part of human genetic endowment is not to say that *all* aspects of language are simultaneously available to the child. Indeed, if this latter were the case, we might expect first language acquisition to be an even faster process than it is. In fact, the account of early sentences which we present in section 24 does not suggest that functional categories are completely *absent* in the early stages; rather, it proposes that they are 'deficient' in certain respects. Whatever view turns out to be correct here, the suggestion that the course of acquisition is at least partly determined by genetic mechanisms remains a live option (***exercise 1***).

Supposing that there is *some* development of functional category systems (i.e. it is not the case that the child completely controls *all* aspects of *all* functional categories from the very earliest stages of acquisition), we can immediately pose another developmental question. We have already seen that even in a language like English, which is relatively impoverished morphologically, there is quite a variety of inflectional endings (third person singular present *-s*, past tense *-ed*, progressive *-ing*, perfect/passive *-en*, plural *-s*, comparative *-er*, superlative *-est*, etc.) along with a rather rich set of derivational and compounding processes and various other functional categories containing free morphemes (members of D, AUX, PRN, etc.). Are these items acquired in any determinate sequence? Indeed, what sort of evidence should we accept for these items being acquired at all? We turn to consideration of these questions.

Apprentices in morphology

Consider the plural morpheme in English. In section 10 (exercise 5a), we have suggested that with a number of well-known exceptions, the allomorphic realisation of this morpheme as /-s/, /-z/ or /-əz/ is predictable by taking account of the phonological characteristics of the final segment in the singular form of a noun. Thus, the plural form of *cats* (/kæts/) will not appear in the lexical entry for *cat*; adults, it is assumed, have access to this regular morphological process, i.e. they control a morphological rule. What reason have we for supposing that young children control this rule?

First note that the mere fact that young children produce appropriately inflected tokens of *cats, dogs* and *buses,* while suggestive, does not provide conclusive evidence for the above proposition. This is because there is every reason to believe that they will have *heard* tokens of the appropriately inflected forms in which we are interested. Surely, they could simply have committed them to memory and either include /kæts/ as part of the lexical entry for *cat*, indicating that it is the plural form (precisely what we would advocate for *feet* and *men*), or, list it as a quite separate lexical entry, thereby failing to acknowledge any systematic relationship between *cat* and *cats*.

In a celebrated experiment reported in 1958, Jean Berko devised a technique which enabled her to distinguish the above alternatives. Acknowledging that existing forms could not be used to demonstrate the child's command of rules, Berko invented some simple words, which she introduced to children in a specific context. For plural allomorphy, her technique was to show the child a picture of a single bird-like creature and say *this is a wug* (/wʌg/). Then, the child was shown a picture of two of these creatures and prompted with *now there are two of them, there are two* . . . The child was to supply an appropriate form. Now, if the mechanism for acquiring plurals requires children to be exposed to every specific example, they should be unable to complete the Berko test. However, the overwhelming majority of children tested responded with *wugs* (/wʌgz/). Note, furthermore, that the form the children supplied contained the correct allomorph of the plural morpheme (/-z/). As well as plurals (for which there were several other items to test other allomorphs), Berko devised ways of investigating other aspects of inflectional and derivational morphology. While her results were not always as clear cut as in the case of plurals, overall she established that children in the age range five to seven do exhibit creative control of a variety of morphological processes. In fact, evidence for this is available from a different source, the spontaneous speech of English-speaking children, and from a much earlier age (***exercises 2 and 3***).

In a seminal study of the 1970s, Roger Brown and his colleagues at Harvard reported the results of their detailed longitudinal work with three children. This study had many aspects, but here we shall concentrate on what Brown referred to as 'fourteen grammatical morphemes'. This set included a number of verbal inflections and here we shall restrict our attention to these. Within this group, Brown distinguished between regular and irregular past tense inflections (as in *jumped* and *came*) and between regular and irregular third person singular present (as in *walks* and *does*, where the latter involves a vowel change as well as the addition of -*s*). Completing his list was the progressive inflection -*ing*.

When we work with samples of naturally occurring production data, it is necessary to formulate a criterion for acquisition. The point is that when children begin to use, say past tense forms, they do not do so consistently, vacillating for some time between the appropriately inflected form and the base form. Brown decided that an appropriate criterion was 90 per cent usage in obligatory contexts, the rationale behind this figure being that once the children in his study satisfied this criterion, they continued to do so; setting the criterion lower would have entailed that children moved from not having acquired a morpheme to having acquired it, only to subsequently return to not having acquired it. With this methodological decision in place, it was then possible to determine the point at which each of the verbal inflections was acquired. The ordering which emerged is in (179):

(179)   1. progressive -*ing*
         2. past tense irregular
         3. past tense regular
         4. third person singular present regular
         5. third person singular present irregular

To begin with, we attend briefly to the fact that the progressive morpheme comes first in this ordering. One possible reason for this is simply its *regularity*. Unlike the past tense and third person singular morphemes, the progressive has no variant realisations as allomorphs (although, see section 16 on the sociolinguistic variable (ing)). As a verbal suffix, it attaches in a fixed form to the vast majority of English verbs, and this, coupled with its relatively transparent semantics in signalling ongoing activities, may be sufficient to account for its accessibility to children. Of the remaining four items, the third person singular present forms will not delay us. There are very few irregular allomorphs of this morpheme (*does, says* [sɛz], *has, is*), and it is perhaps hardly surprising that these forms are relatively late in being acquired.

The surprise package in (179) is provided by the past tense allomorphs, with the irregular forms meeting Brown's 90 per cent criterion before the regular forms. Of course, there are more irregular past tense forms than there are irregular third person singular forms, but they are far outweighed by the regular forms, and in these circumstances, intuition suggests that the regular pattern would prevail first. There are two observations bearing on this order of acquisition. First, the irregular forms, while relatively small in number, include some of the most *frequently occurring* verbs in English (*was, had, came, went, brought, took,* etc.). Second, the regular pattern does indeed prevail but only after a period during which the irregular forms are correctly produced. A consequence of this is the phenomenon of **overregularisation**, when the child incorrectly applies the regular past tense formation rule to a base form which, in the adult language, requires an irregular process. The result is a stage at which the child's performance on such past tense forms as *went* and *came* deteriorates, as these forms are partially replaced by **goed* and **comed*. It is forms such as these, typically occurring in the child's third year, which demonstrate that the child is operating in a rule-governed fashion. Such forms are very uncommon in the speech children hear (adults can be induced to overregularise in this way if, for example, they are asked to produce past tense forms under time pressure) and it would be fanciful to suggest that, having apparently successfully mastered the irregular forms, children abandon their mastery on the basis of a very unusual occurrence. It is more plausible to suggest that overregularisation is indicative of reliance on a rule system (**exercises 4 and 5**).

Turning to a different aspect of morphological organisation, one of the issues which concerned us in section 10 was the relative positioning of derivational and inflectional affixes and the possibility of combining both sorts of affixation with compounding. We also suggested that lexical entries will contain information about *irregular* inflectional forms (*brought, went, teeth, mice,* etc.) but that *regular* forms would not be listed in this way, as they can always be produced by reference to the rules of English morphology. Now, among derivational processes, some appear to be entirely regular including that which adds *-er* to a verb to form an agentive or instrumental noun, and the productivity of this process can readily be attested by noting that we are comfortable with a noun like *e-mailer*, derived from the verb *e-mail*, itself presumably a conversion from the noun *e-mail*. If, in the future, some individuals develop the capacity for transmitting mail mentally (mail which will be unadventurously dubbed *m-mail*), as soon as any English speaker cares to think about it, the transmitters will become *m-mailers*. We must conclude, then, that the process of *-er* suffixation can freely consult the lexical entries of verbs and do its work on whatever it finds there. This capacity for creating new forms also appears to apply to compounding, and one particular such process, alluded to in section 11, combines an *-er* suffixed noun with another noun which could function as an object of the verb from which the *-er* noun is derived. Thus, we find compounds such as those in (180):

(180)　　a. taxi-driver
　　　　　b. road-mender
　　　　　c. horse-rider
　　　　　d. crossword-compiler
　　　　　e. net-surfer

From our present perspective, (180e) is the most interesting of these; it indicates that this compounding process is alive and well, as wasting one's time by surfing the net (indeed, the net itself and surfing in this sense) were unknown until fairly recently.

What the above discussion suggests is that the formation of compounds like those in (180) is entirely rule-governed. Consultation of a lexical entry produces the base form of a verb, which undergoes *-er* suffixation. Further consultation of the lexicon produces a noun which then enters into a compound with the derived nominal (see section 10 for argument that the processes take place in this order rather than the converse). We now consider the interaction of these processes with plural formation.

It is a well-known observation that the nouns appearing in the compounds in (180) cannot be pluralised (**taxis-driver*, **roads-mender*, etc.), despite the fact that a taxi driver usually drives more than one taxi, a road-mender typically mends many roads, etc. This is readily explained if we adopt the account of the previous paragraph and suppose that regular inflectional processes such as plural formation only occur after derivational processes and compounding (this will, of course, enable us to deal with *taxi-drivers*, *road-menders*, etc.). But now consider nouns which have irregular plurals, such as *geese, teeth* and *mice*. Given our assumptions about lexical entries, these forms appear in lexical entries. In principle, therefore, they (unlike regular plurals) are available to be involved in the formation of compounds.

We can pursue this informally by considering a hypothetical situation. Suppose that you live in a house near a lake. During the spring, early in the morning, the local geese mate noisily leading you to lose sleep. Mercifully, you discover that the local supermarket stocks a powder which, when applied in small quantities, quietens geese. Your sleep is saved, but also your linguistic intuitions are aroused because on the packet containing the powder, you see not **goose** *quietener* but **geese** *quietener,* i.e. a compound of the type under discussion which includes a plural noun. Now, while *goose quietener* is OK, it is our view that *geese quietener* is also fine, and, of course, if the irregular *geese* is available to take part in compounding, this is precisely what we would expect.

Now, it seems that children as young as three already have lexical entries and control of morphological processes which match what we are taking to be the adult system. In a simple experiment, Peter Gordon presented children with a puppet who liked to eat various kinds of objects (e.g. buttons, teeth, mice, pins). Pre-tests established whether the children (aged three to five) understood the singular and plural forms of the nouns tested, and they were then asked to tell the experimenter what they would call someone who liked to eat buttons, etc. Depending on whether the noun being tested had a regular or irregular plural, the results were remarkably different. For regular plurals, almost all the children's responses employed the singular form in the compound (*button-eater*); for irregular plurals, a large majority of the responses from those children who had exhibited knowledge of the correct form, used the plural in the compound (*teeth-eater*). This result suggests not only that children can perform quite complex morphological operations by the age of three, but that the *organisation* of their morphological systems and the relationship between this and the form of their lexical entries is already strikingly similar to that of adult English speakers (***exercise 6***).

The semantic significance of early words

Above, we mentioned that one aspect of the early vocabulary of many children is one or more rather general verbs which are used to refer to a wide range of activities. If we turn our attention to the meaning of the child's early vocabulary items, we meet the view that this widening of use is a feature not just of early verbs, but also of nouns used to refer to concrete objects. We begin our discussion by briefly looking at some of the evidence for this claim.

The stories of embarrassment are largely apochryphal, but contain an element of truth. A small child being pushed along the street points to an unknown man and squawks *daddy!* Sometimes, it is the milkman who gets this treatment in the stories, but the general idea is that at a certain stage, children are likely to **overextend** the reference of some of their nouns to include inappropriate objects. Other examples which are often cited include overextending *doggy* to refer to all hairy, medium-sized beasts and overextending *ball* to include all circular objects such as the moon. Early attempts to account for this phenomenon assumed that, for the child, nouns referring to concrete objects had a wider meaning than they have in the adult language; from this perspective, acquiring the meaning of such a noun involved gradually coming to restrict the set of objects to which it applies.

Now, the notion of 'meaning' which was employed in these discussions was the definitional one employing features that we have encountered and been somewhat cautious about in the previous section. Thus, we might suppose that from this perspective, the meaning of *doggie* for an adult might be along the lines of (181):

(181)   doggie – [medium-sized, hair-covered, four-legged, carnivorous . . .]

The claim then is that children have only a subset of these defining conditions. Furthermore, because the child's world is dominated by that which is perceptually present, it is plausible to suppose that this subset consists of those features which are perceptually based. Thus, (181) might be replaced by (182), adopting the assumption that being carnivorous is not a property which is readily perceived by the small child:

(182)   doggie – [medium-sized, hair-covered, four-legged]

Of course, if this is the case, cats, sheep and various other creatures will satisfy the conditions in (182) and a child, confronted with such a creature, will refer to it as a doggie.

Another example is provided by *ball*. Here we might suppose that the semantic representation in the adult lexical entry is along the lines of (183):

(183)   ball – [round object, used in games, . . .]

By contrast, the child relying entirely on perceptually based features, and therefore not having access to [used in games], which concerns the *function* of balls, has (184):

(184)   ball – [round object]

We can immediately see why a child will refer to the moon using *ball* on the basis of (184).

It will come as no surprise that we regard the above proposals as flawed in certain respects. Most obviously, the reliance on definition-like constructs as providing word meanings has been examined in the previous section and, we believe, found to be wanting. To set the child off on the acquisition road with a construct not employed in the adult system, while not totally unintelligible, would require extensive justification. More importantly, overextension of children's early nouns is a fairly short-lived and limited phenomenon. The majority of children's concrete nouns are not overextended, and the truly remarkable aspect of the acquisition of words is the *accuracy* of children's use. Of course, we tend not to notice appropriate usage, but the fallacy of building a theory of lexical development on a minority of aberrant cases should be apparent. Finally, there is an alternative way of thinking about overextension, which in our view is more plausible.

Take the case of *doggie*. Small children with limited lexical resources may find themselves in situations where they wish to draw attention to, say, a sheep. They know that the creature in front of them is not a dog, but they lack a lexical item for referring to it; in these circumstances, they may resort to the strategy of finding the word in their lexicon which most nearly matches in meaning what they are looking for. The plausibility of this way of looking at things is increased if we consider the case of an adult confronted with a novel type of creature. Such an adult may well resort to something along the lines of, 'there's a sort of X over there', where X is an item in this adult's lexicon. In these circumstances, we would not conclude that the adult's meaning of X was too general; rather, we would say that they were doing their best in the face of inadequate lexical resources. We remain uncertain about what the 'matching' required by this account might amount to, because we do not have an adequate theory of the semantic representations appearing in lexical entries. However, this view does not require that the child's semantic representation for *doggie* should be different to the adult representation, and this is consistent with the overwhelming accuracy in child usage to which we have drawn attention.

As a final issue in this section, we would like to sketch what may prove to be a more promising approach to *some aspects* of early lexical development. In the previous section, we introduced the semantic relation of hyponymy and indicated how it defined taxonomies in certain areas of vocabulary. Part of a taxonomy appears in (185):

(185)

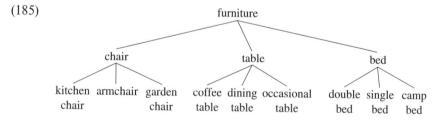

In (185), we refer to the level occupied by *furniture* as the **superordinate** level (note that this is a slightly different use of 'superordinate' to that which was introduced in the previous section), the level occupied by *chair, table* and *bed* is the **basic** level, and the lowest level is the **subordinate** level.

Taxonomies such as the one in (185) are very interesting for a number of reasons. For example, it will not have escaped notice that the move down the taxonomy from the basic to the subordinate level is accompanied by the appearance of morphological complexity; *kitchen chair, armchair*, etc. are compounds (see a similar observation in connection with (142), p. 196). There is no *logical* reason why such complexity appears at this level. The hypothetical (even more partial) taxonomy in (186) categorises the world in exactly the same way as the relevant portion of (185), but here morphological complexity appears at a higher level:

(186)

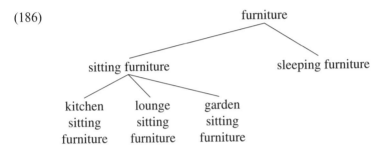

Now, of course, it may be entirely accidental that the level we are referring to as basic has the property of being the most specific level of categorisation which has morphologically simple labels, but what is intriguing is that this *linguistic* observation (which could be extended by considering further taxonomies in English and other languages) is linked to a set of *psycholinguistic* observations (see section 15) and some rather interesting facts about lexical development. Here, we focus on the latter.

The question we raise is: at what level do children 'enter' taxonomies such as (185)? The answer is very clear. Children acquire words such as *chair, table* and *bed* before they acquire *furniture* or any of the subordinate terms. Of course, the subordinate items include the basic level morphemes, so this observation ought not to be too surprising, but if, as our earlier discussion suggested, children's early words are 'too general' in their meaning, we might expect superordinate terms to be early acquisitions. But this is not the case.

Now, consider the fact that a child confronted with a chair is, inevitably, confronted with a piece of furniture (a child being given a carrot is also being given a vegetable, a child eating an apple is also eating a fruit, etc.). Why is it that in these circumstances children inexorably home in on the basic level items? Easy, you might say: this is because *adults* use basic level items in such situations and obviously the child must be exposed to an item in order to acquire it. This is true, but we can continue to ask why this should be, i.e. why do adults label basic level categories rather than superordinate ones? To answer this question, we need to consider the 'information' which categories at different levels in taxonomies contain. To get a sense of what is involved here, we will ask you to conduct a short 'thought experiment'.

Referring to (185), try to think of as many properties as you can which you *reliably* associate with the category of furniture – note that you are not being asked to come up with a definition of *furniture*. You should soon admit to being stumped by this request: there simply are not very many properties that all (or, indeed, most) items of furniture typically have in common. Next do the same thing for the categories of chairs, tables and beds. You should do better – there are quite a few properties that are reliably associated with chairs ('is used for sitting on', 'has a back', 'has a smallish flat part', etc.). Furthermore, these properties *reliably* distinguish chairs from tables and beds, which are other categories at the basic level. Finally, try the same process for the category of kitchen chairs. Naturally, as kitchen chairs are chairs, all your chair properties will carry over to kitchen chairs; it is, however, unlikely that you will be able to come up with very much that is new about kitchen chairs (beyond, 'usually found in a kitchen'!) which distinguishes them from other varieties of chair.

Our thought experiment is complete, and it is time to confess that the genuine experiment has been done by Eleanor Rosch and her colleagues in the 1970s with the results hinted at above. What do these results mean? It appears that the basic level is the most abstract level at which (relatively) large numbers of *diagnostic* (i.e. fairly reliable) properties are associated with categories. In this sense, basic categories are 'informationally rich' – there are many properties which will give you fairly reliable cues that you are confronted by a chair, and not a bed or a table, and this will in turn enable you to predict that the object confronting you has the range of properties generally associated with chairs, even if, for whatever reason, you don't get a good look at it, say. By contrast, there are few, if any, properties that enable you to decide that something is a piece of furniture (excluding, of course, knowing already that what you have is a chair, a table or a bed). Finally, the problem of our relationship with kitchen chairs and other subordinate categories is that the vast majority of properties we associate with them will not serve to distinguish them from other varieties of chair. In short, it appears that categorisation at the basic level can be achieved with reasonable reliability *on the basis of partial information*, whereas this is not true at either the superordinate or subordinate levels. It is not true at the superordinate level because there are *no properties* which predict category membership at this level; it is not true at the subordinate level because the predictors of category membership here are *not reliable*.

The suggestion that a certain level of taxonomic categorisation is informationally rich in this way leads to the provocative idea that children are somehow geared to informational richness (clusters of co-ordinated properties) in their environments. And adults 'know' unconsciously that this is the case. As a consequence, they provide words which small children are 'ready' for. Much remains to be understood in connection with this suggestion, but if it is along the right lines, it provides an illustration of how the maximisation of the informativeness of categories, provides children with ready-made meanings to be matched by the words supplied by their linguistic environment. From this perspective, absence of error is precisely what we would expect in the acquisition of early vocabulary (*exercise 7*).

Exercises

1. In section 11 we distinguished between word-based and stem-based morphology, illustrating the distinction with examples from English and Italian. What difficulties is the acquisition of Italian likely to present for the proposal that the development of functional categories (*including tense and agreement inflections*) is delayed in the child's acquisition of language because of the gradual unfolding of a genetically determined programme? Are these difficulties fatal to the proposal?

2. Devise your own small experiment to test children's control of past tense allomorphy. To do this, you will need to invent a number of verbs referring to actions which can be easily depicted in drawings. For instance, you might draw a cat balancing on its tail and have accompanying text along the lines of: 'This is a cat who knows how to *zid*. He does it most days. Yesterday he did it; yesterday he . . .' The child's task is to complete the sentence and evidence for control of the relevant morphological processes would be provided by a child saying *zidded*.

    If you have access to a small group of children, try your experiment on them and summarise the results. As an alternative, the class can cooperate in devising the experiment and each member of the class for whom it is possible can run the experiment on one or more children, with a subsequent pooling of the results.

3.   Thinking along similar lines to those you have pursued in exercise 2, devise experiments for testing children's control of the comparative (*-er*) and superlative *(-est)* suffixes. Make sure that you include adjectives for which an adult would use the *more* and *most* constructions. Again, run your experiment if you have the opportunity.

4.   It has been noted that when children overregularise past tense morphology, they are more likely to do this with certain types of irregular verbs than with others. For example, English verbs which undergo Ablaut (see section 11) and no other process in forming their past tense (*sing/sang*, *ring/rang*, etc.) are more likely to be overregularised than are verbs which undergo no change (*hit/hit*, *shut/shut*, etc.). When adults are asked to supply past tense forms under time pressure, a similar difference in the amount of overregularisation occurs. Why do you think this might be? (Hint: think of as many no-change verbs as you can and pay close attention to their phonological characteristics in the light of what you know about regular past tense formation.)

5.   The two classes of irregular verbs in exercise 4 do not exhaust the full set of English verbs which have irregular past tense forms. Think of as many irregular past tense forms as you can and classify them in terms of the morphological processes they involve. Informally test adults on their ability to supply irregular forms from your various classes under time pressure (you do this by saying that you are going to present them with a verb and they have to *immediately* produce the past tense form – give them some examples, so that they are clear on what is required). Do you think that the results of such informal testing will generalise to predict frequencies of overregularisation errors in child speech? Does your answer to the question in exercise 4 help in understanding the data you have collected?

6.   In the text, we introduced the compounds *geese-quietener* and *goose-quietener* and suggested that adults are likely to find the former reasonably acceptable (see **ducks-quietener*). By making up a small set of compounds involving regular and irregular plurals, test whether

this is so. You might, for example, provide a context for each of your compounds and then ask adults to rate them for acceptability on a scale of 1 to 5. Note that the important observations to make are comparative: even if people don't like *geese-quietener* much, do they nonetheless clearly prefer it to *ducks-quietener*?

7.   You are to conduct a simple naming experiment with children to ascertain whether they use superordinate, basic or subordinate level expressions to name a variety of common objects. The simplest way to do this is to cut pictures of objects out of magazines and show them to children with the question 'What's this?' Present your results in a systematic way. How might you deal with the objection that the children you tested simply did not know the superordinate and subordinate terms you were interested in eliciting?

14 Lexical processing and the mental lexicon

An adult native speaker of English with a normal speech rate produces more than 150 words per minute – on the average, more than one word every half second. Indeed, under time pressure, for example, when you are calling your friend in New Zealand from a public telephone in Britain or the US, a native speaker can produce one word every 200 msecs, which is less than a quarter of a second, and your friend can still understand what you are saying. The lexicon of an average native speaker of English contains about 30,000 words. This means that in fluent speech you have to continuously choose from these 30,000 alternatives, not just once, but two to five times per second, and there is no clear limit on how long you can indulge in this process. Furthermore, your friend is *recognising* your words at the same rate at the other end of the telephone line. If you wanted to and had enough money, you could make the telephone companies happy by talking to your New Zealand friend for hours, with a decision rate of one word every 200–400 msec. Incredibly, despite the high speed of lexical processing, errors in the production and comprehension of words are very rare. Research has revealed that in a corpus of 200,000 words, getting on for twice the length of this book, only 86 lexical errors were found, i.e., fewer than 1 in every 2,000 words. Thus, lexical processing is speedy, very accurate, and decisions are made at very high processing rates although there are many alternatives.

In this section, we will discuss the sorts of processes that are involved in our production and comprehension of words. We will structure our account around two general questions, which will enable us to raise some of the major issues surrounding the processing of words in contemporary psycholinguistics.

Serial–autonomous versus parallel–interactive processing models

In the light of the figures mentioned above, we can begin by intuitively considering what might be involved in recognising or producing a common word such as *dog*. It ought to be self-evident that these processes can be broken down into a number of subprocesses. Thus, focusing on recognition for the sake of concreteness, in order to recognise that a sequence of sounds imping-ing on your aural receptors constitutes a token of *dog*, it is necessary for you to recognise that the sequence contains an initial /d/, etc. Failure to do this, say by 'recognising' an initial /b/, would result in an obvious misperception, and, under normal conditions, these are uncommon. Obviously, by complicating the word in question, we could offer similar observations for the perception of suprasegmental features such as stress (it is important to your interlocutors that when you say *TORment*, a noun with stress on the initial syllable, they do not 'perceive' *torMENT*, a verb with stress on the final syllable). It is incon-testable that sound properties are generally important in spoken word recog-nition. It is also easy to see that information about the *category* to which a word belongs is important: if you are going to understand a simple sentence such as (187), then you had better categorise the token of *dog* in that sentence as a verb and not as a noun:

(187)   A problem with speech perception dogs me wherever I go

Additionally, it is easy to agree that the *morphological properties* of words must be recognised: *I dog Bill* and *Bill dogs me* are interpreted quite differently, and these different interpretations are due to the choice between nominative *I* and accusative *me* and the related choice between *dog* and *dogs*. Finally, you can make the various decisions we are sketching here, but your decisiveness is unlikely to do you much good unless you also come to a view on what a spe-cific occurrence of *dog* means. Recognising words in the sense introduced above involves *understanding* them, and this presupposes semantic choices.

Now, there are at least two ways in which we can conceptualise these various decisions being made. The first, which gives rise to **serial–autonomous** accounts of processing, maintains that these decisions are taken in sequence, with all decisions of a certain type being taken before decisions of the next type. Furthermore, information which may be available on the basis of later decisions cannot inform earlier decisions. The alternative, **parallel–interactive** approach takes the opposite perspective: in principle, information relevant to any decision is available at any point in processing, and there is no place for a strictly ordered set of subprocesses. We shall now try to be a little more spe-cific.

Serial–autonomous models of lexical processing involve a series of steps in which information is passed from one component of the mental lexicon to the next. One characteristic property of serial–autonomous models is that each stage in the processing of a word is carried out by a specialised module which accepts input only from the previous module and provides output only to the next one. Thus, crudely, we might suppose that word recognition begins with a module which recognises a sequence of sounds, and this module presents its output to an independent module which assigns a morphological analysis to this sequence of sounds. At this point, if a token of (187) is being listened to, the word *dogs* may be analysed as either the verb stem *dog* plus the third person singular present suffix *-s* or as the noun stem *dog* plus the plural suffix *-s*. Now, of course, ultimately, only the first of these analyses is correct, but from the serial–autonomous perspective, the syntactic, semantic and contextual information which will force the listener to this decision is not available at this stage in the perceptual process. To use a notion introduced by Jerry Fodor, each specialised module is **informationally encapsulated** and can take account only of the information supplied by modules which operate earlier in the perceptual process. By contrast, parallel–interactive models claim that language perception (and production) involves the activation of some or all sources of relevant information at the same time. According to this view, then, the morphological analysis of *dogs* as the noun stem *dog* plus the plural suffix *-s* will not be produced in the course of perceiving a token of (187). This is because enough syntactic, semantic and contextual information is already available from earlier parts of the utterance to rule out the possibility of this analysis. We can try to sharpen up the difference between these two approaches even more by considering another (plausible) situation.

Suppose that the telephone companies are experiencing a technical problem, so that the line to your friend in New Zealand is occasionally interrupted by a crackling noise for about a quarter of a second. This occurs while you are saying (188); as a consequence, your friend hears (189):

(188)   I thought you were coming on Wednesday

(189)   I thought you were (krrrrk) on Wednesday

As your friend listens to (189), we can ask whether any lexical recognition is going on during the crackle. According to the serial–autonomous view, the answer would be a definite 'no', while parallel–interactive models would answer with an equally clear 'yes'. In a serial model, there is only one way to get access to a word form such as *coming* and that is through its phonological form (if we were concerned with written word recognition, we would again maintain that there is only one route to recognition, but in this case this would be via an orthographic analysis). Since a phonological analysis is unavailable to your friend in (189), modules which would subsequently analyse *coming* as *come + ing*, assign appropriate morphosyntactic properties to these morphemes and associate meanings with them cannot operate. Generalising, we can say there is no lexical access at this point. Of course, what your friend might do under these conditions is try to guess what you are talking about and to ask for clarification (*Do you think I'm coming/dying/graduating on Wednesday?*), but these kinds of conscious inferences are different from the automatic process of accessing the mental lexicon.

Now consider how a parallel–interactive perspective approaches the same problem. According to this view, all sorts of information are simultaneously used to access the lexicon, regardless of where in the processing system the information comes from. If, as in (189), the phonological information for accessing *coming* is not available, an interactive system can have recourse to information from another source so that lexical processing does not break down because of an inadequate input signal. Suppose, for example, you were talking about your friend's visit to Britain before you produced (188), and that only the exact date still had to be fixed. Then, he or she might understand (189) as (188) despite the degenerate signal, by having access to information from the surrounding context.

A very large number of experimental studies have attempted to differentiate between the two approaches and to argue for the appropriateness of one or the other. Many of these studies involve complex experimental designs, the details of which we cannot engage in the space we have available. We can, however, offer a brief overview of two types of experiment which, intriguingly, lead to opposing conclusions.

Consider first, then, the sentence in (190):

(190)   The young woman had always wanted to work in a bank

Of course, *bank* is ambiguous in English, with the senses 'financial institution' and 'side of a river'. From a parallel–interactive perspective, when listeners to (190) hear *bank*, they take advantage of all the information available to them, including the contextual information supplied by their general knowledge of the world and earlier parts of the sentence. Since this information is incompatible with the 'side of a river' sense of *bank*, this possibility will not be considered and only the 'financial institution' sense will be accessed. The serial–autonomous view, on the other hand, sees lexical access as entirely driven by phonology, and so maintains that both senses will be accessed – the phonology does not differentiate them. Now, suppose that immediately following the aural presentation of (190), subjects are presented with a visual word/non-word decision task, i.e. on a screen in front of them appears an English word, say *garden,* or a non-word sequence, say *brogit.* Their task is to respond as quickly as possible, by pressing one of two buttons, to indicate whether the visual item is a word or not.

In order to convey the major finding of this type of experiment, we need to make one further assumption explicit. This is that words are organised in the mind so that semantically related words (in the sense of section 12) are 'close' to each other. More technically, if you hear a token of *dog,* some (mental) **activation** spreads to semantically associated items such as *cat* or *animal* or *bark,* and we say that these latter items are **primed**. When an item is primed, we would expect it to be more readily available for lexical access than when it is not. We return to our experimental study.

A parallel–interactive approach will maintain that for subjects who have just heard (190), only the 'financial institution' sense of *bank* will be active and only lexemes semantically related to *bank* in this sense, e.g. *money, cheque,* will be primed. For the serial–autonomous theorist, however, both senses of *bank* are activated, so additional items such as *river* and *tow-path* will also be primed. The following experimental conditions are the crucial ones, where the capitalised words are the items presented visually for a word/non-word decision:

(191)   a. The young woman had always wanted to work in a bank. MONEY
         b. The young woman had always wanted to work in a bank. RIVER
         c. The small yellow car was found outside the village. MONEY
         d. The small yellow car was found outside the village. RIVER

Here, (191c) and (191d) are intended to provide **neutral contexts**; neither *money* nor *river* is primed in these contexts, so decisions that the visually presented items are words provide a measure of how long this process takes when these items are unprimed. For both the serial–autonomous and parallel–interactive accounts, (191a) provides a **primed context** for the recognition of *money* as a word. Both approaches predict that subjects' responses to (191a) should be faster than their responses to (191c). For (191b), however, the two approaches make different predictions; this is a primed context only from the serial–autonomous perspective. Thus, this approach predicts that subjects' responses to (191b) will be significantly faster than their responses to (191d); the parallel–interactive approach predicts no significant difference in these cases. Results supporting the serial–autonomous position have appeared in the psycholinguistics literature, thereby suggesting that the perceptual mechanisms are 'stupid' in the sense that they do not avail themselves of all available information. Lest we lose sight of it in the dispute between serial–autonomous and parallel–interactive accounts, we should also note that *any* priming effects depending on semantic similarity, provide experimental support for the view of the structured lexicon we developed in section 12, viz. that the mental lexicon is not just a list of items but rather a structured set over which a notion of psychological 'distance' can be defined, with semantic similarity contributing to this measure of distance.

Alongside studies which support the serial–autonomous view, the psycholinguistics literature contains many reports of experiments which favour the parallel–interactive position. Again, we offer just a brief outline of the thinking behind one of them.

Suppose that experimental subjects are instructed to respond as quickly as possible, by pressing a button, to an occurrence of a designated word, say *party*. They can be presented with tokens of *party* in a variety of contexts, illustrated in (192):

(192)   a. John and Mary shared a birthday last week when their **party** . . .
        b. The giraffe walked rapidly into the bedroom where its **party** . . .
        c. Ghost although out yesterday the runs street which my **party** . . .

These contexts represent three distinct categories. In (192a) we have an example which is syntactically and semantically well formed. The example in (192b) is syntactically well formed but semantically odd, given our knowledge of the world, and (192c) is just a random list of words exhibiting neither semantic nor syntactic structure. Again, we note that the serial–autonomous view regards word recognition as phonologically driven, so this approach ought to predict no differences in recognition times for *party* in these examples. By contrast, the parallel–interactive account expects that subjects will be able to take account of syntactic information in (192b) and of syntactic and semantic information in (192a); this should enable subjects to produce enhanced recognition times in these two conditions when compared with (192c). Using this technique, the parallel–interactive view has been supported with recognition times being fastest for the condition in (192a), slowest for (192c) and of intermediate speed for (192b).

We conclude this brief discussion with some general remarks. Parallel–interactive models of lexical processing are highly efficient in that they almost always compute an output, even in cases such as (189) in which crucial information is not available via phonological recognition. Thus, they lead us to expect that words can be recognised in an appropriate context, even in circumstances where there are no phonological or orthographic cues at all. Serial–autonomous models cannot account for such context effects, except by suggesting that a listener can guess the identity of a particular word, using inference processes which do not themselves belong to the system of language perception. At the same time, however, parallel–interactive models are theoretically unconstrained, and it is therefore difficult to make testable predictions on the basis of such approaches. Given parallel interaction, anything goes, and you can, for example, recognise a word without having any direct cues. This is impossible with the serial autonomy approach. Moreover, as each module has a clearly described task in a serial–autonomous model, an output error or a recognition error can be traced back to the module that caused the error. This is impossible in a parallel–interactive model in which information is distributed over many different places which are all continuously interacting. In sum, parallel–interactive models of word recognition are extremely successful at the product level; in fact, they almost always produce an output, i.e. recognise a word. But they provide little understanding about the actual mechanisms that are involved in understanding words. Serial–autonomous models are theoretically more interesting and they make specific predictions as to which kinds of inputs are required for word recognition, but when the input is faulty or noisy, they are not efficient enough, and they cannot straightforwardly account for context effects.

It should be clear from the above where the lines of this particular dispute are drawn. Both types of model offer a story about how degenerate word forms may be perceived. For the adherent of a parallel–interactive account, such perception is due to the normal functioning of the perceptual system. It is a characteristic of this system that it is always seeking to identify words on the basis of any type of information available to it, and the only difference between a well-formed signal and a degraded signal is that in the latter situation *one* sort of information (the phonological form) is missing. From the serial–autonomous perspective, the lack of phonological form means that the language perception system breaks down at this point and another cognitive system (of guessing or inferencing) comes into play. Devising experiments which will distinguish clearly between these alternatives is a difficult task and we have outlined above two paradigms which produce conflicting conclusions. It is perhaps not accidental that most current models of lexical processing include both serial and parallel–interactive features.

On the representation of words in the mental lexicon

A basic property of words is the arbitrary relationship they exhibit between meaning and form: words have meaning, and they have phonological or orthographic structure, and there is no way of recovering the former from the latter. Note that if this were not the case, we would not expect to find lexical differences between languages: if *cow* is the 'natural' sign for a bovine creature, we should be puzzled by the existence of *vache* in French. Given this **arbitrariness of the linguistic sign**, the lexicon (or the mental dictionary of a language) must include some sort of stored entry for the lexemes of a language. Most psycholinguists believe that the mental lexicon must contain lexical entries which contain a number of separate but interconnected levels. The following model of a lexical entry is based on suggestions of the psycholinguist Pim Levelt:

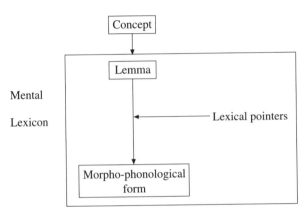

Figure 35 *One view of the structure of the mental lexicon, illustrating the form of a lexical entry*

According to this model, **concepts** must be distinguished from **lexical entries**, and lexical entries consist of two levels, one for the semantic form of the lexical entry, i.e. its meaning or content, and the other for the entry's morphological make-up and its phonological properties. Hence, a lexical entry can be split up into two parts, its **lemma** and its **form** information (note that in this literature the term lexical entry is used to refer to what we called lexemes and that the term lemma refers to the semantic representation of a lexeme). The lemma lexicon and the form lexicon are connected through lexical pointers: each lemma points to its corresponding form, i.e., it can address a particular entry in the form lexicon where the morpho-phonological properties of the lemmas are stored.

What is the evidence for distinguishing between these levels of representation in the mental lexicon? Switching our focus from perception to production, consider first the distinction between concepts and lemmas and suppose a native speaker of English wants to formulate a message about the object/concept represented in figure 36:

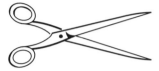

Figure 36   *A simple concept*

According to the model in figure 35, this concept will activate the appropriate lemma in the lexicon, i.e. *scissors* and subsequently the word form /sɪzəz/. Concepts are represented on a prelinguistic level, whereas lemmas must be part of the mental lexicon of a particular language. Thus, for native speakers of English the concept represented in figure 36 is probably the same as for native speakers of German, but at the lemma level there are differences: *scissors* is inherently plural, and is not countable (**one/*two/*three scissors*), but the German equivalent of *scissors* is *Schere* which is inherently singular, and it is a count noun (*eine Schere, zwei/drei/vier Scheren,* 'one scissor, two/three/four scissors'). Similar examples are *trousers* (plural) versus *Hose* (singular), *glasses* (plural) versus *Brille* (singular). The fact that *Schere, Hose* and *Brille* are count nouns, whereas *scissors, trousers* and *glasses* are not, is a semantic difference on the lemma level which is not a consequence of and does not result in different conceptualisations.

What about the distinction between the lemma and the form lexicon? Returning to perception, one important piece of evidence for distinguishing between these two levels of representation comes from our ability to process non-words, i.e. words, for which we have no proper meaning representation. Thus, native speakers of English perceive a clear difference between the items in (193) and (194):

(193)   blatt

(194)   plaupf

The item in (193) is a potential English word, in terms of its phonological form although it does not have any meaning in English. The item in (194), however, is an impossible word in terms of its form properties – specifically, English does not permit the consonant cluster /pf/ to comprise a syllable coda (see section 5). In other words, the difference between (193) and (194) in terms of their phonological form demonstrates that we can make judgements about the form of a lexical entry independently of its meaning. This in turn shows that the mental lexicon cannot be thought of as a set of entities (structured or otherwise) with *direct* form–meaning mappings; the form lexicon, it seems, *can* be accessed independently without activating any links to meaning.

This idea has been confirmed in reaction-time experiments involving the recognition of non-words. In one set of experiments, subjects are presented with strings of four letters and their task is to decide as quickly as possible whether the stimulus letter string is or is not a word of English. Different conditions were tested as indicated in figure 37:

Stimulus	Example	Mean decision time
Word	DESK	708 msec.
Non-word (fully unpronounceable)	SJMF	607 msec.
Non-word (onset unpronounceable)	SJIF	644 msec.
Non-word (coda unpronounceable)	SAJF	680 msec.
Non-word (pronounceable)	SARF	746 msec.

Figure 37 *Five conditions in a word/non-word recognition experiment*

The experiment showed that decision times on totally illegal and unpronounceable sequences such as SJMF are considerably faster than for any other stimulus used; they are even faster than those for existing words of English. This indicates that we possess a rapid process by which globally illegal words can be detected, and this process must be purely form-based.

Failures of lexical access, as for example in speech errors, provide another important source of evidence for discovering the internal structure of the mental lexicon, and we shall now introduce some of the key issues in this area of speech production (see section 7 for speech errors involving phonological units).

Three classes of speech errors, illustrated in (195) to (197), can be distinguished for our purposes:

(195)   **Blends**: two words are fused into one.
    a. Irvine is quite *clear* (← *close* and *near*)
    b. At the end of today's *lection* (← *lecture* and *lesson*)
    c. to determine *whatch* (← *what* and *which*)

(196)   **Substitutions**: mis-selections of words
    a. He's a *high* grader (← *low*)
    b. Don't burn your *toes* (← *fingers*)
    c. I just put it in the oven at a very low *speed* (← *temperature*)

(197)   **Word exchanges**: two words within the speaker's utterance are
exchanged

    a.   You can't cut *rain* in the *trees*

    b.   This spring has a seat in it

Victoria Fromkin and Anne Cutler have collected speech errors over many
years, and the anthologies they have put together provide the most extensive
data base of naturally occurring speech errors we have; the examples mentioned above were taken from these collections.

Speech errors in lexical access all involve failures of lemma retrieval, but the
mechanisms underlying blends, substitutions and exchanges are different. In
general, a speech error occurs when lemma selection is disturbed by the simultaneous activation of two elements. Consider for instance blends and notice
from the examples in (195) that the two words forming the basis for the blend
are roughly equivalent in meaning. Thus, in (195b) lemma selection is disturbed
by the fact that the two closely related elements *lecture* and *lesson* are active at
the same time. But at which processing level are these two elements active?
Given figure 35, there are two possibilities: at the conceptual level and/or at the
lemma level. To answer this question, we must have a closer look at the meaning
relations that hold between the two elements activated in a speech error.

As noted, in blends the two elements are very similar in meaning and are
usually of the same syntactic category. We hardly ever find antonym blends,
i.e., fusion of two words that have opposite meanings (e.g.: *harsy* ← *easy/hard*),
or blends in which one element is a superordinate term for the other one (e.g.:
dealsman ← *dealer/salesman*). In an extensive published list of blends, for
example, there was not a single antonym blend and just three involving a
hyponym and its superordinate.

Compare this with the elements involved in substitution errors in (196). The
most common cases of this type involve antonyms (196a) or other semantic
relations. For example, *fingers* and *toes* are co-meronyms, each entering into
the relation of meronymy with *body*. Moreover, there is a clear frequency effect
in substitutions: high-frequency words are more likely to substitute for a low-
frequency word, but not the other way round and it has been found that in 74
per cent of a large corpus of substitutions, the intruding element had a higher
frequency than the correct item, with only 26 per cent of cases involving a
lower frequency item substituted for one of higher frequency.

Finally, in word exchanges the two elements that are exchanged are typically unrelated in meaning. Rather, they express different concepts, as for example, in (197a, b).

Let us briefly summarise the similarities and differences between these three kinds of speech errors in figure 38:

	BLENDS	SUBSTITUTIONS	EXCHANGES
meaning relation	closely related	closely related	unrelated
antonyms	no	yes	no
co-meronyms, etc.	no	yes	no
frequency effect	no	yes	no

Figure 38 *Differences between types of speech errors*

Given these facts, we conclude that the explanation of word exchanges differs radically from the other two kinds of speech errors. Word exchanges result from different sentence fragments being active at the same time. For example, in producing (197a) there is a point at which the slot for the object of the verb *cut* and the slot for the object of the preposition *in* have to be filled, and at this point two candidate fillers, *rain* and *trees*, are simultaneously active and are somehow exchanged. Thus, the two elements that are involved in word exchanges are neither conceptually nor semantically related; rather they are *syntactically related*. They belong to different phrases, but they have similar syntactic functions in their phrases.

How do substitutions come about? Take example (196b) for illustration. In this case, the speaker wanted to convey a message involving the concept of a finger. Given figure 35, this concept activates the lemma *finger*. In the mental lexicon, lemmas that are semantically related are closely associated (see the discussion of spreading activation earlier in this section). Thus, the lemma *toe* is a close associate of the lemma *finger* in the mental lexicon. For some reason, the activation of *toe* is stronger in this case than that of *finger*, and this produces the substitution. The kinds of errors that occur in word substitutions are familiar from word-association experiments in which subjects are asked to freely associate to a given stimulus. In such experiments, responses such as *last* as a response to *first*, *wine* to *beer*, *later* to *earlier* and *sun* to *moon* are typically found. These responses reflect the semantic structure of the mental lexicon, for example, the fact that a given lemma is closely connected to its antonym(s), synonym(s), co-hyponym(s), etc. The same can be said about word substitutions: generally speaking, word substitutions reflect semantic relations in the mental lexicon.

Consider finally how we might explain the occurrence of blends. Blends occur between two words that are broadly similar in meaning, but unlike in the case of substitutions, semantic relations such as antonymy, hyponymy and meronymy appear to be irrelevant. Thus, as noted, antonym blends and blends involving a word and its superordinate are extremely rare. This suggests that in blends the intrusion of the second element occurs at the *conceptual level*, rather than in the mental lexicon. Take, for example, (195b). The message fragment the speaker wants to convey at this point, namely selecting a reference point of the school/university day, would be compatible with using both concepts, LECTURE and LESSON. These two concepts are closely related and are simultaneously activated. Subsequently, they both activate their corresponding lemmas (see figure 35). Both lemmas are retrieved and inserted into the same slot. In short, blends result from conceptual intrusion. Viewed from the perspective we have sketched above, speech errors are not a random phenomenon, but they rather reflect levels of representation in the mental lexicon (*exercises 1, 2, 3 and 4*).

A rather different set of issues concerning the structure of the mental lexicon arises in connection with our observations at the end of section 12. There we noted that there is psycholinguistic evidence which supports the idea that the notion of *prototype* plays a role in lexical organisation, and we shall now briefly discuss a small sample of this evidence.

Recall that within the category of birds, a robin appears to be prototypical, particularly if it is contrasted with an ostrich. We suggested that this might be a reflection of the lexical entry for *robin* being 'closer' than that for *ostrich* to that for *bird*. One piece of evidence supporting this view is very easily obtained. If subjects are simply asked to list the names of birds, then typically *robin*, *sparrow*, and *eagle* will appear early on such lists, whereas *ostrich*, *emu* and *chicken* will appear late, if at all. If we suppose that presentation and processing of the word *bird* produces activation which spreads 'outwards' from the lexical entry for *bird*, becoming less effective the further it travels, we have a ready explanation for this finding. The lexical entries for *robin*, *sparrow* and *eagle*, being 'close' to that for *bird*, receive a large amount of activation and are thereby primed (see above) and produced on subjects' lists. Lexical entries for other, more remote, bird names are primed to a lesser extent or not at all.

Another very direct approach to this topic is to ask subjects to rate pairs of words for semantic similarity using, say, a five–point scale. Thus, you might be presented with *sparrow* and *hawk* and if you feel that they are very similar semantically, you will score them at five, if you consider them not semantically similar at all, you will give them one, and if you perceive a middling amount of semantic similarity, you will use one of the intermediate numbers. It comes as a surprise to many people that a technique as simple as this produces reliable results across large populations of subjects. As far as our current interest goes, the important finding coming out of such experiments is that pairs such as *robin* and *bird* receive significantly higher scores than pairs such as *ostrich* and *bird*. Again, this is consistent with the lexical representation for *robin* being 'closer' than that of *ostrich* to that of *bird* in psychological space, a conclusion that is not captured by supposing that lexical organisation in this area is merely taxonomic.

Finally, another twist to this story emerges from an experiment conducted by Lance Rips and his colleagues. In this study, subjects were asked to imagine a small remote island populated entirely by various species of birds and were told that all members of one species (e.g. the owls) had been infected with a particularly virulent (for birds) disease. The subjects' task was to judge what proportion of other species succumbed to the disease. In support of what we have seen above, it was found that if the initially infected species was prototypical (e.g. robins), then greater proportions of other species were judged to contract the disease than if the initially infected species was not prototypical (e.g. ducks). Putting this crudely, if the robins started it, more sparrows, eagles, owls, etc. were judged to get the disease than if the ducks started it. Intriguingly, this result applies to specific pairs of birds. For instance, if the disease starts with robins, maybe 60 per cent of ducks are judged to get it; however, if it starts with ducks, only 40 per cent of robins fall ill. This is a rather different result to those which show that the lexical representation of *robin* is relatively 'close' to that of *bird*. What this seems to show is that the 'distance' from the lexical representation of *robin* to that of *duck* is smaller than the distance from the lexical representation of *duck* to that of *robin*, i.e. 'distance' in the mental lexicon might not even be symmetrical!

In general, we can conclude that lexical processing is an extremely rapid and efficient cognitive process, and psycholinguists have only begun to develop appropriate theoretical models for understanding this process. Additionally, the organisation of the mental lexicon, while broadly in line with the ideas that linguists have developed, appears to have some rather unusual properties. Most importantly, while psycholinguists often appeal to non-linguistic notions such as memory and frequency in their studies, the proposals made by linguists on such issues as semantic similarity, categorisation and lexical representation regularly provide the basis for modelling (*exercise 5*).

Exercises

1. Consider the following results of two judgement experiments:
    Subjects were presented with pictures of small and large triangles
    and sticks, such as the following:

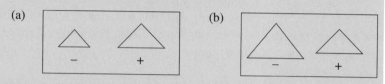

(a)   (b)

The subjects first saw the object marked with '+' in one of the two
fields (a) or (b), and then the second object marked with '−'. The
subjects' task was to indicate, as quickly as possible, whether the
object in the position marked with '+' was bigger or smaller than the
object marked with '−'.

In experiment 1, the task was to SAY *bigger* or *smaller*. In experiment 2, the task was to PRESS A BUTTON when the bigger object
was marked and another button when the smaller object was marked.

The results were different. Experiment 1 produced a strong con-
gruency effect: when the pair of objects was small, as for example in
(a), subjects were quicker in saying *smaller*, but when the objects
were relatively large, as in (b), they were quicker in saying *larger*. In
experiment 2 there was no such difference.

Explain these findings in terms of the model in figure 35.

2. Analyse the following speech errors, by commenting on how they
    might have arisen:

    a. forgot to add the *list* to the *roof*
    b. He rode his bike to school *tomorrow* (← *yesterday*)
    c. gone *mild* (← *wild/mad*)
    d. I got into this *guy* with a *discussion*
    e. he *misfumbled* the ball (← *mishandled/fumbled*)
    f. *Ask* me whether (← *tell*)
    g. that's torrible (← *terrible/horrible*)

3. Consider the following results from object-naming experiments in
    which subjects have to indicate the name of a visually presented
    object, such as a telephone or an hour-glass:

Two conditions were used. In condition 1, the subjects' task was a verbal response, i.e., they had to say *telephone* or *hour-glass* as quickly as possible upon seeing the object picture. In condition 2, the subjects' task was to press a button as quickly as possible every time they saw the object picture; hence, in condition 2 no verbal response was required.

The results were different. In condition 1, a strong frequency effect appeared: pictures with high-frequency names, such as that of a telephone were responded to faster than pictures with low-frequency names, such as that of an hour-glass. In condition 2, the effect disappeared.

Answer the following questions in relation to this experiment:

a. How would you explain the frequency effect in condition 1?
b. At which level of lexical processing in figure 35 does the frequency effect occur?
c. How does the evidence from speech errors fit with the frequency effect found in these object-naming experiments?

4. Consider figure 38 in the text and compare the mean decision times for the examples DESK and SARF. Both are pronounceable English words, but there is still a significant reaction-time difference: the rejection of a non-word takes longer than the acceptance of a real word. This is called the **lexicality effect**. How would you explain this effect in terms of the model in figure 35?

5. You are to conduct a small experiment to investigate the prototype structure of a number of common categories. First, choose your categories by identifying a number of superordinates for which fairly large numbers of hyponyms exist, e.g. *sport, occupation, vegetable, fruit, crime*. Then ask as many subjects as you can muster to write down in thirty seconds as many instances of the category as they can think of – make sure that they write them down in such a way that you can ascertain the *order* in which they appear.

Examine your results for any obvious patterns across your subjects and draw appropriate conclusions on whether your experiment is consistent with the ideas on prototypes which have been discussed in this section.

15   Lexical disorders

In the introduction (pp. 12ff.), we offered some preliminary remarks on the types of language disorders which are of most interest to the linguist. These are **aphasia** and **Specific Language Impairment (SLI)** and it is important that we re-emphasise a very important difference between these. Aphasia is a disorder of language and speech that is caused by a brain lesion which may be due to an accident or a stroke, *after language has been acquired in the normal way*; before the brain lesion occurred, aphasics had normally functioning language systems. By contrast, SLI is a term covering disorders *in the normal acquisition of language* without there being any clear primary deficit. Despite their linguistic problems, SLI children and adults have normal non-verbal IQs, no hearing deficits, and no obvious emotional or behavioural disturbances; unlike aphasics, SLI subjects have never acquired language in the normal way.

Aphasia provides us with a potentially valuable source of information as to how linguistic representations are implemented in the brain. It is reasonable to suppose that we might learn how a machine (or any other physical device, such as the human brain) works by investigating how it goes wrong. In aphasic patients, there is typically some residual language left after brain damage, indicating that the knowledge of language can be **selectively** impaired by brain lesions, and it is by carefully studying the range and nature of such selective impairments that we hope to learn something about the interconnections of the brain mechanisms underlying language. From a different perspective, SLI provides an important strand in the argument for adopting the strong innateness views Chomsky and his followers propose. If our knowledge of language, and, specifically of grammar, is indeed controlled by our genes, then we should expect to find genetically caused disorders of grammatical development, namely in cases in which something has gone wrong with the language genes. SLI subjects provide us with the chance of studying the effects of a rather isolated, and probably genetically determined, deficit in the acquisition of language, specifically of grammar (see the main introduction for reasons for believing that the disorder is genetically determined).

In this section, we will focus on disorders which display their effects at the lexical and morphological level. We will first look at which linguistic properties of words and morphemes are typically lost in aphasics, and then describe which aspects of the lexicon and morphology are hard to acquire for SLI subjects.

Words and morphemes in aphasia

Typically, aphasic patients are reported to have word-finding difficulties, they sometimes mis-name things, or they use circumlocutions to replace difficult words. According to the standard clinical classification of aphasic syndromes, we can distinguish two characteristic types of errors of word usage in aphasia. The first is called **agrammatism** and affects function words such as articles, auxiliaries, complementisers, and bound morphemes such as those marking tense and agreement in English, and also gender, case, etc. in those languages such as Italian and Russian which are inflectionally richer than English. It does not affect content words such as nouns, verbs, and adjectives (see section 9). Agrammatism is considered to be the characteristic symptom of **Broca's aphasia**, and in our main introduction, we saw that this disorder tends to be associated with damage to a particular area of the left cerebral hemisphere. The second type of lexical disorder consists of **paraphasias**, which are errors in the use of content words that typically occur in **Wernicke's aphasics**; function words seem to be unaffected in these cases. Consider, as an illustration, the following two attempts by aphasic patients to describe a picture of a child stealing a biscuit:

(198)   Ah . . . little boy . . . cookies, pass . . . a . . . little boy . . . Tip, up . . . fall

(199)   They have the cases, the cookies, and they were helping each other with the good

The example in (198) comes from a Broca's aphasic. Speech like this is emitted slowly with great effort (a characteristic we have partially indicated by the pauses between different parts of the utterance). Content words such as adjectives (*little*), nouns (*boy, cookies*) and verbs (*tip, fall*) are produced by the patient, whereas function words such as articles and bound morphemes are sometimes omitted. This combination of properties produces the characteristic **telegraphic speech** of Broca's aphasics, a term which has given way to 'agrammatism' in more recent research.

It should be immediately apparent that the example in (199) is quite different to (198). This was produced by a Wernicke's aphasic describing exactly the same picture. The speech of such patients is fluent and effortless, and the rate of production of words can *exceed* the normal rate (see section 14, p. 226). However, the content of the speech can be remarkably empty and convey little information, as illustrated by the sequence . . . *and they were helping each other with the good* in (199). Typically, Wernicke's aphasics do not demonstrate disturbances of grammar and function words, but rather these patients make many errors in content word usage, e.g. *cases* instead of *cookies* in (199). This characteristic of inappropriate content word selection appears also in reading aloud, where, for example, the sentence in (200a) is read as (200b):

(200)   a. The spy fled to Greece
        b. The spy filed to grain

The frequency of such paraphasias ranges from 10 per cent to about 80 per cent of words in extreme cases.

Let us now look at these two characteristic errors in word (and morpheme) usage, agrammatism and content-word paraphasias, in a little more detail.

Agrammatism

According to the standard clinical classification, agrammatism is defined as the omission of function words in speech production, whereas in comprehension, agrammatic patients perform in the normal range. Recent linguistic studies have shown that this traditional clinical picture is too superficial and partly incorrect.

It is true that English-speaking agrammatics omit many function words, but from studies on agrammatism in other languages, we quickly learn that this observation cannot be generalised. Consider, for example, Italian. If Italian-speaking agrammatics were using the strategy of dropping functional elements, specifically bound morphemes, they would produce bare stems such as those in (201):

(201)   *and- ospedal-. Non cred-   parol- . . .
        go   hospital. Not believe word . . .

But these bare stems (*and-, ospedal-,* etc.) are not possible words in Italian, which has a stem-based morphology (see section 11), and utterances such as

(201) are *not* found in the speech of Italian agrammatics. What we do find is that agrammatic patients use 'unmarked' verb forms, for example the infinitive, as in (202), or they produce inflectional errors such as the error in gender marking in (203):

(202)   andare ospedale. Non credere   parola
          to-go   hospital. Not to-believe word

(203)   capucetto   rossa (*capucetto rosso* would be correct)
          riding hood-masc. red-fem.

(Note that both 202 and 203 would be marked with a * in standard Italian – the lack of annotation here indicates that the expressions *do* occur in agrammatic Italian speech.)

Furthermore, the range of errors that aphasics produce is rather restricted and narrowly constrained. Erroneous infinitive inflections occur, as in (202), but only on verbs and never on nouns, and gender mistakes, such as that in (203) are also found, but only on nouns and adjectives and never on verbs. This observation suggests that significant remnants of Italian morphology remain in place.

Studies on other languages, e.g. French, Hebrew and Russian, lead to the same conclusions as may be derived from Italian and justify a number of general conclusions. Specifically, it appears that agrammatics respect:

a.   The word-structure properties of their native language;
b.   The categorial features of bound morphemes;
c.   Inflectional paradigms.

We shall now say a little more about each of (a) to (c).

The generalisation in (a) covers the fact that agrammatics never produce words, stems or roots that would violate word-structure properties of their language. Thus, bound inflectional morphemes are dropped in English-speaking agrammatics, but the consequence of this is the occurrence of stems which *can* function as words (e.g. *walks* → *walk*). However, such morphemes are not dropped, for example in the speech of Hebrew-speaking agrammatics. It therefore seems that the broad distinction between word-based morphology (English) and stem-based morphology (Italian, Hebrew) is retained in the grammars of agrammatics.

The generalisation in (b) describes the fact that agrammatics seem to know the categorial identity of affixes, in the sense that they retain knowledge of the categories to which specific affixes can be attached. Thus, verb inflections, e.g.

infinitive endings, are only attached to verbs, never to nouns; conversely, case suffixes are never attached to verbs but only to nouns.

The third observation in (c) is that agrammatics still have inflectional paradigms. What this acknowledges is that many of the inflectional errors agrammatics produce are exchanges between individual cells of morphological paradigms, e.g. feminine gender is incorrectly used instead of masculine gender, as in (203). It is important to be clear that this is a stronger generalisation than (b), which does not rule out the replacement of one type of nominal affix by another nominal affix, say replacing a gender affix by a number affix. But, in fact, this does not occur and the contents of the inflectional paradigms are typically intact. To take a particular case, it is as if the agrammatic knows that case affixes attach in a specific slot, but makes incorrect choices from the available set of case affixes.

Taken together, these findings indicate that agrammatism cannot be accounted for in terms of a global simplification process by which functional elements are simply deleted from the linguistic output. Rather, the linguistic impairments are more specific, and the proper understanding of agrammatism requires notions such as word-structure properties, categorial features and morphological paradigms. Linguistic theories of agrammatism will be considered in section 26, after we have extended our discussion to include the syntactic disorders that occur in these patients.

Another myth of the clinical classification of aphasias is that Broca's aphasia is mainly a production disorder and that comprehension is largely unimpaired in these patients. This view was mainly based on lack of knowledge, specifically on the fact that in the clinical interview comprehension is not systematically studied. Rather, clinicians ask patients everyday questions such as *How did the stroke come about?*, and agrammatic patients answer such questions appropriately. But this does not mean that comprehension is unimpaired, as the meaning of such questions could be directly inferred from the meaning of the content words and the context in which the question is posed. An important feature of English telegrams, which gave rise to the characterisation of agrammatic speech as 'telegraphic', was the omission of function words (e.g. *ARRIVE HEATHROW TOMORROW 3PM STOP HEAVY BAGS PLEASE MEET STOP JOHN*), and such telegrams were typically understood by their recipients, giving a clear indication that the presence of function words is not always necessary for understanding to occur. In the 1970s, aphasiologists started to carry out experimental studies on agrammatism, the results of which clearly demonstrated that agrammatics have comprehension problems with functional elements which are similar to those they show in production (*exercises 1, 2 and 3*).

Paraphasias

Errors in the use of content words, i.e. paraphasias, are reported to be characteristic of Wernicke's aphasics. What kind of content words cause difficulty and how can we account for the error patterns? First of all, performance of Wernicke's aphasics on content words is affected by the *frequency* of the word in the vocabulary: infrequent words take longer to retrieve and are more often inaccurately retrieved than frequent words. Second, and more importantly, the typical error patterns that occur in paraphasias can be explained in terms of the structures which characterise the mental lexicon such as we have already met in the previous three sections of this part of the book. Consider the data in (204) from object-naming experiments; in such experiments, subjects are presented with a picture of an object and are simply asked to name it:

(204)   target picture: SHARK   subjects' responses:
                                        a. *fish*
                                        b. *trout*
                                        c. *guitar*
                                        d. *rainbow trout*

Among these responses, (204a, b) represent the common types, and we can understand what is going on here by referring to section 13 where we distinguished between three levels of categorisation in taxonomies: the basic level (where we find such words as *trout, shark* and *guitar*), the superordinate level (*fish, musical instrument, fruit,* etc.) and the subordinate level (*rainbow trout, great white shark, bass guitar,* etc.). These notions, as well as being significant in understanding the child's acquisition of words, have also proved important in the study of how visually presented objects are categorised by normal, adult subjects. Such subjects typically categorise an object (e.g. by naming it) at the basic object level, despite the fact that *logically* it could be categorised at a variety of other levels. In object-naming experiments with Wernicke's aphasics by contrast, the subject's typical naming response to the picture of a shark is either the superordinate level term (*fish*) or a *prototypical* element from the basic set (*trout*) (see section 12 for the notion of prototypicality). Wild paraphasic misnaming as in (204c) only occurs in severely impaired subjects, and responses at the subordinate level such as that in (204d) are practically non-existent.

In another set of experiments, the role of phonetic and semantic similarity in aphasics' perception of category names has been tested. Aphasics were asked to select a picture of an object from a set of multiple-choice pictures in response to a test word presented orally by the experimenter. A typical situation is schematised in (205):

(205)   test word: *chair*   subject's choices: a picture of   a. CHAIR
                                                                   b. STAIR
                                                                   c. TABLE
                                                                   d. APPLE

When the aphasics produced errors in this experiment, it was typically an error of type (205c), i.e. an exchange based on the semantic similarity between the test word (*chair*) and the name of the depicted object (*table*) – in this case, the similar items are co-hyponyms. Errors such as (205b), based on phonological similarity, specifically on rhyme, were much less frequent, and wild 'paraphasias' such as (205d) were produced only by severely impaired subjects (note that these subjects did not actually produce these errors in their speech in this study, hence referring to them as 'paraphasias' is an extended use of this expression). These findings indicate that the meanings of words and their associative links in the mental lexicon are accessible to Wernicke's aphasics, and that only in severe cases of vocabulary deficit do the associative processes themselves begin to break down. The examples cited in the last category in (206) below indicate that the notion of 'semantic relatedness' which we are relying on here has to be interpreted fairly liberally if it is not going to exclude significant numbers of cases; the fact remains, however, that the overwhelming proportion of paraphasias do appear to be explicable in terms of one semantic relation or another.

In sum, the following effects have been found in content-word paraphasias from aphasics:

(206)   **I.   Frequency effects**:

Low-frequency content words yield more paraphasias than high-frequency words.

II.   Categorisation-level effects:
a. Hyponym exchanges: *sparrow → owl*
b. Use of superordinates: *sparrow→ bird*

III.   Similarity effects:
a. Semantic exchanges: *hair → comb*
b. Pragmatic exchanges: *flowers → visit*   (flowers and visits are
                                              often associated in
                                              everyday life)

In general, the content-word usage of Wernicke's aphasics is markedly poorer than in normal speakers. Thus there are more errors, but the types of errors (as set out in 206) are familiar from normal subjects. When normal speakers are under stress, or are distracted or confused, their word usage too is influenced by word frequency and semantic similarity, and they produce errors with all the characteristics of paraphasias (see section 14). Thus, there do not seem to exist any *qualitative* differences in content word usage between aphasics and normal speakers, and, apart from severe cases of jargon aphasia, the organisational principles of the mental lexicon, in terms of levels of categorisation and associative processes are not affected by the deficit. We now turn our attention to our second major category of language disorders, SLI (*exercises 4 and 5*).

Dissociations in SLI subjects' inflectional systems

There is a consensus that SLI children have problems in the area of inflectional morphology, and at first sight, the picture we get from examining the language of such children is very similar to that of agrammatism in Broca's aphasia. Specifically, SLI subjects often omit grammatical function words and bound morphemes encoding case, gender, number, person etc., or they use them incorrectly. It also seems that in SLI children, the development of inflectional morphology comes to a standstill at an early stage, and that beyond that point the acquisition process cannot advance without difficulties.

Consider the following examples from a ten-year-old SLI child:

(207)   a. you got *a* tape recorder*s*
         b. the four bus go in Boucherville
         c. when the cup break *he* get repair
         d. *the* Marie-Louise look at the bird
         e. the superman *is say* good-bye and *hiding*
         f. the ambulance arrive

In these examples we see problems in number marking within noun expressions (207a, b), an inappropriate pronominal choice (207c), an inappropriate determiner choice (207d), difficulties with participle forms and auxiliary verbs (207e) and in subject-verb agreement (207c, f).

How can we explain the difficulties of SLI subjects in the area of inflection? One interesting proposal is that SLI individuals' ability to learn inflectional rules is impaired relative to their ability to memorise and store individual words. Consider the two inflected verb forms in (207) which are irregular and correct (*got* and *is*). By contrast, regular verb inflections such as the third person singular *-s* are omitted (*go, break, get, look,* and *arrive*). These data indicate that SLI subjects can retrieve irregular verbs such as *got* and *is* from memory – equivalently from the relevant lexical representations – but that they cannot generate the third person singular forms of verbs. Recall that we are assuming that these do not appear in lexical representations, since they are derivable by regular processes. SLI subjects have problems learning regular inflectional rules, while at the same time their ability to retrieve irregular forms, which are stored as part of a verb's lexical entry remains intact. In short, whereas normal speakers appear to possess two distinct psychological mechanisms for inflection, a rule system that attaches regular affixes, e.g. the third person singular *-s*, to stems, and a set of irregular forms such as *got* and *is* which are stored in memory, SLI subjects' knowledge of inflection is selectively impaired. In support of this rule-deficit hypothesis on the nature of SLI, it has been reported that SLI subjects produce practically no overregularisations of plural or past tense affixes; such overregularisation would, of course, indicate productive use of these affixes (see section 13). This, then, is a further indication that SLI individuals have more problems with regular rules of inflection than with accessing irregulars from memory, and it is this selective impairment which enables us to conclude that two psychological capacities (the ability to implement rules and the ability to retrieve forms from memory) can be *dissociated*.

Results from other SLI studies have indicated that the linguistic deficit is even more selective than has been suggested above. One of these investigated SLI children's performance on two regular inflectional affixes, the plural *-s* (*two book-s*) and the third person singular present *-s* (*she arrive-s*). It was found that the SLI children's usage of the third person singular present *-s* was only 36 per cent correct, whereas 83 per cent of their *-s* plurals were correct, this difference being statistically significant. Despite the fact that both affixes are regular, SLI subjects' performance with the plural is considerably better than with the tense/agreement suffix. Notice also that the two inflectional morphemes tested in this study are homophones, displaying identical phonologically conditioned allomorphy (see section 10); this rules out phonological explanations for the observed difference. Taken together, these findings indicate that the different grammatical functions of the affixes is the controlling factor. SLI subjects seem to be significantly less impaired in their use of noun plurals than in their use of the affix encoding subject-verb-agreement and tense. We will come back to these findings in section 26, after we have discussed the structure of the sentences SLI subjects typically produce (*exercise 6*).

In summary, we have seen that language disorders such as aphasia and SLI do not involve global disruptions of the mental lexicon and the grammar, but rather selective deficits to otherwise normal lexical and morphological systems. In the so-called agrammatic errors produced by Broca's aphasics, word-structure properties, categorial features and inflectional paradigms are respected, and the notion 'agrammatism', literally meaning 'lack of grammar', is in fact a misnomer. Agrammatics have a grammar that is selectively impaired, but the architecture of the system is identical to that of linguistically normal people. A similar point can be made for paraphasias, i.e. errors in content-word usage typically occurring in Wernicke's aphasics. The relevant variables controlling content-word usage in aphasics are the same as for normal subjects, namely word frequency, semantic similarity and categorisation level, thus showing that the basic structure of the mental lexicon does not globally change as a result of the impairment. In the case of SLI, the development of inflection is selectively impaired: the acquisition of regular inflection causes more problems than learning irregulars, and inflectional morphemes encoding tense/agreement seem to be more adversely affected than pluralisation morphemes. The precise basis for this selectivity awaits further insight.

Exercises

1.   Describe the nature of the linguistic deficit that results when people suffer damage to Broca's area of the brain. Given such a deficit, what kind of linguistic ability might Broca's area be responsible for?

2.   Translate the following sentences into agrammatic English and agrammatic French/German/Italian/Spanish (choose one out of these languages); explain each change and characterise the difference between agrammatism in English and agrammatism in the other languages:

   a.   The tall men are beginning to run
   b.   The two boys were sitting in their father's arms
   c.   Louisa and Paula arrived yesterday

3.   Broca's aphasics often perform better in controlled experiments than in spontaneous speech. Sketch a psycholinguistic explanation for this.

4. Characterise the errors in content-word usage that Wernicke's apha-
    sics typically produce and illustrate them using your own examples.

5. Design an object-naming experiment to elicit paraphasias from
    Wernicke's aphasics.

    Comment on at least the following points:
    — experimental procedure/design;
    — subjects (number of subjects, control group, selection criteria,
      pretests, etc.);
    — materials (test items, control items, pictures, oral vs visual presen-
      tation, etc.);
    — theoretical assumptions (explain your views on paraphasias);
    — predictions (explain the expected results of the specific experi-
      ment given your assumptions).

    Try the experiment on your friends and/or relatives. It might be
    unwise to diagnose any of them as aphasic!

6. Discuss the claim that SLI subjects lack regular rules of inflection.

16 Lexical variation and change

Variation in language is multi-dimensional. In sections 3 and 4, we have looked at how variation in social structure is reflected in the sound patterns of language and how this variation is often indicative of language change in progress. We have also seen how geographical variation in language is caused by different levels of contact between different peoples at different times. In this section we are interested in variation in words and in their origins, meanings and contexts of use. We'll also examine change in both the choice of words and the meanings of those words.

Borrowing words

What is the origin of words like *shampoo, pizza, alcohol* and *curry*? When did they enter the English language? And why? Almost certainly, you will be able to answer these questions for at least some of these words, but we can ask the same questions with respect to words which are much less 'exotic'. According to published counts of word frequencies, the items listed in (208) are among the most frequently occurring nouns in English:

(208)   people, way, water, word, man, day, part, place, things, years, number, name, home, air, line

All these words have been part of the English language for centuries, and while most of them date back to Germanic languages which preceded the separate development of English, some had their origins in Latin (*part, place* and *air*, for example). Throughout its history, English has been adding to its lexicon by acquiring new words from other, often unrelated, languages. *Risotto* and *pizza* come from Italian, *vodka* from Russian, *goulash* from Hungarian, *coffee* and *yoghurt* from Turkish, *alcohol* and *sherbet* from Arabic, *sago* from Malay, *ketchup/catsup* from Chinese and *tomato* from Nahuatl (a central American language and the language of the Aztecs). These new words are known as **borrowings**. Of course, as well as having borrowed thousands of words, English has been a great provider too, much to the annoyance, for example, of language purists in France who strive to find native French words to replace *le parking, le hamburger* and *le walkman.*

Why do speakers borrow words from other languages? Perhaps the most obvious reason is sheer necessity. People need to develop words for new and unfamiliar concepts – new technology, new plants and animals, and in the examples above, new and unfamiliar foods. Note that the model of lexical representations discussed in section 14 supposes that there is a distinction between concepts and lexical entries, and from this perspective, there is nothing odd about the suggestion that we have concepts for which we lack words. Another reason is prestige. If certain cultures are associated with particular prestigious activities, it is common for the words associated with that activity to come from the language of that culture. Continuing with the food theme, France was at one time considered the centre of world gastronomy, and hence English has words like *cordon bleu, gourmet, cuisine, restaurant, menu, mousse* and *soup* which it has borrowed from French.

When a word is borrowed, it is often gradually changed so that it fits the phonological and morphological structure of the borrowing language or dialect. So whilst Françoise and Ricardo might go to a cafe [kafe] for a croissant [kʁ wasɑ] and a cappuccino [kaputtʃino], Mavis and Vic, in London, would go to the [kæf] for a [kwasɒnʔ] and a [kapətʃɹinɐʊ]. Similarly, whereas the plural of *pizza* is *pizze* in Italian, English now applies its own plural morpheme to the borrowed word, hence *pizzas.*

Sometimes when new concepts are introduced from other societies, the speakers of a particular language may use their own native linguistic resources to coin a new word. These are known as **calques**. Let's look at some examples of this. Comanche, an American language of the southern USA, has a word *ʔohapltiʔataka-sikikamatl,* which literally means 'orange's brother tastes sour'. It is the word used for a lemon! In Irish Gaelic the words *sciath fearthanna* translate as 'rain shield', and refer to an umbrella. In New Zealand, it is the job of the Maori Language Commission to create new words by using words already in the language. As a consequence, we find examples such as those in (209):

(209)	New Word:	papa patopato	wai mangu	roro hiko
	Literal Meaning:	board knock	water black	brain electric
	Idiomatic Meaning:	keyboard	ink	computer

English tends to resort to Latin and Greek when new words are devised, particularly for referring to new technology. Examples appear in (210):

(210)   television: Greek *tele* ('far') + Latin *visio* ('sight, thing seen')
microscope: Greek *mikros* ('small') + Greek *skopein* ('observe closely')
photograph: Greek *photo* ('light') + Greek *graphos* ('written')

Borrowings, then, are words which originated in one language (or dialect), but which have come to be used in another, even by people who don't speak the 'lending' language. These borrowings are very often assimilated to the phonological and morphological structure of the new host language (*exercises 1, 2 and 3*).

Register: words for brain surgeons and soccer players, hairdressers and lifesavers

A **register** is the specialised vocabulary common to a particular trade, occupation, topic or activity. Hairdressers, soccer players, brain surgeons and undertakers all have specialised words or uses of words which refer to concepts particularly common or specific to their activity or profession. As a soccer player you might *nutmeg* your opponent (kick the ball between their legs) or play a *one-two*; you might ask a hairdresser for a *flat top* or a *bob*, or need a surf lifesaver to rescue you from a *rip* (a dangerous backcurrent on a surf beach), but you are unlikely to ask a brain surgeon for a *lobotomy*. It is of some interest that occupations, interests, etc. can have some impact on the important idea of a basic level of categorisation introduced in section 13. Thus, whereas for many of us, *dog* corresponds to a basic level category, for those of us preoccupied with dogs, the basic level shifts down to that of particular breeds. Similarly, while all of us are familiar with such words as *beech, ash* and *elm*, many of us are not in a position to distinguish these different types of tree. For those of us who are arboreally challenged in this way, it is plausible to suggest that *tree* appears at the basic level in our categorisation systems. However, this is not the case for botanists and tree surgeons. For them, the basic level of categorisation will be that of *beech, ash* and *elm* or, indeed, the more specific level of *copper beech, mountain ash,* etc.

Often, people consider that the registers of doctors and lawyers (and even linguists) hinder communication and understanding. The term 'jargon' is sometimes used to refer to the confusing registers of particular occupations. In some senses, registers are 'in-group' varieties, which lead to accurate and speedy communication of information among those that know and use them, but confuse those who don't. It is obviously important that the doctor tells the nurse that you have had a coronary infarcture or a stress fracture of your left tibia, but what you want to know is that you've had a heart attack or broken your left leg. In this medical example, the use of a special register is clearly a necessity – the leg, for example, has several major bones and it is vitally important for the nurse to know which one you've broken. Some registers, however, are deliberately confusing so as to hinder understanding by outsiders. This may be because the group speaking the particular register wants to maintain a sharply contrasting identity, or maybe has something to hide (*exercise 4*).

Biscuit or cookie? Variation and change in word choice

Consider (211):

(211)   Concept   Word to refer to concept

                                     Britain: *biscuit*
                                     U.S.A.:   *cookie*
                                     Australia: *biscuit/cookie*

The thin flat, often round, usually sweet, hard but crumbly thing we eat during our coffee break is called different things in different English-speaking areas. In Britain it is usually referred to as a biscuit and in the USA it is a cookie. Australia is experiencing the initial stages of language change with the word *biscuit* gradually losing out to the word *cookie*.

Such geographical differences in word choice are well known. Most people are familiar with the US-UK contrasts between *sidewalk* and *pavement*, *gas* and *petrol*, *pants* and *trousers*, *elevator* and *lift*, *vacation* and *holiday*. Just as borrowing is frequent in situations of **language contact**, as we saw earlier, it is also very common when **dialect contact** arises. In the past century, within the English-speaking world, most interdialect borrowings have come from American English, with the newly borrowed words pushing out or beginning to push out older words, usually of British English origin. Thus, we find examples such as those in (212), where in each case, the American English form is replacing or has replaced the British English equivalent:

(212)   **British English**   **American English**
        housey   bingo
        bakery   baker's shop
        minerals   soft drinks
        pictures   movies
        lorry   truck
        chips   fries
        crisps   potato chips

An interesting study of lexical shift from older 'British'-type words to American borrowings has been conducted by Miriam Meyerhoff in New Zealand. As is indicated in figure 39, she found that while some 'British' English words were being retained, many Americanisms were being borrowed, a finding which reflects both the increase in sociocultural contact between the US and New Zealand, and the reduction in such contact between New Zealand and the UK.

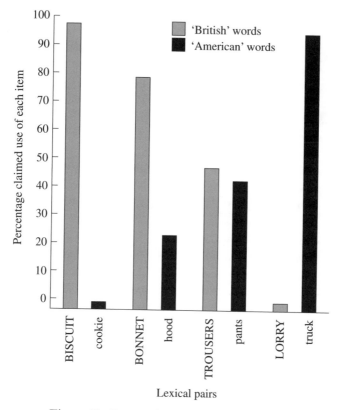

Figure 39 *Reported use of lexical pairs in New Zealand English*

A number of studies have suggested that people are able to acquire new lexical items rather more quickly than they can acquire new phonological features. For instance, Jack Chambers has compared the rate at which a group of Canadian children whose parents had moved to southern England adopted British English lexical and phonological features (see section 3, exercise 7). He selected twenty-five British/Canadian lexical pairs (including *nappy/diaper*, *pushchair/stroller* and *boot/trunk*) and five pronunciation pairs (including [bənɑnə]/[bənænə] and [təmɑtʌʊ]/[təmeɪdʌʊ]) and analysed the extent to

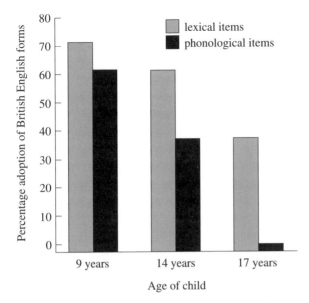

Figure 40 *The adoption of British English by Canadian children: lexicon and phonology*

which the Canadian youngsters adopted the British forms. The graph in figure 40 presents the findings for three of the children he studied. Each child had acquired more of the lexical items than of the pronunciation features. We have therefore seen two examples of dialect contact leading to change in lexical choice: sociocultural contact with North America has led to the adoption of American English words in other English dialects, and contact with British English has led a number of Canadian children to shift away from their indigenous lexical patterns to those of their new home. This dialect contact also has a considerable effect on lexical variation *within* individual English speaking countries. In England, the urbanisation of rural areas has had a devastating effect on the survival of traditional rural dialects. Urban varieties are increasingly being diffused into the surrounding rural areas, the effects of which are particularly visible in the lexicon. Traditional dialect words are losing ground in competition from words from urban or standard dialects. An example of such **lexical attrition** is presented in the map below. A century ago, the word *dwile* (meaning 'floorcloth') was widely used in the Eastern Counties of England. Today it is restricted largely to the adult populations of Norfolk and parts of Suffolk. In a recent study, as indicated in figure 41, the word *dwile* was barely recognised by any of the children surveyed, which strongly suggests that it is unlikely to survive long into the twenty-first century (***exercise 5***).

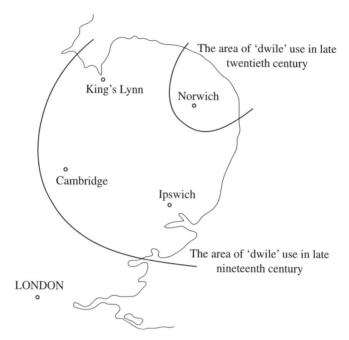

Map 3 *The lexical attrition of the word* dwile *in East Anglia*

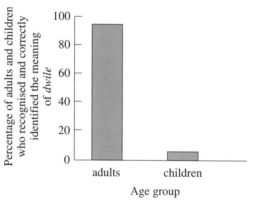

Figure 41 *The lexical attrition of* dwile *in East Anglia*

Same word – new meaning

A 'nice' example to begin our discussion of the way word meanings change is presented by the word *nice* itself. This word entered the English language around the thirteenth century from Old French, a descendent of the Latin word *nescius* meaning 'ignorant'. By the fourteenth century its meaning had already changed to mean 'silly' or 'wanton': a nice person was one from whom favours might easily be obtained. In the fifteenth century, *nice* came to mean 'coy' or 'shy', by the sixteenth it meant 'subtle', and only in the eighteenth century did it reach its present meaning of 'agreeable' or 'good'. Nowadays, the meaning of *nice* appears to be weakening: it has such a bland, general, quality of 'goodness' that in some contexts, such as that illustrated in (213), it means little more than 'OK':

(213)   [conversation between father and daughter]
       HEIDI: Hey, dad, I've just bought a new Golf GTi convertible. What do you reckon?
       ALBERT: Mm. It's nice.

For a more contemporary example of semantic change, consider the word *gay*. Originally, *gay* meant 'full of joy and mirth, light-hearted'. In the middle of the twentieth century, however, it also came to mean 'homosexual', and now this later meaning has almost completely taken over from the former one. Just like linguistic change in phonology, which we discussed earlier (section 4), semantic change is always preceded by semantic variation – in other words, at some stage in the shift from meaning A to meaning B, *both* meanings will be current within a community. At one time, therefore, both 'joyful' and 'homosexual' were meanings of the word *gay*. Gradually, over time, one meaning has begun to be used much more than the other to such an extent that the older meaning is dying out.

If we look back into the history of English, many thousands of words have changed their meaning in the same way that the word *gay* is changing today. In an attempt to establish regularities of semantic change, historical linguists tend to classify meaning changes according to the nature of the semantic shift.

Some changes are due to **semantic broadening**: here the word takes on a wider, more general meaning than it had previously. The word *thing* is a classic example of such broadening. In Old English and Old Norse, this word meant 'a public assembly'. In present-day Icelandic, a language with similar Germanic roots to English, it still does. In Modern English, however, it has now been extended so much that it simply means 'an entity of any kind'. The word *companion* provides another example. It used to mean 'someone who eats bread with you' (see Italian *con* 'with' + *pane* 'bread'); now it means 'someone who is with you'. The word *broadcast*, which only a couple of centuries ago meant 'to sow seeds', has now, in this technological age, been extended to include the spreading of information on television and radio.

Pudding, which today is usually sweet and eaten for dessert, comes from the French word *boudin* which means a sausage made with animal intestines.

The opposite of semantic broadening is **semantic narrowing**, with the word taking on a more restricted meaning than before. In Middle English, a girl was a young person of either sex, a boy was a male person of any age and *lust* simply meant 'pleasure'. A number of words with similar meanings have undergone shifts in different directions of generality. For example, the word *hound* was once the generic word for a canine. This word's meaning has narrowed and the generic canine term is now *dog*, which once referred to a particular breed of dog.

These changes in word meaning have often obscured the Germanic roots of the English language, with many originally Germanic words either changing in meaning or dying out. Consider table 30 below:

Table 30: Equivalences between Modern English and other Germanic languages				
Modern English	**Old English**	**Frisian**	**Dutch**	**German**
meat	flesh	fleis	vlees	Fleisch
animal	deer	dier	dier	Tier
dog	hound	houn	hond	Hund
cloud	wolcen	wolk	wolk	Wolke
die	steorfan	stjerre	sterven	sterben
bird	fugol	fûgel	vogel	Vogel
smoke	reek	rikje	roken	rauchen
poor	earm	earm	arm	arm
air	lyft	lucht	lucht	Luft
take	niman	nimme	nemen	nehmen

In this table, note the similarities between the Old English words and the equivalents in the modern day varieties of the closest cousins of English. Words such as *steorfan* (Modern English: *starve*) and *reek* have been semantically narrowed in the transition from Old English to Modern English, and many of the other words have died out in the face of competition from other English words, or from words borrowed from other languages. For example, *poor* is a word borrowed from Old French.

It is also common to contrast changes involving **amelioration** with those due to **pejoration**. Pejorations involve the development of a *less favourable* meaning or connotation for a particular word. Villains were formerly farm-dwellers, but are now criminals; people who were crafty and cunning in medieval times were strong (see German *Kraft*) and wise, but now are deceitful and evasive. *Grotesque* meant 'resembling a grotto or cave', but now means 'distorted and ugly'. The word *dunce* is taken from the name of a thirteenth-century scholar, John Duns Scotus, whose thinking was discredited long after his death. Ameliorations, or the development of more favourable meanings for words, are fewer in number. Some of the more notable examples are *constable*, the meaning of which has shifted from 'an attendant at the stable' to 'a police officer' and *knight* which in Old English referred to a boy or servant but now has a much more prestigious meaning.

We have now seen a number of examples of semantic changes. But what is it about 'meaning' that allows such changes to take place? How is it possible for the meanings of words to alter so radically? April McMahon has suggested three possible reasons:

a. Most words are **polysemic** – they have a range of meanings – and over time marginal meanings may take over from central meanings (possibly because a borrowing has invaded the semantic space of the central meaning). Note that polysemy must be distinguished from ambiguity. An ambiguous word such as *match* or *bank* corresponds to two (or more) distinct lexemes and normally has two (or more) distinct entries in a conventional dictionary. A polysemous word has only a single lexical entry with a range of closely related meanings. An example illustrating the takeover of central meaning is the word *sloth*, which once had a central meaning of 'lacking in speed'. This central meaning was taken over by the word *slowness* and so the central meaning of *sloth* shifted to what was formerly a more peripheral meaning, namely 'laziness'.

b. Children do not receive a fully formed grammar and lexicon from their parents, but, with help from Universal Grammar, have to figure it out for themselves. The child may therefore acquire a slightly different meaning for a word than that understood by its parents. Earlier we saw that children, in the very early stages of language acquisition, sometimes seem to use certain words with broader meanings than the adults around them e.g. *dog* to mean 'any hairy animal with four legs' (see section 13). As the child gets older, it gradually restricts the meaning of the word more and more. It is not too difficult, however, to imagine that slight semantic shifts may emerge at the end of this restriction process. We did, of course, express some reservations about the extent of such overextended lexical use by small children in section 13, but these reservations need not rule out what we are contemplating here. Consider, for instance the broadening of Old English *dogge*, referring to a specific breed of dog to the current situation where *dog* is the generic term for canines. We suggested in section 13 that children are 'tuned in' to the basic level of categorisation, and we can suppose that for the case in question this is the level of Modern English *dog*. All we need to suppose, then, is that for whatever reason at some point a child was exposed to examples of *dogge* and interpreted them as referring to the basic level generic category. For such a child at this point, the semantic broadening has occurred. Of course, it is still necessary to understand how such a child's 'non-standard' interpretation became established and spread throughout the community, but we do at least have a plausible account of the first important step in semantic change. Overall, the suggestion that children are crucially involved in language change is a very attractive one.

c. The relationship between concepts and the words which conventionally refer to those concepts is arbitrary (see section 14) and so either can vary or change fairly freely through time and across space. Just as different geographical areas may have different words to represent different concepts (**lexical variation**), so also different words may, through time, evolve so as to be associated with different concepts (**semantic change**) (*exercise 6*).

Variation and change in morphology

As mentioned in section 10, English verbs have few inflections, but one which is found is that which marks present tense and agreement with the third person singular subject. This is not the case in all dialects of English, however, and in some dialects this suffix has been lost. Speakers of African American Vernacular English (AAVE) in the USA and the English of East Anglia in the UK produce examples such as those in (214):

(214)   a. this dog chase rabbits
        b. this cat miaow all night
        c. he spend a lot
        d. she dance well

This contrasts with the situation in southwest England, where people would not only say *he spends a lot*, but also produce examples such as those in (215):

(215)   a. they spends a lot
        b. I dances every night

In this area, the *-s* suffix does not mark present tense and agreement (with third person singular subjects) but *only* present tense. Around the English-speaking world, therefore, there is variation both in the presence or absence of the -*s* suffix and in its grammatical function.

Older versions of English, and most other Germanic languages (apart from Afrikaans) have far more extensive systems of inflection than present day Standard English. In Old English, there were four different present tense forms (as there still are today in German, although they are distributed differently), in comparison with two in Modern Standard English. This is illustrated for the verb *help* and its equivalents in table 31:

Table 31: The present tense forms of Modern English *help* and their equivalents in Old English and Modern German					
Old English		**Modern German**		**Modern English**	
ic	helpe	Ich	helfe	I	help
thu	hilpst	Du	hilfst	You (sing)	help
he/heo	hilpth	Er/Sie	hilft	He/She	helps
we	helpath	Wir	helfen	We	help
ge	helpath	Ihr	helft	You (pl)	help
hi	helpath	Sie	helfen	They	help

Similarly, Modern Standard English has lost the three noun genders of Old English illustrated in (216):

(216)   tha stan*as*   the stones (masculine)
         tha gief*a*   the gifts (feminine)
         tha scip*u*   the ships (neuter)

Over the centuries, then, morphological change in English has largely been in a direction of radical reduction and simplification of inflections to an extent not seen in most other Germanic languages.

The reduction of two former Old English inflections -*inde* and -*ingel*-*ynge* to Modern Standard English -*ing* has had a considerable effect on present-day variation in English. In most English speaking countries, there is social variation in the pronunciation of (ing), some pronouncing it [ɪŋ], which is the standard form, and others [ɪn], the widely used non-standard form. Sociolinguists have found variation in (ing) particularly interesting for a number of reasons.

First, a number of studies from around the English-speaking world have found that, all else being equal, women use a higher proportion of the standard [ɪŋ] form than men. Some representative results appear in figure 42:

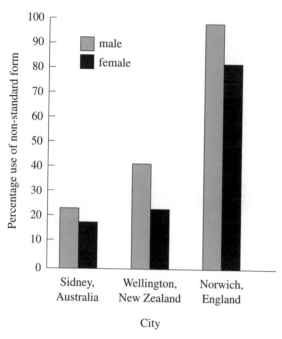

Figure 42 *Speaker sex and the use of (ing) in casual speech in three English-speaking cities*

Secondly, variation in (ing) appears to be fairly stable over the entire speech community of English. In other words, neither form seems to be replacing the other, but there is a pattern of **stable variation**, with [ɪŋ] being the **acrolectal** form (used in higher social classes and in more formal contexts) while [ɪn], the **basilectal** form, is used among working class groups and in more informal contexts. Figures 43a and 43b support this assertion.

Finally, research has shown that people use different proportions of [ɪŋ] and [ɪn] at different stages of their life. A study in Norwich in Eastern England, for example, found that young people predominantly used the non-standard [ɪn] form, but changed their behaviour in middle age to use a greater proportion of the standard form, before reverting to a greater use of the non-standard form again in retirement (see figure 44).

Peter Trudgill, who conducted the Norwich study, has suggested that people come under the pressure of the standard variety more in their economically active years than in their youth or in their retirement and that this would account for the variation in (ing) use across a person's lifespan.

Synchronically, (ing) can be regarded as a phonological variable, the alternation of velar and alveolar nasal realisations of the final segment (ng).

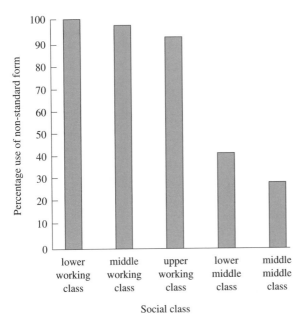

Figure 43a *Social class and the use of (ing) in casual speech in Norwich*

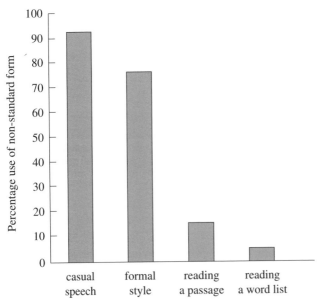

Figure 43b *Speech style and the use of (ing) among upper working class residents of Norwich*

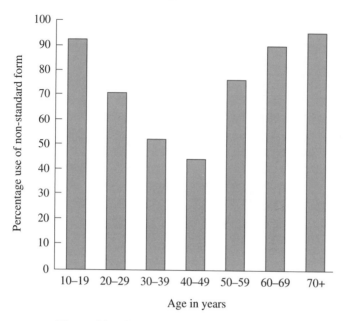

Figure 44 *Changes in the use of (ing) in Norwich across the generations*

Historically, however, it must be considered as a morphological variable since [ɪŋ] and [ɪn] come from two different Old English morphemes and still retain signs of their former grammatical roles within present day variation. The relevant changes between Old English and the English of about 1400 are set out in table 32:

Table 32: Changes in the Old English suffixes -inde and inge/-ynge		
Changes since Old English	**Old English -inde (verbal suffix)**	**Old English -inge/-ynge (verbal noun suffix)**
reduction of final /e/ to /ə/	-ində	-iŋə
loss of final /ə/	-ind	-iŋ
reduction of -nd- cluster	-in	-iŋ
English of about 1400	-in	-iŋ

By the mid fifteenth century , -*ind* had encroached on -*ind*'s territory as a verbal suffix in the south of England, but retained its more restricted role in the north and in parts of East Anglia. In Modern English times, we can see that this geographical variation (-*in* in the north and -*ing* in the south) has evolved nationwide into social and stylistic variation. The former roles of -*inde* and -*inge* are, however, still reflected in present-day variation. Research has demonstrated that [ɪn] is much more likely to be found in progressives (*Madonna is singing again*) and verbal complements (*I don't mind listening to Madonna*) than in nominal -*ing* forms (*I don't like Madonna's singing*). The -*in*/-*ing* alternation, therefore, retains morphological importance, as well as being a salient marker of social and stylistic information around the English-speaking world (*exercise 7*).

Finally in this section we shall consider the role of social contact on morphological variation. In section 4, we saw how the strength of social networks in the speech community has a considerable effect on the maintenance of local dialect forms and susceptibility to language change. In a study carried out on the speech of the African American and White populations of Philadelphia, Sharon Ash and John Myhill have found that there is a strong link between ethnicity, social network ties and the use of certain non-standard morphological features. We have already noted that one prominent characteristic of African American Vernacular English (AAVE) is the absence of the suffix -*s* as a marker of third person singular agreement (see the examples in (214) above). Additionally, possessive -*s* is not used in this dialect and we find examples such as those in (217):

(217)   a. I met his brother wife
         b   His cat name is Peanut

Ash and Myhill's research has revealed that there is a strong relationship between the use of these AAVE features and the levels of social contact between whites and African Americans in Philadelphia. Those blacks who have very little contact with whites use the AAVE features most, while those with more contact with the white population use them less. Similarly those whites who have little contact with the African American community rarely if ever use the AAVE features, while those who have more contact do use these features, albeit rarely (see figure 45). Network links with other ethnic groups have led, in this case, to a weakening in the use of the ethnic variety and the adoption of linguistic features from 'outside'.

In this part of the book, we have introduced a range of concepts which are necessary for coming to terms with the rich variety of processes on which different languages rely for forming complex words, focusing on English in section 10 and taking account of aspects of other languages in section 11. Just as progress in understanding sound systems requires a way for describing sounds accurately (the IPA of section 2), so discussion of word formation is dependent on classification of words into certain types, and we took the first

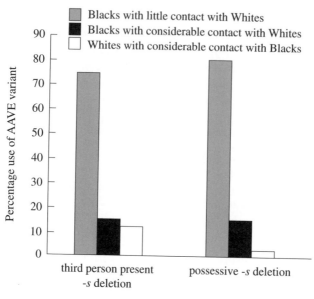

(figures for the fourth category of Whites with little contact with Blacks are too small to show on a graph of this nature)

Figure 45 *Ethnicity, levels of interethnic contact and the use of AAVE morphological features*

steps in this direction in section 9 (see also section 18). A parallel aim throughout sections 9 to 11 has been to sketch a view of the *lexical representations* which are an integral part of a *grammar* (see the introduction, p. 4), constituting, as they do, the *lexicon*. Such representations, as well as having phonological and syntactic aspects (see (114)), also encode the *meanings* of lexical items, and section 12 has examined how such meanings might be described and also raised the issue of how the overall *structure* of the mental lexicon might be understood in terms of meaning relations; that is, as well as coming to terms with the *internal structure* of a lexical representation, we proposed that meaning relations such as *hyponymy* and *meronymy* are useful in determining the ways in which lexical representations are related to each other.

With basic concepts in place, the next three sections of this part have sought to establish their usefulness in the study of the acquisition of words by small children (13), the processing and storage (in a mental lexicon) of words by adults (14) and the difficulties in perceiving and producing words which can arise as a consequence of brain damage (15).

Finally, in section 16 we have examined *variation* with respect to two of the principle components of the lexical entries, the semantic representation and the morphological shape of word forms serving particular grammatical functions. We have seen cases where each of these may be subject to variation within the speech of an individual, across social groups, between dialects and at different stages in the historical development of a language or dialect. For a full description of a speaker's behaviour, then, the simple representations we have presented in section 10 are not fully adequate; however, we can be confident that they constitute the basic core or nucleus over which variation can be defined.

Our last major theme is the sentence, to which we now turn in the final part of the book.

Exercises

1. Check the following list of words in a good dictionary and:

    (a) find out the language of origin of each word;
    (b) ascertain when it is claimed the word entered the English language;
    (c) speculate on WHY the word was borrowed.

jojoba	bog	glacier
banana	cigarette	flamingo
tundra	sauna	curry
jungle	buffalo	orang-utan
wigwam	wombat	yacht
canyon	hashish	pyjama

2. The word *skyscraper* has not been widely borrowed. Instead many languages have used native words to express the notion of 'scraping the sky'. In Dutch, for example, we find *wolkenkrabber*, literally 'cloud-scratcher'. Find out how other languages refer to skyscrapers, and what the component parts of the words they use mean.

3. In Malay, the word *juru* means 'expert'. It can be combined with other words to give labels to particular types of job. So, since the word *bahasa* means 'language', *juru bahasa* means 'interpreter'. What do you think the following Malay words mean?

juruhebah (*hebah* means 'announce')
jurutera (*jentera* means 'motor/engine')
jururawat (*rawat* means 'attend to/look after')
jurutaip (*taip* means 'type')
jurucakap (*cakap* means 'talk, speak')

4.   Examine the registers associated with some of your own sports and pastimes. How large is their technical vocabulary? Why do you use these registers? Why don't you use words everyone can understand?!

5.   When sociolinguists wish to study variation in phonology, they normally rely on an analysis of recordings of natural speech. In an hour's recording, there are usually enough examples of most variables for an adequately representative sample. Attempting to analyse lexical variation and change from recorded speech samples is not so straightforward, however. Suppose we were interested in finding out whether people said 'biscuit' or 'cookie'. We might find that in an hour's recording (or even ten hours' recording) there will be no examples of *biscuit* or *cookie* or any other word associated with the relevant concept. (Let's face it, how often do *you* talk about biscuits or cookies in your everyday conversation?) So how do we find out which word people use? It might be reasonable to assume that we could simply ask: *Do you say 'biscuit' or 'cookie'?* There is evidence that this method is flawed too. Researchers in New Zealand found, for example, that while when asked, people claimed to use the word *trousers*, it was discovered that they used the word *pants* in later conversation. Bearing in mind these data collection problems, how would *you* analyse lexical variation?

6.   **Etymology** is the study of the history of words. Find a good etymological dictionary and examine how the meanings of the following words have changed over time:

treacle	assassin	buxom
botulism	hysteria	parasite
villain	butcher	sinister
bead	clue	cloud
mess	worm	weird
heckle	liquor	saucer

7.   Having asked their permission, make a short recording of a group of your friends conversing. From the recording you have made, listen and note down the pronunciation of each occurrence of (ing). Compare the way males and females in your recording pronounce (ing). What are your results? Do your findings agree with those of other researchers? Can you identify any differences between (ing) in progressives and verbal complements on the one hand and nominal (ing) on the other?

Further reading and references

Many of the topics introduced in sections 9, 10, and 11 are dealt with in more detail by Bauer (1988) and Katamba (1993). Carstairs-McCarthy (1992) provides a good overview of these issues and Spencer 1991 (chapters 1 and 2) gives further details of many of the phenomena discussed. Matthews (1991), though tough going in places for beginners, provides interesting insights into morphology. For more advanced discussion of some of the topics of these sections, see the chapters by Stump (inflection), Beard (derivation), Fabb (compounding), Halpern (clitics), Spencer (morphophonological operations) in Spencer and Zwicky (1998).

A very readable introduction to the use of entailment in studying lexical semantic relations is Cruse (1986), which acknowledges a considerable debt to Lyons (1977, particularly chapters 8 and 9). Arguments against the usefulness of definitions for understanding how meanings are composed can be found in Fodor (1981) and Fodor, Garrett, Walker and Parkes (1980), neither of which is easy to read for beginners. One of the earliest, and most accessible, attempts to argue for the importance of prototypes in the study of meaning is Rosch (1973).

Discussion of the remarkable rate of children's word acquisition appear in Carey (1978, 1985). Valian (1986) is a study of syntactic categorisation in early stages of acquisition, while Radford (1990) was among the first to systematically examine children's difficulties with functional categories. Berko (1958) studied productive morphological processes in children, and Brown (1973) reports the order of morpheme acquisition discussed in the text. There are many discussions of the overregularisation of the English past tense -*ed*; among the most notable are Kuczaj (1977), Bybee and Slobin (1982) and Marcus (1995). Gordon (1985) reports the results on pluralisation of compounds. The classic account of children's word meanings as sets of perceptual features is Clark (1973), and the importance of the basic object level in children's initial categorisations is examined in Rosch, Mervis, Gray, Johnson and Boyes-Braem (1976).

Further discussion of the process of word recognition, introduced in section 14, including relevant experimental evidence can be found in Harley (1995, chapters 3 and 9) and in Garman (1990, chapter 5). The issues we have raised in connection with the representation of words in the mental lexicon are largely based on Levelt (1989, chapter 6). This is an important and very readable book.

For section 15, Garman (1990, chapter 8) provides a brief overview of research in aphasia, and Caplan (1992, chapter 4) is also worth consulting. The discussion of agrammatism contains materials and is based on ideas from Grodzinsky (1990). Leonard (1998, chapters 2 and 3) provides an overview of research into SLI, focusing on English. The materials we rely on in our discussion are from Gopnik (1990)

Both Trask (1996) and McMahon (1994) provide good detail about borrowing and lexical, semantic and morphological variation and change. Research on register can be found in Biber and Finegan (1994). The study on lexical change in New Zealand English, referred to in section 16, was conducted by Meyerhoff (1993). Trudgill (1974, 1988) provides valuable information on (ing) in Norwich (England), and Horvath (1985), Bell and Holmes (1992) and Shuy, Wolfram and Riley (1967) report work on this variable for Sydney (Australia); Wellington (New Zealand) and Detroit (USA) respectively. The work on dialect acquisition was conducted by Chambers (1992). The research on (ing) as a morphological variable can be found in Houston (1991). Ash and Myhill (1986) investigated the relationship between ethnicity, social network strength and the use of African American morphological features. A British newspaper, *The Eastern Daily Press* (10 May, 1993), researched the attrition of *dwile* in East Anglia.

Part 3 Sentences

17 Introduction

In this final part of the book we switch our attention to the study of syntax, focusing on the processes whereby words are combined to form phrases which in turn are combined to form sentences. With many linguists, we share the view that sentences constitute the 'largest' objects which fall under the generative approach to linguistics we are pursuing. Of course, this is not to say that there are no 'larger' linguistic objects which are worth studying. Such larger objects as *conversations, discourses, stories* and *texts* are, without doubt, structured, and, indeed, research into these areas has often assumed that some notion of 'grammar' is applicable to them. This may be so, but we believe that any such 'grammar' will have a very different form to what we are considering here, and will have to take account of a wide range of factors which extend beyond the knowledge of language. To take just one simple example, consider the two-turn conversation in (218):

(218)   SPEAKER A: I'd like a cup of coffee.
        SPEAKER B: The shop across the street is still open.

There is no reason to regard this as anything other than a well-formed conversation, but quite a complex set of assumptions underlie this judgement. For instance, if the shop across the street is known by both participants to be a shoe shop, the well-formedness of (218) immediately evaporates (unless they know the shop's staff well, and know that they will be invited into the back room for a cup of coffee); A and B *knowing that the shop across the street sells coffee* is a condition on the well-formedness of (218), but this has nothing to do with knowledge of language. We maintain that this simple example is typical and that to extend our considerations to include the study of conversations and other 'larger' units would rapidly involve us in trying to model the whole of human knowledge and not just knowledge of language. Of course, in restricting ourselves in this way, we are committing ourselves to the view that knowledge of language (grammar, in our sense) constitutes a coherent

279

domain of enquiry, and we may be misguided in this respect. The important thing to be clear about is that there is no room for dogmatism here: the study of conversations and other linguistic objects beyond the sentence is undoubtedly interesting in its own right, and it may turn out that in order to understand how sentences, words and even sounds work, we need to take account of encyclopaedic knowledge. For the moment, there is no compelling reason to believe that this is so, and this justifies our decision not to go beyond the sentence in this book.

Since Chomsky's ideas began to be influential in linguistics, syntax is probably the area where most research effort has been directed, with the consequence that a rather large number of different theoretical accounts have developed, each with its specialised terminology (for instance, the lexical functional grammar of Joan Bresnan and her colleagues and the head driven phrase structure grammar most closely associated with the work of Carl Pollard and Ivan Sag). What we shall do in this part of the book is introduce one such account which is based on fairly recent work of Chomsky himself. In doing this, we shall be able to bring into the discussion a wide range of basic syntactic ideas which will be transferable to theoretical frameworks which differ from that adopted here. Of course, these frameworks also have their own vocabularies and theoretical constructs, but acquaintance with what follows in this part of the book should enable readers to approach such alternatives with confidence.

Sections 18 to 23 contain the core theoretical ideas of this part of the book. The first of these sections builds on section 9 in introducing basic, traditional terminology for talking about phrases and sentences. Section 19 examines in detail one of the core operations in the theory of grammar, that whereby two linguistic objects are combined to create a third, complex object. Of course, we have already met combinatory processes in morphology (affixation and compounding), but the operation introduced here is different to these. Scientific progress in a field often involves the postulation of theoretical entities with intuitively odd properties (e.g. gravity in Newton's physics, or the properties of subatomic particles in modern physics). Empty categories, that is positions in linguistic structures which are occupied by nothing audible or visible, but which nonetheless have syntactic properties comprise one of the contributions of syntax to this catalogue, and they are introduced in section 20. There is ample evidence to suggest that some linguistic expressions, having combined with others, can subsequently move into another position in a structure. Movement, the second major operation in the syntactic theory we introduce here, is the topic of section 21.

In parts 1 and 2 of the book, we have examined linguistic variation from a sociolinguistic perspective. The applications of this perspective to syntax have to date not been extensive. However, the study of variation *per se,* between varieties of a language, historical periods of a language and between different languages has received a great deal of attention. How variation is dealt with in the theoretical framework developed here is the topic of section 22. Finally, section 23 introduces considerations of Logical Form (see the introduction, p. 6), a level of syntactic representation relevant to the interpretation of sentences, which relies heavily on another construct with unusual properties, *invisible* movement.

The final three sections of this part of the book utilise the theoretical framework in examining the child's acquisition of grammar (section 24), adult processing of sentences (section 25) and syntactic disorders of language (section 26). Certain ideas which can be formulated rather naturally within our framework are argued to be fundamentally important in understanding issues which arise in these areas. Equally importantly, these areas offer additional perspectives for testing and expanding the scope of syntactic theories.

18 Basic terminology

A substantial proportion of the terminology we need in order to embark on the study of syntax has already been introduced, particularly in section 9. However, there are some additional notions which it is important for us to understand, so in this section we shall introduce these, integrating them with ideas with which we are already familiar.

Categories and functions

It is traditionally said that sentences are structured out of words, phrases and clauses, each of which belongs to a specific **grammatical category** and serves a specific **grammatical function** within the sentence containing it. The lexical and functional categories from section 9 are examples of grammatical categories, and as our discussion proceeds, we shall see how phrases and clauses can be categorised. The smallest type of sentence which we can produce is one containing a single clause, such as (219):

(219)   John smokes

This comprises the noun *John*, which is traditionally claimed to serve the function of being the **subject** of the clause (in that it denotes the person performing the act of smoking), and the verb *smokes* which serves the function of being the **predicate** of the clause (in that it describes the act being performed). Consider next the slightly longer clause in (220):

(220)   John smokes cigars

Here we have the subject *John*, the predicate *smokes* and a third item, *cigars*, which is the **complement** (*cigars* refers to the entities on which the act of smoking is being performed). The subject *John* and the complement *cigars* are the two **arguments** of the predicate *smokes* (i.e. the two entities involved in the act of smoking). A **clause** is an expression which contains a subject and a predicate, and which may also contain other types of element (e.g. the clause in (220) contains a complement as well, and so is of the form *subject + predicate + complement*).

There are a number of morphological and syntactic properties which differentiate subjects from complements. For one thing, the two occupy different positions within the clause: in English, subjects generally precede predicates and complements follow them. Moreover (with an exception to be noted later), subjects generally have different **case** properties to complements. The different case forms of typical pronouns and noun expressions in English are given in (221):

(221)	**nominative**	**objective**	**genitive**
	I	me	my
	we	us	our
	you	you	your
	he	him	his
	she	her	her
	it	it	its
	they	them	their
	who	who(m)	whose
	the dog	the dog	the dog's

Subjects typically carry **nominative** case, whereas complements typically carry **objective** case. This isn't immediately obvious from (220), since nouns like *John* and *cigars* aren't overtly inflected for the nominative/objective case distinction. However, if we replace *John* by an overtly case-marked pronoun, we require the nominative form *he*, not the objective form *him*; and conversely, if we replace *cigars* by an overtly case-marked pronoun, we require the objective form *them*, not the nominative form *they*:

(222)   a. He/*Him smokes cigars
        b. John smokes them/*they

A third difference between subjects and complements is that, as we have noted on several occasions, in English verbs agree in Person and Number with their subjects. However, they don't agree with their complements. So, if we have a third person singular subject like *he* or *John*, we require the corresponding third person singular verb-form *smokes*; but if we have a first person singular subject like *I*, or a first person plural subject like *we*, or a second person singular or plural subject like *you*, or a third person plural subject like *they*, we require the alternative form *smoke*:

(223)   a. He smokes/*smoke cigars
          b. I/We/You/They smoke/*smokes cigars

If, however, we change the complement, say replacing the plural form *cigars* with the singular *a cigar* in (220), the form of the verb in English is unaffected:

(224)   John smokes cigars/a cigar

Overall, then, we can differentiate subjects from complements in terms of whether they normally precede or follow the verb, whether they have nominative or objective case, and whether or not they agree with the verb.

Now consider the even longer clause in (225):

(225)   The president smokes a cigar after dinner

This clause comprises three **constituents** (i.e. structural units) the function of which is already familiar – namely the subject *the president*, the predicate *smokes* and the complement *a cigar*. But what is the function of the expression *after dinner* which also occurs in (225)? Since *after dinner* does not refer to one of the entities directly involved in the act of smoking (i.e. it isn't consuming or being consumed), it isn't an argument of the predicate *smokes*. On the contrary, it simply serves to provide additional information about the time when the smoking activity takes place. In much the same way, the italicised expression in (226) provides additional information about the location of the smoking activity:

(226)   The president smokes a cigar *in his office*

An expression which serves to provide (optional) additional information about the time or place (or manner, or purpose, etc.) of an activity is said to serve as an **adjunct**. So, *after dinner* in (225) and *in his office* in (226) are both adjuncts.

Now consider the following kind of clause (characteristic of colloquial styles of English):

(227)   Cigars, the president never smokes them in front of his wife

The function of the constituents contained in the part of the clause following the comma is straightforward to analyse: *the president* is the subject, *smokes* is the predicate, *them* is the complement, and *never* and *in front of his wife* are both adjuncts. But what is the function of the expression *cigars* which precedes the comma? The traditional answer is that *cigars* functions as the **topic** of the clause, in the sense that it serves to indicate that the clause tells us something about cigars; the part of the clause following the comma is said to be the **comment**. It is interesting to contrast (227) with (228):

(228)   Cigars, the president never smokes in front of his wife

In (227) *cigars* is the clause topic, and *them* (which refers back to *cigars*) is the complement of the verb *smokes*. By contrast, in (228), *cigars* seems to serve both functions, and hence is the topic of the overall clause as well as being the complement of the verb *smokes*.

Now consider the clause in (229):

(229)   The president was smoking a cigar for relaxation

Again, this comprises a number of constituents with familiar functions: *the president* is the subject, *smoking* is the predicate, *a cigar* is the complement, and *for relaxation* is an adjunct. But what is the function of the auxiliary *was*? The answer is that it serves to mark **Tense**, indicating the time at which the activity took place (viz. the past). English has a binary (i.e. two-way) tense system, so that in place of the past tense form *was* in (229), we could use the corresponding present tense form *is*. Although this distinction is traditionally said to be a past/present one, many linguists prefer to see it as a past/non-past distinction, since the so-called present tense form can be used with future time-reference (e.g. in sentences such as *our guest is arriving at 3 p.m. tomorrow*). However, since the term 'present tense' is a familiar one, we'll continue to use it below.

Complex sentences

So far, we have looked at **simple sentences** – i.e. sentences which comprise a single clause (hence, all the clauses in (219), (220) and (222)–(229) above are *simple* sentences). However, alongside these we also find **complex sentences** – i.e. sentences which contain more than one clause. In this connection, consider the structure of the following sentence:

(230)   Mary knows John smokes

If we take a clause to be a structure comprising (at least) a subject and a predicate, it follows that there are two different clauses in (230) – the *smokes* clause on the one hand, and the *knows* clause on the other. The *smokes* clause comprises the subject *John* and the predicate *smokes*; the *knows* clause comprises the subject *Mary*, the predicate *knows* and the complement *John smokes*. So, the complement of *knows* here is itself a clause. The *smokes* clause is a **complement clause** (because it serves as the complement of *knows*), while the *knows* clause is the **main clause**. The overall sentence in (230) is a complex sentence because it contains more than one clause. In much the same way, (231) below is also a complex sentence:

(231)   The president may secretly fear Congress will ultimately reject his proposal

Once again, it comprises two clauses – one containing the predicate *fear*, the other containing the predicate *reject*. The main clause comprises the subject *the president*, the auxiliary *may*, the adverbial adjunct *secretly*, the verbal predicate *fear* and the complement clause *Congress will ultimately reject his proposal*. The complement clause in turn comprises the subject *Congress*, the auxiliary *will*, the verbal predicate *reject*, the complement *his proposal* and the adjunct *ultimately*.

Now contrast the two different types of complex sentence illustrated below:

(232)   a. We expect [John will win the race]
         b. We expect [John to win the race]

Both sentences comprise two clauses – a main clause and a bracketed complement clause. The main clause in (232a) comprises the subject *we*, the verbal predicate *expect* and the complement clause *John will win the race*; the main clause in (232b) is identically constituted except that the complement clause is *John to win the race*. The complement clause in (232a) comprises the subject *John*, the auxiliary *will*, the verbal predicate *win* and the complement *the race*; the complement clause in (232b) comprises the subject *John*, the infinitive particle *to*, the verbal predicate *win* and the complement *the race*. So, superficially, at least, the two sentences appear to have much the same structure.

Yet, there are important differences between the two complement clauses they contain. In (232a), the auxiliary *will* is a tensed form (more specifically, a non-past form), as we see from the fact that if we transpose the whole sentence into the past tense, we use the corresponding past tense form *would* instead of *will*:

(233)   We expected [John *would* win the race]

By contrast, if we transpose (232b) into the past tense, the infinitive particle *to* remains invariable:

(234)   We expected [John *to* win the race]

So, we can say that the bracketed complement clause in (232a) and (233) is **tensed**, whereas its counterpart in (232b) and (234) is **untensed** (i.e. unspecified for tense).

A further difference between the two types of complement clause can be illustrated in relation to (235):

(235)   a. I didn't know [John wears glasses]
         b. I've never known [John wear glasses]

In (235a), the verb *wears* agrees with its third person singular subject *John*; but the corresponding verb *wear* in (235b) doesn't agree with *John*. More generally, complement clauses like that bracketed in (235a) contain a verb inflected for agreement with its subject, whereas complement clauses like that in (235b) contain a verb form which lacks agreement.

There is a third important difference between the two types of complement clause in (232a, 235a) and (232b, 235b), as we can see from the fact that if we replace the subject *John* by a pronoun overtly marked for case, we require the nominative form *he* in (232a, 235a), but the objective form *him* in (232b, 235b):

(236)   a. We expect [he/*him will win the race]
         b. We expect [him/*he to win the race]

(237)   a. I didn't know [he/*him wears glasses]
         b. I've never known [him/*he wear glasses]

To use the relevant grammatical terminology, we can say that an auxiliary or a verb is **finite** if it inflects for tense/agreement and has a nominative subject, and **non-finite** if it doesn't inflect for tense or agreement and doesn't have a nominative subject. By extension, we can distinguish between a **finite clause** (i.e. a clause with a nominative subject which contains a verb/auxiliary inflected for tense/agreement) and a **non-finite clause** (i.e. a clause which doesn't have a nominative subject, and which doesn't contain a verb/auxiliary inflected for tense/agreement). Thus, the complement clauses in (232a) and (235a) are finite clauses, but those in (232b) and (235b) are non-finite.

We observed in section 9 that verbs in English can have up to five distinct forms, as illustrated in (238):

(238)   *-s*   *-d*   base   *-n*   *-ing*
         shows   showed   show   shown   showing

The *-s* and *-d* forms are finite forms, the *-s* form being the third person singular present tense form, and the *-d* form being the past tense form. By contrast, the *-n* and *-ing* forms are non-finite forms, since they are not inflected for either tense or agreement (recall that the *-n* form often ends in *-ed*!). At first sight, it might seem odd to claim that the *-n* and *-ing* forms are untensed, since *-ing* forms are sometimes referred to in traditional grammars as ***present** participles* and *-n* forms as ***past** participles*. However, it is clear from sentences like (239) that the tense of the clause is marked by the auxiliaries *is/was*, not by the verb form *going*:

(239)   a. He is going home
         b. He was going home

But if the *-ing* inflection on *going* doesn't mark tense, what does it mark?

The answer, as we have noted, is that *-ing* serves to mark **aspect** (a term used to describe the duration of the activity described by a verb, e.g. whether the activity is ongoing or completed). In sentences such as (239), the *-ing* form indicates that the action of going home is still in progress at the time indicated by the auxiliary: hence (239a) can be loosely paraphrased as 'He is now still in the process of going home', and (239b) as 'He was then still in the process of going home.' Thus, the *-ing* forms like *going* in (239) mark **progressive aspect**. By contrast, *-n* forms such as *gone* in (240a, b) mark the completion of the act of going home:

(240)   a. He has gone home
         b. He had gone home

Hence (240a) can be loosely paraphrased as 'He has now completed the action of going home' and (240b) as 'He had by then completed the action of going home.' Tense is marked by the choice of *has* or *had*, and we say that *-n* forms like *gone* in (240) mark **perfect aspect** (i.e. they indicate *perfection* in the sense of completion of the relevant act). We have, of course, already met *-ing* forms and *-n* forms in section 10, where they were respectively referred to as *progressive participles* and *perfect participles*. Since participles mark aspect (not tense or agreement), they are non-finite forms.

So far, we have argued that the *-s* and *-d* forms of verbs are finite, but the *-ing* and *-n* forms are non-finite. But what about the uninflected base forms of verbs (the forms which appear in dictionaries of English)? The answer is that the base form of the verb has a dual status, and can function either as a finite form or a non-finite form (i.e. it corresponds to more than one grammatical word in the sense of section 10). In uses like that italicised in (241) below, the base form serves as a finite present-tense form:

(241)   I/We/You/They/People *show* little interest in syntax these days

But in uses like those italicised in (242), the base form is non-finite and is traditionally termed an **infinitive** form:

(242)   a. She didn't want him to *show* any emotion
         b. He didn't *show* any emotion
         c. You mustn't let him *show* any emotion

Base forms also have other uses which we will come across subsequently (e.g. the imperative use of *keep/tell* in 244c and 245c below).

Up to now, all the complex sentences we have looked at have comprised a main clause and a complement clause. But now consider the rather different kind of complex sentence illustrated in (243):

(243)   I couldn't find anyone who could help me

There are two clauses here – the *find* clause and the *help* clause. The *find* clause comprises the subject *I*, the negative auxiliary *couldn't*, the verbal predicate *find* and the complement *anyone who could help me*. The complement in turn comprises the pronoun *anyone* followed by the clause *who could help me*. Since the pronoun *who* in this clause 'relates to' (i.e. refers back to) *anyone*, it is called a **relative pronoun**, and the clause containing it (*who could help me*) is called a **relative clause**. The relative clause in turn comprises the subject *who*, the auxiliary *could*, the verbal predicate *help* and the complement *me*. The relative clause is a finite clause, since (although it doesn't inflect for agreement) the auxiliary *could* is a past tense form (as we see from the fact that it carries the past tense suffix -*d*, see *I couldn't find anyone who helps/helped in the kitchen*), and its subject *who* carries nominative case (in formal English, the corresponding objective form would be *whom*, and this would be inappropriate here – see **anyone whom could help me*) (***exercise 1***).

The functions of clauses

One aspect of the syntax of clauses which we have so far overlooked is that different clauses have quite different functions. In this connection, consider the functions of the following simple (single-clause) sentences:

(244)   a. He failed the exam   b. Did he help you?
         c. You keep quiet!   d. What a fool I was!

The sentence in (244a) is said to be **declarative** in function, in that it is used to make a statement; by contrast, (244b) is **interrogative**, since it serves to ask a question and (244c) is an **imperative** sentence used to issue an order or command. Finally, (244d) is an **exclamative** sentence, used to exclaim surprise or delight. In complex sentences, each clause has its own function, as we can see in relation to the examples in (245):

(245)   a. He asked who had helped me
         b. Did you know he had escaped?
         c. You tell him what a great time we had!

In (245a), the main (*asked*) clause is declarative, whereas the complement (*helped*) clause is interrogative; in (245b), the main (*know*) clause is interrogative, whereas the complement (*escaped*) clause is declarative; and in (245c), the main (*tell*) clause is imperative, whereas the complement (*had*) clause is exclamative. The structure of the main clause in (245c) is particularly interesting. It comprises the subject *you*, the predicate *tell* (which is an imperative verb form in this use), the pronoun complement *him* and the clause complement *what a great time we had!* So, (245c) shows us that some verbs may have more than one complement – in this case, *tell* has both a pronoun complement and a clause complement, and this is a reflection of the fact that *tell* has three arguments corresponding to someone doing the telling, someone being told, and something being told (*exercise 2*).

Our discussion here has shown that sentences are built up out of one or more clauses: each clause contains a subject and a predicate, and may contain one or more complements and/or adjuncts as well. As we shall see in the next section, clauses too have a complex internal structure, and are typically built up out of a sequence of **phrases**. We can illustrate the difference between a phrase and a clause in terms of the two different kinds of reply which speaker B can give to speaker A's question in the following dialogue:

(246)   SPEAKER A: When does the president smoke cigars?
         SPEAKER B: He smokes cigars after dinner. (Reply 1)
                     After dinner. (Reply 2)

Here, reply 1 is clearly a clause, since it comprises the subject *he* and the predicate *smokes*, as well as the complement *cigars* and an adjunct *after dinner*. By contrast, reply 2 isn't a clause, since it contains no subject and no predicate: in traditional terms, it is a phrase. For our purposes, we can define a phrase informally as a sequence of two or more words which is not a clause (because it does not contain a subject and/or predicate), but which can nevertheless serve as a free-standing expression, and be used e.g. as a reply to an appropriate kind of question. In the next section, we turn to look at how words can be combined together to form phrases, phrases combined together to form clauses, and clauses combined together to form complex sentences.

Exercises

1. In relation to the sentences below, say what case each of the bracketed pronoun or noun expressions carries, and whether each italicised verb/auxiliary is finite or non-finite.

    (a) [She] *loves* [you]
    (b) [Mary] *thought* [he] *had hidden* [the money]
    (c) [Someone] *has stolen* [the president's] papers

(d) [People] *want* [politicians] to *reduce* [taxes]

(e) [The FBI] *don't want* [the CIA] *interfering* in [their] affairs

(f) [You] *mustn't let* [friends] *pressurise* [you]

(g) Students [who] *work* hard *achieve* the success [which] [they] *deserve*

2.   Analyse the structure of the clauses in the examples below:

(a) The prisoners escaped

(b) The prisoners shot a guard

(c) That kind of incident, nobody could foresee

(d) The prisoners brutally attacked the guard who spotted them

(e) They don't yet know which prisoners planned the escape

(f) Has anyone told the press the prisoners were carrying knives?

(g) The comments which the governor made have antagonised the guards whom the prisoners attacked

(h) Which prison officer claimed the prisoners had secretly made keys?

More specifically, say how many clauses each sentence contains, what the grammatical function of each clause is (e.g. main clause, complement clause, relative clause), what type each clause is (e.g. declarative, interrogative, imperative, exclamative), what the constituents of each clause are, and what function each constituent serves within its containing clause (e.g. subject, predicate, complement, or adjunct).

19 Sentence structure

In this section, we shall look at the way in which words are combined together to form phrases, phrases are combined together to form clauses, and clauses are combined together to form complex sentences. This involves the introduction of our first core syntactic operation, that of merger.

Merger

To put our discussion on a concrete footing, let's consider how an elementary two-word phrase such as that produced by speaker B in the following mini-dialogue is formed:

(247)   SPEAKER A: What is the government planning to do?
        SPEAKER B: *Reduce taxes.*

As speaker B's reply illustrates, the simplest way of forming a phrase is by combining two words together: for example, by combining the word *reduce* with the word *taxes* in (247), we form the phrase *reduce taxes*. There is clear evidence that the grammatical properties of phrases are determined by one of the words in the phrase. For example, when we combine a verb like *reduce* with a noun like *taxes*, the resulting phrase *reduce taxes* seems to have verb-like properties (as opposed to noun-like properties or properties which are neither verb-like nor noun-like). This can be seen from the fact that the phrase *reduce taxes* can occupy the same range of positions as a verb like *resign*, and hence, for example, occur after the infinitive particle *to*:

(248)   a. The government ought to *resign*
        b. The government ought to *reduce taxes*

By contrast, *reduce taxes* cannot occupy the kind of position occupied by a plural noun such as *taxes*, as we see from (249):

(249)   a. *Taxes* are at the heart of the debate about policy

b. **Reduce taxes are at the heart of the debate about policy*

So, it seems clear that the grammatical properties of a phrase like *reduce taxes* are determined by the verb *reduce*, and not by the noun *taxes*. We can say that the verb *reduce* is the **head** of the phrase *reduce taxes,* and conversely that the phrase *reduce taxes* is a **projection** (i.e. a phrasal expansion) of the verb *reduce* (note that the use of 'head' introduced in connection with compounding in section 10 is not to be identified with what we are talking about here). Since the head of the resulting phrase is the verb *reduce*, the phrase *reduce taxes* is a **verb phrase**: and in the same way that we abbreviate category labels like verb to V, we can abbreviate the category label verb phrase to VP. If we use the labelled bracketing technique (section 10) to represent the category of the overall phrase *reduce taxes* and of its component words *reduce* and *taxes*, we can represent the structure of the resulting phrase as in (250):

(250)   [_VP [_V reduce] [_N taxes]]

What (250) tells us is that the overall phrase *reduce taxes* is a verb phrase (VP), and that it comprises the verb (V) *reduce* and the noun (N) *taxes*. The verb *reduce* is the *head* of the overall phrase, and the noun *taxes* is the complement of the verb *reduce*. The operation by which the two words are combined together to form a phrase is called **merger**.

Although we have used the labelled bracketing technique to represent the structure of the verb phrase *reduce taxes* in (250), we have seen in section 10 that an alternative way of representing this sort of structure is in terms of a **labelled tree diagram** such as (251):

(251)

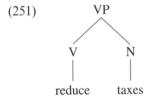

The tree diagram in (251) is entirely equivalent to the labelled bracketing in (250), in the sense that the two provide us with precisely the same information about the structure of the phrase *reduce taxes*: so (251) – like (250) – tells us that *reduce* is a verb (V), *taxes* is a noun (N), and *reduce taxes* is a verb phrase (VP). The differences between a labelled bracketing like (250) and a tree diagram like (251) are purely notational: each category is represented by a single **node** (i.e. point) in a tree diagram, but by a *pair of brackets* in a labelled bracketing.

We can generalise our discussion at this point and hypothesise that all phrases are formed in essentially the same way as the phrase in (251), namely by merging two categories together to form a larger category. In the case of (251), the resulting phrase is formed by merging two words. However, not all phrases contain just two words, as we see if we look at the structure of B's reply in (252):

(252)   SPEAKER A: What's the government's principal objective?
         SPEAKER B: *To reduce taxes*

The italicised phrase in (252) appears to be formed by merging the infinitive particle *to* with the verb phrase *reduce taxes*. What's the head of the resulting phrase *to reduce taxes*? There is evidence which indicates that this head is the infinitive particle *to*, so that the resulting string (i.e. continuous sequence of words) *to reduce taxes* is an **infinitive phrase**. The evidence is that strings such as *to reduce taxes* have a different distribution from verb phrases, as is indicated by sentences such as those in (253) and (254):

(253)   a. They ought [to reduce taxes]
         b. *They ought [reduce taxes]

(254)   a. They should [reduce taxes]
         b. *They should [to reduce taxes]

If we assume that *reduce taxes* is a verb phrase whereas *to reduce taxes* is an infinitive phrase, we can then account for the data in (253) and (254) by saying that *ought* is the kind of word which requires an infinitive phrase after it as its complement, whereas *should* is the kind of word which requires a verb phrase as its complement.

The infinitive phrase *to reduce taxes* is formed by merging the infinitive particle *to* with the verb phrase *reduce taxes*. Using I as a convenient abbreviation for infinitive particle and IP as an abbreviation for infinitive phrase, we can say that the phrase *to reduce taxes* is an infinitive phrase (IP) formed by merging the infinitive particle (I) *to* with the verb phrase (VP) *reduce taxes*, and so has the structure in (255) (note that the category label I will shortly be given a rather broader interpretation):

(255)

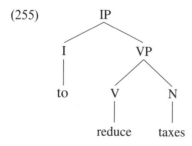

The resulting IP is headed by the I *to*, and the VP *reduce taxes* is the complement of *to*.

What is implicit in our discussion up to this point is the idea that we can build up complex structures by successively merging pairs of categories to form ever larger phrases. For example, by merging the infinitive phrase *to reduce taxes* with the verb *try*, we can form the phrase produced by speaker B in (256):

(256)   SPEAKER A: What will the government do?
         SPEAKER B: *Try to reduce taxes.*

The resulting phrase *try to reduce taxes* is headed by the verb *try*, as we see from the fact that (like a typical verb phrase) it can be used after the infinitive particle *to* in sentences like those in (248) above (see *The government ought to try to reduce taxes*). This being so, the italicised phrase in (256) is a VP which has the structure in (257):

(257)

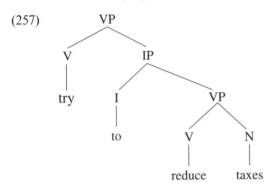

The head of the overall VP is the verb *try*, and its complement is the IP *to reduce taxes*. Now, (257) illustrates the important property of recursion, which we introduced in section 10, when discussing English compounds. Our analysis is claiming that *try to reduce taxes* is a VP which itself contains another VP, *reduce taxes*, and it is easy to see that further applications of merger will yield a larger VP *expect to try to reduce taxes* including the VP in (257). We thus see that this simple operation of merger, as a core operation in the theory of grammar, immediately deals with the fact that English, and any other language, has a potentially *infinite* number of sentences (see the introduction, p. 4).

So far, we have restricted our discussion to the question of how *phrases* are formed. However, as we saw in the previous section, linguists draw a distinction between *phrases* and *clauses*. For example, the reply given by speaker B in (258) below is a clause, containing the subject *they* and the predicate *try*:

(258)   SPEAKER A: What will the government do?
         SPEAKER B: *They will try to reduce taxes.*

An obvious question to ask is how clauses are formed – or, in more concrete terms, what the structure of speaker B's reply is in (258).

Before we attempt to answer this question, we should note that there are interesting similarities between infinitival *to* and auxiliaries like *will/would, shall/should, can/could, may/might,* etc. For example, *to* typically occupies the same position in a clause as an auxiliary like *would* (viz. between the subject *John* and the verb *show* in (259a, b)):

(259)   a. They expected [John *would* show some interest]
         b. They expected [John *to*   show some interest]

Moreover, just as *would* requires after it a verb in the infinitive form (see *would show/*would showing/*would shown*), so too does infinitival *to* (see *to show/*to showing/*to shown*). Furthermore, infinitival *to* behaves like a typical auxiliary (e.g. *should*) but unlike a typical verb (e.g. *want*) in allowing ellipsis (i.e. omission) of its complement:

(260)   a. I don't really want to go to the dentist's, but I know I *should*
         b. I know I should go to the dentist's, but I just don't want *to*
         c. *I know I should go to the dentist's, but I just don't *want*

The fact that *to* patterns like the auxiliary *should* in several respects strengthens the case for regarding them as belonging to the same category. But what category?

Some years ago, Noam Chomsky suggested that the resulting category (comprising finite auxiliaries and infinitival *to*) be labelled **inflection** (abbreviated in earlier work to INFL and more recently to I). The general idea behind this label is that finite auxiliaries inflect for tense/agreement, and infinitival *to* serves much the same function in English as do infinitive inflections in languages like Italian which have overtly inflected infinitives (so that Italian *cantare* is equivalent to English **to** *sing*). We can thus say that both auxiliaries like *should* and the infinitive particle *to* belong to the category I/INFL. The convention we shall adopt from now on is to use INFL/IP in text (as use of I can lead to confusion with the first person nominative pronoun form) and I/IP in trees. Note also that our category AUX from section 9 is now subsumed under INFL.

Having established that auxiliaries like *will* are assigned to the category INFL, let's now return to the question of how clauses like that produced by speaker B in (258) are formed. The simplest assumption (and hence the most desirable theoretically) is to posit that clauses are formed by exactly the same binary (i.e. pairwise) merger operation which leads to the formation of phrases. This being so, we can suggest that the clause *They will try to reduce taxes* is formed by first merging the auxiliary *will* with the verb phrase *try to reduce taxes* to form the expression *will try to reduce taxes*, and then merging this larger expression with the pronoun *they* to form the complete clause *They will try to reduce taxes*.

At first sight, it might seem plausible to claim that the expression *will try to reduce taxes* is an IP, and that when combined with the pronoun *they* it forms a pronoun phrase. But this can't be right, since it would provide us with no obvious way of explaining why it is ungrammatical for speaker B to reply as in (261) below:

(261)   SPEAKER A: What will the government do?
         SPEAKER B: *Will try to reduce taxes.*

If complete phrases can be used to answer questions, and if *will try to reduce taxes* is a complete IP, how come it can't be used to answer A's question in (261)?

The answer which we shall give to this question here is that *will try to reduce taxes* is an *incomplete* phrase. Why? Because auxiliaries require a subject, and the auxiliary *will* doesn't have a subject in (261). More specifically, let's assume that when we merge an auxiliary (i.e. an INFL) with a verb phrase (VP), we form an incomplete inflection phrase which we shall denote as Ī (= I′ = I-bar, in each case pronounced 'eye-bar'); and that only when we merge the relevant INFL with its subject do we form an IP (i.e. a complete inflection phrase). Given these assumptions, the clause *They will try to reduce taxes* will have the structure in (262):

(262)

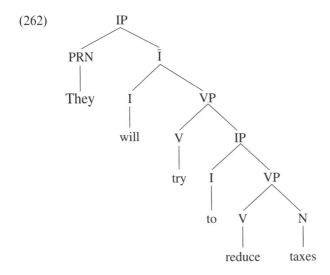

In a structure such as (262), the position occupied by the pronoun (PRN) *they* which serves as the subject of *will* is said to be the **specifier** position within IP. It is important to be clear that *specifier*, like *subject, predicate*, and *complement* is the label of a grammatical *function* and not a grammatical *category*; thus, in (262) the function of specifier is fulfilled by the PRN (a category label) *they*. A specifier precedes the head of the phrase containing it, whereas a complement follows its head: so, the PRN *they* precedes *will* in (262) because it is the specifier (and also subject) of *will*, whereas the VP *try to reduce taxes* follows *will* because it is the complement of *will*; likewise in a determiner phrase (DP) such as *such a pity*, *such* is the specifier of (and so precedes) the head determiner (D) *a*, and *pity* is the complement of (and so follows) *a* – for discussion of DP structures, see section 20; similarly in a prepositional phrase (PP) such as *right inside it*, *right* is the specifier of (and so precedes) the preposition (P) *inside* and *it* is the complement of (and so follows) *inside*.

Tests for constituency

Tree diagrams such as (262) provide a visual representation of what we take to be the syntactic structure of the corresponding sentences: they make specific claims about the operations which form part of grammars. But this raises the question of how we can tell whether the claims made about structure in tree diagrams are correct. One way to deal with this question is to note that there are a number of traditional tests which we can use to determine structure. We shall look at just one of these, relating to the phenomenon of **co-ordination**. English and other languages have a variety of co-ordinating conjunctions like *and*, *but* and *or* which can be used to co-ordinate (that is conjoin or join together) expressions such as those bracketed below (see section 9, p. 153):

(263)   a. [fond of cats] and [afraid of dogs]
         b. [slowly] but [surely]
         c. [to go] or [to stay]

In each of the phrases in (263), a co-ordinating conjunction has been used to conjoin the bracketed pairs of expressions. Clearly, any adequate grammar of English will have to provide a principled answer to the question: 'What kinds of strings (i.e. sequences of words) can and cannot be co-ordinated?'

It turns out that we can't just co-ordinate any random set of strings, as we see by comparing the grammatical reply produced by speaker B in (264) below with the ungrammatical reply in (265):

(264)   SPEAKER A: What did he do?
          SPEAKER B: Run *up the hill* and *up the mountain*.

(265)   SPEAKER A: What did he do?
          SPEAKER B: *Ring *up his mother* and *up his sister*.

Why should it be possible to co-ordinate the string *up the hill* with the string *up the mountain* in (264), but not possible to co-ordinate the string *up his mother* with the string *up his sister* in (265)? We can provide a principled answer to this question in terms of *constituent structure*. More specifically, we can maintain that the string *up the hill* in (264) is a constituent of the phrase *run up the hill* (*up the hill* is a prepositional phrase – a PP, in fact), and so can be co-ordinated with another similar type of phrase (e.g. a PP such as *up the mountain*, or *down the hill*, or *along the path*, etc.). Conversely, however, we can maintain that the string *up his mother* in (265) is not a constituent of the phrase *ring up his mother*, and so cannot be co-ordinated with another similar string (*up* is associated with *ring* in such constructions, and the expression *ring up* forms a complex verb which carries the sense of 'to telephone'). On the basis of contrasts such as these, we can suggest that the *constraint* (i.e. grammatical restriction) in (266) is part of an adequate grammar of English:

(266)   Only *like* constituents can be conjoined; non-constituent strings cannot be conjoined

We are thus supposing that processes for combining words and phrases in native speakers' grammars are constrained by (266), and that (266) comprises part of English native speakers' competence.

Having established (266), we can now make use of it as a way of testing the tree diagram in (262) above. A crucial claim made in (262) is that the strings *reduce taxes*, *to reduce taxes*, *try to reduce taxes*, and *will try to reduce taxes* are all constituents (of various different types). Evidence for the correctness of this claim comes from co-ordination facts in relation to sentences such as those in (267):

(267)   a. They will try to [reduce taxes] and [increase pensions]
          b. They will try [to reduce taxes] and [to cut bureaucracy]
          c. They will [try to reduce taxes] and [attempt to eliminate poverty]
          d. They [will try to reduce taxes] but [may not succeed]

Given the crucial premise (266) that only strings of like constituents can be conjoined, example (267a) provides evidence for analysing *reduce taxes* as a VP, since it can be conjoined with another VP like *increase pensions*. Likewise, (267b) indicates the correctness of analysing *to reduce taxes* as an

IP, since it can be co-ordinated with another IP like *to cut bureaucracy*. Similarly, (267c) shows us that *try to reduce taxes* is a VP, since it can be conjoined with another VP like *attempt to eliminate poverty*. And in much the same way, (267d) tells us that *will try to reduce taxes* is an I-bar because it can be co-ordinated with another I-bar like *may not succeed*. Overall, then, we see that the assumptions about the structure of clauses embodied in tree diagrams like (262) receive independent support from tests like the *co-ordination test* (**exercise 1**).

Constraints on merger: features and checking

Although we've suggested that all phrases and sentences are formed by a simple binary merger operation, it's clear that we can't randomly combine any pair of categories, as examples like the following illustrate:

(268) a. *He* has seen them
       b. **I/* We/* You/*They* has seen them
       c. **Him* has seen them

Given the analysis we are assuming here, a sentence such as (268a) will have the structure in (269):

(269)

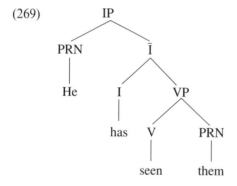

In terms of the structure (269), what the examples in (268) illustrate is that the auxiliary *has* requires a specifier/subject with specific person, number and case properties. The reason why (268b) is ungrammatical is that *has* requires a third person singular specifier (i.e. subject) like *he, she, John, the president*, etc. and doesn't allow any other kind of specifier. Similarly, the reason why (268c) is ungrammatical is that *has* allows only a nominative pronoun like *he* as its specifier, not an objective pronoun such as *him*. Thus, overall, *has* requires a *third person singular nominative* expression as its specifier/subject.

Now consider contrasts such as the following:

(270)   a. He has *seen* them
          b. *He has *seeing* them
          c. *He has *see* them

Examples such as these suggest that the auxiliary *has* allows only a certain type of complement: more specifically, *has* requires a complement headed by the -*n* form of a verb such as *seen*, i.e. the perfect participle form. This requirement is satisfied in (270a), where the complement of *has* is the VP *seen them*, the head verb of which is the perfect participle *seen*. The requirement would equally be satisfied in a simple sentence such as *He has **gone***, where the complement of *has* is not a VP, but rather a simple V *gone* in the perfect participle form. However, the requirement for *has* to have a complement either identical to the -*n* form of a verb or headed by such a form is not satisfied in (270b) where the complement is a VP *seeing them* headed by a verb *seeing* in the progressive -*ing* form, nor in (270c) where the complement of *has* is a VP *see them* headed by a V *see* in the (uninflected) infinitive form.

Now consider the following contrasts:

(271)   a. He has seen them
          b. *He has seen they
          c. *He has seen

What (271a) and (271b) tell us is that the verb *see* allows an objective pronoun like *them* as its complement, but not a nominative pronoun like *they*: verbs which allow an objective pronoun complement are called transitive verbs (see section 9). What the ungrammaticality of (271c) tells us is that *see* requires a complement of an appropriate kind when used in structures like (271c), and so can't be used *without* a complement (though the picture is complicated by the fact that *see* occurs without a complement in other uses – see *I see, I can't see*, etc.).

It is interesting to compare (271a) above with sentences like those in (272):

(272)   a. John has seen the dog
          b. The dog has seen John

If we assume that *has* requires a nominative subject and *see* takes an objective complement, one suggestion which we might make is that noun expressions like *John* and *the dog* can serve both as nominative and as objective expressions, even though they don't overtly inflect for nominative/objective case.

The more general point illustrated by our discussion here is that syntactic structures are projections of lexical items (i.e. words), and so must satisfy the individual properties of the words they contain. Let's suppose that these properties are described in terms of sets of **grammatical features** of various kinds. One set of features which words possess is **head features** (which determine the kinds of head word positions they can occupy, and mark their intrinsic properties); a second type is **specifier features** (which determine the range of specifiers which they do or don't allow); and a third is **complement features** (which determine the range of complements which they can or can't take). So, in a structure such as (269), the head features of *has* include the fact that it is a present tense auxiliary, its specifier features tell us that it requires a third person singular nominative subject, and its complement features indicate that it takes a complement identical with or headed by the *-n* form of a verb. We might suppose that the grammatical features carried by every word in a structure must be **checked**, and that a feature is erased once checked, in much the same way as you cross items off a shopping list after checking that you have bought them. Any grammatical feature which remains unchecked (i.e. which hasn't been erased via checking) results in an ungrammatical sentence. These are the central concepts of **checking theory**, a fundamental component of the human language faculty in Noam Chomsky's recent work (*exercise 2*).

Exercises

1.   Analyse the following sentences, showing how their structure is built up in a pairwise fashion by successive merger operations. Show how the *co-ordination test* can be used to provide evidence in support of the structures you posit.

(a) He was behaving badly
(b) We must talk to her
(c) He may feel sorry for her
(d) She is trying to solve the problem
(e) I would imagine she has forgotten them
(f) They are expecting you to contact them
(g) Ruraville has become the capital of Ruritania
(h) They don't seem keen to approve the plan to cut the budget

Assume that the sentences are derived by first merging the last two words in the sentence to form a larger category, then merging the category thereby formed with the third-from-last word to form an even larger category, then merging this even larger category with the fourth-from-last word, and so on. (It should be noted, however, that while this procedure will work for the sentences in this exercise, it requires modification to handle more complicated sentences.) In addition, assume that *don't* is a single word which belongs to the same category as words like *must*, *might*, etc., and that infinitival *to* sometimes (but not always) has a specifier/subject of its own. Finally, assume that not just auxiliaries and verbs, but also determiners, nouns, prepositions and adjectives can merge with a following complement to form a determiner phrase (DP), noun phrase (NP), prepositional phrase (PP), or adjectival phrase (AP) (so that e.g. when the D *the* merges with the N *budget*, it forms the DP *the budget*).

2.   Draw tree diagrams to represent the structures of the sentences below, and say how the case/agreement features carried by the pronouns, verbs and auxiliaries in the grammatical sentences are checked, and which feature or features remain unchecked (and why) in the ungrammatical sentences.

(a) He was helping us
(b) *He am helping us
(c) *Him was helping we
(d) *He was help us
(e) They may see her
(f) *Them may see she
(g) She has tried to contact them
(h) *She have tried to contact them
(i) *Her has trying to contact they
(j) *She has try to contacting them

20 Empty categories

So far, we have tacitly assumed that syntactic structures are projections of **overt** constituents (i.e. of words, phrases and clauses which have an overt phonetic form). However, as understanding of syntax has deepened, it has been argued that syntactic structures can also contain what are variously referred to as **covert, null** or **empty** constituents – i.e. 'silent' constituents which have no overt phonetic form. In this section, we will introduce a number of different types of empty category along with the arguments for supposing that such categories play a role in the grammar of English. In section 25, we shall see that evidence from a different source, psycholinguistic experiments, points to the importance of empty categories in sentence processing.

Empty INFL

As a first example, consider how we might analyse the following set of examples from African American Vernacular English (AAVE) – see section 16 for discussion of the (ing) variable in this variety in connection with forms such as *playin'*:

(273)   a. I'm playin' baseball
        b. We/You/He/They playin' baseball

Example (273a) contains an overt form of the auxiliary *be* – namely the contracted form *'m*. However, the examples in (273b) contain no overt form of *be*, yet there are good reasons to suppose that they contain a covert/null/empty variant of *are/is* which we will symbolise as φ. If this is so, (273a, b) will have essentially the same structure, viz., (274a, b):

(274)

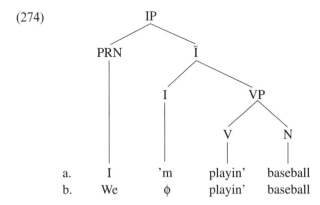

a.   I   'm   playin'   baseball
b.   We   φ   playin'   baseball

Since (274b) is an IP headed by a null variant (φ) of *are,* we can provide a straightforward account of why the subject *we* is nominative (because φ is a variant of the auxiliary *are*, and it is a specifier-feature of auxiliaries like *are* that they require a nominative subject), and of why the complement verb *playin'* is in the *-ing* form (because φ is a variant of *are*, and it is a complement-feature of the auxiliary *are* that it selects a complement headed by a verb in the *-ing* form).

Further evidence that structures like (274b) contain a null auxiliary come from AAVE examples reported by Ralph Fasold such as the following (where *gonna* = *going to*):

(275)   He gonna be there, I know he *is*

In structures like (275), the italicised auxiliary in the second clause (i.e. the clause after the comma) is a copy of that in the first clause in familiar varieties of English. The examples in (276) illustrate this:

(276)   a. You *can* do it, I know you *can/*are/*have*
         b. He *is* trying, I know he *is/*must/*did*
         c. They *will* come, I know they *will/*were/*do*

So, the fact that the auxiliary *is* appears in the second clause in (275) suggests that the first clause contains a null counterpart of *is*.

Although standard varieties of English don't allow the use of a null auxiliary in sentences like (273), there are specific types of constructions in which auxiliaries can be null. In this connection, compare the two sentences in (277):

(277)   a. He *was* laughing and she *was* crying
         b. He *was* laughing and she — crying

The second sentence seems to contain a 'gap' in the position marked —. The auxiliary *was* has been omitted in (277b) to avoid repetition, and we say that it has undergone a particular kind of ellipsis known as **gapping** (for the obvious reason that it leaves a gap in the middle of the sentence), so resulting in the structure in (278) below:

(278)

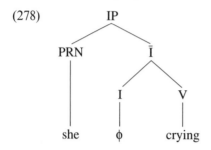

That is, the clause is an IP headed by a null auxiliary φ. If we assume that φ here is a null variant of *was*, we can account for the fact that the subject is *she* (since *was* requires a third person singular nominative subject like *he* or *she*), and the verb *crying* is in the progressive *-ing* form (since *is* requires a complement headed by a verb in this form).

If we extend this reasoning a little further, we can account for sentence pairs such as (279a, b) in a similar fashion:

(279)   a. He didn't enjoy syntax
        b. He enjoyed syntax

Here (279a) is clearly an IP headed by an overt auxiliary (INFL) *didn't* which is a past tense form: using the convention of describing grammatical properties like tense in terms of grammatical features, we can say that the INFL constituent containing *didn't* carries the tense feature [PastTns]. In order to maximise the structural symmetry between (279a) and (279b), we can then propose that whereas (279a) is an IP headed by an overt past tense INFL constituent, (279b) is an IP headed by a covert past tense INFL constituent: this means that (279a, b) have the structures in (280a, b):

(280)   a.   b.

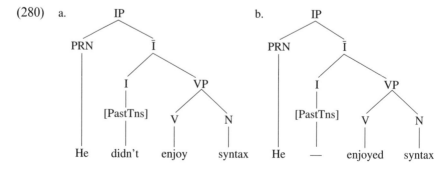

Let's also assume that where INFL contains an auxiliary, the tense feature which INFL carries is realised on the auxiliary in INFL, so that *didn't* carries the past tense ending *-d* in (280a); but where INFL doesn't contain an auxiliary and is unfilled, the tense feature carried by INFL is realised on the head verb of the verb phrase, so that *enjoyed* carries the past tense ending *-d* in (280b). Such an analysis allows us to attain a unitary characterisation of the syntax of clauses, and to posit that all clauses are IPs which comprise a subject expression, an (overt or covert) INFL head which contains a tense feature, and a verb (phrase) complement.

Evidence that auxiliariless finite clauses contain an abstract INFL constituent which carries (present/past) tense properties comes from so-called **tag questions**. Examples of typical tag questions are given in (281) below (where the part of the sentence following the comma is called the **tag**):

(281)   a. He *must* be mad, *mustn't* he?
        b. He *can* speak Swahili, *can't* he?
        c. You *will* help us, *won't* you?
        d. They *might* suspect him, *mightn't* they?
        e. He *could* plead guilty, *couldn't* he?

As examples like these show, the tag in such questions generally contains a (negative) auxiliary which copies grammatical features of the auxiliary which occupies the INFL position in the main clause (both auxiliaries are italicised in 281). So, for example, the main clause in (281a) contains the auxiliary *must* (which is a present tense form expressing necessity), and this is copied in the tag in the negative form *mustn't*. If auxiliaries in tags copy grammatical features carried by the INFL constituent in the main clause, consider how we account for the fact that a sentence like (279b) *He enjoyed syntax* is tagged by (a negative form of) the past-tense auxiliary *did* in (282):

(282)   He enjoyed syntax, *didn't* he?

If we assume, as in (280b) above, that (279b) is an IP headed by an unfilled INFL constituent which contains the tense feature [PastTns], and that INFL in tags contains an overt auxiliary which encodes the features carried by INFL in the main clause, it follows that we should expect the tag to contain a past-tense *dummy* auxiliary like *did* (which encodes only past tense, not modal notions like necessity or possibility) – precisely as we find in (282).

A direct consequence of the IP analysis of clauses is that auxiliaries and verbs occupy different positions within the clause: auxiliaries occupy the head INFL position of IP, whereas verbs occupy the head V position of VP. An interesting way of testing whether this is correct is in relation to the behaviour of items which have the status of auxiliaries in some uses, but of verbs in others.

One such word is *have*. In the kind of use illustrated in (283a) below, *have* is a *perfect auxiliary* (since it takes a complement headed by a verb in the perfect participle *-n* form), whereas in the kind of use illustrated in (283b) it functions as a *causative* verb (because it has a meaning akin to that of the verb *cause*):

(283)   a. He *had* gone to Paris
          b. He *had* a specialist examine the patient

By standard tests of auxiliarihood (see section 9), perfect *have* is an auxiliary, and causative *have* is a verb: e.g. perfect *have* can undergo inversion (*Had he gone to Paris?*), whereas causative *have* cannot (**Had he a specialist examine the patient?*). In terms of the assumptions we are making here, this means that *have* occupies the head INFL position of IP in its perfect use, but the head V position of VP in its causative use.

Evidence in support of this claim comes from facts about cliticisation, a process by which one word attaches itself in a leech-like fashion to another (see section 10). The word *had* can cliticise onto the pronoun *he* in (283a) (forming *he'd*), but not in (283b), as we see from (284a, b):

(284)   a. *He'd* gone to Paris
          b. **He'd* a specialist examine the patient

How can we account for this contrast? If we assume that the perfect *had* in (283a) is an auxiliary which occupies the head INFL position of IP, but that causative *had* in (283b) is a verb occupying the head V position of VP, then prior to cliticisation the two clauses will have the respective (simplified) structures indicated by the labelled bracketings in (285a, b) below (the INFL constituent in 285b is empty and so carries only the tense feature [PastTns]):

(285)   a. [$_{IP}$ He [$_I$ had] [$_{VP}$ [$_V$ gone] to Paris]]
          b. [$_{IP}$ He [$_I$ PastTns] [$_{VP}$ [$_V$ had] a specialist examine the patient]]

If we assume that *have*-cliticisation is possible only when *have* immediately follows the expression to which it cliticises and is blocked by the presence of an intervening constituent, it should be obvious why *had* can cliticise onto *he* in (284a) but not in (284b): *had* is immediately adjacent to *he* in (285a), but separated from *he* by a null INFL constituent, which contains only an abstract syntactic feature, in (285b). A crucial premise of this account is that *have* is positioned in the head INFL of IP in its perfect use, but in the head V of VP in its causative use. So, *have*-cliticisation facts lend support to the claim that all clauses are IPs of the form *subject + INFL + complement*, and that clauses which have no overt INFL constituent contain a covert INFL which carries abstract tense properties (and which can block cliticisation).

In much the same way, we can argue that so-called **bare infinitive clauses** (i.e.

clauses which contain a verb in its uninflected infinitive form, but which lack the overt infinitive particle *to*) contain a covert counterpart of *to*. In this regard, consider the syntax of the bracketed infinitive clauses in (286a, b):

(286)   a. I have never known [you to lie]
         b. I have never known [you lie]

The two bracketed clauses in (286) are infinitive clauses (since in both cases the verb *lie* is in the infinitive form), and each serves as the complement of the verb *known* (so that each of the bracketed clauses is a complement clause). The bracketed complement clause in (286a) is an IP headed by the INFL (infinitive particle) *to*, and has the structure (287a) below. In order to maximise the symmetry between *to* infinitives and bare infinitives, we can analyse the bracketed bare infinitive complement clause in (286b) as an IP headed by a covert infinitive particle (symbolised below as φ) as in (287b):

(287)   a. 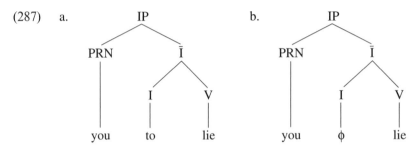   b.

Evidence in support of positing a covert infinitive particle in bare infinitive clauses comes from the fact that *have* cannot cliticise onto *you* in the bracketed bare infinitive clause in (288) below (the % prefix means that this type of structure is found only in some varieties of English):

(288)   a. %I wouldn't let [*you have* done it]
         b. * I wouldn't let [*you've* done it]

Why should cliticisation be blocked here? The answer is that bare infinitive clauses are IPs headed by a null infinitive particle φ, as shown in simplified form in (289):

(289)   I wouldn't let [you φ have done it]

The presence of the intervening null infinitive particle is sufficient to prevent *have* from cliticising onto *you* (a complication is that sentences like (288a) are ungrammatical for some speakers of English who prefer the variant *I wouldn't have let you do it*: the crucial point, however, is that people who find sentences like (288a) grammatical nonetheless find sentences like (288b) ungrammatical).

The overall conclusion to which our discussion leads us is that all clauses are IPs of the form *subject + INFL + complement* (with INFL containing an overt or covert auxiliary or infinitive particle). However, this assumption proves potentially problematic in respect of certain types of infinitive clause which appear at first sight to be subjectless, and consideration of such cases leads us to another type of empty category.

PRO: the empty subject of infinitive clauses

Compare the structure of the bracketed infinitive clauses in (290a, b):

(290)   a. We would like [*you* to stay]
         b. We would like [to stay]

Each of the bracketed infinitive clauses in (290) is an IP headed by the infinitive particle *to*, and each bracketed IP serves as the complement of the verb *like* and so is a complement clause. An apparent difference between the two is that the bracketed infinitive clause in (290a) has an overt subject *you*, whereas its counterpart in (290b) appears to be subjectless. However, we shall argue that apparently subjectless infinitive clauses contain an understood *null* subject. Since the null subject found in infinitive clauses has much the same grammatical properties as pronouns, it is conventionally designated as **PRO**.

Given this assumption, sentence-pairs such as (290a, b) have essentially the same structure, except that the bracketed IP has an overt pronoun *you* as its subject in (290a), but a covert PRO as its subject in (290b). These structures appear as (291a, b) below:

(291)

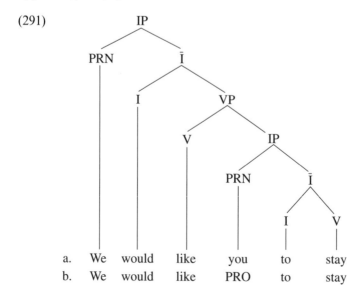

a.	We	would	like	you	to	stay
b.	We	would	like	PRO	to	stay

Introducing the relevant technical term, we can say that the null subject PRO in (291b) is **controlled** by (i.e. refers back to) the subject *we* of the *would* clause, or equivalently that *we* (i.e. the expression which PRO refers back to) is the **controller** or **antecedent** of PRO. Verbs such as *like* which allow an infinitive complement with a PRO subject are said to function (in the relevant use) as **control verbs**.

An obvious question to ask at this juncture is why we should posit that apparently subjectless infinitive complements like that bracketed in (290b) have a null PRO subject. Part of the motivation for positing PRO is semantic in nature. In traditional grammar it is claimed that subjectless infinitive clauses have an *understood* or *implicit* subject – and positing a PRO subject in such clauses is one way of capturing the relevant intuition. The implicit subject becomes explicit if the relevant clauses are paraphrased by a clause containing an auxiliary like *will*, as we see for the paraphrase for (292a) below given in (292b):

(292) a. The president hopes [to be re-elected]
　　　 b. The president hopes [*he* will be re-elected]

The fact that the bracketed clause in (292b) contains an overt (italicised) subject makes it plausible to suppose that the bracketed clause in (292a) has a covert PRO subject.

There is also syntactic evidence in support of claiming that subjectless infinitive clauses have a covert PRO subject. Part of this evidence comes from the syntax of **reflexives** (i.e. *-self/-selves* forms such as *myself/yourself/himself/themselves*, etc.). As examples such as the following indicate, a reflexive generally requires a *local* (i.e. 'nearby') antecedent:

(293) a. They want [*John* to help *himself*]
　　　 b. *They want [John to help *themselves*]

In the case of structures like (293), a *local antecedent* means 'an expression which the reflexive can refer back to within the same (bracketed) clause'. Thus, (293a) is grammatical because it satisfies this *locality requirement*: the antecedent of the reflexive *himself* is the noun *John*, and *John* is contained within the same bracketed *help*-clause as *himself*. By contrast, (293b) is ungrammatical because the reflexive *themselves* does not have a local antecedent (i.e. it does not have any expression it can refer back to within the bracketed clause containing it); its antecedent is the pronoun *they*, and *they* is part of the *want*-clause, not part of the bracketed *help*-clause. In the light of this locality requirement, consider how we account for the grammaticality of the following:

(294) John would like [to prove himself]

Given that a reflexive needs a local antecedent, the reflexive *himself* must have an antecedent within its own (bracketed) clause. This requirement will be satisfied if we assume that the bracketed complement clause has a PRO subject, as in (295):

(295)   John would like [PRO to prove *himself*]

We can then say that *himself* has an antecedent within the bracketed clause containing it, since *himself* refers back to PRO. Because PRO in turn refers back to *John*, this means that *himself* refers to the same person as *John*.

The claim that apparently subjectless infinitive clauses have a null PRO subject enables us to maintain the definition of a clause as a *subject + predicate* structure which we gave earlier. If there were no PRO subject for the bracketed clause in (294), the predicate *prove* would have no subject of its own, and hence it would be impossible to maintain the assumption that every clause contains a subject as well as a predicate.

The overall conclusion to be drawn from our discussion up to now is that clauses are IP structures of the form *subject + INFL + complement*: the subject is an overt or covert pronoun or nominal (i.e. noun-containing) expression, INFL is occupied by an overt or covert auxiliary or infinitive particle, and the complement is a verb or verb phrase. So far, we have not discussed the possibility of complements being covert. We now turn to this.

Covert complements

Just as both INFL and its subject can be covert, so too the complement of INFL can be covert in structures where it undergoes ellipsis. For example, in a dialogue such as (296) below, speaker B's reply is understood as an elliptical form of *He may resign*:

(296)   SPEAKER A: Do you think he will resign?
         SPEAKER B: *He may*.

We might accordingly suggest that the auxiliary *may* has a null complement, and that the sentence *He may* has the structure (297):

(297)

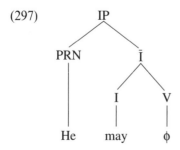

In (297) φ is understood as having the same grammatical and semantic features as *resign*, differing from *resign* only in that it has no phonetic features (and so is 'silent'). If this is so, clauses are always IPs of the form *subject + INFL + complement,* and the subject may be overt or covert, INFL may be overt or covert, and the complement may be overt or covert.

Empty constituents in nominal phrases

The kind of reasoning we have used here to argue that all clauses are IPs can be extended to the analysis of nominal (i.e. noun-containing) expressions. In this connection, consider the italicised nominals in the clauses below:

(298)   a. *The Italians* do love *the opera*
         b. *Italians* do love *opera*

The italicised determinate (i.e. determiner-containing) nominals *the Italians* and *the opera* in (298a) comprise a determiner (D) *the* and a following noun (N) *Italians/opera*, and so can be analysed as **determiner phrases (DPs)**. This means that the overall clause in (298a) will have the structure in (299):

(299)

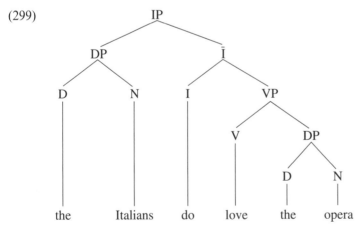

But what of the structure of the indeterminate (i.e. determinerless) nominals *Italians* and *opera* in (298b)? In order to maximise the structural symmetry between determinate and indeterminate nominals, we shall suppose that indeterminate nominals too are DPs, and differ from determinate nominals only in that they are headed by a null determiner (symbolised below as φ). If this is so, the clause in (298b) will have the structure (300):

(300)

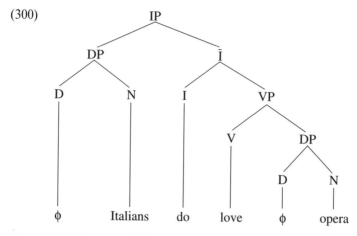

Thus, (298b) has essentially the same structure as (298a), except that the head D positions of the DPs are filled by the overt determiner *the* in (298a) but by the covert determiner φ in (298b).

There is evidence to support the postulation of covert determiners which goes beyond a desire to maximise structural symmetry. If English does indeed have such a determiner, we'd expect it to have much the same semantic properties as overt determiners (e.g. quantifying determiners such as *all* or *some*). In this connection, consider the interpretation of the italicised indeterminate nominals in sentences such as (301) and (302):

(301)   a. *Eggs* are fattening
          b. *Bacon* is fattening

(302)   a. I had *eggs* for breakfast
          b. I had *bacon* for breakfast

The nouns *eggs* and *bacon* in (301a, b) have a **generic** interpretation, and hence are interpreted as meaning 'eggs/bacon in general'. By contrast, in (302a, b) they have a **partitive** interpretation, roughly paraphrasable as '*some* eggs/bacon'. If we say that indeterminate nominals are DPs headed by a null generic/partitive determiner φ, we can say that the semantic properties of φ determine that bare nominals will be interpreted as generically or partitively quantified.

Moreover, just like some overt determiners, the null determiner φ can be used to quantify only specific types of nominal expression. For example, as indicated by (303), the overt determiner *enough* can be used to quantify a non-count noun like *machinery* or a plural count noun like *machines*, but not a singular count noun like *machine*:

(303)   We don't have [*enough* machinery/machines/*machine]

(*Machine* is a **count noun** in that we can say *one machine* and *two machines*; but *machinery* is a non-count noun in that we can't say **one machinery* or **two machineries*.) We can therefore say that *enough* can only be used to quantify a *non-individual* noun expression (i.e. an expression headed by a noun which is not a singular count noun). Significantly, the hypothesised null determiner φ has precisely the same quantificational properties as *enough*, and can be used to quantify a non-count noun like *machinery* or a plural count noun like *machines*, but not a singular count noun like *machine*, as we see from (304):

(304)   Never trust [φ machinery/machines/*machine]

The fact that the covert determiner φ has the same quantificational properties as overt determiners such as *enough* increases the plausibility of a null determiner analysis for indeterminate nominals.

If we conclude that nominal expressions are DPs headed by an overt or covert D, an obvious question to ask is how we deal with so-called 'pronouns'. In this connection, compare the italicised expressions in (305a, b) below:

(305)   a. *We Yanks* do envy *you Brits*
          b. *We* do envy *you*

The expressions *we Yanks* and *you Brits* in (305a) can plausibly be analysed as DPs comprising a D (*we/you*) and a noun complement (*Yanks/Brits*). Thus, (305a) will have the structure (306):

(306)

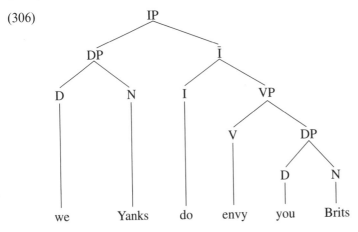

But what is the structure of (305b)?

In (306) in structures such as *we Yanks* and *you Brits*, the pronouns *we* and *you* function as determiners which take nouns (*Yanks* and *Brits*) as their complements. Simple pronouns like *we* and *you* in (305b) are therefore ana-lysed as determiners used without any noun complement. Thus, our earlier category PRN is systematically subsumed under D. With this analysis, (305b) has the structure (307):

(307)

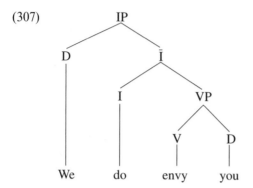

The analysis in (307) enables us to provide a unitary account of the syntax of nominal and pronominal expressions, and to hypothesise that they are all pro-jections of a head determiner constituent. In structures such as (306), the determiner *we* is used *prenominally* (with a following noun as its complement), whereas in structures such as (307) it is used *pronominally* (i.e. on its own without any following noun complement). The determiner analysis of pro-nouns also provides us with a straightforward account of the fact that most determiners can be used either prenominally (*these books are exciting, each child has a desk*) or pronominally (*these are good, each has a desk*).

Another advantage of the determiner analysis of pronouns is that it might help us to understand why two-year-old children sometimes produce struc-tures such as that observed by David McNeill in (308):

(308)   Get it ladder!

Suppose the child producing (308) analyses *it* as a determiner, and wrongly assumes that (like most determiners) it can be used not only pronominally, but also prenominally; this would mean that *it ladder* in (308) is a DP for such a child with the structure in (309):

(309)

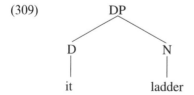

The analysis in (309) assumes that the child uses the definite pronoun *it* in (308) in much the same way as an adult would use the definite prenominal determiner *the*.

However, the analysis in (309) raises the interesting question of why *it* can be used pronominally but not prenominally in adult English, and conversely why *the* can be used prenominally but not pronominally – in other words, how we should account for the contrasts in (310):

(310)   a. I walked under *the ladder*   b. *I walked under *it ladder*
        c. I walked under *it*   d. *I walked under *the*

The answer lies in the specific *complement features* of individual words. More precisely, let us say that it is a complement feature of most determiners that they can be used with or without a following noun (or noun phrase) complement: however, a determiner like *the* has the complement feature that it requires a complement headed by a noun; and conversely, a determiner like *it* has the complement feature that it doesn't allow a complement of any kind. Then, given the notion of feature checking mentioned at the end of section 19, the ill-formedness of (310b, d) will follow because complement features of *it* and *the* are not checked in these structures.

The assumption that pronouns are determiners leads us towards the goal of attaining a unitary characterisation of the syntax of nominal and pronominal expressions as projections of a head determiner constituent: determinate nominals are DPs headed by an overt determiner; indeterminate nominals are DPs headed by a null determiner; pronouns are determiners used without a complement (and, by extension, the null pronoun *PRO* is also a null determiner used without a complement). We can then conclude that all nominal and pronominal expressions are projections of an (overt or covert) D constituent, and so we arrive at a uniform characterisation of nominals as **D-projections** (in much the same way as we earlier analysed all clauses as **I-projections**).

The general approach which we have adopted here should now be clear. We assume that our theory of grammar (UG) provides us with a 'template' for the structure of particular types of expression. So, clauses are universally I-projections, and (pro)nominals are universally D-projections. Clauses which appear to lack an INFL constituent have a *covert* INFL; nominals which appear to lack a D-constituent have a *covert* D. As will become clearer as our exposition unfolds, *empty categories* play a central role in the theory of syntax which we are outlining here (*exercises 1 and 2*).

Exercises

1.   Below are a number of tree diagrams representing the structures of a variety of different sentences. For each of the five numbered positions in each structure, say what kinds of item (overt or covert) can occupy the position, and what determines the choice of item occupying each position.

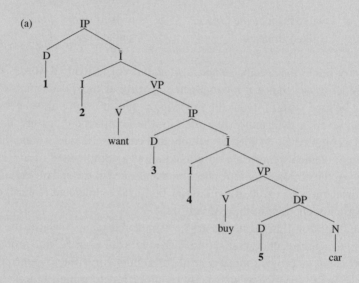

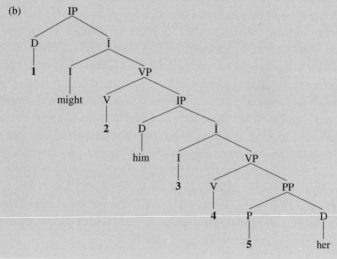

(c)

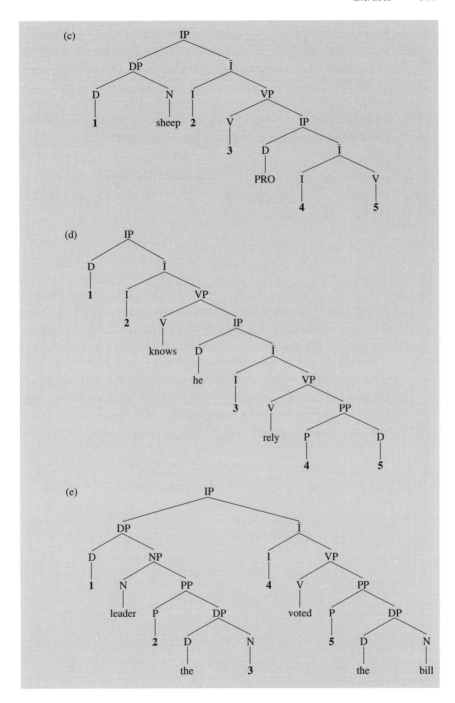

(d)

(e)

Bear in mind that in many cases, a given position can be occupied by a wide range of different elements, though the choice of element in one position may be dependent on the choice of element in another position.

2.   Discuss the syntax of the following sentences, drawing a separate tree diagram to represent the structure of each sentence:

(a) He had decided to protect himself
(b) He had them repair the car
(c) He may let you have a boat
(d) We students hate exams
(e) He promised to behave
(f) He wants to try to help others
(g) They made plans to grow bananas
(h) People know power corrupts politicians

Assume (as in the text) that all clauses are I-projections (and comprise an overt or covert subject, an INFL constituent containing an overt or covert auxiliary or infinitive particle, and a complement comprising a verb or verb phrase); likewise, assume that all nominals are D-projections (i.e. overt pronouns like *him*, reflexive pronouns like *himself* and the covert pronoun *PRO* are D-constituents, and nominal expressions are DPs comprising an overt or covert determiner followed by a noun or noun phrase complement).

21 Movement

Hitherto, we have assumed that all clauses are IP constituents of the form *subject + INFL + complement*, and that each of these three constituents can be either overt or covert. However, a potential complication for this analysis is posed by the fact that many clauses are introduced by functional elements such as *that* (e.g. *He admitted **that** he stole it*), *for* (e.g. *She's keen **for** you to go*) or *if* (e.g. *I doubt **if** he understands*): these are known as **complementisers** (see section 9) and are referred to by the label **COMP** in earlier work and **C** in more recent analyses. This is because they are typically used to introduce a complement clause. In this connection, consider speaker B's reply in (311):

(311)   SPEAKER A: What did he want to know?
          SPEAKER B: *If the president was lying.*

Given what we have said so far, we can assume that the auxiliary (INFL) *was* merges with the verb *lying* to form the I-bar *was lying*; and the resulting I-bar in turn merges with the DP *the president* to form the IP *the president was lying*. But where does the complementiser (C) *if* fit into the sentence? The answer we propose is that C merges with the IP *the president was lying* to form the complementiser phrase (CP) structure in (312):

(312)

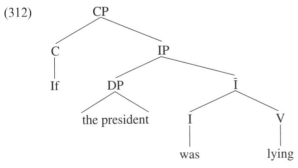

(Note that (312) does not provide details of the internal structure of the DP *the president*, since these are irrelevant to the point under discussion.)

Given the analysis in (312), the overall clause has the status of a CP which comprises a head C *if* and an IP complement *the president was lying*. Having extended our framework in this way, so as to acknowledge that some clauses are CPs, we are now in a position to introduce our second core syntactic operation (the first being merger). This is **movement**, and there are several types.

Head movement

Let's begin by comparing the clause *If the president was lying* produced by speaker B in (311) above with the question used by speaker B in (313):

(313)   SPEAKER A: What's the question that everyone's asking?
         SPEAKER B: Was the president lying?

In the question in (313), the auxiliary *was* is traditionally said to have been *inverted* with respect to the subject *the president*. What this means is that although auxiliaries are normally positioned after subjects (e.g. in statements such as *The president was lying*, where the auxiliary *was* is positioned after the subject *the president*), in questions like that in (313) an auxiliary can undergo inversion and *move* into some position in front of the subject. But what position does an inverted auxiliary move into?

Since the inverted auxiliary *was* appears to occupy the same presubject position in B's utterance in (313) that the complementiser *if* occupies in (312), a natural suggestion to make is that the inverted auxiliary actually moves into the head C position of CP. If this is so, we'd expect to find that an inverted auxiliary and a complementiser are mutually exclusive (on the assumption that only one word can occupy a given head word position like C): in other words, if both complementisers and inverted auxiliaries occupy the head C position of CP, we'd expect to find that a clause can be introduced by *either* a complementiser *or* an inverted auxiliary, but not by the two together. In the event, this prediction turns out to be entirely correct, as we see from the ungrammaticality of speaker B's reply in (314):

(314)   SPEAKER A: What did the journalist from the *Daily Dirge* ask you?
         SPEAKER B: *If was the president lying.

The fact that no clause can contain both a complementiser and an inverted auxiliary provides us with strong evidence that inverted auxiliaries occupy the same structural position as complementisers – i.e. that both occupy the head C position in CP.

But how can it be that an auxiliary like *was* (which normally occupies the head INFL position within IP) comes to be positioned in the head C position of CP? The answer is that auxiliaries move out of their normal postsubject position into presubject position in structures like (313), by an operation often referred to as *inversion*. In terms of the framework being used here, this means that an inverted auxiliary moves from the head INFL position in IP into the head C position in CP, in the manner indicated by the dotted line in (315):

(315)

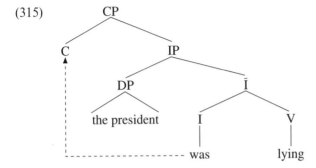

This type of inversion operation involves movement of a word from the head position in one phrase into the head position in another phrase (in this case, from the head INFL position of IP into the head C position of CP), and so is known as **head movement**.

An important question raised by the I-to-C movement analysis of inversion is what happens to the head INFL position of IP once it is vacated by movement of the inverted auxiliary into C. What has been argued in work since the 1970s is that when a constituent moves from one position in a structure to another, the position out of which it moves remains intact, and is filled by an empty category; more specifically, a moved expression leaves behind an empty **trace** of itself in the position out of which it moves (the romantics among you can think of traces as being rather like the footprints you leave behind in the sand when walking on the beach in Mallorca or Malibu). If we use the conventional symbol *t* to denote the trace of a moved constituent, a sentence such as *Was the president lying?* will have the structure in (316):

(316)

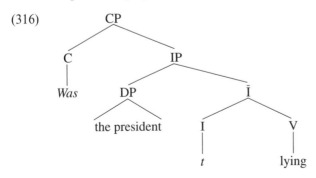

In (316), the head INFL position of IP is occupied by the trace *t* of the moved auxiliary *was*. The trace serves as a way of indicating that the INFL position 'belongs to' (i.e. was formerly occupied by) *was*, and so cannot be filled by another auxiliary (e.g. we can't insert *is* in INFL in (316), as we see from the ungrammaticality of *Was the president is lying?*). There are also other considerations in support of positing a trace of *was* occupying INFL.

From a purely theoretical perspective, we have supposed up to now that all phrases and clauses are projections of a head word category. If we are to retain this principle, IP in (316) must be headed by an INFL constituent: and if there is no overt INFL constituent in (316), there must be a covert one. The trace of the moved auxiliary fulfils this requirement.

There is also interesting *developmental* evidence in support of the claim that auxiliaries leave behind traces when they undergo inversion. Two-year-old children often produce *auxiliary copying* structures such as the following (produced by a boy Sam at age 2;9, whose father, Ian Crookston, kindly provided the data):

(317)   a. *Did* the kitchen light *did* flash?
         b. *Can* its wheels *can* spin?
         c. *Is* the steam *is* hot?
         d. *Was* that *was* Anna?

What is going on here? The answer appears to be that when Sam inverts the relevant auxiliary and thereby moves it from INFL to C, he leaves behind an *overt* trace of the auxiliary in INFL (in the form of a *copy* of the moved auxiliary), so that the auxiliary appears in both INFL and C. This means that a sentence like (317a) is derived in the manner indicated in (318) in Sam's early grammar:

(318)

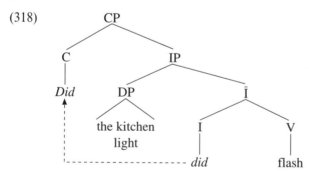

If this analysis is correct, child sentences such as (317) (which have also been reported from other children) lend plausibility to the claim that moved constituents leave behind traces in the positions out of which they move. The difference between Sam's grammar and that of an adult is that traces left behind by auxiliary inversion are *overt* in Sam's grammar, but are *covert* (i.e. 'silent') in adult grammars of English.

In addition to evidence from child grammars, there is also evidence from adult grammars for claiming that a moved auxiliary leaves behind a silent trace. Part of this evidence comes from facts about cliticisation. In this connection, note that *have* can cliticise to *they* in sentences such as (319) below, but not in (320):

(319)　　a. *They have* gone
　　　　　b. *They've* gone

(320)　　a. Will *they have* gone?
　　　　　b. *Will *they've* gone?

Why should cliticisation of *have* onto *they* be possible in (319) but not in (320)? We can give a straightforward answer to this question if we suppose that inversion of *will* in (320) leaves a trace behind in the position out of which *will* moves, i.e. in the position marked by *t* in (321):

(321)　　*Will* they *t* have gone?

We can then say that the presence of the intervening trace *t* prevents *have* from cliticising onto *they* in inversion structures such as (321).

Operator movement

So far, we have implicitly assumed that CP comprises a head C constituent (which is filled by a complementiser in some structures and by a preposed auxiliary in others) and an IP complement. However, one question which such an analysis raises is where the bold-printed pre-auxiliary constituents are positioned in structures such as (322):

(322)　　a. **What languages** *can* you speak?
　　　　　b. **No other colleague** *would* I trust

Each of the sentences in (322) contains an italicised inverted auxiliary (*can/would*) occupying the head C position of CP, preceded by a bold-printed phrase of some kind (viz. *what languages/no other colleague*). Each of the pre-auxiliary phrases contains a word which is sometimes classed as an **operator**: thus, *what* is an *interrogative operator* (or *wh-operator*) and *no* is a *negative operator*. Expressions containing such operators are called *operator expressions*.

It seems clear that each of the operator expressions in (322), despite its position, functions as the *complement* of the verb at the end of the sentence. One piece of evidence leading to this conclusion is the fact that each of the examples in (322) has a paraphrase in which the operator expression occupies the canonical (i.e. typical) complement position after the relevant verb:

(323)   a. You can speak *what languages?*
        b. I would trust *no other colleague*

Structures like (323a) are sometimes referred to as *wh-in-situ* questions, since the wh-operator expression *what languages* does not get preposed, but rather remains *in situ* (i.e. 'in place') in the canonical position associated with its grammatical function as complement of *speak*. Structures such as these are used primarily as *echo questions*, to echo and question something previously said by someone else (e.g. if a friend boasts 'I just met Lord Lickspittle', you could reply – with an air of incredulity – 'You just met *who?*'). Sentences such as those in (323) make it plausible to suppose that the operator phrases in (322) originate as complements of the relevant verbs, and subsequently get *moved* to the front of the overall sentence. But what position do they get moved into?

The answer is obviously that they are moved into some position preceding the inverted auxiliary. Now, if inverted auxiliaries occupy the head C position in CP, we might suppose that preposed operator phrases are moved into some prehead position within CP. Given that *specifiers* are typically positioned before heads, an obvious suggestion to make is that preposed operator phrases occupy *the specifier position within CP* (abbreviated to *spec-CP*). If this is the case, then the sentences in (322) will be derived as in (324):

(324)

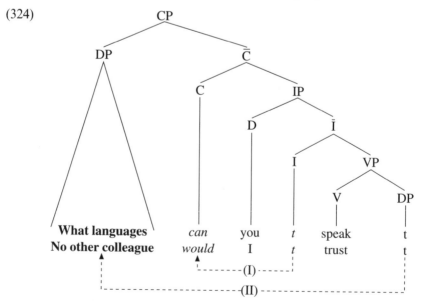

(We have assumed in (324) that *what* and *no* are both determiners of some kind, and hence that the phrases *what languages* and *no other colleagues* are DPs.) Two different kinds of movement (indicated by the dotted lines) are involved in (324): movement (I) is movement of a *head* (the italicised auxiliary *can/would*) from INFL to C, and, as already discussed, this type of movement operation is referred to as head movement; movement (II) involves movement of an operator expression into the specifier position within CP, and this very different kind of movement operation is known as **operator movement**.

An assumption made in the analysis of operator movement in structures like (324) is that just as a moved head (e.g. an inverted auxiliary) leaves behind a trace in the position out of which it moves, so too a moved operator expression leaves behind a trace at its *extraction site* (i.e. the position out of which it is extracted or moved). The bold trace (**t**) in (324) makes this explicit: it serves to mark that the DP position containing the trace 'belongs to' (i.e. was formerly occupied by) the preposed complement, and so cannot be filled by any other constituent (hence the ungrammaticality of e.g. **What languages can you speak any Italian?*, where the DP *any Italian* illicitly occupies the DP position which belongs to the trace). Evidence in support of traces again comes from facts about *have* cliticisation. The form *have* of the perfect auxiliary has the clitic variant *'ve* and can cliticise to an immediately preceding word which ends in a vowel or diphthong. Significantly, however, cliticisation is not possible in sentences such as (325a) below, as we see from the fact that the sequence *say have* cannot contract to *say've* in (325b) (and so isn't pronounced in the same way as *save*):

(325)   a. Which students would you *say have* got most out of the course?
        b. *Which students would you *say've* got most out of the course?

What prevents *have* from cliticising onto *say* here? Let's assume that prior to being moved to the front of the sentence by operator movement, the operator phrase *which students* is the subject of *have*, as in the echo question counterpart to (325a) in (326):

(326)   You would say *which students* have got most out of the course?

If we also assume that when the phrase *which students* is fronted, it leaves behind a trace in the position out of which it moves, then the structure of (325a) will be (327):

(327)   *Which students* would you say *t* have got most out of the course?

This being so, we can account for why *have* cannot cliticise onto *say*: it is not immediately adjacent to it, the two words being separated by the intervening trace – hence the ungrammaticality of (325b).

An interesting extension of our analysis of the syntax of operators is suggested by complement clause questions such as that bracketed in (328):

(328)   I'm not sure [which senators the president has spoken to]

The bracketed interrogative (i.e. question-asking) clause in (328) is a complement clause since it serves as the complement of *sure*. In (328), the operator expression *which senators* clearly originates as the complement of the preposition *to* (as we see from echo questions such as *The president has spoken to **which senators**?*). But where does it move to? So far we have assumed that wh-operator expressions move into the specifier position within CP, to the left of C. But how can this be the case in (328), since the bracketed complement clause contains no overt C constituent. A natural answer to give to this question within a theory which posits that specific positions in a structure can be occupied by empty categories is to suppose that the head C position in the bracketed CP in (328) is filled by a covert complementiser φ, so that the bracketed clause in (328) is a CP derived as in (329):

(329)

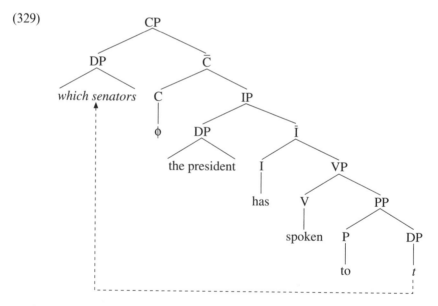

There are a number of reasons for suggesting that the bracketed complement clause in (329) contains a covert complementiser. One is that this enables us to maintain a unitary characterisation of operator movement as involving the movement of an operator expression into a specifier position to the left of an (overt or covert) C constituent. Another is that such an analysis provides a straightforward account of why auxiliary inversion is not permitted in complement clause questions in (standard varieties of) English, as we see from the ungrammaticality of (330):

(330)   *I'm not sure [which senators has the president spoken to]

Recall that in relation to the ungrammaticality of speaker B's utterance in (314) above, we suggested that the presence of an overt complementiser like *if* blocks auxiliary inversion: it seems a natural extension of this idea to suppose that the presence of the covert complementiser ɸ also prevents an auxiliary from moving from INFL to C. A third reason is that, as observed by Alison Henry for a variety of English spoken in Belfast, we can find complement clause questions which contain an overt complementiser, as in (331):

(331)   %I'm not sure [which senators *that* the president has spoken to]

(Recall that the % sign in front of the sentence indicates that the sentence is grammatical in only some varieties of English.) Since it is clear that in structures such as (331) the operator expression *which senators* is positioned to the left of the italicised complementiser *that*, it is reasonable to suppose that in structures like (328) *which senators* is positioned to the left of a covert complementiser ɸ.

An interesting question to ask at this stage is *why* wh-operators should be moved to the front of the relevant interrogative clause in wh-questions. We can put this question rather differently by asking 'What is it that makes us interpret the bracketed clause in (331) as a question?' The answer clearly isn't the choice of complementiser heading the clause, since *that* isn't interrogative (hence the *that*-clause in *I didn't know **that he was cheating*** can't be interpreted as a question in Belfast English). So, it would seem that it is the presence of the interrogative phrase *which senators* in the specifier position of CP which ensures that the bracketed clause is interpreted as interrogative. Generalising, we can hypothesise that a clause is interpreted as a question in English if it has an interrogative specifier. We can then say that the wh-operator expression *which senators* in (329) moves into spec-CP in order to ensure that the clause containing it has an interrogative specifier, and so is interpreted as a question.

But why should it be that in questions containing more than one wh-operator such as (332) below, only one wh-operator can be preposed, not more than one?

(332)   a. **Who** do you think will say *what*?
         b. **What* **who** do you think will say?

The sentence in (332a) is derived as in (333):

(333)

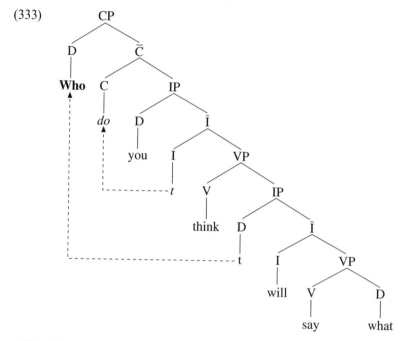

We will incorporate into our theory of grammar an **economy principle** along the lines of (334):

(334)   **economy principle**
Minimise grammatical structure and movement operations (i.e. posit as little structure as possible, and move as few constituents as possible the shortest distance possible)

Obviously, (334) is consistent with general scientific guidelines which require us to always seek the simplest and most elegant theory which is consistent with the data we need to explain. Now, if a clause is to be interpreted as a question, it requires an interrogative specifier in Spec-CP. It does not require *more than one* such interrogative specifier, and it follows from (334) that we can prepose only one of the two interrogative operators (*who* and *what*) in (333) in order to satisfy the requirement for CP to have an interrogative specifier: preposing both would be superfluous (in that it would involve two applications of operator movement rather than one), and hence is ruled out by the economy principle. Furthermore, (334) requires that it is the nearest wh-operator expression which moves to spec-CP in a multiple wh-question (because (334) favours shorter movements over longer ones). Thus, we can account for why it is *who* and not *what* that moves to spec-CP in (333). It is clear from the schematic structures in (335) that *what* must move further than *who* to get to the spec-CP position:

(335)   a.   Who do you think t will say what?

b.   *What do you think who will say t?

Yes–no questions

The assumption that questions are CPs which contain an interrogative specifier runs into apparent problems in relation to *yes–no questions* such as (336):

(336)   Are you having any problems?

Even though (336) is obviously a question, it doesn't seem to contain an interrogative specifier of any kind. So, it would appear that our existing analysis wrongly predicts that sentences such as (336) can't be interpreted as questions. How can we overcome this problem?

One answer to this question suggested by Jane Grimshaw and Ian Roberts in independent research is to suppose that in yes–no questions, the specifier position within CP is filled by a covert yes–no question operator, which we might symbolise as **?** (since the question-mark *?* is the conventional way of marking a sentence as interrogative). If we take *?* to be an adverb of some kind, this would mean that (336) has the derivation in (337):

(337)

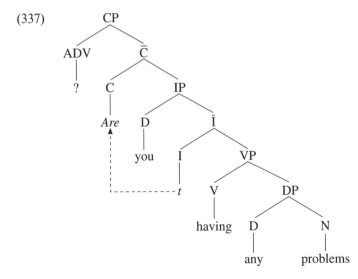

We can then say that the overall structure is interpreted as a question by virtue of the fact that it contains the covert interrogative operator *?* in spec-CP. In this case, the operator has not moved to this position from elsewhere in the structure; rather, it appears here as a result of our earlier operation of merger (more specifically, by being merged with the following C-bar).

The suggestion that yes–no questions contain an abstract question operator is by no means as implausible at it might at first sight seem. It is noteworthy that yes–no questions in Shakespearean English could be introduced by the overt question operator *whether*, as in (338):

(338)   *Whether* had you rather lead mine eyes or eye your master's heels?
(Mrs Page, *Merry Wives of Windsor*, III. ii)

It seems likely that *whether* occupies spec-CP in (338). If we assume that yes–no questions in present-day English contain a covert counterpart of *whether* in spec-CP, we can argue that questions in present-day English have essentially the same structure as their counterparts in Shakespearean English, the only difference between the two varieties lying in whether the question operator they contain is overt or covert.

A further piece of evidence in support of positing a null interrogative operator in yes–no questions in present-day English comes from facts relating to a class of expressions generally known as **polarity items** (because they seem to have an inherent negative/interrogative polarity). As we see from examples like (339) below, the quantifying determiner *any* (in *partitive* uses where it means more or less the same as *some*) is generally restricted to occurring after a negative or interrogative expression:

(339)   a. *Nobody* has any money
         b. *How* can any progress be made?
         c. *He has any money
         d. *Any progress can't be made

However, as we see from sentences such as (336) above, the polarity item *any* can occur in yes–no questions. How come? If we suppose that (336) has the derivation (337) and contains the null question operator *?* in spec-CP, we can immediately account for the grammaticality of (336) by observing that *any* occurs after the covert interrogative operator *?* in this structure. Thus, our generalisation about the distribution of the polarity item *any* is preserved.

We can extend the null-operator analysis to complement clause yes–no questions introduced by *if*, such as that bracketed in (340):

(340)   I asked [if he was having any problems]

It will then be the case that the bracketed clause in (340) is a CP which has the partial structure in (341) below (simplified by not showing the structure of the IP complement of *if*):

(341)

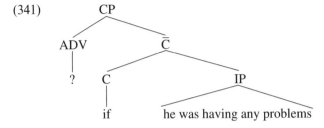

We can then say that the interrogative operator *?* licenses (i.e. allows us to have) the polarity item *any* which is contained in the following IP.

From a theoretical perspective, the main advantage of the null-operator analysis of yes–no questions is that it enables us to attain a unitary analysis of the syntax of questions (as clauses which contain an overt or covert interrogative specifier), and a unitary analysis of polarity items (as items restricted to occurring after a negative or interrogative operator).

Other types of movement

Having discussed the syntax of head movement and operator movement at some length, we now turn to briefly consider two further types of movement operation. One is found in the so-called **passive** construction. Traditional grammarians maintain that the italicised verb in a sentence such as (342a) is in an *active* form, whereas the italicised verb in the corresponding (b) sentence is in the *passive* form (see section 9):

(342)   a. The thieves *stole* the jewels
         b. The jewels were *stolen* (by the thieves)

There are four main properties which distinguish passive sentences from their active counterparts. One is that passive (though not active) sentences generally contain some form of the auxiliary *be* – see *were* in (342b). Another is that the verb in passive sentences is in the *-n* participle form (see *stolen*), known in this use as the *passive participle* form. A third is that passive sentences may (though need not) include a *by*-phrase which contains an expression which seems to have much the same role as that of the subject in the corresponding active sentence: for example, *the thieves* in the active structure (342a) serves as the subject of *stole the jewels*, whereas in the passive structure (342b) it serves as the complement of the preposition *by* (though in both cases it seems to have the semantic role of *agent* – i.e. the person perpetrating the relevant act). The fourth difference is that the expression which serves as the *complement* of the active verb surfaces as the *subject* in the corresponding passive construction: for example, *the jewels* is the complement of *stole* in the active sentence (342a), but is the subject of *were stolen by the thieves* in the passive structure (342b). Here, we focus on this fourth difference (setting the other three aside).

It has often been claimed that passive subjects 'originate' as the complements of their verbs. Alternations such as those in (343) below suggest that this is a plausible assumption:

(343)   a. *The names of the directors* are listed below
         b. Below are listed *the names of the directors*

In (343a), the italicised passive subject occupies the typical pre-auxiliary subject position, preceding *are*. But in the curious construction in (343b), the italicised expression is positioned after the verb *listed*, suggesting that it does indeed originate as the complement of this verb.

But if the subject of a passive clause originates as the complement of the relevant passive participle, how does it get from complement position into subject position? In the framework we are developing here, it is proposed that passive subjects are *moved* from complement position within VP into subject/specifier position within IP. Given this proposal, a sentence such as (342b) will be derived as in (344):

(344)

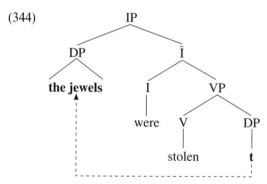

The analysis in (344) claims that the DP *the jewels* originates as the complement of the verb *stolen* and is then moved into spec-IP (i.e. the specifier position within IP) to become the subject (and specifier) of the passive auxiliary *were*. The type of movement operation indicated in (344) is traditionally referred to as **passivisation**: however, because the passivised DP moves from complement position to subject position (hence from one argument position to another, see section 18 for the notion of argument), this type of movement operation is referred to more generally as **A-movement** (an abbreviation for **argument movement**).

The final type of movement operation we shall look at here can be illustrated by sentences such as the following:

(345)   You must realise [that *this kind of behaviour* no teacher can tolerate]

Here, the italicised DP *this kind of behaviour* appears to function as the complement of *tolerate*, and we might therefore suppose that it originates in postverbal position (see *You must realise that no teacher can tolerate **this kind of behaviour***). It is then *topicalised* (i.e. made into the topic of the bracketed *that*-clause) by being moved into a more prominent position at the front of the clause. But where exactly is the italicised phrase moved to? Clearly, it is moved to a position somewhere between the complementiser *that* and the following IP which begins with *no teacher*. The analysis of this kind of structure we adopt here maintains that the topicalised expression undergoes an operation known as **adjunction** by which it is adjoined (i.e. attached) to the left of IP, and that it leaves a trace behind in the position out of which it moves, so that the *that*-clause in (345) is derived as in (346):

(346)

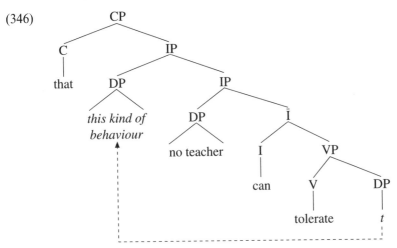

Adjunction is an operation whereby a given type of category is expanded into a larger category of the same type by the addition of another expression. In the case of (346), the original IP *no teacher can tolerate this kind of behaviour* is expanded into the larger IP *this kind of behaviour no teacher can tolerate t* by moving the DP *this kind of behaviour* and adjoining it to the left of the original IP, leaving behind a trace as the complement of *tolerate*.

Our discussion of the movement operations *head movement, operator movement, A-movement/passivisation* and *adjunction* has interesting implications for the overall organisation of a grammar. It means that the **derivation** of a structure (i.e. the way in which a given structure is formed) involves not only a series of *merger* operations combining pairs of categories together to form larger and larger phrases and clauses, but may also involve one or more *movement* operations, moving words or phrases from one position in a structure to another. We shall say a little more about the general structure of a grammar from the perspective we are adopting in section 23 (***exercises 1 and 2***).

Exercises

1.   Discuss the syntax of the following sentences, drawing a separate tree diagram to represent the structure of each of them (using arrows to show what has moved from where to where):

(i)   a. No-one could do anything
       b. Nothing could anyone do
(ii)   a. What can anyone do?
       b. Can anyone do anything?
(iii) a. What did you say had happened to who?
       b. *Who did you say what had happened to?
(iv)   a. Aren't I losing any weight?
       b. *I aren't losing any weight
(v)   a. What you doing? (colloquial English)
       b. You doing anything? (colloquial English)
(vi)   a. Nobody was arrested
       b. Was anyone arrested?
(vii) a. The neofascists, I wouldn't want to win the election
       b. *The neofascists, I wouldn't wanna win the election

For the purposes of this exercise, make the following set of assumptions about the above sentences. The clauses containing an inverted auxiliary (i.e. an auxiliary positioned in front of its subject) are CPs, but the other types of clause are IPs. The words *no-one, nothing, anyone* and *anything* are pronominal determiners, and so belong to the category D. Some auxiliaries have a null variant ϕ in colloquial English. Some auxiliary forms are inherently interrogative and have to move to the head C position of an interrogative CP. The inherently negative forms *aren't* and *wouldn't* are single-word auxiliaries which originate in the head INFL position of IP. The form *wanna* results from cliticisation of *to* onto *want* (forming *wanta* which in colloquial speech can become *wanna*); cliticisation is blocked by an intervening constituent or its trace.

2.   In one variety of Belfast English described by Alison Henry we find complement-clause questions such as those italicised below:

(a) I don't know *which exams that he has failed*
(b) I don't know *which exams has he failed*
(c) *I don't know *which exams that has he failed*
(d) I don't know *which exams he has failed*
(e) They didn't know *if he had failed the exam*
(f) *They didn't know *if that he had failed the exam*
(g) *They didn't know *if had he failed the exam*
(h) They didn't know *had he failed the exam*

By contrast, in standard varieties of English only sentences like (d) and (e) are grammatical. Discuss the syntax of the italicised complement clauses, drawing a separate tree diagram to represent the structure of each of them. Try to pinpoint key differences between Belfast English and Standard English. For the purposes of the exercise, assume that the relevant interrogative clauses are CPs whose head C position is filled by an overt or covert complementiser or preposed auxiliary, and whose specifier position is filled by an overt or covert interrogative operator expression.

22 Syntactic variation

So far, our discussion of syntax has focused largely on a variety of English which we might call Modern Standard English (MSE). But since we find numerous dimensions of variation in language (e.g. variation from one style to another, from one regional or social variety to another, from one period in the history of a language to another, and from one language to another), an important question to ask is what range of **syntactic variation** we find in the grammars of different languages or language varieties. Of course, having answered this question, further issues arise. For instance, if we are considering what are regarded as varieties of the same language, we might be concerned with understanding the social and contextual factors which determine when speakers use one variety or another. This is the sort of concern which our discussion of variation in parts 1 and 2 focused on, but here we shall adopt the less ambitious goal of seeing how our syntactic framework can come to terms with a small sample of within- and across-language variation.

Inversion in varieties of English

The most obvious manifestation of structural variation in syntax lies in word order differences. As we shall see below, these are typically attributable to differences in syntactic structure or in the movement operations which apply within a given type of structure. In the previous section we have met one manifestation of auxiliary inversion in MSE questions. Looking at this movement in other varieties of English, we shall see that on the one hand, some such varieties allow auxiliary inversion in contexts where MSE doesn't, and conversely others don't allow inversion in contexts where MSE does.

Let's begin by looking at the following type of inversion structure (the examples are from the research of Peter Sells and his colleagues) found in African American Vernacular English (AAVE) but not in MSE:

(347)   a. Can't nobody beat 'em
         b. Didn't nobody see it
         c. Ain't no white cop gonna put his hands on me

Why should we find inversion in negative structures like these in AAVE, but not MSE? A clue to the answer to this question may lie in a further difference between the two varieties illustrated by the MSE sentence (348a) and its AAVE counterpart (348b):

(348)   a. I said nothing (MSE)
         b. I didn't say nothin' (AAVE)

In the MSE structure, the sentence is negated by the single negative expression *nothing*; but in the AAVE structure, the sentence is negated by two negative expressions – *didn't* and *nothin'*. For obvious reasons, therefore, AAVE is popularly said to use *double negation* (or, in the jargon used by linguists, *negative concord*).

If we look at what's going on in AAVE more carefully, we'll see that the essence of negative concord in this variety seems to be a *constraint* (i.e. structural restriction) to the effect that negative expressions like *no/nothin'/nobody* in AAVE must be preceded by a negative auxiliary such as *can't/don't/didn't*, etc. This constraint obviously doesn't operate in MSE, since MSE doesn't use double negatives. In the light of this difference between the two varieties, consider what distinguishes the MSE sentence (349) from its AAVE counterpart (347a):

(349)   Nobody can beat them

One important difference between the two is that MSE uses the positive auxiliary *can*, whereas AAVE uses its negative counterpart *can't*, this being attributable to the fact that AAVE has negative concord, but MSE does not. But a further difference is that the auxiliary *can't* undergoes inversion in the AAVE structure (347a), whereas *can* does not in the MSE (349). More specifically, *can't* in (347a) moves from INFL to C in the manner shown in (350):

(350)

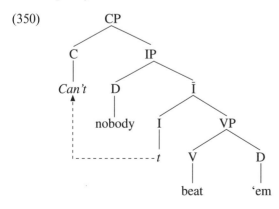

But why should *can't* undergo inversion in this way? The answer is that *can't* moves from INFL into C in order to get into a position where it precedes the negative pronoun *nobody*, and so can satisfy the requirement that a negative expression like *nobody* should be preceded by a negative auxiliary. Auxiliary inversion is used as a *last resort*, in order to satisfy this requirement. Since the requirement is not operative in MSE, there is no motivation for auxiliary inversion in MSE structures of this type, or for projecting the clause beyond IP into CP. Hence, the corresponding MSE sentence (349) has the simpler IP structure (351):

(351)

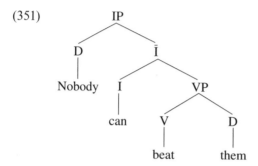

The fact that the MSE structure in (351) is an IP (rather than a CP) can itself be seen to follow from the economy principle of the previous section, which bans superfluous structure.

Our brief illustration of negative auxiliary inversion reveals two interesting (and interrelated) syntactic differences between AAVE and MSE – namely that negative clauses like (347a) in AAVE are CPs and involve auxiliary inversion, whereas their counterparts in MSE are IPs and don't involve inversion. This underlines the point made at the beginning of this section, namely that word order variation is typically attributable to differences in structure and movement operations.

So far, we have looked at a case where auxiliary inversion occurs in one variety of English (AAVE) in contexts where it is not allowed in MSE. Now let's look at the opposite kind of variation – namely, where inversion is required in MSE but not in some other variety. In this connection, consider the differences between a MSE question like (352a) below and its counterpart in Jamaican Vernacular English (JVE) in (352b), as reported in research by Beryl Bailey:

(352)   a. How many coconuts did he sell?
         b. Homuch   kuoknat im   en sel?
            How-much coconut him did sell

The crucial syntactic difference between the two is that in MSE questions, the auxiliary *did* moves from its normal position in INFL into C, whereas in JVE questions, its counterpart *en* remains *in situ* in INFL, and doesn't move to C. Thus, the two sentences (352a, b) have the respective structures (353a, b) below (To simplify discussion, we don't show the internal structure of the determiner phrases *how many coconuts/homuch kuoknat*):

(353)

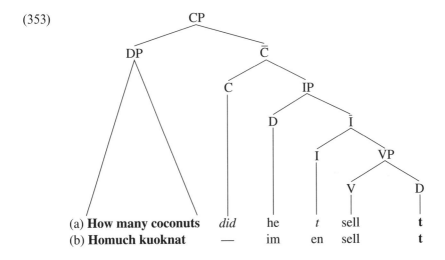

| | (a) **How many coconuts** | *did* | he | *t* | sell | **t** |
| | (b) **Homuch kuoknat** | — | im | en | sell | **t** |

In both varieties, the bold wh-operator expression **how many coconuts/homoch kuoknat** moves from complement position in VP into specifier position in CP. However, the two varieties differ in that in the MSE structure (353a), the auxiliary *did* moves from INFL to C, leaving behind a trace in INFL, whereas in the JVE structure (353b), the corresponding auxiliary *en* remains *in situ* in INFL, so that C is unfilled (as indicated by —).

The key question raised by the analysis in (353) is why auxiliaries should move from INFL to C in MSE questions, but remain in INFL in JVE questions. Using an idea developed by Noam Chomsky in recent research, we might suggest that C in questions is **strong** in MSE, but is **weak** in JVE, and that a strong position has to be filled. Since main clauses in English can't be introduced by complementisers like *that/for/if* (which, as their very name suggests, are typically used to introduce complement clauses), the only way of filling a strong C position in a main clause is by movement of an auxiliary out of INFL into C as in (353a), thereby satisfying the requirement for the strong C in MSE questions to be filled. By contrast, in JVE, the head C position of CP is a weak position, and so doesn't need to be filled. Hence, in consequence of the economy principle from the previous section, which requires us to minimise movement operations and not move anything unless it is absolutely necessary, there is no auxiliary inversion in JVE questions (*exercise 1*).

Syntactic parameters of variation

What the analysis in (353) claims, then, is that questions have the same CP/IP/VP structure in JVE and in MSE (and perhaps universally), but that the two languages differ in respect of whether C is a *strong* or a *weak* head in the relevant type of structure. Generalising at this point, we might suggest that languages (and varieties) vary in their structure along a number of specific **parameters** (i.e. 'dimensions'), and that one such parameter of variation (which we might call the **C parameter**) relates to whether C is strong or weak in a particular type of clause (questions) in a given language. The assumption that C is restricted to being *either* strong *or* weak (i.e. there is no third value it can take on) also suggests that parameters may be inherently **binary**, i.e. they have one of two values in any given language.

We can illustrate a related kind of **parametric variation** in relation to word-order differences between negative sentences containing *not* in MSE and Early Modern English (EME), as reflected in Shakespeare's plays written around the year 1600. In EME (as in MSE), clauses containing an auxiliary were typically negated by positioning *not* between the auxiliary and the verb (phrase) following it. The EME examples in (354) illustrate this:

(354)   a. She shall *not* see me (Falstaff, *Merry Wives of Windsor*, III. iii)
        b. I do *not* like thy look (Dogberry, *Much Ado About Nothing*, IV. ii)
        c. I will *not* hear thy vain excuse (Duke, *Two Gentlemen of Verona*, III.i)

As *not* is a *negative particle*, we can categorise it as belonging to the syntactic category NEG. But what position does *not* occupy within the structure of clauses?

One analysis assumes that *not* serves as an **adjunct** of some kind (since it doesn't seem to be a subject, predicate or complement), and a common way of analysing adjuncts is as expressions which attach to a particular kind of constituent and expand it into a larger constituent *of the same type* (see the discussion of topicalisation in the previous section). Taking *not* to be the kind of adjunct which merges with a VP (expanding VP into a larger VP), sentence (354a) will have the structure (355):

(355)

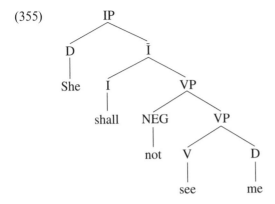

What (355) claims is that the verb *see* merges with its complement *me* to form the VP *see me*, and that the resulting VP is then merged with the negative adjunct *not*, so forming the larger (negative) VP *not see me*.

Now, what is particularly interesting about Shakespearean English is that in auxiliariless finite clauses, the (italicised) finite verb is positioned in front of *not*:

(356)   a. My master *seeks* not me (Speed, *Two Gentlemen of Verona*, I. i)
        b. I *care* not for her (Thurio, *Two Gentlemen of Verona*, V. iv)
        c. Thou *thinkest* not of this now (Launce, *Two Gentlemen of Verona*, IV, iv)

Given that *not* in (355) is adjoined as the leftmost constituent of VP, how can we account for the fact that the verb (which would otherwise be expected to follow the negative *not*) ends up positioned in front of *not* in sentences like (356)? An obvious answer is that when INFL is not filled by an auxiliary, the verb moves out of the head V position in VP into the head INFL position in IP, so moving across the negative particle *not* which is adjoined to VP. If this is what happens, (356a) has the derivation in (357):

(357)

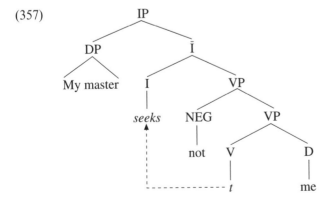

Interestingly, questions in Early Modern English seem to have involved the same *inversion* operation as in Modern Standard English. Now if (as we showed in the previous section) inversion in questions involves movement from INFL to C, an obvious prediction made by the assumption that verbs move from V to INFL in EME is that they can subsequently move from INFL to C, so resulting in sentences such as those in (358):

(358)   a. *Saw* you my sister? (Speed, *Two Gentlemen of Verona*, I. i)
        b. *Speakest* thou in sober meanings? (Orlando, *As You Like It*, V. ii)
        c. *Know* you not the cause? (Tranio, *Taming of the Shrew*, IV. ii)
        d. *Spake* you not these words plain? (Grumio, *Taming of the Shrew*, I. ii)

It follows from this suggestion that an EME question such as (358c) is derived in the manner represented in (359):

(359)

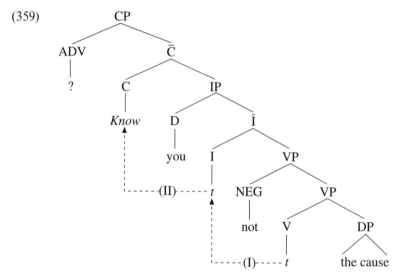

The fact that the verb *know* is positioned to the left of the subject *you* indicates that it is raised first from V to INFL and then from INFL to C by two successive applications of head movement (numbered I and II respectively in (359)).

Why should it be that negatives like (356) and interrogatives like (358) are no longer grammatical in MSE? What is the nature of the change that has taken place in the course of the evolution of the language? The answer seems to be that it was possible for finite (non-auxiliary) verbs to move to INFL in EME, but that this is no longer possible in MSE; hence, for example, verbs could move to INFL across an intervening *not* in EME structures such as (357) and from INFL subsequently move to C, as in interrogatives like (359); but no movement to INFL (and thence to C) is possible for verbs in MSE.

But why should finite non-auxiliary verbs be able to move to INFL in EME, but not in MSE? The answer is that INFL was *strong* in EME, but is *weak* in MSE. A strong INFL, just like a strong C, has to be filled, and so if the INFL position isn't occupied by an auxiliary, a strong INFL will 'lure' the verb out of the head V position in VP into the empty head INFL position in IP, as in EME structures such as (357) above (more precisely, we should say that a strong INFL has to be filled *at some stage of derivation*, since a verb which moves into INFL doesn't have to stay there but can go on to move to C, as in (359)). By contrast, a weak INFL does not have to be filled: if it contains an auxiliary, it will be filled, but a weak INFL doesn't have the strength to 'lure' a non-auxiliary verb out of V into it, so that INFL in such a language will remain unfilled in auxiliariless clauses.

Generalising at this point, we can say that a further parameter of structural variation between languages (which we might refer to as the **INFL parameter**) relates to whether INFL is strong or weak. Like the C parameter, this too turns out to be *binary* (in that INFL can be *either* strong or *weak* – it cannot be both or neither). In EME, INFL and C are both strong, whereas in MSE, INFL is weak but C (in questions) is strong.

An interesting question which arises at this point is why we can't form questions in MSE by directly moving a verb from the head V position in VP to the head C position in CP, as in (360):

(360)

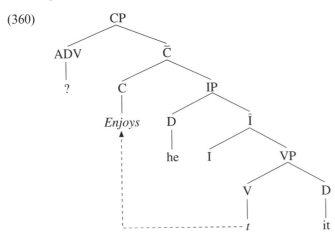

After all, C is strong in MSE questions and so needs to be filled: so why can't we fill C by moving the verb *enjoys* directly from V to C? Why is the resulting sentence **Enjoys he it?* ungrammatical?

The most satisfying answer we can give to this question is to suppose that some universal grammatical principle rules out the type of movement indicated in (360). But what principle? Some years ago, Lisa Travis suggested that head movement is universally subject to the *constraint* stated informally in (361) (a *constraint* being a principle which imposes restrictions on how grammatical operations work):

(361)   **head movement constraint (HMC)**
        A moved head can move only into the head position in the next highest phrase containing it

Given this constraint, we can provide a principled account of why the movement indicated in (360) leads to ungrammaticality: the movement of *enjoys* from V to C violates HMC, because the V *enjoys* is contained within the VP *enjoys it*, the next highest phrase containing this VP is IP, and the head of IP is the unfilled INFL constituent. This means that HMC rules out the possibility of *enjoys* moving directly from V to C, because the verb would thereby be moving too far 'in one go'. In fact, the economy principle from the previous section provides us with an alternative account of the same restriction, since the movement from V to C can be regarded as 'too long' in the context of a possible shorter move from V to INFL.

But this in turn raises the question of why we can't move *enjoys* into C in two successive steps as in (362):

(362)

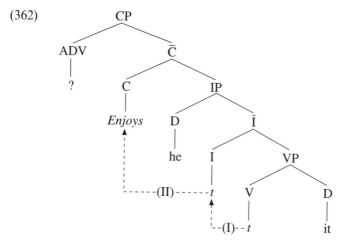

Here, *enjoys* moves first from V to INFL, and then from INFL to C, just like in the EME structure (359). This would involve two successive applications of head movement; each application would itself satisfy HMC, since in moving from V to INFL *enjoys* moves into the head position in the next highest phrase above VP (namely IP) and in moving from INFL to C, it moves into the head position within the next highest phrase above IP (namely CP). Equally, these moves are the 'shortest' available, so this proposal appears to be consistent with the economy principle. So why is the resulting sentence *Enjoys he it?*

ungrammatical? The answer is in fact provided by the economy principle. Movement (I) of *enjoys* from V to INFL in (362) is ruled out because INFL is a *weak* head in MSE, and this means that it doesn't have to be filled. Given that it doesn't have to be filled, by the economy principle, it *won't* be filled by movement, since any move to fill it is unnecessary.

It is interesting to note that the question counterpart of *He enjoys it* in MSE is formed by the use of the auxiliary *do* as in (363):

(363)   *Does* he enjoy it?

Why should we require *do* in questions like (363), but not in the corresponding statement *He enjoys it*? The answer is that statements like *He enjoys it* are IPs headed by a weak INFL which therefore does not need to be filled, whereas questions are CPs headed by a strong C which can only be filled by moving an auxiliary like *does* from its normal INFL position into C – as shown informally in (364) below (where [PresTns] in (364a) is the present tense feature carried by the unfilled INFL constituent):

(364)   a. [$_{IP}$ He [$_I$ PresTns] [$_{VP}$ [$_V$ enjoys] it]]
         b. [$_{CP}$? [$_C$ *Does*] [$_{IP}$ he [$_I$ *t*] [$_{VP}$ [$_V$ enjoy] it]]]

In (364b), the auxiliary *does* (like other auxiliaries) originates in the head INFL position of IP, and then moves into C because C is strong and so must be filled. Since the auxiliary *do* has no semantic content of its own (and hence is usually called a *dummy* auxiliary), it is used purely as a *last resort*, as a way of satisfying the requirement for a strong C to be filled.

The null subject parameter

So far, we have looked at two different parameters, one relating to the strength of C, the other to the strength of INFL. Now let's turn to look at a rather different kind of parametric variation. Early Modern English has the interesting property that it allowed the subject of a finite verb or auxiliary to be *null*, as we see from the fact that the italicised words in (365) below don't have overt subjects:

(365)   a. *Hast* any more of this? (Trinculo, *The Tempest*, II. ii)
         b. *Sufficeth*, I am come to keep my word (Petruchio, *Taming of the Shrew*, III. ii)
         c. *Would* you would bear your fortunes like a man (Iago, *Othello*, IV. i)
         d. *Lives*, sir (Iago, *Othello*, IV. i, in reply to 'How does Lieutenant Cassio?')

Since the null subject in sentences like (365) occurs in a nominative position (as we see from the fact that we could use nominative *thou* in place of the null subject in (365a)), it is generally taken to be a null nominative pronoun, and is designated **pro** (affectionately known as 'little pro', in order to differentiate it from the rather different 'big PRO' subject found in infinitives in MSE, see section 20). We say that languages like EME which have a null nominative pronoun are **null subject languages**. By contrast, Modern Standard English is not a null subject language, as we see from the fact that the present-day counterparts of (365) given in (366) require (italicised) overt subjects:

(366)   a. Have *you* got any more of this?
         b. *It's* enough that I have come to keep my word
         c. *I* wish you would bear your fortunes like a man
         d. *He* is alive, sir

We might therefore say that a further parameter of variation between languages is the **null subject parameter** (NSP) which determines whether finite verbs and auxiliaries do or don't license (i.e. allow) null subjects. Like the two parameters we have already discussed, NSP is binary in nature, so that finite verbs and auxiliaries in a given language either do or do not license null subjects (as well as overt subjects).

But why should it be that finite verbs and auxiliaries licensed null subjects in EME, but no longer do so in MSE? There are two differences between EME and MSE which seem to be relevant here. The first is a syntactic one: verbs raise to INFL in EME (and so come to be contained within the IP constituent which contains the null subject), but not in MSE. The second is a morphological one, in that verbs carried a richer set of agreement inflections in EME than they do in MSE. Whereas third person singular -*s* is the only regular agreement inflection found on present tense verbs in MSE, verbs in EME had both second person and third person inflections (e.g. present tense verbs carried -*st* in the second person singular, and -*s* or -*th* in the third person singular). Shakespearean examples illustrating this are in (367):

(367)   a. Thou see*st* how diligent I am (Petruchio, *Taming of the Shrew*, IV. iii)
         b. The sight of love feed*eth* those in love (Rosalind, *As You Like It*, III. v)
         c. Winter tame*s* man, woman and beast (Grumio, *Taming of the Shrew*, IV. i)

This means that (in singular forms, at least), first, second and third person verb forms were distinct. It is reasonable to suggest that in a language like EME, in which the verb moves into INFL and so is contained within the same phrase (=

IP) as the null subject, the relatively rich agreement inflections carried by verbs and auxiliaries served to **identify** the null subject (e.g. the *-st* inflection on *seest* in (367a) is a second person singular inflection, and hence allows us to identify the null subject as a second person singular subject with the same properties as *thou*). But in a language like MSE there are two factors which prevent the use of null subjects. Firstly, verbs don't raise to INFL (and we are assuming that only a verb in INFL can identify a subject in spec-IP); and secondly, agreement morphology is too impoverished to allow identification of a null *pro* subject (since first and second person verb forms aren't generally distinct in MSE).

Parametric differences between English and German

So far, our discussion of parametric variation has been limited to different varieties of English. What of parametric variation between different languages? To illustrate interlanguage variation, we'll conclude this section with a brief look at clause structure in a language, German, which is closely related to English in historical terms, but which is sufficiently different to illustrate further the nature of syntactic variation. As a starting point for our discussion, consider the following sentence:

(368)   Ich weiss [dass der Adrian das Buch gelesen hat]
          I   know [that the Adrian the book   read   has]
          'I know that Adrian has read the book'

(Names like *Adrian* in colloquial German can be premodified by a determiner like *der* 'the', suggesting that they are indeed DPs; we can also use a null determiner in place of *der*.) The bracketed clause in (368) has the structure (369) below (we don't show the internal structure of the two DPs *der Adrian* and *das Buch*, since this is of no immediate concern):

(369)

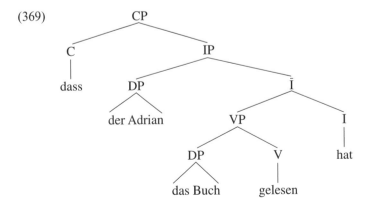

One important word order difference between German and English which is immediately apparent from (369) is that verbs and auxiliaries are positioned *after* their complements in German but before their complements in English: so, in English we have **bought** *a book* and **has** *bought a book*, whereas in German we find (the equivalent of) *a book* **bought** and *a book bought* **has**. This suggests that a further parameter of variation between languages (which we will call the **head parameter**) relates to the relative ordering of heads with respect to their complements: more specifically, we say that English has **head-first** word order within VP and IP (because a head verb or auxiliary precedes its complement), whereas German has **head-last** order within VP and IP; but both have the same head-first order within CP and DP, since complementisers and determiners in both languages precede their complements. Note that this parameter (like the others we have already examined) is binary, in that heads can *either* precede *or* follow their complements.

But now contrast the bracketed clause in (368) with the clause in (370):

(370)   Das Buch hat der Adrian gelesen
          The book has the Adrian read
          'The book, Adrian has read'

There are three important differences between the two. Firstly, the clause in (368) contains the complementiser *dass* 'that' (because it is a complement clause, here serving as the complement of the verb *weiss* 'know'), but that in (370) doesn't (because it isn't a complement clause). Secondly, the auxiliary *hat* 'has' is positioned at the end of the clause in (368), but in front of the subject *der Adrian* in (370). And thirdly, the complement *das Buch* 'the book' is positioned immediately in front of the verb *gelesen* 'read' in (368), but in front of the auxiliary *hat* 'has' in (370). How can we account for the change in word order between (368) and (370)?

Given our framework, the obvious analysis is to say that those constituents which have changed their position in (370) relative to the position they occupy in (368) have undergone movement. Thus, the auxiliary *hat* 'has' originates at the end of the clause (as in (369)), but is then moved into the complementiser position at the beginning of the clause – precisely as happens in the case of auxiliary inversion in English; and the DP *das Buch* 'the book' is preposed from its original complement position immediately in front of the verb *gelesen* 'read' and moved into the specifier position within CP (in much the same way that operator phrases are in English). As a result, (370) will be derived as in (371):

(371)

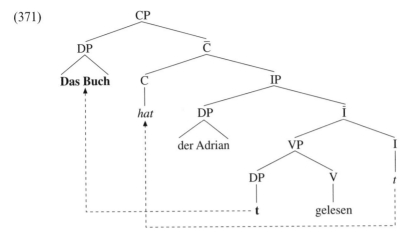

Here, we see that the auxiliary *hat* 'has' originates in INFL and moves to C, and the DP *das Buch* 'the book' originates in complement position within VP and moves into specifier position within CP.

Now consider the following sentence:

(372)   Der Adrian hat das Buch gelesen
The Adrian has the book read
'Adrian has read the book'

Since the auxiliary *hat* 'has' doesn't occupy its normal position at the end of the clause here, it seems once again to have moved from INFL to C. And this time, the subject *der Adrian* is positioned in front of the auxiliary, so seems to have moved from specifier position in IP into specifier position within CP. This means that (372) has the derivation in (373):

(373)

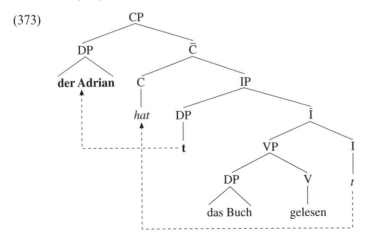

This structure shows that the auxiliary *hat* 'has' has moved from INFL to C, and the subject *der Adrian* has moved from spec-IP to spec-CP.

It is interesting to note in passing that whereas the German sentence (372) is a CP with the structure (373), its English counterpart *Adrian has read the book* is simply an IP. More generally, it would appear that all clauses are CPs in German, whereas only clauses including operator phrases (like *What can I do?* or *Nothing would he say*) or clauses introduced by an overt complementiser are CPs in English (other clauses being IPs).

Next consider (374):

(374)   Welches Buch las   der Adrian?
   which   book read the Adrian
   'Which book did Adrian read?'

What's going on here? It seems clear that the operator phrase *welches Buch* 'which book' has moved into the specifier position within CP (as in English). But how does the verb come to be positioned after it and in front of the subject *der Adrian*? The obvious answer is that (much as in Early Modern English), the verb moves out of the head V position in VP, into the head INFL position in IP, and from there into the head C position in CP, as indicated in (375):

(375)

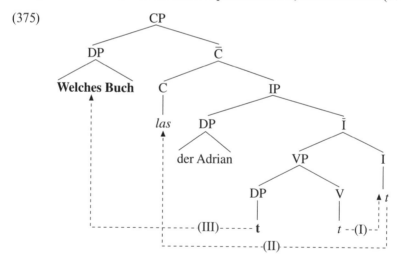

The movement (I) in (375) is head movement of the verb *las* 'read' from V to INFL; movement (II) is again head movement of the verb *las* 'read' from INFL to C; and movement (III) is operator movement of the DP *welches Buch* 'which book' from complement position within VP into specifier position within CP. Since the verb *las* can move from V to INFL and from there to C, it follows that both INFL and C must be strong in German (and hence have to be filled at some stage of the derivation). Note that in consequence of the head movement constraint (361) (or the economy principle requiring 'short' moves), the verb *las* cannot move directly from V to C, but rather must move first to INFL, and then from INFL to C.

An interesting property which the German CPs in (370), (372) and (374) share is that in each case the specifier position within CP must be filled – though this is not true of (369) where *dass* 'that' appears to have no specifier. This means that where the head C of CP is filled by a preposed verb or auxiliary (as in (370), (372) and (374)), CP must have a specifier.

The assumption that clauses in which C is occupied by a preposed verb or auxiliary require a specifier has interesting implications for how we analyse yes–no questions such as (376):

(376)   Las   der Adrian das Buch?
         Read the Adrian the book
         'Did Adrian read the book?'

Here, the overall clause (like all clauses in German) is a CP, and the head C position of CP is filled by the preposed verb *las* 'read'. If we posit that CPs headed by a preposed verb or auxiliary require a specifier, how can we account for the fact that there appears to be no CP-specifier preceding the verb *las* in (376)? Recall that in section 20 we suggested that yes–no questions contain an abstract question operator *?* which occupies the specifier position within CP, and which is required if a sentence is to be interpreted as a question. This being so, (376) will have the derivation in (377):

(377)

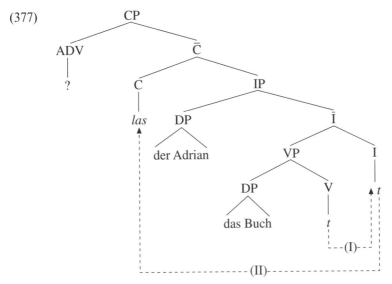

The verb *las* originates in the head V position of VP and then moves from there first into the head INFL position of IP, and then into the head C position of CP (since C is strong in German and so always has to be filled). The requirement for the specifier position within CP to be filled where C contains a preposed verb or auxiliary is satisfied by the null question operator *?* which occupies spec-CP, and which serves to mark the clause as a yes–no question.

Our discussion of structural variation in this section has important implications for the development of a theory of grammar. In previous sections, we have assumed that principles of Universal Grammar (UG) determine that certain aspects of syntactic structure are invariant across languages (e.g. every phrase or clause is a projection of a head; subjects universally occupy the specifier position within IP; questions are universally CPs containing an interrogative operator in spec-CP; categories can universally be overt or covert, etc.). But in this section, we have seen that there is a certain amount of structural variation across languages and language varieties, and that this can be characterised in terms of a set of binary parameters. This leads us towards the **principles and parameters theory** (PPT) developed by Noam Chomsky and many others over the past two decades, in which those aspects of syntactic structure which are invariant across languages are attributable to principles of UG, while those aspects of structure which vary from one language to another are described in terms of a set of (binary) parameters (*exercises 2 and 3*).

Exercises

1. Discuss the structure of the following sentences in African American Vernacular English (AAVE) and how they differ from their Modern Standard English counterparts:

    (a) He don't mess with no cops
    (b) Don't nobody mess with the cops
    (c) Everybody knows [don't nobody mess with the cops]
    (d) *Everybody knows [that don't nobody mess with the cops]

    For the purposes of this exercise, assume that the bracketed structures in (c, d) are CPs which serve as the complement of the verb *knows*. Can you suggest a structural reason why (d) is ungrammatical?

    In addition, discuss the syntax of the following yes–no question in Jamaican Vernacular English (JVE):

(e) Yu   en   si   eniting?
You did see anything
'Did you see anything?'

How can we account for the polarity item *eniting* in (e)?

2.   Draw tree diagrams showing the derivation of the following Early Modern English sentences, giving arguments in support of your analysis. In what ways is EME similar to German?

(a) What sayst thou? (Olivia, *Twelfth Night*, III. iv)
(b) What didst not like? (Othello, *Othello*, III. iii)
(c) Saw you my master? (Speed, *Two Gentlemen of Verona*, I. i)
(d) Can'st not rule her? (Leontes, *Winter's Tale*, II. iii)
(e) Knows he not thy voice (First Lord, *All's Well That Ends Well*, IV. i)
(f) Seawater shalt thou drink (Prospero, *Tempest*, I. ii)
(g) This fail you not to do! (Othello, *Othello*, IV. i)
(h) What visions have I seen! (Titania, *Midsummer Night's Dream*, V. i)

Assume that all the clauses in (a) to (h) are CPs, that *thy voice* in (e) is a DP comprising the D *thy* and the N *voice*, and that *what visions* in (h) is a DP comprising the D *what* and the N *visions*. As noted in section 18, sentences like (g) which are used to issue an order are *imperatives*, while sentences like (h) which are used to exclaim surprise or delight are *exclamatives*.

     If all the sentences in (a) to (h) are CPs, it might be suggested that all finite clauses in Shakespearean English are CPs, and that they require the head and specifier positions within CP to be filled. What implications would this have for the analysis of sentences such as the following:

(i) He heard not that (Julia, *Two Gentlemen of Verona*, IV. ii)

What would then be the difference(s) between sentences like (a) to (i) in EME and their MSE counterparts?

3.   Discuss the derivation of the following German sentences, commenting on points of interest (italics mark emphasis):

(a) Er ist nach Berlin gefahren
    He is to   Berlin gone
    'He has gone to Berlin'
(b) Nach Berlin ist er gefahren
    To   Berlin is he gone
    'He has gone *to Berlin*'
(c) Er fährt nicht nach Berlin
    He goes not to   Berlin
    'He's not going to Berlin'
(d) Nach Berlin fährt er nicht
    To   Berlin goes he not
    'He isn't going *to Berlin*'
(e) Fährt er nicht nach Berlin?
    Goes he not to   Berlin
    'Isn't he going to Berlin?'

(With many verbs of motion, German uses the counterpart of *be* as a perfect auxiliary, rather than the counterpart of *have*.) Assume that *nicht* is a VP-adjunct, and that *nach Berlin* 'to Berlin' is a prepositional phrase (PP); don't concern yourself with the internal structure of this PP.

23   Logical Form

To date, we have had nothing to say about how sentences are interpreted, but, as pointed out in the introduction, an adequate grammar of a language should contain a component which specifies how the **Logical Form (LF)** of a sentence is derived. In this section, we shall introduce some properties of LF for certain types of sentence and see how a further variety of movement can be used to enable us to derive appropriate LFs for the sentences we focus on. First, it is necessary to establish some preliminary notions.

Preliminaries

Consider the simple sentences in (378):

(378)   a. The king smokes
        b. The queen snores

It is obvious that (378a, b) differ in interpretation, and to some extent, this is determined by the words they contain. To see this, we simply note that if we substitute the noun *queen* for the noun *king* in (378a), the interpretation of the sentence we thereby produce (379) differs from that of (378a):

(379)   The queen smokes

On this basis, we can formulate a first version of **The Principle of Compositionality** as in (380):

(380)   The interpretation of a sentence is determined by the interpretations of the words the sentence contains

Now, it is easy to see that (380) is not adequate. Consider, for example, the sentences in (381):

(381)   a. The dog chased a rabbit
         b. The rabbit chased a dog

These two sentences are differently interpreted, yet each of them contains exactly the same words. In this case, we can readily see what this difference in meaning rests on: the words in the two sentences occur in different orders, with different sequences fulfilling different grammatical functions (see section 18). For instance, the sequence *the dog* constitutes a subject in (381a), whereas this function is fulfilled by the sequence *the rabbit* in (381b). In drawing attention to these differences, we focus on the *syntax* of the two sentences, and this suggests that a more adequate version of the Principle of Compositionality might be formulated as in (382):

(382)   The interpretation of a sentence is determined by the interpretations of the words occurring in the sentence *and* the syntactic structure of the sentence.

If we understand *the, dog, chased, a* and *rabbit*, and if we know that *the dog* serves as subject, *chased* as predicate and *a rabbit* as complement in (381a), then we are equipped to understand the sentence.

The Principle of Compositionality in (382) is vital in understanding the phenomenon of **structural ambiguity**, illustrated by examples such as those in (383) (see also section 10, p. 172):

(383)   a. Frank spotted the man with a telescope
         b. Frank spotted the man with a wooden leg

While it may not be immediately obvious, each of these sentences has two different interpretations. For (383a), the most likely interpretation is that Frank looked through a telescope and spotted the man. However, it is easy to see another interpretation, whereby the man had a telescope and Frank spotted him (by some means or other). Here, then, we have a single sequence of words with two interpretations, and (382) suggests that this is possible so long as the sequence can be associated with two syntactic structures. Focusing on the VP *spotted the man with a telescope*, we might propose the two structures in (384a, b) as arising from merging constituents in different orders:

(384)   a.   b.

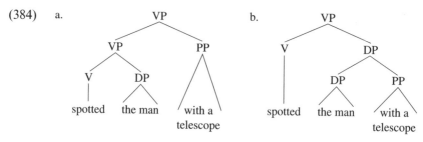

(Here, we do not specify the internal structure of the DP *the man* and the PP *with a telescope*, both of which are irrelevant to the point under discussion.) For (384a), having formed the DP *the man*, we merge this as a complement with the head V *spotted* to give the VP *spotted the man*; then having formed the PP *with a telescope*, this is merged as an adjunct with the VP *spotted the man* to form the larger VP *spotted the man with a telescope*. This structure corresponds to the interpretation in which the telescope is used for spotting. The operations involved in producing (384b) are different. Here, having formed *the man* and *with a telescope*, these are merged with the PP serving as an adjunct to the DP, so as to form the larger DP *the man with a telescope*. Then, this DP, functioning as a complement, is merged with the head V *spotted* to give the VP *spotted the man with a telescope*. This structure is appropriate for the interpretation where the man who is spotted has a telescope.

What of (383b)? At first sight, you may feel that this sentence is unambiguous, its only interpretation being that the man has a wooden leg and Frank spotted him (by some means or other) – equivalently, the only structure for (383b) is one analogous to (384b). However, we suggest that a second interpretation, parallel to that readily available for (383a), can be provided for (383b). To get this interpretation, all we need to do is suspend our beliefs about what people *typically* use as aids for looking at the world and imagine that a wooden leg is fitted out so that Frank's spotting works better if he looks through it. In short, as far as *language* is concerned, (383b) is every bit as ambiguous as (383a); however, beliefs we hold about the world make the ambiguity *less accessible* in the case of (383b), a fact to always bear in mind when investigating the interpretive possibilities for particular sentences.

On the basis of our discussion so far, we can see that any theory of the interpretation of sentences is going to have at least two prerequisites: an account of the semantic contributions of the words appearing in sentences and an account of the syntactic structure of sentences. In section 12, we briefly examined some of the issues which arise in the study of word meaning, and previous sections of this part of the book have developed a syntactic theory to a point where we can associate semantically appropriate syntactic structures with examples such as (381) and (383). However, consideration of a wider range of examples indicates the need to further extend our syntactic resources. Before seeing why this is so, it will be useful to look at one way in which philosophers have studied the meanings of sentences.

A philosophical diversion

Consider the sentence in (385) and suppose, for the sake of argument, that the name *Shirley* is the name of a specific sheep:

(385)   Shirley snores

A view adopted by many philosophers and linguists, is that at least part of what is involved in understanding a sentence in a language (i.e. grasping its interpretation) is knowing what the world *would* be like if the sentence were *true*; to know this is to know the **truth conditions** of the sentence. Note that knowing the truth conditions of a sentence does not require that we know that the sentence *is* or *is not* true; to know this latter for every sentence you understand would be to approach omniscience, and it would be absurd for linguistics to claim that knowledge of a language has (near-)omniscience as a consequence.

You can persuade yourself that the position outlined in the previous paragraph is plausible by considering a small experiment that you might undertake. Suppose you take a picture and construct some simple English sentences which are true or false of the picture; then you present the sentences and the picture to someone in whose linguistic competence you are interested, asking them to respond with 'true' or 'false' to each of the sentences. If their responses were incorrect in some cases, you would probably conclude that they did not *understand* those particular sentences; if their responses appeared to be random across the set of sentences, you would probably conclude that they did not understand English at all – imagine the responses you would get from a monolingual French speaker who is told (in French) to respond with *vrai* ('true') or *faux* ('false') to a set of *English* sentences.

At least part of what (385) means, then, can be identified with its truth conditions. What might these conditions look like? Well, *Shirley* is a particular type of DP (perhaps with a null determiner), a proper name, and, we might suppose for simplicity, that it names a unique individual, the sheep called Shirley. The verb *snores* names a property, the property of snoring. Then, we might state the truth conditions for (385) as in (386):

(386)   The sentence *Shirley snores* is true just in case the individual named by *Shirley* has the property of snoring

At this point, you may feel that while (386) is true, it is pretty unhelpful, since what it says is so trivial. But this reaction is due to the fact that in (386) we are using English to talk about English – more technically, we are using English as a **metalanguage** to talk about English as an **object language**. Obviously, if we are going to present the truth conditions for a sentence, we are going to have to use some language or other to do this. Readers of this book understand English, so our metalanguage is English throughout, but now suppose that we want to consider the truth conditions for the French sentence in (387):

(387)   Delphine ronfle
         'Delphine snores'

And suppose, again for simplicity, that the DP *Delphine* names a unique individual. Using English as our metalanguage, the truth conditions for (387) appear in (388):

(388)   The sentence *Delphine ronfle* is true just in case the individual named by *Delphine* has the property of snoring

Now, if you don't know French, but you do understand English, (388) will tell you *something* about the interpretation of (387); the reason you feel that (386) tells you nothing about the interpretation of (385) is entirely due to the fact that (386) uses English to tell you something about English, a language you understand.

It is easy now to generalise on the basis of additional examples of sentences consisting of a proper name and an intransitive verb that we might care to construct. Some such sentences appear in (389) and a generalisation is formulated in (390):

(389)   a. Smythe smokes
         b. Jones jogs
         c. Stevens stammers

(390)   For any sentence consisting of a DP α followed by an intransitive verb β, the sentence is true just in case the individual named by β has the property named by β

Note how this begins to acknowledge the Principle of Compositionality in (382), by stating how the interpretation of a sentence (its truth conditions) is determined by the semantic properties of its component words (names refer to individuals and intransitive verbs to properties) and the sentence's syntax (the DP precedes the intransitive verb). Obviously, we have deliberately chosen a very simple type of sentence and the only aspects of syntax to which we have referred are the categorial status of the constituents and their order. However, this is sufficient to enable us to contrast the sentences in (385) and (389) with those in (391):

(391)   a. Every sheep snores
         b. Most sheep snore
         c. No sheep snores
         d. Which sheep snores?

Take (391a); as *every sheep* is a DP, consisting of the D *every* and its complement N *sheep*, and *snores* is an intransitive verb, its syntactic structure fits the description in (390), but if we try to apply (390) to formulate the truth conditions of (391a), we run into a major problem. This problem concerns the DP in subject position, *every sheep*. The question (390) raises is: what individual is named by *every sheep*? But it is not sensible to ask this question of this expression. Arguably, it is even less sensible to ask it of *most sheep* in (391b), and just plain nonsense to ask it of *no sheep* in (391c) and *which sheep* in (391d). These expressions, while evidently DPs, do not name individuals in the straightforward way that proper names do, and it appears that (390) is simply not applicable to sentences containing such phrases.

The problem we have arrived at here was already appreciated at the end of the nineteenth century by the German philosopher, Gottlob Frege, and his British contemporary, Bertrand Russell. The solution to it that they developed can be sketched by talking informally about the truth conditions for (391a). We have seen that we cannot formulate these truth conditions in terms of an individual named by *every sheep* which has the property of snoring. Instead, what we need to do is examine each individual sheep (none of which is every sheep) in turn, checking whether *it* has the property of snoring. If the answer is 'Yes' for every sheep, the sentence is true. But this seems to require that *from a semantic perspective*, the simple syntactic representation of (391a), whereby it contains just a DP subject and an intransitive verb, is not appropriate (we are simplifying our syntactic assumptions by ignoring INFL and its projections – taking account of these would not affect the point under discussion). What we appear to need is a *syntactic representation* which enables us to make it explicit that in determining the truth conditions of (391a), we have to consider a number of individuals in turn, checking whether each of them has the relevant property. We can achieve this by introducing into the syntactic representation an expression which, unlike a proper name, does not pick out a unique individual, but instead can *vary* in the individuals it picks out. Such an expression is a **variable**, and the sort of representation we need for semantic purposes appears in (392):

(392)   (every sheep x)(x snores)

Here x is a variable and (392) is read as 'for every individual x which is a sheep, x snores'. If we now suppose that (391a) can be somehow linked to (392), the truth conditions of (391a) can be formulated as in (393):

(393)   *Every sheep snores* [or *(every sheep x)(x snores)*] is true just in case for every value of x which is a sheep, x has the property of snoring

Traditionally, (392) is referred to as the **logical form** of (391a). It is a syntactic representation containing the constituents *every sheep x* and *x snores*. The expression *every sheep x* looks like some kind of DP and *x snores* is a clause with the variable *x* functioning as its subject and *snores* as its verbal predicate. However, at this stage, we are not concerned with the details of this syntactic structure – what is important is that, taking account of the Principle of Compositionality in (382), it is appropriate for determining the truth conditions of (391a). By contrast, the *superficial* syntax of (391a) is inappropriate for this purpose. As we have noted, (391a) contains nothing beyond a subject DP and an intransitive verb; specifically, nothing corresponding to a variable appears in this structure, and thus it is not possible to see this structure as providing the appropriate basis for the operation of the Principle of Compositionality.

Now, (391b, c) will yield to this sort of intuitive treatment readily enough, to give us the logical forms in (394) and (395) respectively:

(394)   (most sheep x)(x snores)

(395)   (no sheep x)(x snores)

And, each of (394) and (395) provides appropriate *syntactic* formats for the statements of truth conditions in (396) and (397):

(396)   *Most sheep snore* or [*(most sheep x)(x snores)*] is true just in case for most values of *x* which are sheep, *x* has the property of snoring

(397)   *No sheep snores* or [*(no sheep x)(x snores)*] is true just in case for every value of *x* which is a sheep, *x* does not have the property of snoring

To summarise up to this point, and putting (391d) to one side for the moment, we are suggesting that the superficial *syntactic form* of the other sentences in (391) is not appropriate for revealing their semantic properties. For (385) *Shirley snores* and similar sentences, there is a straightforward relationship between syntactic form and the computation of truth conditions; in the syntax, there are two entities, the subject DP and the intransitive verb, which are matched directly by the individual picked out by the name and a property in the semantics. In (391a, b, c), however, we find a different situation: again, there is a subject DP – in each case a **quantificational** DP – and an intransitive verb, but, in these cases, there is no individual picked out by the former; instead, the semantics requires some means of considering a range of objects, and this is achieved by introducing a variable into the logical form. Accordingly, for these sentences, their logical forms do not appear to be directly reflected in their syntactic structures. For Frege, who was concerned to develop a *semantic* account of quantification for use in logical inference, this was of no concern, and he was at liberty to *stipulate* whatever representations were necessary and to rely on his own skill in ensuring that the logical forms he stipulated were appropriate. For a linguist, however, confronted with trying to produce an explicit theory of human linguistic competence, such stipulation and reliance on the skill of a nineteenth-century German logician is not comfortable; at this point, we must acknowledge an unacceptable gap between what syntax provides and what semantics needs in the case of sentences containing quantified noun phrases.

Covert movement and Logical Form

A resolution to the dilemma posed above is approached via (391d). An obvious point is that, as (391d) is an interrogative, it doesn't make much sense to talk about its truth-conditions, but putting this to one side, we can ask whether its logical form is more appropriately construed along the lines of (385) or similarly to (391a, b, c). Specifically, we can ask whether its interpretation involves reference to an individual picked out by the phrase *which sheep* or whether we need representations like those in (392), (396) and (397) to make this interpretation more transparent. The answer is obvious. There is no *which sheep* being referred to in (391d), just as there is no *no sheep* being referred to in (391c), in contrast to the individual picked out by *Shirley* in (385). We are therefore led to the logical form for (391d) in (398):

(398)   (which sheep x)(x snores)

We can immediately note that (398) captures something important about the interpretation of (391d); someone who understands (391d) knows that it asks for a search through a set of sheep looking for one which has the property of snoring. The fact that we have a variable in (398) taking as values individual sheep provides us with a device for conducting such a search.

But now, for this example at least, we can note an interesting and important correspondence between what semantics requires and what syntax supplies. Recall our discussion of movement in section 21 and the observation made there that a class of *operator expressions*, including wh-phrases, move from the position they occupy as a result of merger operations to a clause-initial position, viz. spec-CP. In the earlier discussion, the moved wh-phrases originated in complement position as in (324) repeated as (399a) with the derivation in (399b):

(399)   a.   What languages can you speak?

b.

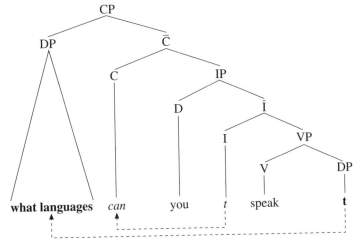

Furthermore, it was argued in section 21 that this movement leaves a *trace* (**t** in 399b) of the moved operator expression behind in the argument position, and that the appearance of a wh-operator position in spec-CP is necessary if this clause is to be interpreted as interrogative. Now, (391d) is interrogative, and we can propose that *which sheep* moves in this example from its original position in spec-IP to the spec-CP position as indicated in (400):

(400)

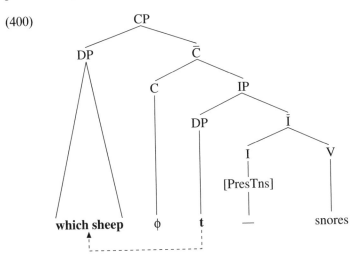

Obviously, in (400) the derived position occupied by *which sheep* and its initial argument position are linked, and it is conventional to indicate this linking by the notational device of **co-indexing** the moved item and its trace (up to now, we have used either bold or italic type to perform this function). If we do this, (400) can be roughly represented as in (401) (ignoring the covert C and unfilled INFL positions):

(401)   (Which sheep$_i$) (t$_i$ snores)

But now reverting to (398), we can see that precisely the same link is signalled by use of the variable x in that representation. In other words, it turns out that if we suppose that wh-phrases move into spec-CP, we derive a *syntactic* representation which has characteristics strikingly similar to that required by the semantics. It is important to be clear that this conclusion has been reached by relying on a generalisation of the empirical argumentation from section 21 (that wh-phrases move to spec-CP leaving behind a trace) and not by arbitrary stipulation.

This is progress, but where does it leave us with (391a, b, c), examples where the semantics again seems to require something like (398), but where there is nothing in the overt syntax to suggest anything beyond what a superficial syntactic analysis would produce? Or is there? We conclude this section by sketching just two of the many arguments for there being a *syntactically motivated* level of logical form for sentences including quantified noun phrases, a level at which the syntax provides the right sort of structures for the semantics to work as outlined above. It should be noted that when we offer syntactic arguments for this level of representation, we use initial capitals for Logical Form; this distinguishes it from the philosopher's stipulated representations.

For the first argument, consider the examples in (402):

(402)   a. Frank loves his hamster
         b. Who loves his hamster?
         c. Every boy loves his hamster

The pronoun *his* can be interpreted in two distinct ways in each of these sentences. Take (402a): *his* can refer either to Frank or to some other male human being, say, George. In the former case, we say that *Frank* and *his* are **co-referential**, and we indicate that this is the interpretation we are concerned with by using co-indexing, as in (403):

(403)   Frank$_i$ loves his$_i$ hamster

For the latter case, the sentence means that Frank loves George's hamster and that *his* refers to someone other than Frank is indicated by contra-indexing, as in (404):

(404)   Frank$_i$ loves his$_j$ hamster

For (402b), we again have an interpretation with *his* referring to, say, George, and in this case, the sentence means: 'for which person x does x love George's hamster?' Additionally, however, *his* can have what is referred to as a **bound variable interpretation**, in which case it has the interpretation: 'for which person x, does x love x's hamster?' Note that co-reference is an inappropriate notion in this case, as *who* (just like *which sheep* in 391d) does not *refer* to anyone. Again, it is conventional to indicate the bound variable interpretation using co-indexing as in (405):

(405)   Who$_i$ loves his$_i$ hamster

Finally, (402c) is similar to (402b): *his* can refer to, say, George or it can have a bound variable interpretation. In the former case, the sentence means 'for every boy x, x loves George's hamster'; in the latter, 'for every boy x, x loves x's hamster'. The latter interpretation is signalled as in (406):

(406)   Every boy$_i$ loves his$_i$ hamster

Now, alongside the examples in (402), consider those in (407):

(407)   a. His$_i$ hamster loves Frank$_i$
         b. *Who$_i$ does his$_i$ hamster love?
         c. *His$_i$ hamster loves every boy$_i$

Co-reference is possible in (407a) (i.e. this sentence can mean 'Frank's hamster loves Frank'), but the bound variable interpretation of *his* is not an option in either (407b) or (407c). That is to say, (407b) cannot be interpreted as meaning 'for which person x, does x's hamster love x', and (407c) cannot be interpreted as meaning 'for every boy x, x's hamster loves x' (of course, if *his* were to be interpreted as referring to George, all these sentences are fine, but in these circumstances, we would use contra-indexing, as in (408)):

(408)   a. His$_j$ hamster loves Frank$_i$
         b. Who$_i$ does his$_j$ hamster love?
         c. His$_j$ hamster loves every boy$_i$

The challenge is to account for these observations, and we can start by applying our assumptions about movement to (407b). After *who* has moved to spec-CP and *does* has moved to C, we have the structure in (409):

(409)

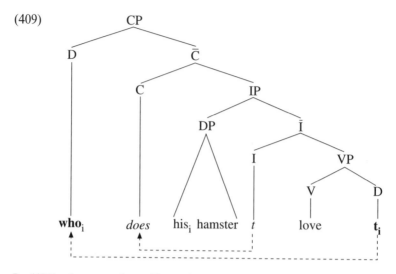

In (409), the moved auxiliary *does* and its trace are italicised, whereas the moved wh-operator *who* and its trace are bold-printed. Additionally, we have co-indexed *who* and its trace in accordance with the convention introduced above. Finally, *who* and *his* are also co-indexed, thereby showing that it is the bound variable interpretation of *his* which concerns us.

Now, we know that (409) is an illegitimate derivation, since the bound variable interpretation for *his* is not a possibility here, so we can ask what's wrong with (409). Note that in this derivation the movement of *who* has *crossed over* the position occupied by *his*, the pronoun with which it is co-indexed on the ill-formed interpretation. In this respect, (409) contrasts with (410), which indicates how (405) is derived:

(410)

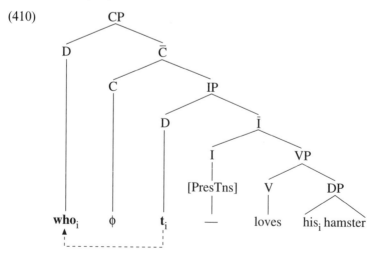

In (410), *who* does not cross *his* in moving to spec-CP, and the bound variable interpretation of *his* is possible.

On the basis of these observations, we can formulate the **Crossover Principle** in (411):

(411)   An operator expression may not be moved across a co-indexed pronoun.

This principle now accounts for the ill-formedness of (407b), contrasted with the well-formedness of (405), and since proper names like *Frank* do not move, it does not impinge on (403) or (407a), both of which allow the pronoun to be co-indexed with the proper name.

At this point, (407c) falls outside the Crossover Principle, yet it appears to exhibit the same sort of phenomenon as (407b) – the impossibility of a pronoun being interpreted as a bound variable. We can accommodate it to (411), however, if we suppose that there is, at some level of syntactic representation, **covert** (i.e. invisible) movement of the quantified DP *every boy* to some clause-initial position. For concreteness, suppose that this position is that occupied by overtly moved topics as described in section 21, i.e. adjoined to IP. After this covert movement of *every boy* in (407c), we obtain the structure in (412) (note that there is no system of C-projections in this declarative structure in accordance with the conclusions of the previous two sections):

(412)

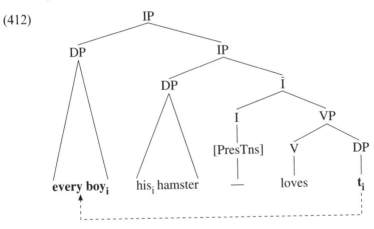

The derivation in (412) violates the Crossover Principle in (411), so long as we see (411) as applying to *all* movements, overt and non-overt, i.e. by postulating non-overt movement of the quantified DP *every boy*, we extend the coverage of our theoretical principle in (411), and we ensure that the ill-formed examples (407b, c) are accounted for *in the same way*. From the point of view of standard scientific practice, this is a positive result. Furthermore, there is a bonus which is particularly important in the current context. The representation in (412) with the quantified DP moved out of its argument position and a co-indexed trace in this argument position has the right sort of form for understanding the truth-conditions of sentences which contain quantified DPs; and, rather than being *stipulated*, as it was by Frege, the representation is *justified by independent syntactic argumentation*.

To be entirely clear on what is being suggested here, consider (413), a sentence which contains the quantified DP *many sheep* in complement position:

(413)   Sharkey sheared many sheep

Semantic considerations require that this sentence should have a logical form along the lines of (414):

(414)   (many sheep x)(Sharkey sheared x)

Syntactic arguments have now been advanced to suggest that quantified DPs (covertly) adjoin to IP at the *covert* syntactic level of **Logical Form (LF)**. For (413), this gives the (partial) LF in (415):

(415)

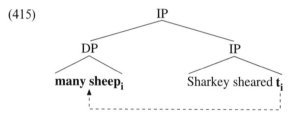

And (415), because of its similarity to (414), provides an appropriate representation for the semantics of quantified DPs to proceed in the required fashion. The structure in (415) is a *well-formed LF*, but (412), the LF for (407c) is *ill-formed* by virtue of violating (411), a principle we are supposing to apply to all movement.

If, finally, we return to our set of examples in (391), we can see that in all cases, their LFs will be semantically appropriate. These appear in schematic form in (416):

(416)   a. every sheep$_i$ [t$_i$ snores]
         b. most sheep$_i$ [t$_i$ snore]
         c. no sheep$_i$ [t$_i$ snores]
         d. which sheep$_i$ [t$_i$ snores]

The only relevant difference in these examples is that for (416d) the movement of the operator phrase is overt to spec-CP, whereas for (416a, b, c) the movement of the quantified DP is covert in the derivation of LF, and involves adjoining the quantified DP to IP. Having introduced the possibility of covert movement into our theory of grammar, we can now sketch the overall organisation of a grammar as in (417):

(417)

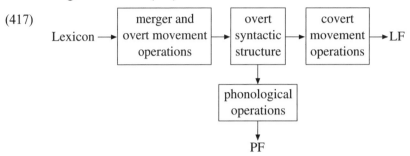

According to this organisation, a derivation proceeds with a selection of items from the lexicon. These then undergo merger and overt movement, as described in sections 19 and 21. When these operations are complete, the derivation is passed on to the phonological component which determines how a structure is pronounced, taking account of issues which have been introduced in parts 1 and 2 of this book – obviously, the phonological component must have access to the results of overt movements. Additionally, however, the derivation is passed on to the interpretive component, where covert movements (operations which are not seen by the phonology and not 'heard' by native speakers) convert the representation to a Logical Form (*exercise 1*).

More evidence for covert movement

While the argument we have sketched above involving a quantified DP crossing a pronoun is an interesting one, the suggestion that such phrases move non-overtly is an abstract and somewhat difficult idea which would benefit from additional support. We now turn to a cross-linguistic argument for the same general conclusion.

Consider the English sentences in (418), where co-indexed traces indicate the merged position of the (overtly) moved wh-operator phrase:

(418)   a. Who$_i$ does John think the dog chased t$_i$?
         b. John wonders who$_i$ the dog chased t$_i$

In (418a) we have a main clause question and in (418b) an indirect question, and we can rephrase this by saying that in (418a) the semantic **scope** of interrogation is the whole sentence, whereas in (418b) it is only the embedded clause – note that (418b) is not used as a question which requires an answer. Of course, this difference in semantic scope correlates with the position of the overtly moved wh-phrase: it appears in the main clause spec-CP in (418a) and in the embedded Spec-CP in (418b) (*exercises 2 and 3*).

In contrast to (418a, b), consider the ill-formed (419a, b):

(419)   a. *John thinks who$_i$ the dog chased t$_i$
         b. *Who$_i$ does John wonder the dog chased t$_i$

How are we to account for these examples? The natural place to seek an explanation lies in the nature of the verbs *think* and *wonder*. In section 19, we introduced the idea that heads of phrases possess sets of features including *complement features*. These latter determine the types of complement a particular head can or cannot co-occur with. So, suppose that the lexical entry for *think* includes a complement feature which indicates that if its complement is clausal, it must be a *declarative* clause, whereas the lexical entry for *wonder* indicates that it must take an *interrogative* CP complement.

With these assumptions in place, a straightforward account of the data in (418) and (419) is now available. Recall that we have argued that in order to be interpreted as interrogative, an English clause must have a wh-operator in its spec-CP position. If we represent (unfilled) interrogative C by a feature [+ Q], the pre-movement structure for (418a) is (420):

(420)   [$_{CP}$[$_C$ + Q] John thinks [$_{IP}$ the dog chased who]]

The [+ Q] introducing the main clause indicates that the structure is interrogative and it follows that *who* must be moved into the spec-CP position in the main clause, giving us (418a). But why can't we construct an alternative derivation starting from the pre-movement structure in (421)?

(421)   [$_{IP}$ John thinks [$_{CP}$ [$_C$ + Q] the dog chased who]]

Here, the [+Q] in the embedded C position is a signal that the embedded clause is to be interpreted as interrogative, so this should require movement of *who* to the embedded spec-CP position, enabling us to derive (419a). But in fact this derivation will be ill formed, because the complement feature of *think*, which requires that its clausal complement be declarative, i.e. non-interrogative, will not be checked, and it is a principle in our framework that all such grammatical features need to be checked.

Next consider (418b). Before any movement takes place, we have the structure in (422):

(422)   [$_{IP}$ John wonders [$_{CP}$[$_C$ + Q] the dog chased who]]

The [+Q] feature in the embedded C position requires *who* to be moved to the embedded spec-CP and this gives us a well-formed derivation for (418b). But again we should ask why we can't construct a derivation starting from (423):

(423)   [$_{CP}$ [$_C$ + Q] John wonders [$_{IP}$ the dog chased who]]

The [+Q] feature in the main clause C requires *who* to be moved to the main clause spec-CP position, giving (419b) which is ill formed. But we are now supposing that the verb *wonder* has a complement feature which, in order to be checked, requires the presence of an interrogative complement clause. In (423), there is no such clause; as a consequence the complement feature of *wonder* will not be checked and the derivation will not be well-formed, as required. We now turn to non-overt movement (*exercise 4*).

Mandarin Chinese is unlike English in not exhibiting overt movement of the equivalent of wh-phrases. In this language, we find simple sentences such as (424) (Mandarin Chinese is a tone language, but we suppress tones since they are not relevant to the point under discussion, see section 2):

(424)   ni   yao   shenme?
         you want what
         'what do you want?'

Now consider the equivalents of (418a, b) in Mandarin Chinese:

(425)   a. Guo renwei gou zhui   shei?
            Guo think   dog chase who
            'who does Guo think the dog chased?'
         b. Guo xiang-zhidao gou zhui   shei
            Guo wonder   dog chase who
            'Guo wonders who the dog chased'

In (425a, b), the equivalent of a wh-phrase *shei* ('who') appears in the position in which it is merged with the verb *zhui* 'chase' (Chinese is a language like English in which the basic word order in a simple sentence is subject–verb–complement). But despite *shei* appearing in identical positions in these two sentences, the *scope* of interrogation matches what we find in the corresponding English sentences, i.e. (425a) is a main clause question, whereas (425b) contains an indirect question with interrogative scope restricted to the subordinate clause. How might we account for this? For English, we have proposed that in order for a clause to be interpreted as interrogative, it must contain an interrogative expression in its spec-CP position. This looks like a good candidate for a universally valid condition on representations, but it immediately appears to be contradicted by Chinese. However, we can retain our condition, if we suppose that whereas in English the spec-CP position must be overtly filled, in Chinese it can be filled as a consequence of covert movement.

What we are suggesting, then, is that the Chinese verbs *renwei* 'believe' and *xiang-zhidao* 'wonder' have identical complement features to their English equivalents and that both languages share the requirement that an interrogative clause must have an interrogative expression in its spec-CP position *at LF*. In the case of English, this condition is satisfied via overt movement in overt syntax, but in Chinese, it requires covert movement of operator expressions to the appropriate position. The upshot of this is that the LFs for (425a, b) are (426a, b) respectively:

(426)   a.

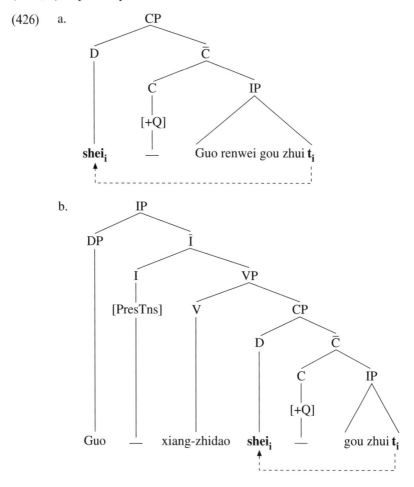

A consequence of this way of looking at things is that, whereas the overt syntactic structures of (425a, b) are quite different to their English counterparts, the LF structures in (426a, b) are strikingly similar to the LFs for the corresponding English sentences (for the latter, there will be no significant change from the overt syntax, since the relevant conditions have been satisfied by overt movement). Furthermore, (426a) has only the interpretation of a direct question (the operator appearing in spec-CP of the main clause) whereas (426b) has only the interpretation of an indirect question (the operator appearing in spec-CP in the subordinate clause).

Our brief discussion of English and Chinese raises one final question. Why is it necessary for the requirement that an interrogative clause have an interrogative expression in its spec-CP position to be satisfied in overt syntax in English whereas it can be satisfied in covert syntax in Chinese? It will come as no surprise that we suggest that this is another example of a parametric difference between grammars. Extending an idea introduced in section 21, we propose that Spec-CP in questions can be strong or weak. If it is strong (as in English), it must be filled *overtly*; if it is weak (as in Chinese), it will not be filled overtly. Since covert movement will never lead to a position being filled overtly, the covert movement of wh-phrases in Chinese is clearly consistent with the weakness of spec-CP in this language (*exercises 5 and 6*).

Exercises

1.   Consider the sentence in (a):

   (a) John visited London after Mary did

   It is often assumed that the interpretation of such a sentence involves 'copying' the VP from the clause *John visited London* into the position of *did* in the second clause to give (b) and that this 'VP-copying' process is part of the procedure of deriving the LF for such a sentence.

   (b) John visited London after Mary visited London

   Suppose that this is correct, and consider (c):

   (c) John [$_{VP}$saw [$_{DP}$everything that Mary did]]

   In (c), we have the VP *saw everything that Mary did* which is produced by merging the head V *saw* with the complex quantificational DP *everything that Mary did*. What problem arises if you apply VP-copying to (c)? Does the same problem arise if VP-copying takes place *after* covert movement? Using these questions, you should be able to construct another argument for the necessity of covert movement.

2.   A common observation is that a sentence such as (a) is ambiguous:

(a) Some student voted for every candidate

The interpretations are: (i) there is some particular student who voted for all candidates; (ii) for each candidate, it is possible to find a student who voted for that candidate. This ambiguity is referred to as a **scope ambiguity**, and we say that for (i), *some student* has wide scope and *every candidate* narrow scope. These relative scopes are reversed for (ii). In the text, we have informally suggested that semantic scope might be linked to 'height' in the structure of LF, with 'higher' operator expressions having wider scope. Try to develop an account of how the ambiguity in (a) might be represented using the ideas developed in this section.

3.   Contradicting the claim appearing in exercise 2, it has sometimes been suggested that the relative scope of quantified DPs can be read directly off their surface order. Thus, (a) in exercise 2 has been claimed to be unambiguous, allowing only the interpretation where *some student* has wide scope and *every candidate* has narrow scope. Certainly, this interpretation appears to be *preferred*, and we can, it seems, reverse this preference by passivising the sentence, as in (a′) below:

(a′) Every candidate was voted for by some student

Here the interpretation where every candidate is voted for but not by the same student (the second interpretation from exercise 2) is strongly preferred. Use the examples in (b) and (c) below and any others you consider relevant to assess the generality of this 'surface' account of scope:

(b) Some worker in every factory likes ice cream
(c) Every voter in some constituency voted for Pratt

4.   Alongside *think* and *wonder*, English has verbs such as *know*, which appear in both (a) and (b):

(a) Who$_i$ does John know the dog chased t$_i$?
(b) John knows who$_i$ the dog chased t$_i$

How might these examples be dealt with in the framework sketched in this section? How, within this framework, would you account for the ill-formedness of (c):

(c) *Who does John know who the dog chased

5.   In Chinese, the verb *zhidao* corresponds to English *know*. The sentence (a) below is ambiguous. Describe its two interpretations and show how they can be linked to two distinct LF-representations:

(a) Guo zhidao gou zhui   shei
    Guo know   dog chase who

6.   In section 21 (p. 330) we suggested that the *economy principle* can be utilised to account for why only one wh-phrase moves to spec-CP in multiple questions such as (a):

(a) Who saw what?

Consider the sentence in (b):

(b) Who wonders what goes where?

This sentence is ambiguous between the following interpretations. First, it can be a direct question on *who* alone and it might be answered by (c):

(c) Bill wonders what goes where

Alternatively, it can be taken as a direct multiple question on *who* and *where*, in which case it will solicit answers such as (d):

(d) Mary wonders what goes in the dining room and John wonders what goes in the kitchen

Note that it cannot be interpeted as a direct question on *what* under any circumstances. Evaluate the extent to which these observations are consistent with the economy principle. What are the consequences of extending this principle so that as well as minimising grammatical structure and grammatical operations, it also favours covert movement over overt movement?

24 Children's sentences

The *principles and parameters theory* (PPT) outlined at the end of section 22 has interesting implications for the development of a theory of language acquisition, and in particular for how we answer the question: 'What is it that children have to learn about the syntax of their native language?' Clearly, a major part of the task of acquiring a first language involves **lexical learning** (i.e. learning words and their idiosyncratic properties, see section 13). However, the question we shall focus on here is what **structural learning** is involved in first language acquisition – i.e. what children have to learn about the structure of sentences in the language they are acquiring. (Note that we shall be concerned here only with how children acquire their native languages, not with the very different question of how children or adults acquire foreign languages.)

Within the PPT model, certain aspects of sentence structure are assumed to be determined by *UG principles* (i.e. principles of Universal Grammar), and hence are invariant across languages. If we further assume that principles of UG are part of the child's innately endowed *language faculty*, it follows that universal aspects of sentence structure will not have to be learned (see the introduction, pp. 8f.). For example, if clauses are universally CP/IP/VP structures and this is part of the child's innate linguistic competence at birth, it will not have to be learned. Similarly, if noun/pronoun expressions are universally D-projections (and hence comprise either a pronominal determiner, or a prenominal determiner with a noun or noun phrase complement) and this is also part of the child's innate knowledge, this too will not have to be learned. In other words, the child does not have to learn those aspects of sentence structure which are universal by virtue of being determined by innately endowed UG principles.

So what do children have to learn about sentence structure in their native language? The answer is that they have to learn those aspects of structure which vary in a parametric fashion from one language to another. A key assumption of the PPT model is that all structural variation between languages can be characterised in terms of a set of parameters, each of which is binary and hence has two possible values (e.g. the *head parameter*, which specifies that a particular type of phrase is head first or head last, the *INFL parameter*, which indicates whether INFL is either strong or weak, *the wh-parameter*, which does or does not require that wh-operators move overtly into spec-CP, the *null subject parameter*, which states that finite verbs do or do not license null subjects). It follows from this that the only *structural learning* which children face in acquiring their native language is the task of determining the appropriate value of each of the structural parameters along which languages vary.

If our reasoning here is along the right lines, it leads us to the following view of the language acquisition process. The central task which the child faces in acquiring the structural properties of a language is to construct a grammar of the language. The child's language faculty incorporates a theory of Universal Grammar which includes (i) a set of universal *principles* of grammatical structure, and (ii) a set of structural *parameters* which impose severe constraints on the range of structural variation permitted in natural languages (perhaps limiting the range of variation to a series of binary choices). Since universal principles of grammatical structure don't have to be learned, the child's structural learning task is limited to that of **parameter-setting** (i.e. determining an appropriate *setting* for each of the relevant structural parameters).

The assumption that acquiring the syntactic structure of a language involves the relatively simple task of setting a number of structural parameters at their appropriate value provides a natural way of accounting for the fact that structural learning is a remarkably rapid and error-free process in young children.

Setting parameters: two examples

A good example to illustrate the approach we have just outlined is provided by examining the acquisition of word-order. Young children acquiring English as their native language show evidence from the very earliest two- and three-word sentences they produce of knowing (tacitly, not explicitly, of course) that phrases in English uniformly have *head-first* word order. Accordingly, the earliest verb phrases and prepositional phrases produced by English children consistently show verbs and prepositions positioned before their complements, as structures such as the following illustrate (produced by a young boy called Jem at age 1;8; head verbs or prepositions are italicised):

(427)   a. *Touch* heads. *Cuddle* book. *Want* crayons. *Want* malteser. *Open*
         door. *Want* biscuit. *Bang* bottom. *See* cats. *Sit* down.
         b. *On* mummy. *To* lady. *Without* shoe. *With* potty. *In* keyhole. *In*
         school. *On* carpet. *On* box. *With* crayons. *To* mummy.

So, children acquiring English set the *head parameter* at the head-first setting appropriate to all types of phrases in English from the very earliest multiword utterances which they produce. They do not use different orders for different words of the same type (e.g. they don't position the verb *see* after its complement but the verb *want* before its complement), or for different types of words (e.g. they don't position verbs before and prepositions after their complements).

Just as children acquiring English seem to know from the outset that English is the type of language which positions heads before complements, so too they also seem to know that English is the type of language which positions a wh-operator expression at the beginning of an interrogative clause (in spec-CP). Some evidence that this is so comes from the examples in (428) below, which illustrate typical wh-questions produced by a girl called Claire at age 2;0–2;1 (the recordings were made by Jane Anne Collins Hill):

(428)   a. Where girl go? Where pencil go? Where cow go? Where the horse
         go?
         b. What kitty doing? What squirrel doing? What lizard doing? What
         the dog doing? What the cow say?

Although various constituents which would be obligatory in the corresponding adult questions are omitted (e.g. *Where go?* shows omission of the auxiliary *does* and the subject *it)*, all the sentences in (428) show correct positioning of the wh-operators *where/what* at the beginning of the sentence.

A natural question to ask at this juncture is how we can account for the fact that from the very outset of multiword speech we find English children correctly positioning heads before their complements, and wh-expressions at the beginning of interrogative clauses. The principles-and-parameters model enables us to provide a principled explanation for how children manage to learn word-order properties like these in such a rapid and error-free fashion. The answer provided by the model is that learning these aspects of word order involves the comparatively simple task of setting a binary parameter at its appropriate value. This task will be a relatively straightforward one if the head parameter determines that the only possible choice is for a given type of phrase in a given language to be *uniformly head-first* or *uniformly head-last*, and likewise if the wh-parameter determines that the only possible choice is for wh-operators to be preposed (and moved into spec-CP) or to remain in situ. Given such an assumption, once a child hears (and can parse) a verb phrase such as *help daddy*, the child will immediately be able to infer that English is a head-first language. Likewise, once a child hears (and is able to parse) a wh-question like *What are you doing?* the child will immediately infer that English is a wh-fronting language which has overt movement of wh-operators. So, child structures like (427) and (428) are consistent with the parameter-setting model of acquisition outlined above. However, there is what at first sight appears to be some puzzling counter-evidence to the claim that children set parameters at their appropriate value at a very early age.

Null subjects in early Child English

In influential research in the early 1980s, Nina Hyams observed that children acquiring English at around two years of age frequently omit sentence subjects and produce sentences such as those in (429):

(429)   Play it. Eating cereal. Shake hands. See window. Want more apple. No go in.

Hyams maintained that sentences like these have an *implicit* (i.e. 'understood') subject, a claim which is made more plausible by the fact that when children produce a seemingly subjectless sentence, they sometimes produce an expanded variant of the sentence immediately afterwards in which the 'understood' subject is made explicit – as in the following examples (collected by Martin Braine) produced by Stevie at ages 2;1–2;2:

(430)   a. Go nursery . . . Lucy go nursery
        b. Push Stevie . . . Betty push Stevie
        c. No touch . . . This no touch
        d. Want that . . . Andrew want that
        e. Plug in . . . Andrew plug in

Hyams went on to argue that apparently subjectless child sentences such as those in (430) have null nominative 'little *pro*' subjects (like those found in Early Modern English, see section 22), so that a child sentence like *Want more apple* would have the fuller structure indicated informally in (431):

(431)   *pro* want more apple

Here, the child is viewed as using the null nominative pronoun *pro* where an adult would use the overt nominative pronoun *I*. The more general conclusion which Hyams drew was that Child English (at the relevant stage) is a *null subject language* – i.e. a language which allows finite verbs to have a null *pro* subject. If this were so, it would provide an obvious challenge to the claim that children correctly set parameters from the outset, since adult English is not a null subject language.

However, there are reasons to be sceptical of Hyams' claim that English children initially mis-set the null subject parameter and hence misanalyse English as a language which allows finite verbs to have a null nominative *pro* subject like that found in Early Modern English (EME). We saw in our earlier discussion of EME (section 22, pp. 347ff.) that null nominative *pro* subjects are only licensed in EME because finite verbs raise to INFL and (by virtue of the rich agreement inflections they carry) can locally identify a null *pro* subject in spec-IP. However, in Child English verbs never raise to INFL (as we see from the fact that children never produce sentences like **Teddy likes not spaghetti* in which the verb *likes* moves from V to INFL across the intervening negative particle *not*), and often children's verbs carry no agreement inflection at all (e.g. they may say *Teddy want ice-cream* rather than *Teddy wants an ice-cream*). For reasons such as these, it is unlikely that children's 'missing' subjects are instances of the null nominative pronoun *pro* found in EME.

An alternative analysis has been produced in more recent work by Luigi Rizzi, who argues that omission of the subject in child sentences like (429) is attributable to a separate phenomenon of **truncation** whereby sentence structure can be truncated in such a way that the initial constituent of the sentence can be null. This phenomenon of truncation is also found in colloquial adult English, e.g. in sentences such as (432):

(432)   a. Can't find it (= *I* can't find it)
         b. You know anything about it? (= *Do* you know anything about it?)
         c. Time is it? (= *What* time is it?)

As these examples illustrate, truncation typically affects the first word in a sentence (*I* in 432a, *do* in 432b and *what* in 432c). In children's grammars, it even seems to extend to wh-pronouns, which are sometimes omitted from questions (resulting in *null operator* questions). So, alongside overt operator questions like (428), Claire (at the same age) produced null operator questions such as (433):

(433)   a. Bunnies doing? (= *What* are the bunnies doing?)
         b. Mommy gone? (= *Where* has Mommy gone?)
         c. This go? (= *Where* does this go?)

If children's null operator questions like (433) are the result of truncation, a natural suggestion to make is that children's null subject sentences like (429) are also the result of truncation (and not of a missetting of the null subject parameter).

Empirical evidence in support of the *truncation* analysis of children's 'missing' subjects comes from research done by Virginia Valian. She noted that English children only omit subjects in main clauses, never in complement clauses. If Child English were a genuine null subject language which allowed any finite verb to have a null subject, we should expect that children would omit subjects in finite complement clauses just as frequently as they omit them in finite main clauses. But Valian's study showed that while English children frequently omit subjects in finite main clauses, they never do so in finite complement clauses (whereas a group of young Italian children she studied frequently omitted subjects in finite complement clauses, as we would expect if they had correctly identified Italian as a null subject language). This seems to provide us with conclusive evidence that the null subjects used by English children are not the result of missetting the null subject parameter, but rather are the consequence of some independent process such as truncation. And this in turn enables us to continue to maintain the parameter-setting model of acquisition under which children from the very outset quickly arrive at a correct setting for each parameter.

But there is a further complication which we need to take account of before we can be sure that our conclusion is correct, and this relates to the fact that children often omit subjects in wh-questions. So, for example, alongside wh-questions with overt subjects such as (428) and (433), Claire (at the same age) produced wh-questions with null subjects like (434):

(434)   a. What doing? (= What are *you* doing?)
         b. Where go? (= Where did *it* go?)
         c. What do? (= What shall *I* do?)

The null subject in such sentences cannot be the result of truncation, since a subject pronoun can only be truncated if it is the first word in a sentence, and it seems reasonable to assume that the wh-pronouns *what/where* are the first words in the sentences here, not the 'missing' subject pronouns *you/it/I*. So what precisely is the nature of the null subject in the examples in (434)?

An important clue comes from the fact that the clauses in (434) appear to be *non-finite*, in the sense that they contain no finite verb or auxiliary (e.g. they lack the finite auxiliaries *are/did/shall* which appear in their adult counterparts). Now, we already know from our earlier discussion in section 20 that non-finite clauses in adult English (such as those bracketed below) allow a null 'big PRO' subject:

(435)   a. I intend [PRO going to Sri Lanka for my holidays]
         b. I intend [PRO to go to Sri Lanka for my holidays]

This suggests that the 'missing' subject in the non-finite wh-questions in (434) may also be PRO, and hence that (434a), for example, has the simplified structure (436):

(436)   What PRO doing?

Evidence in support of this analysis comes from the fact that English children typically don't use null subjects in finite wh-questions – i.e. they don't produce sentences such as the following (the asterisk here serves to indicate a non-occurring structure):

(437)   a. *What are doing? (= What are *you* doing?)
         b. *What did say? (= What did *he* say?)
         c. *Where have been? (= Where have *you* been?)

Why not? The answer is that children's null subjects in wh-questions are instances of PRO, and PRO can only occur as the subject of a non-finite clause, not as the subject of a clause containing a finite auxiliary like *are/did/have*) (***exercise 1***).

Non-finite clauses in Child English

Having argued that English children produce non-finite wh-questions like (436) with a null PRO subject, let's take a closer look at the structure of such sentences. In keeping with the assumptions underlying the principles and parameters model, we will assume that UG principles determine that wh-phrases must move to spec-CP at LF, and that the wh-parameter determines whether this movement is overt or wh-operators remain *in situ* in overt syntax (the choice depending on the setting of the parameter in a given language). Since we have already argued from wh-questions like (428) that children show evidence of having arrived at the correct setting of the wh-parameter from the very earliest questions they produce, we can conclude that the wh-pronoun *what* (which originates as the complement of *doing*) moves overtly to spec-CP in (436). Hence, (436) must contain a CP projection. If we make the standard assumption that C universally selects an IP complement, and if we also assume (as we have throughout) that subjects occupy spec-IP, it follows that (436) will also contain IP. Finally, since (436) contains the lexical verb *doing* (and since INFL selects a VP complement), it will also contain VP. So, our assumptions lead us to the conclusion that (436) is a CP/IP/VP structure derived in the manner outlined (in simplified form) in (438):

(438)   [$_{CP}$ **What** C [$_{IP}$ PRO INFL [$_{VP}$ doing **t**]]]

Its adult counterpart *What are you doing?* will have the derivation in (439):

(439)   [$_{CP}$ **What** [$_C$ *are*] [$_{IP}$ you [$_I$ *t*] [$_{VP}$ doing **t**]]]

An important difference between the two structures is that the adult structure (439) is a *finite* clause (headed by the finite auxiliary *are*) with a nominative *you* subject, whereas its child counterpart (438) is a non-finite clause with a null PRO subject. Since INFL in English can only be filled by a finite auxiliary (and only finite auxiliaries can move from INFL to C), it is scarcely surprising that (438) contains no overt auxiliary.

There are two interesting conclusions which our discussion of children's non-finite questions lead us to. The first is that there is essential **structural continuity** between adult and child grammars: this (in a fairly obvious sense) is what the principles and parameters model would lead us to expect. After all, if some aspects of sentence structure are determined by innate UG principles and so do not have to be learned, and if other (language-specific) aspects of structure involve children in the comparatively simple learning task of parameter-setting, we should expect to find that the very earliest sentences children produce are similar in structure to their adult counterparts.

A second conclusion which we can draw is that children sometimes use non-finite clauses like *What doing?* in contexts where adults require a finite clause like *What are you doing?* More specifically, young children tend to alternate between finite and non-finite clauses in finite contexts (i.e. in contexts where adults require a finite clause). We can illustrate this in terms of the negative sentences in (440) below, produced by a girl called Kathryn between ages 1;10 and 2;0 (the data are from a study by Lois Bloom):

(440)   a. Can't see. I can't open it. I don't go sleep. I don't need pants off. I
            don't want those shoes. This one don't fit.
         b. No like celery, Mommy. No want this. No go outside. Not going
            away. No going home. Man no go in there. Kathryn not go over
            here. Kathryn no fix this. Kathryn no like celery. Mommy no play
            'corder. Kathryn not quite through.

Sentences in colloquial English are usually negated by a finite negative auxiliary such as *don't*, *won't*, *can't*, *isn't*, etc., and it is clear from the examples in

(440a) that Kathryn already knows this. However, alongside the finite negative sentences in (440a) she produces non-finite auxiliariless negatives like (440b), sometimes negated by *no*, sometimes by *not* (confusion between *no* and *not* is typical of young children).

So, in contexts where adults require a finite clause, young children alternate between finite and non-finite clauses. An interesting reflex of the difference between these two types of child clause is that their subjects are differentially case-marked, as examples such as those below illustrate:

(441) a. *I'*m pulling this
       b. *Me* going make a castle (Holly 2;0)

(442) a. *She'*s gone
       b. *Her* gone school (Domenico 2;0)

(443) a. *He'*s kicking a beach ball
       b. *Her* climbing up the ladder there (Jem 2;0)

(444) a. *I* can mend it
       b. *Me* finding something (Adam 2;2)

(445) a. *I'*m having this
       b. *Me* driving (Rebecca 2;2)

In finite clauses like the (a) examples we find nominative subjects, whereas in non-finite clauses like the (b) examples we find objective subjects: for example, nominative *I* is used as the subject of the finite contracted auxiliary *'m* in (441a), but objective *me* is used as the subject of the non-finite verb *going* in (441b). Why should this be?

Interestingly, these case-marking errors turn out to be predictable if we assume that by the age of two, children have acquired the adult English case-marking system. Adult English is said to have **structural case**, in that the case carried by a pronoun is determined by the position it occupies in the structure containing it, in accordance with the following (simplified) generalisation:

(446) A (pro)nominal expression carries:
       a. nominative case if it is the subject of a finite clause
       b. genitive case if it is the possessor in a possessive structure
       c. objective case otherwise (by default)

We can illustrate how (446) works for adult English in terms of the italicised pronouns in the examples below (A and B represent different speakers in the c, e and f examples):

(447)   a. *He* has lost *his* tax return
      b. Remember *me* to *them*!
      c. A: You've been lying   B: What! *Me* lie to you? Never!
      d. *I* always hated syntax, *me*
      e. A: Who did it?   B: *Me*
      f. A: Who is it?   B: It's *me*

In (447a), *he* is nominative because it is the subject of the finite auxiliary *has*, and *his* is genitive by virtue of its possessive function. In (447b), *me* and *them* receive objective case by default – i.e. by virtue of the fact that neither is used as a finite clause subject or possessor: hence, objective case is said to be the *default* case in English. In (447c), *me* is the subject of the non-finite *lie* clause (*lie* here is a non-finite infinitive form) and so receives objective case by default. In (447d), *I* is nominative by virtue of being the subject of the finite verb *hated* and the dislocated pronoun *me* at the end of the sentence receives objective case by default. In (447e), *me* is used as a sentence fragment, and hence carries default objective case. And in (447f), *me* is used as a predicative pronoun (i.e. a pronoun which serves as the complement of the copular verb *be*), and again carries default objective case.

In the light of our discussion of how (446) works, let's return to the question of how we account for the fact that children alternate between structures like *I'm playing* and *Me playing*. Given our assumption that subjects are in spec-IP, both clauses will be IPs. Since *I'm playing* contains a finite auxiliary in INFL but *Me playing* does not, let's assume that INFL is finite in the first case and non-finite in the second. Using the feature [±fin] as a convenient way of marking the difference between a finite and a non-finite INFL, we can say that the two have the respective (simplified) structures indicated in (448):

(448)   a.   b.

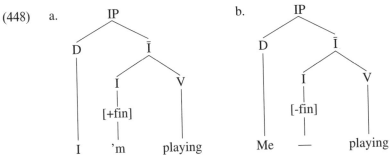

INFL is filled by '*m* in (448a) but is null in (448b) because only a finite INFL can be filled by an auxiliary, not a non-finite INFL (and we can assume that children leave a given position empty when they have no suitable lexical item which can fill it). Let's further assume that by the age of two, children have acquired the adult English case-marking system in (446), so that (at the relevant stage) there is continuity between adult and child case systems. It follows that the subject in (448a) will have nominative case by (446a) and so appear as *I*; and conversely that the subject in (448b) will have default objective case by (446c) and so appear as *me*.

We can extend the analysis proposed here to account for the fact that many two-year-olds alternate between saying, for example, *I want one* and *Me want one*. Let's suppose that when *want* is used with an objective subject like *me*, it is a non-finite form (i.e. the same non-finite form that we find in adult infinitive structures such as *He seems to **want** one*). In terms of the analysis outlined here, this means that the two sentences have the respective structures in (449) below (with *want* being a finite form in 449a and a non-finite infinitive form in 449b):

(449)   a. $[_{IP}$ I $[_{I}$ +fin] $[_{VP}$ $[_{V}$ want] one]]
       b. $[_{IP}$ Me $[_{I}$ −fin] $[_{VP}$ $[_{V}$ want] one]]

On this view, children alternate between using finite verbs and infinitives in contexts where adults use finite verbs: for this reason, Ken Wexler and his co-researchers have dubbed the relevant stage the **optional infinitive stage** (sometimes abbreviated to **OI stage**). This stage typically lasts until around the child's fourth birthday (with the use of non-finite clauses in finite contexts gradually becoming less and less frequent as the child gets older) (*exercises 2 and 3*).

A related phenomenon which we find during the relevant stage is that children alternate between using tensed and untensed verb forms in contexts where adults require tensed verbs (i.e. verbs inflected for present/past tense). This pattern is illustrated by the sentences in (450) below (produced by Claire at ages 2;0–2;1):

(450)   a.   David did it. Claire did it. Bear did it. Claire fell down. Claire woke up. Happened the hammer? Look I found. That goes little one. That one goes another one. There goes another one. Goes there. Goes here.
       b.   Pixie eat dinner. Jane help dinner time. Bunny stand up. Cow fall down. Claire close it. Claire do puzzle. Jane do it. That go there. Chair go there. That one fit. Daddy sit in chair. Raggedy Ann sit down. Raggedy Ann lie down. Porcupine lie down. Raggedy Ann stay there. Raggedy Ann to wake up. Jane see Mommy. Pig say oink (reply to 'What does the pig say?').

The sentences in (450a) are finite clauses containing a finite verb like *happened/goes* overtly inflected for tense, but those in (450b) appear to be non-finite clauses containing an untensed verb like *eat/go*. In terms of the framework we are using here, *Claire fell down* and *Claire fall down* will have the respective simplified structures (451a, b):

(451)   a. [$_{IP}$ Claire [$_I$ +fin] [$_{VP}$ [$_V$ fell] down]]
         b. [$_{IP}$ Claire [$_I$ −fin] [$_{VP}$ [$_V$ fall] down]]

Both clauses are IPs, but they differ in that INFL is finite in (451a) and so the verb *fell* is overtly inflected for past tense, whereas INFL is non-finite in (451b) and so the verb remains in the uninflected form *fall* (i.e. the same form as we find in infinitives). Once again, we see the familiar pattern of children alternating between finite and non-finite forms in finite contexts.

Children's nominals

Up to this point, we have concentrated on the clause structures produced by young children, noting that they sometimes produce non-finite clauses in finite contexts, and so, for example, omit auxiliaries where adults require them. We find a similar pattern of development in relation to children's nominal structures. From around two years of age, children start to produce adult-like DP structures of the form *determiner + noun*, using both definite determiners like *the/this/that* and indefinites such as *a/another/some*. However, alongside determinate nominals containing overt definite or indefinite determiners, we also find children producing bare nominals which contain a noun but no determiner (in contexts where adults would require a determiner), as illustrated by the following sentences produced by Claire at ages 2;0–2;1:

(452)   a. There's *the hat*. Piggie see *the water*. Baby drink *the coffee*. Daddy sitting in *the chair*. Horsie swimming in *the pool*. Do *the green one*. Put *that mommy* in *the carriage*.
         b. It's *a baby*. It's *a dolly*. It's *a girl*. There's *a spider*. There's *a bunny*. There's *another one*. There goes *another one*. Put *another fence*.
         c. Daddy sit in *chair*. Girl sleeping. *Baby* eating *dinner*. *Baby* eating *juice*. Claire do *puzzle*. *Pig* say oink. Read *book*. Ring *bell*. See *flower*.

The italicised nominals in (452a) are DPs headed by the definite determiners *the/that*, and likewise those in (452b) are DPs headed by the indefinite determiners *a/another*. Since Claire is clearly able to form DPs at this stage, it seems reasonable to assume that all her nominals are DPs (as indeed must be the case if principles of UG specify that all nominals are D-projections). But this in turn means that bare nominals such as those italicised in (452c) must also be DPs; and since they contain no overt determiner, they must be headed by a null determiner. Note that Claire doesn't just use null determiners in contexts where adults do (e.g. with proper names like *Claire*), but also in contexts where adults require an overt determiner (e.g. modifying a singular count noun like *chair/girl/puzzle*, etc.). In other words, just as she omits auxiliaries in obligatory contexts, so too she omits determiners in obligatory contexts (i.e. in contexts where adults would require an overt determiner).

Research conducted by Nina Hyams and Teun Hoekstra has suggested that there are systematic parallels between the role of INFL in clauses and the role of D in nominals. They note that just as the tense specification of INFL serves to anchor a clause in time, so too the definiteness specification of D serves to anchor a nominal in space. On this basis, they argue that definiteness and tense are two different manifestations of a single common property, which they refer to as *finiteness*. In the terminology of Hyams and Hoekstra, nominals which contain an overt determiner are finite, whereas those which lack an overt determiner in a context where adults would require one are non-finite. This means that a sentence such as *Pig say oink* (which Claire used in reply to 'What does the pig say?') will have the structure (453) below (We have assumed that *oink* is an onomatopoeic word which doesn't belong to any syntactic category):

(453)

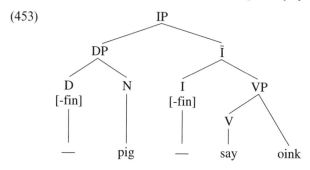

In the same way as the overall clause (IP) is non-finite by virtue of being headed by a non-finite INFL, so too the subject DP is non-finite by virtue of being headed by a non-finite D.

Hoekstra and Hyams argue that children's finite clauses always have finite subjects (so that they say *The doggy is barking* but not **Doggy is barking*), but that their non-finite clauses can have both finite and non-finite subjects (so that they say both *The doggy barking* and *Doggy barking*). They maintain that this follows from UG principles – more specifically from the specifier-head agreement relation which holds (universally) between a finite INFL and its subject. Since there is no agreement relation between a non-finite INFL and its subject, there are no finiteness restrictions on the choice of subject in a non-finite clause (***exercise 4***).

What our discussion here shows is that just as children alternate between finite and non-finite clauses, so too they alternate between finite and non-finite DPs. One way in which this has been described is to say that children sometimes leave functional categories **underspecified** with respect to the features they encode. So, for example, INFL can be underspecified for its tense/agreement features, and D can likewise be underspecified for its definiteness/agreement features. An underspecified functional category will be null where children have no suitable item in their lexicon which can fill the relevant slot – as we can see from the fact that D and INFL are null in (453). For obvious reasons, this proposal is generally known as the **underspecification** analysis of child grammars (see section 6 for a similar sense of underspecification in child phonology).

The overall conclusion we arrive at in this section is that there is essential structural continuity between adult and child grammars. Innate principles of Universal Grammar determine that clauses are universally CP/IP/VP structures, and that nominal expressions are D-projections; and we have evidence that children as young as two years of age are able to produce CP and DP structures. There is also evidence that parameters like the head parameter, the wh-parameter and the null subject parameter are correctly set from the very earliest stages of acquisition (with apparent null-subject sentences found in child English being instances of either truncation or sentences with PRO subjects). The principal difference between adult and child structures is that children sometimes omit functional elements in obligatory contexts (e.g. they omit auxiliaries, determiners and tense/agreement inflections where adults require them). They thus alternate between finite and non-finite clauses, and between finite and non-finite nominals. As we noted, one way of describing this is to say that functional categories in child grammars may optionally be underspecified (i.e. they may lack some of the features they have in adult grammars) (*exercise 5*).

Exercises

1.   The sentences below illustrate typical null subject sentences which English children do and don't produce. (An asterisk indicates a non-occurring structure):

(a) Can't find it (= I can't find it)
(b) Goes in there (= It goes in there)
(c) Want 'nother one (=I want another one)
(d) Gone home (= He's gone home)

(e) Where going? (= Where are you going?)
(f) *Can help me? (= Can you help me?)
(g) *What are doing? (= What are you doing?)
(h) *Teddy says likes chocolate (= Teddy says he likes chocolate)

Discuss the nature of the null subject in each case, and say why the subject can be omitted in some of the sentences but not others. What conclusions about parameter-setting can we draw from the relevant data?

2.   The sentences below illustrate ways in which two-year-olds typically do (and don't) use case-marked pronouns. (An asterisk marks a structure which children don't generally produce):

(a) I'm playing with them
(b) Me driving my car
(c) He wants a drink
(d) Him like chocolate
(e) *Me am helping daddy
(f) *Him wants to go to bed
(g) *Daddy won't help my
(h) *You can't drive I car

Analyse each of the sentences, and say why children do or don't produce them. Are such sentences consistent with the view that by two years of age children have generally acquired the adult case system?

3.   Two-year-olds produce negative sentences such as (a) to (d), but not (e):

(a) He doesn't like cabbage
(b) Doesn't like cabbage
(c) Him no like cabbage
(d) No like cabbage
(e) *Him doesn't like cabbage

How can we account for this?

4.   The sentences below illustrate the kinds of sentence structures in which children do or don't omit determiners in contexts where adults require them:

(a) The car's broken
(b) The car broken
(c) Car broken
(d) The car goes in there
(e) The car go in there
(f) Car go in there
(g) *Car's broken
(h) *Car goes in there

How can we account for these data?

5. Corresponding to adult questions like *What's the man/he doing?*, two-year-olds typically produce structures such as the following:

(a) What's the man doing?
(b) What the man doing?
(c) What man doing?
(d) Man doing?
(e) What's he doing?
(f) What him doing?
(g) What doing?

By contrast, they don't generally produce questions like those below:

(h) *What's man doing?
(i) *What's him doing?
(j) *What's doing?

Analyse the syntax of the child question structures in (a) to (g), and try to explain why children don't generally produce sentences like those in (h) to (j).

25 Sentence processing

In section 14 we discussed how words are accessed and retrieved from the mental lexicon. In this section, we shall look into the processing of sentences, focusing on sentence comprehension. Notice first that there is a fundamental difference between lexical and syntactic processing: the lexemes in a language, being finite in number, are *stored* in the mental lexicon. Sentences, however, typically are not stored in any kind of mental list (if they were, then we would be unable to produce any new sentences, i.e. sentences that we have never heard or read before). Indeed, sentence repetition and sentence recognition experiments have shown that normally syntactic structures are extremely transient: memory for syntax is unreliable only half a minute after a sentence has been heard or read (was the second sentence in this paragraph *Focusing on sentence comprehension, in this section, we shall look into the processing of sentences* or *In this section, we shall look into the processing of sentences, focusing on sentence comprehension*?). Hence, whereas word recognition can be described as a retrieval process with the goal of finding an entry in the mental lexicon, sentence processing does not involve accessing and retrieving entries from a mental repository.

If the representations of sentences are not retrieved from a memory store, this means that they are constructed on-line (in a step-by-step fashion) in accordance with syntactic principles or rules. It follows that sentence comprehension involves segmenting the sentence into relevant processing units and constructing a syntactic representation for the sentence (the technical term for this is **parsing**).

But how do we go about processing sentences? According to one view (which is favoured by many psychologists), speakers/listeners rely on parsing and production strategies that have nothing much to do with the units and operations that linguists employ in their syntactic analyses of sentences. According to this view, the detailed tree structures we have been associating with sentences throughout this part of the book bear no relationship to the procedures native-speakers employ when parsing. Alternatively, it has been suggested that such structures do play an important role in sentence processing, to an extent to be determined by psycholinguistic research. Proponents of this alternative view claim that when producing or comprehending a sentence, we make use of essentially the same processing units and operations that are used in linguistic analysis, such as constituents, tree structures, and movement rules. If this is correct, it means, for example, that listeners segment sentences into VPs, IPs, CPs, etc., and that linguistically complex sentences are more difficult to comprehend than simple ones. In other words, the more complex the syntactic derivation (in terms of the operations it involves), the more difficult the sentence is to process. This view came to be known as the **Derivational Theory of Complexity (DTC)**, and many psycholinguists have explored the extent to which the DTC actually holds. When this research began, in the late 1960s, the idea that a generative grammar could provide not just a theory of syntactic knowledge (competence), but at the same time a theory of syntactic processing (a central aspect of performance) was adopted with considerable enthusiasm. Subsequently, however, these rather naive ideas have been abandoned, and more complex questions are now being asked. In what follows, we will look at two sets of experimental results which suggest that the syntactic constructs theoretical linguists have postulated are in fact used by normal listeners when they process sentences. Positive results of this kind do not, of course, constitute a comprehensive theory of sentence perception. They do, however, indicate that a grammar, as we have understood this notion throughout this book, will be a central component of such a theory.

Click studies

The purpose of click studies is to determine whether listeners *segment* sentences to which they are listening into units similar to those postulated in syntactic theory, namely phrases and clauses. In this type of experiment, sentences such as (454) are recorded on tape, and superimposed on each sentence is a 'click' or 'beep', i.e. a short acoustic signal, which may be located at any one of a number of different places within the sentence.

(454)   The man [who nobody likes] is leaving soon

Immediately after hearing the sentence (including the superimposed 'click'), subjects are given a written copy of it and are asked to indicate the point in the sentence at which they perceived the click. In sentences like (454), the bracketed clause is a *relative clause*, in which the relative pronoun *who* 'relates to' the preceding expression *the man* (see section 18, p. 289). The possible locations of the click for subjects hearing this sentence are indicated by + in (455):

(455)   a. The + man [who nobody likes] is leaving soon
      b. The man [who + nobody likes] is leaving soon
      c. The man + [who nobody likes] is leaving soon

In (455a) the click occurs *before* the relative clause boundary, in (455b) it occurs *after* this boundary, and in (455c) it is located *exactly at* the boundary. Subjects hear a range of sentences of this (and other) structural types with the position of the click systematically varied.

The basic finding in such studies is that subjects misplace clicks *towards or into major clause boundaries*. An early click, which in the stimulus is objectively located immediately before the noun *man* in (455a), is reported as occurring towards or at the clause boundary (i.e. in the word *man* or between *man* and *who*). Similarly, a late click located after the clause boundary in (455b) is reported as occurring earlier, again towards or at the clause boundary. By contrast, clicks objectively located at the clause boundary are accurately perceived as having occurred in this position. Similar results have been obtained with respect to the second clause boundary position in (454), i.e. between *likes* and *is*, and using a variety of different clause types.

Click experiments are deliberately constructed in such a way as to overstretch a subject's processing capacity. The task is extremely demanding as it involves two processing tasks to be undertaken simultaneously, the comprehension of the sentences (which can be tested by asking subjects questions) and the location of the clicks. The idea is that because of the demands of the task the experiment produces errors in click location, and this is in fact what happens. What is most interesting here is the types of errors that the subjects make, which are not random. First, of the three possibilities, click misplacements tend not to occur for (455c) and other sentences, where the click is located at the clause boundary. By contrast, errors are common in the 'early' and 'late' conditions of respectively (455a, b). Second, click mislocations tend to go into the clause boundary. These results suggest two things, namely (i) that the placement errors reflect the way the stimulus sentences are segmented into structural units, and (ii) that the clause is the major sentence processing unit. Using the same technique with different stimuli has yielded evidence for perceptual segmentation at constituent boundaries within clauses, too, specifically for a constituent boundary before VP, but these clause-internal boundaries give rise to a weaker effect than do major clause boundaries such as that in (454).

Finally, it is important to be clear that 'common sense' does not provide an explanation of these findings. For instance, it might be thought that there is a clear 'acoustic gap' between *man* and *who* in (454) and that it is this superficial aspect of the signal which is 'attracting' clicks. But this is not so: acoustic analysis of stimuli used in these experiments indicates that there is no such 'acoustic gap' – the speech signal is continuous – and reinforces the conclusion that subjects are relying on a *linguistic* segmentation of the input signal in their perception of the sentence.

Processing empty categories

As we have seen in section 20, syntactic theory postulates a range of so-called empty categories, phonetically null place-holders that occupy specific phrase-structure positions. Among these are the traces left behind by syntactic movement, discussed at some length in section 21. In fact, it is more accurate to refer to such objects as *covert categories*, since – if the theory is correct – they are not in fact empty of syntactic information. For example, PRO has the categorial status of a D and traces, by virtue of being linked to moved items, retain the syntactic characteristics (as a D-trace, V-trace, etc.) of those items. Is there any evidence from psycholinguistic experiments which independently confirms that empty categories are involved in the processing of sentence structure?

The answer to this question is 'yes'. Before we turn to experimental results, consider (456), which contains a covert category, namely the trace (t_i) of the bracketed wh-phrase *which paintings* (recall that one convention for indicating the relationship between a moved item and its trace is to use co-indexing):

(456)   [Which paintings]$_i$ did you speak to Mary about t_i?

In this structure, the wh-phrase originates as the complement of the preposition *about*, and then moves to spec-CP, leaving a trace behind in the prepositional complement position. The trace is in effect an invisible 'copy' of the wh-phrase, and so has the same grammatical properties as the phrase. Psycholinguists refer to the relationship between the moved wh-element and its trace as a **filler-gap dependency**: the higher overt wh-phrase *which paintings* is regarded as the filler for the lower gap, i.e. the position occupied by the trace.

To study filler-gap dependencies experimentally, psycholinguists have used several different techniques. One such technique is the *probe-recognition task*. In a study employing this task, subjects are asked to read sentences such as (456) from a computer screen, and are then asked to determine as quickly as possible whether certain probe words (e.g. *did* or *to*) appeared in the sentence – typically the probe word is displayed by subjects pressing a button as soon as they have read the sentence on the screen and they then press further buttons to indicate whether the word displayed occurred in the sentence or not. The result for a sentence like (456) is that reaction times (RT) for more recent items such as *to* are shorter than for more distant elements such as *did*. In other words, subjects show a faster reaction time in recognising elements they have recently perceived (probably because they are still present in short-term memory) than for those which are further away from the end of the sentence.

This kind of *recency effect* can be used to investigate the role of traces of movement. Consider the following examples:

(457)   a. John argued that Alex had seen the **boys**
         b. The **boys** argued that Alex had seen John
         c. The **boys** argued that Alex had seen *them*
         d. [Which **boys**]$_i$ did Alex argue that he had seen t_i?

In all cases, the probe is the word *boys*, i.e. subjects have to decide as quickly as possible whether *boys* has occurred in the sentence they had just read (of course in an actual experiment, there will be many different sentences with many different probes, and the order of presentation of examples will be carefully controlled). For (457b), RTs are significantly longer than they are for (457a). This can be put down to the recency effect we have just described. Interestingly, RTs to (457c) are also significantly faster than they are to (457b), despite the fact that *boys* is equally distant from the end of the sentence and the appearance of the probe in both cases. However, (457c) contains *them*, which can be interpreted as co-referential with *the boys*, as a very recent item. It is plausible, therefore, to suppose that *the boys* in (457c) behaves *as if* it were in the position occupied by *them*, thereby giving rise to a recency effect. The most interesting result, however, is that RTs to the probe *boys* in (457d) are similar to those in (457c), and again significantly shorter than those in (457b). This means that there is a recency effect in (457d), too – and the only candidate for explaining this in (457d) is the trace of the moved wh-expression.

What this finding shows is that when subjects process wh-questions such as (457d) and reach the position from which the wh-expression has been extracted (i.e. the position marked t_i in (457d)), the syntactic information contained in the wh-phrase is *reactivated*. Otherwise, there would be no recency effect for the probe word *boys*. The observed effect in (457d) suggests that the wh-trace functions like a pronoun (see (457c)). The experiment also shows that listeners reconstruct the relationship between a trace and its antecedent (i.e. the moved item to which it is related) (*exercise 1*).

Strategies of sentence processing

So far, in this section, we have shown that some notions from syntactic theory such as constituent structure and empty categories are useful for understanding human sentence processing. This, of course, is consistent with the theory of grammar being directly interpreted as a theory of linguistic performance. However, we shall now see that certain *processing principles* or *strategies*, which have no place in a theory of competence, must also be operative when we process sentences. Specifically, we will look at three types of processing difficulties (involving structural ambiguities, centre-embeddings, and garden-path sentences), which demonstrate that some sentences are difficult to process even though they are perfectly grammatical and do not contain any difficult words.

Structural ambiguity (see section 23) may cause processing difficulties. In fact, many of the sentences that we hear in our everyday conversations are ambiguous. Typically, however, these ambiguities do not impede communication. Indeed, we are rarely even aware of the occurrence of an ambiguity, and we generally come up with only one interpretation for each sentence, which, in the vast majority of cases, is the correct one.

Suppose, for example, that somebody who knows the grammar of English but who is unfamiliar with regional British culture is confronted with the following sentence:

(458)   Scotsmen like whisky more than Welshmen

This sentence has two interpretations, which can be paraphrased as (459a, b):

(459)   a. Scotsmen like whisky more than Scotsmen like Welshmen
          b. Scotsmen like whisky more than Welshmen like whisky

The question of which interpretation is the appropriate one cannot be decided by just looking at the individual words in (458), as their meaning remains the same on both readings. The ambiguity of (458), then, must be a structural one. In other words, the grammar of English allows two different syntactic representations to be assigned to (458), each of which is associated with a different interpretation. Hence, the difficulty of comprehending (458) results from its structural ambiguity, and since in the case of (458) there is no preferred interpretation, people typically rely on non-linguistic clues that indicate to them which interpretation is the intended one. For the case under discussion, if we equip our listener with the knowledge that whisky is the national drink of Scotland, this might be sufficient to establish a preference for the interpretation in (459b). However, this preference would not be strong and would almost certainly be overridden in a context where Scotsmen were observed fighting Welshmen.

To understand how the ambiguity of (458) arises, consider again (459a, b). Now assume that there exists a process of *ellipsis* which can erase words in the second clause that have already occurred in the first clause, but that these deleted elements remain visible to interpretation, (one way to make this explicit is to suggest that the elided material is covertly *reconstructed* at LF, see exercise 1 in section 23). Under these assumptions, (458) can be seen as a 'shortened' version of either (459a) or (459b), depending on how ellipsis and reconstruction are implemented. The two options are illustrated below (notice that *Welshmen* functions as the complement of the verb *like* in 460a, but is a subject in 460b):

(460)   a. Scotsmen like whisky more than [~~Scotsmen like~~ Welshmen]
         b. Scotsmen like whisky more than [Welshmen ~~like whisky~~]

In other cases of structural ambiguity we seem to strongly prefer one interpretation over the other quite independently of linguistic and non-linguistic context, and it is in connection with examples of this type that perceptual strategies become very significant. Consider the example in (461):

(461)   John helped the students who lost out

This sentence again has two interpretations, paraphrases of which are given below:

(462)   a. John supported the students who *lost out*
         b. John *helped out* the students who lost

The first interpretation (462a), in which the preposition *out* is associated with the verb *lose*, is clearly preferred by most listeners, but the second interpretation (462b), in which *out* is associated with *help*, is also perfectly grammatical. Ambiguities such as those in (461) are less likely to occur in spoken language comprehension, as different stress patterns lead hearers to prefer certain interpretations; for example, if the speaker introduces a noticeable pause after *lost* in (461), then the particle *out* is likely to be understood as linked to the main verb *helped*. Obviously, such cues are not available in written language comprehension. Notice also that the separation of a particle from the verb is actually quite common in English, and does not normally produce any processing difficulties. Compare, for example, (461) and (463):

(463)   Betty *put* the big Persian cat *out*, before she left the house.

We can roughly indicate the structural ambiguity of (461) by the different bracketings in (464a, b):

(464)   a. John helped [the students who lost] out
         b. John helped [the students who lost out]

But why do listeners prefer the bracketing in (464b) to that in (464a)? Given that both structures are equally grammatical, we have to look beyond mere structural descriptions to find an answer to this question. Recall that syntactic theory accounts for the *existence* of certain types of structural ambiguity by deriving them from different structural representations, as for example in (460a, b). But syntactic analysis itself cannot explain how it is that people resolve such ambiguities in the way they do on specific occasions, nor why they often prefer one structure over another in a manner independent of context, as, for example, with (461). In short, we need to find out what additional strategies or principles listeners employ when they parse sentences.

The fact that listeners prefer interpretation (464b) over (464a) is indicative of a fairly general property of sentence processing: the idea is that as the parser builds a structure, whenever there is a choice between a local and a distant attachment possibility, as in the case of *out* in (461), it favours the more local one. Put differently, listeners prefer to construe any given word *as part of the constituent being processed at that time*, rather than as part of a different constituent. With respect to (461), this means that the preposition *out* is construed as a constituent of the nearest VP, which is the VP headed by the verb *lose*, rather than with the VP headed by *help*, which is further away from *out*. The structure in (465) illustrates this:

(465)

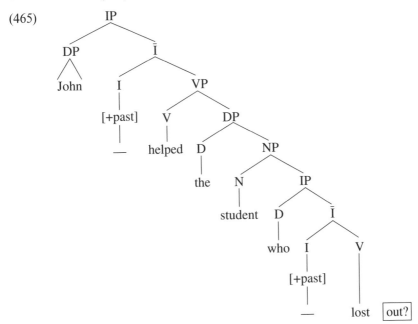

The structure in (465) is based on the assumption that syntactic parsing is like reading or speaking in that it proceeds from left to right and that it is done on-line, i.e. whenever the parser comes across a new word in its left-to-right journey through the sentence, it has to incorporate the word into the tree which is available at that point. In (465), we have got to the point where the parser encounters *out*, and the options for the attachment of this item are indicated in (466a, b) – we assume that *out* adjoins to either *lost* (466a) or *helped* (466b) to produce the complex verb forms *lost out* or *helped out*:

(466)   a.   b.

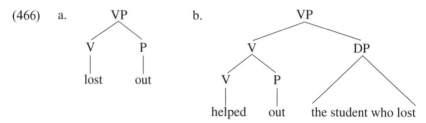

The listener's *grammar* provides the information that *out* can adjoin to either *lost* or *helped*. However, attaching *out* to *lost* as in (466a) is a **local attachment** and is therefore preferred. The alternative of attaching *out* to *helped* as in (466b) involves the parser in looking back to the earlier verb in the sentence and re-considering the structure of the higher VP (a procedure known as *backtracking*). In general, the parser will avoid backtracking and rearrangement of constituents as much as possible. With (466a), no such backtracking is required, and this parse is consistent with the local nature of human parsing.

Another type of grammatical sentence which does not involve structural ambiguity but which yields considerable processing difficulties is one which includes **centre-embedding**. Compare the sentences in (467):

(467)   a. The pen the author the editor liked used was new
         b. The pen which the author whom the editor liked used was new
         c. The editor liked the author who used the pen which was new

These sentences are paraphrases of each other, with no significant meaning differences, and none of them violates any grammatical rule of English. But on several processing measures (e.g. RTs, accuracy of paraphrasing, etc.), (467a) proves more difficult to parse than (467b), and (467b) proves more difficult than (467c). Notice that this holds despite the fact that in terms of the number of words involved, (467a) is actually shorter than both (467b) and (467c). How do we explain these processing differences?

The main factor distinguishing (467a) from (467c) is that in the latter parsing can proceed locally, whereas this is not possible in the former. In

(467c), the three basic clauses (*the editor liked the author, the author used the pen* and *the pen was new*), separated by commas, can be straightforwardly parsed from left to right. Thus, when the parse for the first clause is closed, it can be cleared from short-term memory, as can that for the second clause. In (467a), however, the three basic clauses must all be kept in short-term memory until the end of the sentence is reached; only at this point can the listener attach the appropriate verb to each of the three sets of arguments to form the three basic clauses. A very fundamental finding in research on short-term memory is that its capacity is severely limited (see how many digits you can remember in the sequence in which they are presented to you), so we might plausibly suppose that one difficulty with (467a) is that its processing over-loads short-term memory – importantly, this is not a *linguistic* difficulty. Another aspect of (467a) that prevents local parsing decisions being taken is that the sequence *the pen the author the editor* does not contain any cues as to the grammatical function (subject or complement) fulfilled by these DPs in the various clauses of the sentence. Compare this with (467b). In this case, the relative pronouns *which* and *whom* provide cues which allow the parser to assign grammatical functions to these elements. As the parser can make some decisions early on in (467b) which cannot be made in (467a), parsing (467b) is more local than parsing (467a), and hence again is less burdensome for short-term memory.

We consider finally a phenomenon touched on briefly in our introduction (pp. 11f.), that of garden-path sentences or **syntactic illusions**, as this also requires a processing explanation. In syntactic illusions, a certain decision about interpreting a sentence which is locally tenable leads to the (incorrect) conclusion that a grammatical structure is ungrammatical. Consider, for example, (468a) which is a perfectly grammatical sentence as can be seen from inserting the relative pronoun *which* and the auxiliary verb *was* in the appro-priate positions (468b):

(468)   a. The elephant squeezed into a telephone booth collapsed
        b. The elephant which was squeezed into a telephone booth col-
           lapsed

Despite their well-formedness, many listeners are confused by garden-path sentences such as (468a). The illusion can be explained in terms of processing considerations, specifically by the parser's preference for making local process-ing decisions. To be maximally efficient the parser attempts to close phrases and clauses as soon as possible. In the case of (468a), however, this strategy leads the parser up a garden-path: taking the sequence *the elephant squeezed into a telephone booth* from (468a), the parser assumes that the clause is closed, and this requires that *the elephant* is the (logical) subject of *squeezed,* a clear mistake – in fact, *the elephant* has to be interpreted as the complement of the passive participle form *squeezed,* and to have undergone movement from complement to subject position, as described in section 21. Thus, when the parser reaches the second verb (*collapsed* in this case), time-consuming and laborious re-processing is necessary to escape from the illusion. Indeed, such is the strength of this illusion that some native-speakers experience considerable difficulty in escaping from it at all.

In this section, we have looked at some aspects of how people assign structures to strings of words with two main themes in mind. First, we wanted to establish that the grammatical constructs developed by linguists as part of their theory of grammar do play a role in sentence processing. Of course, it would be a puzzling situation if a mentally represented grammar (theory of competence) were not put to work in sentence perception and production (linguistic performance). Nevertheless, it is reassuring to find experimental evidence which indicates that constituent structure and antecedent-trace relations are actively involved in processing.

Secondly, we have acknowledged that the theory of grammar does not provide a *complete* account of sentence processing, and we have looked at different kinds of sentences that cause processing difficulties, even though they are perfectly grammatical. Processing considerations which go beyond the rules and principles of grammar are necessary to understand these phenomena. The idea that the human parser has a strong preference for operating with *local* operations is a key idea in this area of research (*exercises 2, 3, 4 and 5*).

Exercises

1. Explain the differences between lexical and syntactic processing.

2. Both of the following sentences are perfectly grammatical, but only (b), not (a), is ambiguous. Explain the difference between (a) and (b), guess what the preferred interpretation of (b) is, and explain the preference in terms of processing considerations:

    (a) Anne put the book that Mary had been reading in the study
    (b) Anne threw the book that Mary had been reading in the study

3. Centre-embeddings are difficult to process because the parser prefers not to process more than *two* basic clauses at once. Consider this

claim in the light of the following data and explain the processing differences illustrated by the sentences:

(a) The gazelle the lion chased escaped
(b) The cat the dog the man the baby tripped up bit scratched collapsed
(c) The snow the match the grill heated lit melted
(d) The very beautiful woman the man the girl loved met on a cruiseship in Maine died of cholera in 1912
(e) Though Mary claimed that she will be the first woman president yesterday she announced she'd rather be an astronaut

4. In the following sentences which are highly similar in structure only (a) and (b), but not (c), (d) and (e) produce garden-path effects. How would you explain the differences and why is there no garden-path effect in (c), (d) and (e)?

(a) The log floated down the river sank
(b) John warned the girl came round every evening
(c) John knew the girl came round every evening
(d) The bird found in the store died
(e) The rag-doll washed in the machine fell to pieces

5. In some of the following sentences parsing strategies may explain why they are difficult to process or strange in some way in their written form. Try to find out which of them are candidates for a processing explanation and sketch out an explanation for each of these cases:

(a) The sergeant drilled the holes in the roof
(b) The workman drilled the troops in the parade-ground
(c) She loves rocking chairs
(d) She didn't love him because he looked ugly
(e) The question the girl the lion bit answered was complex
(f) The horse raced past the barn fell

26   Syntactic disorders

The study of syntactic errors in language-disordered patients is an area in which linguists, psychologists and speech therapists have collaborated extensively. Recent syntactic theories have been applied to neurolinguistic data and have led to a better understanding of patients' linguistic problems; in turn, theoretical linguists have gained a new source of data from syntactic errors to test their theories.

Generative linguists in particular have shown interest in syntactic disorders. Recall that many generative linguists (particularly Noam Chomsky and his followers) claim that humans possess a language-specific cognitive system (embodying principles of Universal Grammar) that underlies the production and comprehension of sentences. Syntactic principles are said to be unique to language, and autonomous of non-linguistic cognitive systems such as vision, hearing, reasoning, or memory (see the introduction, p. 14). This view of syntax makes two interesting predictions about language disorders. First, we would expect to find cases of language disorders in which knowledge of syntax is impaired while other cognitive systems remain unaffected: if the syntactic system is indeed autonomous, then it should be possible for it to be selectively impaired, for example as a result of brain lesions or genetic deficits. The second prediction is that syntactic disorders should involve impairments of both language production and language comprehension. If the linguistic view is correct, and there is indeed only one underlying system of syntactic principles which is crucially involved in both sentence production and sentence comprehension, then an impairment of the underlying system should manifest itself not only in sentence production but also in sentence comprehension and in grammaticality judgement tasks.

These predictions have mainly been tested in the context of the phenomenon of agrammatism which typically occurs in Broca's aphasics and (to a lesser extent) on the so-called **paragrammatic errors** from Wernicke's aphasics. In addition to these two areas of enquiry, psycholinguists have recently started to investigate developmental language disorders, particularly Specific Language Impairment (SLI), from a syntactic perspective. These three cases of language disorders are unique, in that patients show syntactic impairment while, at the same time, other cognitive functions seem to be unimpaired. In this section, we will describe the syntactic errors that typically occur in agrammatism, paragrammatism and SLI, and we will show what we can learn from applying syntactic theory, as it has been introduced in this part of the book, to the study of these disorders.

Agrammatism

Recall from the introduction (p. 14) that according to the classical clinical description of aphasias, the sentences Broca's aphasics produce in spontaneous speech are characterised by their simplicity or reduced syntactic complexity. These sentences are often incomplete, with functional elements (including grammatical inflections) being omitted. These problems also usually occur in writing, whereas sentence comprehension is said to be more or less unaffected. Consider (469), where we see examples of Broca's aphasics' attempts to produce some simple English sentences, for illustration:

(469) **Reconstruction of Target**   **Realisation**
   a. He's going *on the* bus   He going bus
   b. *When did* this happen?   This happened?
   c. *The* woman is packing the case   Woman is packing the case
   d. *I* only passed my test *in the*   Only passed my test afternoon
      afternoon
   e. *They are* pulling it   Pulling it

As is shown by the reconstructions of the targets in (469), we can paraphrase the deviant or simplified utterances produced by Broca's aphasics by normal English sentences which differ only minimally from the actual realisations. In all cases, the realisations are syntactically less complex than the target reconstructions, and omissions and simplifications typically affect functional projections (DP, IP and CP). For example, in (469a), the head INFL position of IP is left empty instead of being filled by the auxiliary *is*, and the determiner *the* is omitted from the head D position of the target DP *the bus* (in addition, the preposition *on* is omitted from the target PP *on the bus*). Similarly, in (469b), the wh-operator *when* is omitted from spec-CP, and the preposed auxiliary *did* is omitted from C. In (469c) and (469d), the determiner *the* is omitted from the head D position of the target DPs *the woman* and *the afternoon*, and in the latter, the pronominal D *I* in spec-IP is missing (and the preposition *in* is omitted from the target PP *in the afternoon*). And finally, in (469e) the auxiliary *are* is omitted from the head INFL position of the target IP *They are pulling it*, along with the pronominal D *they* in spec-IP.

According to the clinical definition, agrammatism in Broca's aphasics is modality-specific. That is, agrammatic errors are believed to occur in one modality only, namely in language production, with sentence comprehension unimpaired. If this were correct, then agrammatism would be a disorder of some peripheral language-production mechanism, with the central cognitive system underlying the knowledge of grammar still being intact. Research in linguistic aphasiology, however, provides us with a somewhat different picture. It has been shown, for example, that Broca's aphasics have problems in comprehending functional categories as well as in producing them. Such findings suggest that the agrammatic deficit involves impairment of the underlying linguistic system as well, and not just a disturbance in one modality.

Sentence comprehension in Broca's aphasics can only be studied through structured experiments. Aphasiologists have recently begun to adopt different psycholinguistic techniques, e.g. linguistic judgement tasks, lexical decision experiments and reaction-time techniques in order to assess agrammatics' knowledge of grammar. Let's look in some detail at one experiment which investigated a single, well-defined syntactic phenomenon, namely the fact that sentences like (470a, b), differing only in the positioning of the definite article *the* have quite distinct interpretations:

(470)   a. The man showed her baby the pictures
         b. The man showed her the baby pictures

In (470a) the DP *her baby* functions as what is sometimes known as the 'recipient' complement of the verb (it refers to the individual who receives something – in this case, visual stimulation – in the action referred to by the verb) and the DP *the pictures* is the 'theme' complement (it refers to whatever is generally affected in the action referred to by the verb). By contrast, in (470b), *her* is the 'recipient' complement and *the baby pictures* is the 'theme' complement. The crucial factor underlying this distinction is the determiner *the*. Since in (470a) *the* appears between *baby* and *pictures*, we cannot analyse these two nouns as parts of a noun compound in this structure. (Note that noun compounds don't allow determiners between the two nouns: we have such compounds as *loft space* and *armchair*, but not *loft-the-space* and *arm-the-chair*.) In (470b), however, the compound-based interpretation is possible, due to the absence of *the* between *baby* and *pictures*.

Returning now to agrammatism, in the study we are concerned with, the contrast between (470a) and (470b) was exploited to conduct an interesting experiment on sentence comprehension in agrammatic patients. It was argued that if sentence comprehension was unimpaired in agrammatic aphasics and patients were relying on syntactic clues to process sentences – *such as the presence and position of a determiner* – then sentences like (470a, b) should be correctly interpreted by these patients, just as they are for normal adult speakers of English. If, however, the agrammatic deficit also affects comprehension, and if agrammatics ignore the function word *the* in comprehension in the same way as they omit it in production, as in (469a, c), then (470a, b) should be ambiguous for them in the same way as (471) is for normal adults:

(471)   The man showed her baby pictures

A moment's reflection should reveal that either *her* or *her baby* can be interpreted as the recipient, with the theme being correspondingly either *baby pictures* or *pictures*.

To test this prediction, a sentence-picture matching task was used in which subjects had to choose from four alternative pictures that were presented for each sentence. Suppose the presented sentence was (470a). Then one picture (the correct one) illustrated a man showing pictures to a woman's baby, while a second (incorrect) contained a man showing pictures of a baby to a woman. Two further pictures (both incorrect) were included to test for lexical comprehension, examples being appropriate pictures for the sentences in (472):

(472)   a. The man showed her girls the hats
         b. The man showed her the girls' hats

The results of this experiment demonstrated that agrammatics made few lexical errors, i.e., they hardly ever chose pictures appropriate to (472a, b) when the presented sentence was (470a), but in nearly half of the trials they picked the picture portraying the nominal-compound reading, i.e. the picture appropriate for (470b). In other words, the agrammatic patients appeared to treat (470a) (and 470b) as *ambiguous*, an interpretation which is consistent with them failing to process the definite article *the* and thus treating both sentences as if they were (471). Given that the comprehension disorder found in this experiment is parallel to the syntactic errors that occur in agrammatic production in that both involve errors with function words, we may conclude that agrammatism is a fundamental disorder of the linguistic representational system (i.e. the grammar), rather than a peripheral impairment to one specific modality only.

But how can we characterise agrammatism? The most widely known syntactic theory of agrammatism is Yosef Grodzinsky's hypothesis of an impairment to the internal feature specification of functional projections. This theory is controversial, but it provides a very clear and explicit account. Recall from section 15 (pp. 245f.) that in languages such as Hebrew and Italian, in which many inflections cannot be dropped without violating word-structure properties, agrammatics produce many inflectional errors, e.g. gender errors, number errors, etc. A typical example of such an inflectional error from an Italian agrammatic patient appears in (473):

(473) quest-o   macchin-a
       this-masc.   car-fem
       'this car'

Notice, however, that in this error (and others like it), the categorial identity of the inflections in question is always respected; that is, agrammatics do not, for example, attach verbal affixes (e.g. infinitive endings) to nouns or adjectives and vice versa. How can we account for such a selective impairment in syntactic terms?

Like all heads, functional categories are each associated with a set of properties. A general syntactic property of the category INFL, for example, is that it always takes a VP as its complement. In addition, as we have seen in section 20, INFL is specified for abstract grammatical features such as tense ([PresTns] or [PastTns]), which determine the temporal value of the sentence (e.g. present or past). D, on the other hand, which requires a nominal complement, is associated with features such as number, gender and definiteness. The basic idea is that in agrammatism the specific values of the features associated with functional categories are lost or unspecified – in other words, although categories like INFL or D are present, they are underspecified (see section 24 for a similar idea in connection with the early speech of children). Consider, for illustration, the syntactic representation of the sentence *The boy kissed the girl* in normal standard English (474a) and in agrammatic English (474b):

(474) a.

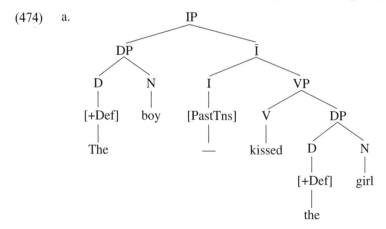

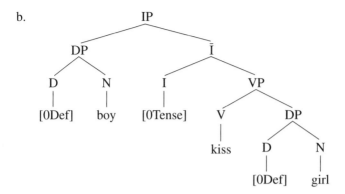

Compare the feature contents of the D- and the I-heads in (474a) and (474b). Grodzinsky argues that the crucial property in (474b) is that the internal feature specifications of these two heads have unspecified feature values, indicated by the '0' (we adapt the notation to make it consistent with earlier parts of this book – see p. 111). This means that the D-head and the I-head are left unspecified with respect to definiteness and tense: in contrast to unimpaired English, the head positions of DP and IP in agrammatism are *not* specified for a definite [+Def] or an indefinite [−Def] determiner, or for a particular tense form which has to be used to fill the INFL position. As a consequence, English-speaking agrammatics leave the functional category heads empty, which results in 'telegraphic' sentences such as *boy kiss girl*.

In languages such as Hebrew, Russian and Italian, in which the option of omitting inflections is not generally available, agrammatics randomly choose some inflectional element to fill the slot, and this choice typically results in inflectional errors. Consider the gender error in (473) above. In Italian, DPs have to be specified for gender features such as [MascGen] or [FemGen], and an expression such as *questa macchina* ('this car') has the structure in (475):

(475)

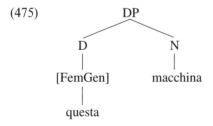

Agrammatic patients have lost the values of syntactic features such as gender, and in their grammars, the features have no specifications; see the structure in (476).

(476)

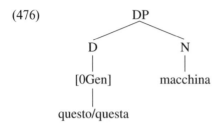

This means that agrammatics can insert any kind of gender inflection into the D-position. This sometimes produces gender errors as in (473), although Italian agrammatics will also produce the correct agreement pattern *questa macchina* on occasions. But the option of omitting gender affixes entirely is not available in this case, as this would produce illicit words such as **quest-* in Italian, and agrammatics do not violate word-structure contraints of their particular language.

Thus, despite performance differences, i.e. *omissions* of functional elements in English-speaking agrammatics and *inflectional errors* in Hebrew- and Italian-speaking agrammatics, the underlying deficit is the same: the functional categories in their syntactic representations have lost their internal feature specification (**exercises 1 and 2**).

Paragrammatism

At first sight, the spontaneous speech of Wernicke's aphasics appears to be fluent, with normal prosody and syntactic structure. However, although the sentences these patients produce are quite long and complex, they are not always syntactically well formed and contain various kinds of errors, e.g. word exchanges and exchanges of whole constituents as well as blends of different constituents. This cluster of properties is called paragrammatism in the clinical literature. Consider as an illustration the various attempts in (477) by a Wernicke's aphasic to name a lady's shoe that was shown to him.

(477)   Experimenter: What is this? (= a lady's shoe)
         Patient: Yes sir. Now there there I remember. I have you
                          there what I thought was the . . . a lady. one. another.
                          with a very short. very very clever done. do that the
                          one two. go. but there's the liver. and there is the new.
                          and so on. It is a document. late . . .

These utterances are spoken at a very high speed with only a few pauses, and the sentences are not so much characterised by a reduction of syntactic complexity (as in the case of agrammatism) as by the juxtaposition of incompatible sequences. There seems to be a consensus among aphasiologists that paragrammatic errors do not result from an independent syntactic disorder, but that they are just indicative of patients' lexical problems, specifically their word-finding difficulties which we briefly examined in section 15. It has been found that blends and syntactic errors typically occur at points at which the patient is trying to retrieve content words, particularly nouns. They start to produce a sentence, and at points at which they experience word-finding problems change the sentence plan or start again. Crucially, however, the syntactic structure of the various fragments including the internal structure of functional projections is the same as that of normal speakers. Thus, paragrammatism is not a genuine syntactic disorder, but rather a secondary effect of patients' lexical disorder (*exercises 3 and 4*)

Specific Language Impairment (SLI)

Finally, we will look at the syntactic errors in the speech of specifically language-impaired children. We will focus on word order, and we will also briefly comment on SLI therapy. English-speaking SLI children do not have problems with word order. That is, the same children who demonstrate great difficulty with inflection and omit functional elements such as determiners or subject–verb–agreement markers (see section 15) may produce perfectly well-formed yes–no questions. However, as the word-order system of English is rather simple, it might well be that SLI subjects do show word-order problems in a language which has a more complex system. Hence, the questions we are going to consider are: do SLI children have genuine word-order problems? and: does the picture we get from English-speaking SLI children hold in general, so that SLI can be said to affect inflection, but not word order?

Let us look at German-speaking SLI children in the light of these questions. Speech therapists have noticed that the most salient syntactic error in the speech of German SLI children is that they almost always place the verb at the end of the clause, as, for example, in (478a, b):

Reconstruction of Target	**Realisation**
(478) a. Ich *fahre* auch ein Auto	is auch ein auto *fahr*
I drive also a car	I also a car drive
'I also drive a car'	
b. Einen Sitz *brauche* ich	ein titz is *brauch*
A seat need I	a seat I need
'I need a seat'	

The speech therapists' view has been confirmed. In several empirical studies, it has been found that between 60 per cent and 70 per cent of the main clauses produced by German SLI children have the verb in clause-final position. Similar results have been obtained in sentence-imitation tasks; when SLI children have been asked to imitate German sentences such as the targets in (478), in 60 per cent of cases they have changed the given word orders to patterns with the verb appearing at the end of the clause.

Speech therapists have taken the frequent use of verb-final patterns by SLI children as an indication of a severe word-order deficit, and have developed sentence pattern drills and other therapeutic techniques for teaching the children 'proper' German word order. However, this therapy has turned out to be unsuccessful, suggesting that the supposed word-order deficit is resistent to therapy.

At this point, a linguistic perspective can help to resolve the issue, and may in fact contribute to specifying appropriate therapeutic goals for children suffering from SLI. A syntactic analysis of the verb-final patterns German SLI children produce shows that their sentences are not in fact as deviant as might be thought at first sight. Verb-final patterns are in fact possible in German main clauses, but *only for non-finite verbs*. For illustration, consider the example in (479). Note that verbs can, in principle, appear in two different positions in German main clauses: finite verbs must appear in the second structural position, like, for example, *hat* in (479), whereas non-finite verbal elements (i.e. infinitives or participles) appear in final position, like *angestellt* in (479). In syntactic terms, we say that VP in German is head-final, whereas the functional projection that hosts the finite verb (i.e. CP) is head-initial (see the tree diagram in (480) and section 22):

(479)   Adrian *hat* das Radio *angestellt*
         Adrian has the radio on-turned
         'Adrian has turned on the radio'

(480)

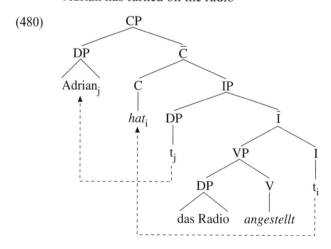

In terms of this analysis, it might be suggested that SLI children have in fact acquired the correct word-order system, that is, they know that VP in German is head-final. Recall that SLI children typically produce *non-finite verb forms*, *like infinitives or simple verbal stems* as in the realisations in (478a, b), and that these appear in clause-final position. The few finite verb forms they produce are correctly placed in second position. Note, for example, that the same child who produced the verb-final patterns in (478), also produced sentences such as (481) with the finite modal auxiliary *will* 'want' in second position and the infinitive *haben* 'to have' in clause-final position, the correct pattern for German:

(481)   ich will auto haben
       I   want car   have
      'I want to have the car'

Thus, it seems that with respect to word order, the grammar of SLI subjects is in fact identical to that of unimpaired speakers, as all the verbs they use appear in the correct positions. The only difference between SLI subjects and normal children is that SLI children do not produce as many finite verb forms as the language requires. This is why sentence-pattern drills aimed at teaching SLI subjects verb-second patterns, in which the finite verb has moved to C, fail to show any effect: they simply miss the point. A more sensible goal for therapy would be to help the SLI subjects overcome their problems with finite verb formation.

We conclude that the grammatical problems of SLI subjects lie mainly with inflection, and that word order is in fact unimpaired. Within the area of inflection, subject–verb agreement, case marking, gender and auxiliaries appear to be more strongly affected than, for example, noun plurals (*exercises 5 and 6*).

In this section, we have looked at different language disorders from a syntactic perspective. The phenomenon of agrammatism is perhaps the clearest case of an impairment to the central cognitive system that underlies the production and comprehension of sentences. We saw that agrammatism affects both sentence production and comprehension, and that the deficit can be characterised in syntactic terms, namely as an impairment to the internal feature specification of functional categories. The phenomenon of paragrammatism, by contrast, does not seem to involve a genuine syntactic deficit. Rather, the paragrammatic errors such as blends, constituent substitutions, etc. that Wernicke's aphasics typically produce result from a *lexical disorder*, specifically from word-finding problems. We also saw that in SLI subjects, the normal development of grammar is selectively impaired, and that the impairment mainly affects inflection. Word order, on the other hand, appears to develop normally in SLI subjects. The importance of the properties of functional categories and inflection which has emerged in this discussion is, of course, reminiscent of what we saw in our discussion of the syntax of normal children. The view that these aspects of linguistic structure hold the key to the essential nature of language and the human language faculty is one which is informing a great deal of current work, and we fully expect this to continue to be the case for the foreseeable future.

Conclusion

As we arrive at the end of the book, it is perhaps appropriate to take stock of what we have achieved with respect to the issues raised in our main introduction.

It will be recalled that there (p. 6) we offered an initial sketch of a grammar as a system containing at least four components: a lexicon, a syntactic component, a component dealing with phonetic form (PF) and a component deriving the semantic (logical) form of a sentence (LF). The way these various components fit together is illustrated in (417) (p. 371), and we have provided extensive discussion of each of these components in the preceding sections. Thus, the syntactic component, with its core operations of merger and overt movement and its reliance on a variety of empty categories has been described in detail in sections 18 to 22; LF and its employment of covert movement has been the topic of section 23; the structure of the lexicon and the nature of lexical entries was our theme throughout much of part 2; and PF, as a system linking levels of phonological representation via phonological processes has been illustrated in part 1, particularly section 5.

It would be misleading to suggest that we have presented a complete and final picture of the organisation of linguistic knowledge in the course of these discussions, and there are a number of factors which justify modesty in this connection. Firstly, like any science, linguistics is a vibrant and developing discipline, with new ideas and novel observations continuing to make their impact on a regular basis. Undoubtedly, the future will see some of what we have presented here replaced by more adequate approaches, but this is inevitable and should be positively regarded as symptomatic of a continued deepening of understanding, itself a trait which appears to be unique to human beings as they pursue scientific activity. Secondly, as noted in the main introduction, our discussion of the theory of grammar and its impact on language acquisition, psycholinguistics and neurolinguistics has been greatly influenced by the ideas of Noam Chomsky. We hope that the preceding pages provide some justification for this emphasis, but we must also acknowledge that there are other approaches to the study of language which may ultimately prove to be more fruitful. However, we also believe that much of what we have presented could be reformulated within different frameworks; to the extent that this is true, the book will have provided a valuable foundation for students who subsequently wish to pursue alternative approaches. Finally, even within the approach we have adopted, there are many outstanding problems which we have deliberately avoided. To offer just one example, we have remained reticent on the location of the morphological processes described in sections 10 and 11 within the model in (417). In some cases, such as compounding, it seems most appropriate to see these processes as taking place within the lexicon, thereby giving rise to new lexemes; in others, it seems more plausible to locate the processes in the syntactic component itself or in PF. As we write, there are no comprehensive and compelling views as to whether the grammar should contain a single morphological component; as a consequence we have felt justified in restricting ourselves to providing the basic descriptive apparatus which will enable readers to recognise different morphological processes, while leaving the major theoretical stone unturned.

Whatever the long-term fate of the Chomskian view of linguistic theory, the coherence which this view has established for the related studies of language acquisition, linguistic processing and language disorders is an impressive achievement. As for language acquisition, we have seen in the relevant sections of the book (6, 13 and 24) that proper consideration of children's achievements leads, almost inexorably, to the conclusion that they approach first language acquisition with remarkably sophisticated knowledge of phonological, morphological, syntactic and semantic representations. All of this points strongly to the correctness of the view that an innate system of UG provides the child with tightly constrained (and, therefore, useful) information about the form of a grammar for a possible human language.

Turning to the *use* of language, particularly sentence comprehension, experimental demonstrations of the need to refer to such theoretical grammatical constructs as empty categories (see section 25) are now plentiful. Overall, there is considerable justification for the view that an individual's mentally represented grammar is normally involved in language use. Note that this does not amount to the claim that the grammar provides a *complete* theory of language use – garden-path sentences argue against this – nor that the grammar is the *only* route to comprehension (for instance, suitable *lists* of words, such as *car, tree, bang, blood, ambulance, hospital* exhibiting no syntactic structure, *can* be interpreted as conveying messages). However, if it is plausible to posit a grammar as a model of native speaker *competence*, it would be perverse to deny this grammar a role in accounting for normal linguistic *performance*, and the discussions we have provided suggest that such perversity is not at play.

As regards our understanding of language disorders, we have argued (sections 15 and in this final section) that the postulation of a mentally represented grammar, broken down into various components and distinguished from the general conceptual system, allows us to formulate views of some disorders which go much deeper than noting that patients have general difficulties with language comprehension or global production problems. As we have seen, the major problem for agrammatics appears to be the selection of appropriate inflectional forms within otherwise intact grammars, and the locus of difficulty for SLI patients is a subset of inflections. We firmly believe that without the modular, autonomous view of language adopted in this book, such insights and their interpretation in terms of selective impairment would remain remote.

Finally, as we noted in section 17, our discussion of syntactic variation in section 22 was very different in character to those of sound variation in section 3 and lexical variation in section 16. Whereas sound and lexical variation were both approached from a sociolinguistic perspective, whereby values of variables are correlated with specific social factors, our discussion of syntactic variation was restricted to using our adopted theoretical framework to *describe the variants*, e.g. Modern English vs. Shakespearian English or English vs. German. We did not focus on factors determining the *choice* of these variants, since we did not consider the situation of one individual simultaneously having access to both variants. However, in a world where the majority of people are (at least) bilingual, such a choice is often available, although the factors determining it may sometimes be rather obvious – an English–German bilingual will normally use English in London when addressing monolingual William and German in Berlin when addressing monolingual Wilhelm. But, of course, this can be seen as a case of *audience design*, a concept introduced in section 3 to account for choice between the values of phonological variables, and there is no reason to believe that other *social variables*, which have arisen in our discussions of language varieties will not also play a role in the syntactic domain, particularly when we focus attention on bidialectalism.

This brief consideration of bilingualism and bidialectalism allows us to draw our discussion to a close by raising an outstanding problem for linguistic research. Throughout our discussions of grammars, we have implicitly adopted an important *idealisation*, viz. that we are concerned with understanding the nature of the internalised linguistic system of a monolingual (indeed, monodialectal) native speaker, functioning in a monolingual (monodialectal) environment. Now, idealisation is a necessary strategy in scientific enquiry, and we maintain that the successes which have been achieved by adopting this idealisation amply justify it. At the same time, sociolinguistic research reveals the extent of the idealisation and raises the question: what is the nature of the internalised system of linguistic representation for someone who is bilingual (or bidialectal)? More specifically, does such a person have two grammars and the facility for switching between them, or a single grammar within which choices can be made? Unfortunately, we do not have the space to pursue these questions here, and it may be that such pursuit, with the attendant dropping of our idealisation, is unlikely to yield much insight from our current level of understanding. It is, however, worthy of note that whereas the sociolinguistic research to which we have drawn attention earlier in this book is quite properly concerned with *external* determinants of language choice, the issues we are now considering are formulated so as to be consistent with Chomsky's *internalist* perspective. We therefore see another sense in which the sociolinguistic perspective can be seen as complementing the position which has informed most of our discussion in this book.

Exercises

1. The following data come from a repetition experiment in which an aphasic subject (S) was asked to produce an exact word-for-word repetition of the experimenter's (E) sentences:

   (a) E: No, I do not like fish   P: No.fish
   (b) E: One morning the girl was   P: One morning the . . . the girl
       pushed by the man   is push push boy
   (c) E: The girl is running to   P: The girl running the . . . the
       the man   girl is running on man

   Analyse the grammatical errors, determine the syndrome and give reasons for your answer.

2. Agrammatics have problems with sentence comprehension. Experimental studies have shown that they can easily understand (a) and (b), but that they have trouble understanding (c) and (d). Explain the comprehension problems of agrammatics and give reasons for the differences in performance between the four sentences below:

(a) The apple that the tiger saw was yellow
(b) The car was driven by Bill
(c) The tiger that the lion chased was yellow
(d) Mary was kissed by Bill

3. Analyse and evaluate all the errors in the following response produced by an aphasic patient to the question 'Did you have lunch today?' Determine the syndrome and justify your choice.

Ooh, I didn't late before, no, yesterday I simply went with my. breakfas with my. er. thing. one. then again at twenty. and a tik (ea?) thing. Nothing to. But I would work tomorrow. tomorrow I would. league er. barrack stuff then. but not . not the rowl thing because I'm waiting. I've been very much waiting. what to do. For years I've been second to just be. keen whether or not I got it.but I've been necking to.get.quite well . . .

4. Provide arguments for the view that paragrammatism is not a genuine syntactic disorder.

5. The syntactic errors that occur in agrammatic production are very similar to those that occur in SLI subjects. Point out the similarities and think of how a linguist would account for them.

6. Consider the following somewhat simplified data from a German SLI child (age 7;5):

(a) *Ich das Buch les-en
       I   the book read-infinitive
(b) Paul soll   das Buch lesen
     Paul should the book read
(c) *Maria das Buch les-en
     Maria the book read-infinitive
(d) Das Buch ist auf dem Schrank
     The book is on   the cupboard
(e) *Wenn Maria das Buch les-en,   ich geh-en.
       If   Maria the book read-inf., I   go-inf.

The * indicates that a string produced by the child is ill formed in adult German.

  (i)   Characterise the linguistic impairment(s) illustrated in these examples by providing tree diagrams for sentences (a) to (e).

 (ii) Does this child have genuine word-order problems? (Hint: analyse the form of the verbs in connection with their position in the sentence.)

(iii) Sketch some goals for language therapy based on your linguistic analysis.

Further reading and references

The model of syntax presented in sections 18 to 22 is a simplified version of that developed in Chomsky (1995b). The CP/IP analysis of clauses outlined in section 20 derives from Chomsky (1981, 1986b), while the DP analysis of nominals is based on Abney (1987). The discussion of African American Vernacular English in section 20 is based on research by Labov (1969) and Fasold (1980); the observation that children produce sentences like *Get it ladder* is taken from McNeill (1966). The analysis of Belfast English questions presented in section 21 is based on Henry (1995); the null operator analysis of yes–no questions is inspired by Grimshaw (1993) and Roberts (1993). The analysis of negative auxiliary inversion in African American Vernacular English in section 22 derives from Sells, Rickford and Wasow (1994); the analysis of Jamaican Creole questions is adapted from Bailey (1966); the Head Movement Constraint is taken from Travis (1984). Most of the works referred to above are technical in nature and unsuitable for beginners; more appropriate follow-up reading for beginners would be a textbook introduction to minimalist syntax. (See e.g. Radford 1997a for a short introduction and Radford 1997b for a longer one.)

The arguments for covert movement in section 23 are based on the classic treatment of LF in May (1985), and the observations on Chinese first appeared in Huang (1982). Both of these works are very technical and not recommended for beginners. A summary of these and several other arguments can be found in Hornstein (1995, chapter 2), a work which goes on to develop a view of LF linked to the minimalist framework outlined in sections 18 to 22. Textbook treatments of LF are Chierchia and McConnell-Ginet (1990, particularly chapter 3) and Larson and Segal (1995).

The Claire data in section 24 are taken from the appendix to Hill (1983); the Kathryn data are from Bloom (1970); the analysis of English as a null subject language is from Hyams (1986); the truncation analysis of children's clauses is adapted from Rizzi (1994); the optional infinitive stage is discussed in Wexler (1994) and Hoekstra and Hyams (1998); the underspecification analysis of child grammars is outlined in Schütze (1997). All the works on acquisition cited above are technical: for a recent textbook study of children's syntactic development, see O'Grady (1997).

For section 25, Harley (1995, chapter 5) and Mitchell (1994) provide detailed reviews of the research literature on sentence processing. Gorrell (1995) is a more specialised but readable account of human sentence parsing.

The account of agrammatism in section 26 is largely based on Grodzinsky (1990, chapter 3), an often-quoted piece of work in the field of aphasiology which is, however, somewhat difficult to read. As an alternative, Caplan (1992, chapter 8) is a useful overview. Leonard (1998) presents a review of SLI studies for languages other than English. The materials used in our discussion are from Clahsen (1998).

Bibliography

Abney, S. P. (1987) 'The English noun phrase in its sentential aspect', Ph.D. dissertation, MIT.

Aitchison, J. (1991) *Language Change: Progress or Decay*, Cambridge University Press. (1998) *The Articulate Mammal*, Routledge, London (4th edn).

Ash, S. and J. Myhill (1986) 'Linguistic correlates of inter-ethnic contact', in D. Sankoff (ed.), *Diversity and Diachrony*, Benjamins, Amsterdam.

Atkinson, M. (1992) *Children's Syntax: An Introduction to Principles and Parameters Theory*, Blackwell, Oxford.

Bailey, B. L. (1966) *Jamaican Creole: A Transformational Approach*, Cambridge University Press.

Bailey, G., Wikte, T., Tillery, J. and L. Sand (1991) 'The apparent time construct', *Language Variation and Change* 3: 241–64.

Bauer, L. (1988) *Introducing Linguistic Morphology*, Edinburgh University Press.

Bell, A. (1984) 'Language style as audience design', *Language in Society* 12: 145–204.

Bell, A. and J. Holmes (1992) 'H-Droppin: two sociolinguistic variables in New Zealand English', *Australian Journal of Linguistics* 12: 223–48.

Berko, J. (1958) 'The child's learning of English morphology', *Word* 14: 150–77.

Biber, D. and E. Finegan (eds.) (1994) *Sociolinguistic Perspectives on Register*, Oxford University Press.

Bloom, L. (1970) *Language Development*, MIT Press, Cambridge MA.

Borden, G. and K. Harris (1984) *Speech Science Primer* (2nd edn.), Williams and Wilkins, Baltimore, MD.

Brown, R. (1973) *A First Language*, Harvard University Press, Cambridge MA.

Bybee, J. L. and D. I. Slobin (1982) 'Rules and schemas in the development and use of the English past tense', *Language* 58: 265–89.

Caplan, D. (1992) *Language: Structure, Processing and Disorders*, MIT Press, Cambridge MA.

Carey, S. (1978) 'The child as word learner', in M. Halle, J. Bresnan and G. Miller (eds.), *Linguistic Theory and Psychological Reality*, MIT Press, Cambridge MA.

Carey, S. (1985) *Conceptual Change in Childhood*, MIT Press, Cambridge MA.

Carstairs-McCarthy, A. (1992) *Current Morphology*, Routledge, London.

Chambers, J. (1992) 'Dialect acquisition', *Language* 68: 673–705. (1995) *Sociolinguistic Theory*, Blackwell, Oxford.

Chambers, J. and P. Trudgill (1980) *Dialectology*, Cambridge University Press.

424

Chierchia, G. and S. McConnell-Ginet (1990) *Meaning and Grammar: An Introduction to Semantics*, MIT Press, Cambridge MA.

Chomsky, N. (1965) *Aspects of the Theory of Syntax*, MIT Press, Cambridge MA.
(1966) *Cartesian Linguistics: A Chapter in the History of Rationalist Thought*, Harper & Row, London.
(1972) *Language and Mind* (enlarged edn), Harcourt Brace Jovanovich, New York.
(1975) *Reflections on Language*, Pantheon Books, New York.
(1980) *Rules and Representations*, Columbia University Press, New York.
(1981) *Lectures on Government and Binding*, Foris, Dordrecht.
(1986a) *Knowledge of Language: Its Nature, Origin and Use*, Praeger, New York.
(1986b) *Barriers*, MIT Press, Cambridge MA.
(1988) *Language and Problems of Knowledge: The Managua Lectures*, MIT Press, Cambridge MA.
(1995a) 'Language and nature', *Mind* 104: 1–61.
(1995b) *The Minimalist Program*, MIT Press, Cambridge MA.

Chomsky, N. and M. Halle (1968) *The Sound Pattern of English*, Harper and Row, New York.

Clahsen, H. (1998) 'Linguistic perspectives on specific language impairment', in W. C. Ritchie and E. K. Bahtia (eds.), *Handbook of Language Acquisition*, Academic Press, London.

Clark, E. (1973) 'What's in a word?', in T. Moore (ed.) *Cognitive Development and the Acquisition of Language*, Academic Press, New York.

Coupland, N. (1984) 'Accommodation at work: some phonological data and their implications', *International Journal of the Sociology of Language* 46: 49–70.

Cruse, D. (1986) *Lexical Semantics*, Cambridge University Press.

Fasold, R. (1980) 'The relation between black and white speech in the south', manuscript, School of Languages and Linguistics, Georgetown University, Washington DC.

Ferguson, C. A., Menn, L, and C. Stoel-Gammon (eds.) (1992) *Phonological Development: Models, Research, Implications*, York Press, Timonium MD.

Fodor, J. A. (1981) 'The present status of the innateness controversy', in J. A. Fodor, *Representations*, Harvester Press, Hassocks.
(1983) *Modularity of Mind*, MIT Press, Cambridge MA.

Fodor, J. A., Garret, M. F., Walker, E. C. T. and C. H. Parkes (1980) 'Against definitions', *Cognition* 8: 263–367.

Fromkin, V. A. (ed.) (1973) *Speech Errors as Linguistic Evidence*, Mouton, The Hague.
(1980) *Errors in Language Performance*. Academic Press, New York.

Garman, M. (1990) *Psycholinguistics*, Cambridge University Press.

Goodluck, H. (1991) *Language Acquisition: A Linguistic Introduction*, Blackwell, Oxford.

Gopnik, M (1990) 'Feature blindness: a case study', *Language Acquisition* 1: 139–64.

Gordon, P. (1985) 'Level ordering in lexical development', *Cognition* 21: 73–93.

Gorrell, P. (1995) *Syntax and Parsing*, Cambridge University Press.

Grimshaw, J. (1993) 'Minimal projection, heads and optimality', manuscript, Rutgers University.

Grodzinsky, Y. (1990) *Theoretical Perspectives on Language Deficits*, MIT Press, Cambridge MA.

Gussenhoven, C. and H. Jacobs (1998) *Understanding Phonology*, Arnold, London.

Harley, T. A. (1995) *The Psychology of Language*, Psychology Press, Hove, East Sussex.

Henry, A. (1995) *Belfast English and Standard English: Dialect Variation and Parameter Setting*, Oxford University Press.

Hill, J. A. C. (1983) *A Computational Model of Language Acquisition in the Two Year Old*, Indiana Linguistics Club, Bloomington, IN.

Hoekstra, T and N. Hyams (1998) 'Aspects of root infinitives', manuscript, UCLA and HIL-RU Leiden.

Holmes, J. (1992) *An Introduction to Sociolinguistics*, Longman, London.

Hornstein, N. (1995) *Logical Form: From GB to Minimalism*, Blackwell, Oxford.

Horvath, B. (1985) *Variation in Australian English: The Sociolects of Sydney*, Cambridge University Press.

Houston, A. (1991) 'A grammatical continuum for (ing)', in P. Trudgill and J. Chambers (eds.), *Dialects of English: Studies in Grammatical Variation*, Longman, London.

Huang, C.-T. J. (1982) 'Logical relations in Chinese and the theory of grammar', Ph.D. dissertation, MIT.

Hudson, R. (1996) *Sociolinguistics*, Cambridge University Press.

Hyams, N. (1986) *Language Acquisition and the Theory of Parameters*, Reidel, Dordrecht.

Ingram, D. (1989) *First Language Acquisition: Method, Description and Explanation*, Cambridge University Press.

Katamba, F. (1993) *Morphology*, MacMillan, Basingstoke.

Kuczaj, S. A. II (1977) 'The acquisition of regular and irregular past tense forms', *Journal of Verbal Learning and Verbal Behavior* 16: 589–600.

Labov, W. (1969) 'Contraction, deletion, and inherent variability of the English copula', *Language* 45: 715–62.

(1972) *Sociolinguistic Patterns*, Blackwell, Oxford.

(1994) *Principles of Linguistic Change*, Blackwell, Oxford.

Ladefoged, P (1993) *A Course in Phonetics* (3rd edn.), Harcourt Brace Jovanovich, New York.

Larson, R. and G. Segal (1995), *Knowledge of Meaning: An Introduction to Semantic Theory*, MIT Press, Cambridge MA.

Laver, J (1994), *Principles of Phonetics*, Cambridge University Press.

Leonard, L. (1998) *Children with Specific Language Impairment*, MIT Press, Cambridge MA.

Levelt, W. (1989) *Speaking*, MIT Press, Cambridge MA.

Lyons, J. (1977) *Semantics* (2 vols.), Cambridge University Press.

McMahon, A. (1994) *Understanding Language Change*, Cambridge University Press.

McNeill, D. (1966) 'Developmental psycholinguistics', in F. Smith and G. A. Miller (eds.), *The Genesis of Language: A Psycholinguistic Approach*, MIT Press, Cambridge MA.

Marcus, G. F. (1995) 'The acquisition of the English past tense in children and multi-layered connectionist networks', *Cognition* 56: 271–9.

Matthews, P. (1991) *Morphology* (2nd edn.), Cambridge University Press.

May, R. (1985) *Logical Form: Its Structure and Derivation*, MIT Press, Cambridge MA.

Meyerhoff, M. (1993) 'Lexical shift in working class New Zealand English: variation in the use of lexical pairs', *English World-Wide* 14: 231–48.

Milroy, J. (1992) *Linguistic Variation and Change*, Blackwell, Oxford.

Milroy, L. (1987a) *Language and Social Networks*, Blackwell, Oxford.

(1987b) *Observing and Analysing Natural Language*, Blackwell, Oxford.

Mitchell, D. (1994) 'Sentence parsing', in M. A. Gernsbacher (ed.), *Handbook of Psycholinguistics*, Academic Press, London

O'Grady, W. (1997) *Language Development*, Chicago University Press.

Petyt, K. (1985) *Dialect and Accent in Industrial West Yorkshire*, Benjamins, Amsterdam.

Pinker, S. (1995) *The Language Instinct: The New Science of Language and Mind*, Penguin, London.

Radford, A. (1990) *Syntactic Theory and the Acquisition of English Syntax: the Nature of Early Child Grammars of English*, Blackwell, Oxford.

(1997a) *Syntax: A Minimalist Introduction*, Cambridge University Press.

(1997b) *Syntactic Theory and the Structure of English: A Minimalist Approach*, Cambridge University Press.

Rizzi, L. (1994) 'Some notes on linguistic theory and language development: the case of root infinitives', *Language Acquisition* 3: 371–93.

Roberts, I. (1993) *Verbs and Diachronic Syntax*, Kluwer, Dordrecht.

Roca, I. (1994) *Phonological Theory*, Routledge, London.

Rosch, E. (1973) 'On the internal structure of perceptual and semantic categories', in T. Moore (ed.), *Cognitive Development and the Acquisition of Language*, Academic Press, New York.

Rosch, E., Mervis, C. B., Gray, W. D., Johnson, D. M. and P. Boyes-Braem (1976) 'Basic objects in natural categories', *Cognitive Psychology* 8: 382–439.

Schütze, C. (1997) 'INFL in Child and Adult Language: Agreement, Case and Licensing', Ph.D. dissertation, MIT.

Sells, P., Rickford, J. and T. Wasow (1994) 'An optimality theoretic approach to variation in negative inversion in AAVE', manuscript, Stanford University.

Shuy, R., Wolfram, W. and W. Riley (1967) *Linguistic Correlates of Social Stratification in Detroit Speech*. USOE Final Report No. 6-1347.

Smith, N. V. (1973) *The Acquisition of Phonology*, Cambridge University Press.

(1989) *The Twitter Machine*, Blackwell, Oxford.

Spencer, A. (1986) 'Towards a theory of phonological development', *Lingua* 68: 3–38.

(1988) 'A phonological theory of phonological development', in M. Ball (ed.), *Theoretical Linguistics and Language Development*, Arnold, London.

(1991) *Morphological Theory*, Blackwell, Oxford.

(1996) *Phonology*, Blackwell, Oxford.

Spencer, A. and A. Zwicky (eds.) (1998) *Handbook of Morphology*, Blackwell, Oxford.

Trask, R. L. (1996) *Historical Linguistics*, Arnold, London.

Travis, L. (1984) 'Parameters and the effects of word order variation', Ph.D. dissertation, MIT.

Trudgill, P. (1974) *The Social Differentiation of English in Norwich*, Cambridge University Press.

(1988) 'Norwich revisited: recent linguistic changes in an English urban dialect', *English World-Wide* 9: 33–50.

(1995) *Sociolinguistics: An Introduction to Language and Society* (3rd revised edition), Penguin, London.

Valian, V. (1986) 'Syntactic categories in the speech of young children', *Developmental Psychology* 22: 562–79.

(1990) 'Null subjects: a problem for parameter-setting models of language acquisition', *Cognition* 35: 105–22.

Vihman, M. M. (1994) *Phonological Development. The Origins of Language in the Child*, Blackwell, Oxford.

Wardaugh, R. (1998) *An Introduction to Linguistics*, Blackwell, Oxford.

Wexler, K. (1994) 'Optional infinitives, verb movement and the economy of derivations in child grammar', in D. Lightfoot and N. Hornstein (eds.), *Verb Movement*, Cambridge University Press.

Wolfram, W. (1991) *Dialects and American English*, Prentice Hall, Englewood Cliffs NJ.

Wolfram, W. and N. Schilling-Estes (1998) *American English*, Blackwell, Oxford.

Index

Ablaut 188f., 224
accent (*see* phrasal stress)
accusative case (*see also* objective case) 158
acquired language disorders 15, 243
acquisition of language 1, 7ff., 105ff., 211ff., 281, 378ff.
acrolect 266
activation 230, 236f., 238
active articulator 33
active voice 155, 333
additions in speech errors 127
adjectives 148; in child language 212; comparative 148, 160, 209, 224; and derivational morphology 166f.; dimensional 199, 210f.; incorporation 184f.; superlative 148, 160, 224
adjuncts 284, 342
adjunction 335, 369
adverbs 148f., 166
affixes 163, 280
affricates 32, 96
African American Vernacular English (AAVE) 264, 269f., 304f., 338ff., 354; double negation in 339; possessives in 269f.
Afrikaans 265
age and variation in language use 266
age-graded sociolinguistic variables 18
agent 334
agglutinating 180f., 186, 192
agrammatism 244ff., 252, 406, 407f., 415, 418, 419f.; errors in comprehension 408; errors in production 407f.
agreement 154, 156, 167, 182, 213, 264, 283, 287, 348, 382, 390; in AAVE 264; in East Anglian English 264; in SLI 250; in south western English 264
allomorphs 175f.

allomorphy 175ff., 178, 190f.; past tense 178; plural 178, 214; third person singular present 178
allophones 86, 98ff.
allophonic variation 86
allophony 86, 175
alternation in phonology 28, 93ff.
alveolars 32, 120f.
alveopalatals (*see* palato-alveolars)
ambiguity (*see also* structural ambiguity) 6, 20, 376, 377
amelioration in semantic change 262f.
American English 29, 43, 45, 55, 59, 69, 70, 77, 78, 102, 257f.
A-movement 325
Ancient Egyptian 132
antecedent 311f.
anterior 97
anticipations in speech errors 127, 129
antonyms 199, 236, 237f.
antonymy 199, 201, 209
aphasia 13ff., 200f., 243ff.
Apophony (*see* Ablaut)
apparent-time method 18, 72f.
approximants 36; in child phonology 110ff.
Arabic 91, 131, 191f., 254
arbitrariness of the linguistic sign 232f., 264
arguments 148, 282
argument movement (*see* A-movement)
Armenian alphabet 132
articles (*see also* determiners) 148, 151
Ash, S. 269
aspect 288; perfect 168, 288; progressive 169, 288
aspiration 38, 84ff., 97ff. 101f.
assimilation (*see also* harmony) 5, 109; in Farsi 54; partial 109; target of 109; total 110; trigger for 109

audience design 57, 62f., 125, 418
Australian English 41, 55f., 67, 69, 78, 79
auxiliary copying in children 324f.
auxiliary inversion 323f., 325, 328f., 338ff.
auxiliary verbs 151f., 296, 307f., 322f.; dummy
    307, 347; and gapping 306; in SLI 250

babbling 105f.
backtracking in parsing 402
back vowels 40
Bailey, B. 340
bare infinitive clause 308f.
Bantu 180
basic level of categorisation 220ff., 225, 248,
    256, 264
basilect 266
Behaviourism 127
Belfast English 56, 329, 337
Bell, A. 57, 62f.
Berko, J. 214
Bengali 85
bidialectalism 418
bilabials 32
bilingualism 418
binarity, of parametric values 342, 345, 348,
    354, 379, 380; of phonological features 95
blends 235ff., 412f.
body of tongue (see dorsum)
borrowing 254f., 271
bound morphemes 162f., 177, 180, 181; in
    aphasia 244; in SLI 250ff.
bound variable interpretation of pronouns
    367ff.
bound word 174
brain, representation of language in 1, 12ff.
Braine, M. 381.
Bresnan, J. 280
British English 41, 63f., 67, 69, 75f., 77, 79,
    257, 258f.
broad transcription 86
Broca, P. 14
Broca's aphasia 244, 250, 252, 406, 407
Broca's Area 14
Brown, R. 215f.
Bulgarian 94

C parameter 342
calque 255f.
Cambodian 42
Canadian English 64
Cantonese 88, 91
Cardiff 57

Caribbean English 71
case (see also nominative, genitive, objective)
    158, 283, 290f.; errors in agrammatism 247;
    marking in Child English 386ff., 392;
    marking in English 386ff.; structural 386ff.
categorical perception 125
causative verb 308
central vowels 40, 44
centre-embedding 399, 402f., 404f.
cerebral cortex 13
cerebral hemispheres 13
chain shift 72f.
child grammar 281, 378ff.
child phonology 105ff.
Celtic languages 189
Chambers, J. 64f.
checking theory 302, 303, 317, 372f.
Cherokee 132
Chinese 48, 132, 180, 254, 373f.; weak spec-
    CP in 375
Chomsky, N. 1, 14, 243, 280, 296, 302, 341,
    354, 406, 416, 419
Chukchee 183, 184ff., 190f.
circumfix (see confix)
clauses 283, 295f., 307, 309f., 312, 313, 321,
    376; bare infinitive 308f.; complement 285f.;
    finite in German SLI 415; finite verb in 287,
    290f.; function of 289f.; in German 352;
    infinitive 308f., 310ff.; as I-projection 317;
    non-finite verb in 287, 290f.; as processing
    unit 396; relative 289, 395f.; tensed 286;
    untensed 286
click studies 395ff.
clitics 173f.
cliticisation 308, 309, 325, 327, 337
cluster (see consonant cluster)
codas of syllables 88ff., 234
cognitive synonymy 198f., 208
cognitive system, language as 1ff., 406
co-hyponyms 196, 237f.; in Wernike's aphasia
    249
co-indexing 366, 397
Comanche 255
co-meronyms 197, 236
comparative adjective 148, 160, 209, 224
comment (vs topic) 284f.
competence 3, 10, 130, 211, 299, 364, 395,
    399, 404, 417
complement 148, 155, 282ff., 298; covert 312;
    interrogative expressions as 326
complement clause 285f.
complement clause question 328, 337

complement clause yes–no question 332f.
complement features 302, 305, 317, 372f.
complementaries 200, 209
complementarity 200, 201
complementary distribution 85, 101
complementiser 153, 213, 321f.; covert 328
complex sentence 285ff.
compounds 171ff., 177, 184f., 186, 221, 224f.,
    280, 408; in language acquisition 216ff.;
    structural ambiguity in 172; synthetic 186
comprehension of language (*see also* speech
    perception, sentence comprehension) 1; in
    agrammatism 247
concatenative morphology 187
concept (vs lexical entry) 233, 238, 255
confix 187
conjugation class 156f., 182f.
consonants 31ff.; categorical perception of
    125; syllabic 46; three-term description of
    37, 66; in writing systems 131
consonant change 66ff.
consonant cluster 45; deletion in 58f.;
    simplification in child language 107
consonant harmony 109
consonant insertion 69
consonant loss 68
consonant mutation 189
constituency tests 298ff.
constituents 284; covert (*see* empty
    categories)
content words 151; in aphasias 244f., 253
continuous perception of vowels 122f.
contour tone 48
contrastive sounds 85
control 311
conversations 279
conversion 165, 177, 216
co-ordinating conjunction 153, 298
co-ordination 298
co-ordination constraint 299
co-ordination test 300, 302f.
co-referential interpretation of pronouns
    366ff.
coronal 37
count noun 234, 314f.
Coupland, N. 57
covert movement 364ff., 416
covert question operator 331f., 353f.
Crossover Principle 369f.
cumulation 181f., 186, 189, 190
Cutler, A. 236
Czech 41, 91

data of linguistics 2, 130, 193
declarative 289, 372f.
declension 158f.
default cases in phonology 101
definitions 204ff., 219
delinking 113f.
demonstratives 151
dentals 32f., 120f.
Derivational Theory of Complexity (DTC)
    395
determiners (*see also* articles) 151, 213;
    prenominal 316; pronominal 316; in SLI
    250
determiner phrase (DP) 298, 313ff.; in Child
    English 389ff., 392f.
derivations: in phonology 95ff.; in syntax 336,
    371
derivational morphology 150, 162, 165ff., 177;
    in language acquisition 216ff.
despecification 113f.
developmental linguistics 1, 7ff.
DhoLuo 188f.
diachronic method in historical linguistics 17,
    66
diacritic 38
dialect contact 257ff.
dictionaries 204ff.
diphthongs 42f.
diphthongisation in language change 70
discourse marker 16
discourses 279
discrimination experiment 122ff.
distinctive features 95, 102f., 132, 138ff., 201
distribution 85
dorsals 37
dorsum 33
double negation in AAVE
D-projections 317, 378, 389
drag chain 73
dual lexicon model of child phonology 110ff.
dummy auxiliary 307, 347
Dunedin 81
Dutch 262, 271

Early Modern English (EME) 342ff., 347f.,
    352, 355, 381f.; strong INFL in 345
East Anglian English 70, 259f., 264
echo question 326
Economy Principle 330f., 340, 341, 346f., 353,
    377
education level and language use 54
Egyptian cuneiform 132

Eimas, P. 105
elision 5
ellipsis 400
Elsewhere Condition 101f.
empty categories 280, 304ff., 323, 416; in psycholinguistics 304, 417; in sentence perception 397f.
empty INFL 304ff.
enclitic 174
entailment 194ff., 207
environment, in phonological rules 98ff.
errors in speech 125ff., 133, 235ff., 240
Estonian 42
ethnic group and language use 55
etymology 272
Even 101
exchanges in speech errors 235f.
exclamative 289
exponent 167, 176, 183
extended exponence 183, 186, 190
external perspectives on language use 419
extraction site 327

Farsi (Persian) 54
Fasold, R. 305
feature matrix 97, 141
features, distinctive in phonology 95ff., 102f., 132, 138ff., 201; grammatical 302, 306; grammatical in agrammatism 410ff.; morphological 176, 188; semantic 200ff., 209; semantic in acquisition 219f.
filler-gap dependencies 397f.
finiteness in language acquisition 390
finite verbs 287, 290f.
Finnish 109, 180
flap 38, 102
flapping 67
floating features 111ff., 116
focus bar 98
Fodor, J. 228
form (vs lemma), in lexical entries 233ff.
free morpheme 162f., 181
Frege, G. 362f., 370
frequency effect, in paraphasias 248f.; in substitution errors 236
French 32, 45, 85, 245, 255, 262
fricatives 32
Frisian 262
Fromkin, V. 236
front vowels 40
function words 151
functional categories 150ff., 415f.; in aphasia

244ff., 407ff.; in language acquisition 212f., 223, 391; in SLI 250ff.

gapping 306
garden-path sentences 11f., 20, 399, 403f., 405, 417
gender, as grammatical feature 159; errors in agrammatism 247, 410; in Old English 265
gender and language use 54f., 63f., 265f., 273
generative grammar 5
generative theory of phonology 107ff.
generic interpretation, of determiners 314
genetic endowment and language 8ff., 15f., 213, 223, 243
genitive case 283
Georgian alphabet 132
German 91, 183f., 187, 188, 234, 262, 263, 265, 349ff., 355f., 413; SLI in 413ff., 420f.; strong C in 352, 354; strong INFL in 352; yes–no questions in 353f.
Germanic 188, 254, 262, 265
glides 36
global aphasia 13
glottal fricative 35, 52f.
glottalisation 57, 78f., 91f.
glottal plosive (glottal stop) 37f.
Gordon, P. 218
grammar 3ff., 90, 132, 153, 170, 270, 279f., 299, 371, 404
grammatical categories 282; in sentence comprehension 227
grammatical functions 282, 298
grammatical word 169, 177, 182, 288
Greek 183
Greek alphabet 131
grey matter 13
Grimshaw, J. 331
Grodzinsky, Y. 409ff.
gutturals 87

Halliday, M. 106
hard palate 35
harmony, consonant 109; lateral 110ff.; velar 109; vowel 109
Hawaiian 91
head, of compounds 171, 186; of a phrase 293
head driven phrase structure grammar 280
head features 302
head first word order 350, 379f.
head last word order 350
head movement 322ff., 344, 352

Head Movement Constraint (HMC) 346, 353
head parameter 350, 379f.
Hebrew 131, 245, 410, 411f.
Henry, A. 329, 337
high vowels 40
historical linguistics 17f.
Hoekstra, T. 390
host for clitic 174
Hungarian 42, 109, 180, 183f., 254
Hyams, N. 381, 390
hyponyms 195, 201, 204, 206, 207, 208, 220, 236ff., 270; in Wernike's aphasia 249
hyponymy 194ff.

Icelandic 261
idealisation 418f.
identification experiment 122ff.
identification of null subject 349, 382
identity of meaning (*see* synonymy)
imaging techniques 15
imperative 288, 289
implicational scale 60f., 64
incomplete phrase 297
incorporation 185
independence of language faculty 14, 406
indicative mood 156
infinite nature of language 4, 295
infinitive 156, 288
infinitive phrase (IP) 294
infix 187
INFL parameter 345, 376
inflection 154f., 166, 179; in grammar 296, 415f.
inflectional allomorphy 182, 190
inflectional classes 156ff.
inflectional errors in agrammatism 245, 410
inflectional formative 167, 181
inflectional languages 180f.
inflectional morphology 162, 165ff.; in language acquisition 216ff.; In SLI 250ff.
inflectional piece 167
inflectional properties 155
inflectional rules (*see* morphological processes)
'information' in categories 222f.
informational encapsulation 228
innateness hypothesis 8f., 105, 211, 243, 417
input representations in child phonology 113
interaction, and variation 57f.
interdentals 34
internal perspective on language use 419
interrogative 289, 372f.

interrogative operator 325
intonation 48f., 125
intonational change 78, 83
Inuit 85, 132
inversion, in questions 323; in varieties of English 338f., 344
IPA (International Phonetic Association) 30ff., 132f. 137
I-projection 317
Irish Gaelic 255
Iroquoian 185
isolating 180f.
Italian 156f., 177, 181, 182, 183f., 190, 223, 244, 254, 261, 296, 410, 414; aphasic speech in 245f.

Jamaican Vernacular English (JVE) 340ff., 354f.; weak C in 341
Japanese 41, 42, 88, 91, 132, 183
Jones, D. 30

kinship vocabulary 209
Koryak 191

labelled bracketing 160f., 163, 293
labelled tree diagram 293
labials 37
labiodentals 34
Labov, W. 18, 21, 23, 61f., 72, 74, 76
language change 17f., 61ff.
language faculty 8f., 15, 20, 302, 376f., 416
language games 130, 134
language shift 17
language use, and the structure of society 16
language variation 17
laryngeal fricative (*see* glottal fricative)
larynx 30
Lashley, K. 127
lateral harmony 110ff.
laterals 36, 110ff.
Latin alphabet 132
lax vowels 42, 86f.
lesions, of the brain 13
levels of linguistic analysis 85f., 116, 132
level tones 48
lexical categories 147ff.
lexical diffusion 75f., 83
lexical entry 4f., 88, 146, 147, 156, 157, 170f., 176, 193, 200ff., 216ff., 232ff., 251, 255, 270
lexical stress (*see* word stress)
lexical substitutions in speech errors 235ff.
lexical tone 47f.

lexicon 4f., 146, 155f., 170f., 193, 200, 205, 216ff., 226ff., 230, 248, 252, 270, 371, 394, 416; grammatical properties in 5; phonological properties in 4; semantic properties in 5
LF component of a grammar 6, 416
Linear B 132
linguistic experience of the child 8f.
linguistic variables and language use 53ff.
linguistically determined variation 58ff.
liquids 36
Liverpool 68
localisation of brain function 13ff.
Logical Form (LF) 6, 281, 357ff.; reconstruction at 400
logical object 6, 11
logical subject 6, 11, 404
London 70f.
low vowels 40

Macken, M. 118
McMahon, A. 263
Malay 254, 271f.
manner of articulation 32; and language change 68
Maori 185, 255
Maximal Onset Principle 91f., 101f.
Mayan languages 185
meaning, in sentence perception 227; of words 193ff., 359
meaning inclusion 195, 202
meaning opposites 194, 199f., 208f.
merger 292ff., 322, 336, 358f., 371, 416; constraints on 300ff.
meronyms 197, 236
meronymy 197, 208, 236ff., 270
metalanguage 360
Middle English 262
mid vowels 40
mid closed vowels 42
mid open vowels 42
Milroy, J. 56
Milroy, L. 56
Milton Keynes 78f.
minimal pair 84f.
minimal responses 16
Modern Standard English (MSE) 338, 342ff., 348, 354, 355; strong C in 341, 347; strong spec-CP in 375; weak INFL in 345, 347
modifiers in compounds 171
monophthongisation 70
monophthongs 42

monosyllabic words 46
mood 156
morphs 175f.
morphemes 162ff.; in aphasia 244ff.
morphological change 264ff.
morphological development in children 214ff.
morpholological operations 186ff.
morphological processes 176, 181, 224, 417; dissociation of in SLI 251f.; phonological conditioning of 175, 178, 251; realisations of 176; voicing as 188f.; vowel change as 188
morphological properties in sentence perception 227
morphological variation 264, 268f.; social contact and 269f.
morphology 162ff.; phonological processes in 187ff.
morphosyntactic word 169
motor control 120, 125
movement in syntax 280, 321ff., 371, 416
Myhill, J. 269

Nahuatl 185, 254
narrow transcription 86
nasalisation 45
nasals 32, 96
native speakers as source of data 2
natural classes in phonology 99f., 103f.
Navajo 93, 183
negation 152; in Child English 392
negative concord in AAVE 339
negative operator 325
negative particle 342
Neogrammarians 74f.
neurolinguistics 1, 12ff.
neutral context in lexical decision tasks 230
neutralisation processes 117
New York 21ff., 61f.
New Zealand English 41, 62f., 70, 78, 79, 258
nodes in tree diagrams 293
nominal phrases 313f.; in Child English 389ff.; as D-projections 317
nominative case 158, 283, 287
nominative subjects in Child English 386ff.
noun incorporation 185
nouns 147f.; in language acquisition 202, 218ff.; and derivational morphology 166f.; and person 153; in taxonomies 198
non-concatenative morphology 189
non-finite clauses 287, 290f.; in Child English 384ff.; in German 414

non-finite verbs 287, 290f.
non-rhotic dialects 41
non-standard dialects 17
Norfolk 71f., 259f.
Northern Cities Chain Shift 72, 74
Northern English 71, 76, 79
Norwich 266f.
nucleus of syllable 46, 88ff.
null constituents (see empty categories)
null determiner 313f.; in Child English 390
null infinitive particle 309
null operator questions in Child English 382
null subjects, in Child English 381ff., 391f.; in
    infinitive clauses 310ff.; in wh-questions
    383f.
null subject language 348, 381f.
null subject parameter 347ff., 379, 381ff.
number 152, 158; in SLI 250

object 155, 186
objective case (see also accusative case) 283,
    287; subjects in Child English 386f.
object language 360
obstruents 37, 89
Old English 261, 262, 263, 265, 268
Old French 261, 262
Old Norse 261
omissions in speech errors 127
onsets of syllables 88ff.; in poetic systems
    130f.; in speech errors 126f.
operator movement 325ff., 352, 364f.
operators 325
Optional Infinitive (OI) Stage 388f.
order in phonological processes 117f.
orthography (see also writing systems) 29, 93f.
output representations in child phonology
    113
overextension in children's word use 218ff.,
    263
overregularisation, in morphological
    development 216, 224; lack of in SLI 251

palatalisation 158
palatals 35
palato-alveolars 35
paragrammatic errors 406, 412f., 415, 420
parallel–interactive processing models 226ff.
parameters 342ff.
parameter setting 379ff., 391
parametric variation 342ff., 375
paraphasia 244, 248ff., 252, 253
parser 10f.

parsing 394ff.
partial exponent 182
partial suppletion 175, 179
partitive interpretation of determiners 314,
    332
part–whole relationship (see meronymy)
passive articulator 33
passive participle 155, 169, 170f., 179
passive voice 155, 168, 333f.
passivisation 334
past tense allomorphy 178
past tense morpheme in acquisition 215f.,
    223f.
peak of syllable (see nucleus)
pejoration and semantic change 262
perception of language (see also speech
    perception, sentence comprehension) 1
perfect aspect 168, 288
perfect auxiliary (vs causative verb) 308
perfect participle 154, 168, 170f., 176, 179,
    180, 288
performance (vs competence) 3, 10, 395, 399,
    404, 417
perseverations in speech errors 127, 129
person 152
PF component of a grammar 5, 88, 94ff., 132,
    416
pharyngeals 39
Philadelphia 70, 269
Phoenician 131
phonemes 84ff., 121, 131, 132, 175
phones 86, 175
phonetic conditioning of sound change 74
phonetic form (PF) 5, 97
phonetic transcription 29ff.
phonological component of a grammar 5, 28,
    371
phonological conditioning of morphological
    processes 175, 178 251
phonological features 95ff., 102f.
phonological perception in children 105, 107,
    110ff.
phonological processes 5, 28, 92ff., 97ff., 104,
    132, 416; in language acquisition 106ff.;
    context-free 109; context-sensitive 109; in
    morphology 187ff.; pronunciation rules as
    113, 116; selection rules as 113, 115f.
phonological production in children 105,
    107ff.
phonological rules 93ff.
phonological variant 52ff.
phonological variation 21, 52ff.

phonotactic constraints 90, 129
phrasal affix 174
phrasal stress 47
phrase 290, 292ff.
Pig Latin 134
pitch 47ff.
place of articulation 32ff., 96; and language change 67f.
plosives 32
plural allomorphy 178, 214
plural morpheme in acquisition 214; in SLI 251
poetic devices 130
polarity items 332f., 336, 355
politeness 16
Polish 45, 93
Pollard, C. 280
polysemy 263
polysyllabic words 46
polysynthetic 184ff.
possessives 174, 178; in AAVE 269f.
poverty of the stimulus argument 9
predicate 282
prefix 163
prefixation 186f.
prepositional phrase (PP) 298
prepositions 149, 166
present participle 154
prevocalic voicing 108, 116
primed context in lexical decision tasks 230
priming 230
principal exponent 183
Principle of Compositionality 357ff., 361, 363
Principles and Parameters Theory (PPT) 354, 378, 385
pro 348f., 381
PRO 310ff., 348, 383ff., 391, 397
probe recognition task 397f.
proclitic 174
progressive aspect 169, 288
progressive form 154, 288; in acquisition 215
projection 293
pronouns 152, 174, 315f.; interpretations of 366ff.; personal 152f.; relative 289; in SLI 250
propositional attitude verbs 198
prosodic phenomena 46ff.
prototypes 206, 209f., 238f., 241f.; in Wernike's aphasia 248
psycholinguistics 1, 10ff., 184, 206, 226ff., 394ff.
Puerto Rican English 59f.
push chain 73

quality in vowels 41
quantificational DPs 363, 366ff., 370
quantity in vowels 41
question operator 332
questions 322ff.; in Child English 383ff., 393; formation of 152, 322ff.; interpretation as 329; wh-in-situ 326; yes–no 331ff.

rapidity of first language acquisition 8
reduplication 188f.
Received Pronunciation (RP) 40, 75
recency effects in psycholinguistics 398
recipient 408
reconstruction at LF 400
recursion, in compounds 172; in sentence structure 295
redundancy in feature specifications 96
reflexives 311f.
regional dialects 16
register 256f., 272
regularity of sound change 74f., 83
resonance 30
retroflex 36, 39
rhotic dialects 41, 61f.
rhyme (rime) 88; in poetry 130
Rips, L. 239
Rizzi, L. 382
Roberts, I. 331
Romance 174
root 163, 168, 177
Rosch, E. 222
rounding 40, 44
rule deficit hypothesis in SLI 251
Russell, B. 362
Russian 32, 42, 85, 88, 91, 158f., 177, 181f., 183f., 244, 245, 254, 411

Sag, I. 280
Samoan 85, 185
scan-copier model of speech production 128f., 133
schwa 39, 93ff.
scope 371ff.
scope ambiguity 376
segments 45, 84; in speech errors 126
selective impairment of brain function 14, 243
Sells, P. 338
semantic broadening 261f.
semantic change 260ff.
semantic narrowing 262
semantic variation 261

sentence comprehension 394ff.
sentence processing 281; strategies of 399ff.
Senufo 91
Separation Hypothesis 177, 180, 190
Serbo-Croatian 47
serial–autonomous processing models 226ff.
Shakespearean English (*see also* Early Modern English) 332
short-term memory 403
short vowels 39f.
Sign Languages 10, 27, 120
simple sentences 282ff.
Smith, N. 117
social class and language use 53f.
social contact and morphological variation 269f.
social dialects 16
social nature of language 1
social network links 56, 269
sociolinguistics 16ff., 52ff., 254ff.
sociological variables 52ff.
soft palate (*see* velum)
sonorants 37, 89, 96
sonority 89f., 101
Sonority Principle 90, 115
sound change 66ff., 133
sound source 30
South African English 74, 79
Spanish 32, 85, 93, 174, 183f.
species-specificity of the language faculty 10, 15, 125
Specific Language Impairment (SLI) 15f., 21, 243, 250ff., 407, 413ff., 420f.; therapy for 413; word order and 413ff.
specifier 298, 326, 329
specifier features 302, 305
speech perception 120ff.
speech production 120, 125ff., 235ff.
spirantisation 68
spoonerisms 126, 129
spreading 111ff.
stable sociolinguistic variables 18
stable variation 266
standard languages 17
stem 168, 179, 181, 184
stem-based inflection 184, 223, 245f.
stopping 108
stops 96
stories 279
Stray Deletion (Stray Erasure) 116
stress 46f., 175; in language change 76ff.; and phonological alternations 93ff.; phrasal 47;

secondary 46; word 46f.; in word recognition 227
structural ambiguity, in compounds 172; in sentence structure 358, 399f., 404
structural continuity in language acquisition 385, 391
structural learning 378; as parameter setting 379
stylistic variation 57f.
subject 148, 155, 282ff., 297
subjunctive 156
subordinate level of categorisation 220ff., 225, 248
substitutions in speech errors 127
suffix 163
suffixation 186f.
Suffolk 259f.
Sumerian cuneiform 132
superordinate 195, 236
superordinate level of categorisation 220ff., 225, 248
suppletion 175
suprasegmental change 76ff.
suprasegmental level 45ff.
suprasegmentals 45ff.
surface representation (surface form) 94ff., 107ff., 111ff.
Swahili 183, 192
syllabification 91f.
syllables 45f., 88ff., 101f., 130, 132; in child phonology 108, 114f.; in poetry 130; in speech errors 126ff.; in writing systems 132
syllable template 115, 118f.
Sydney 55f.
synchronic method in historical linguistics (*see also* apparent-time method) 18, 66
syncretism 182, 186, 190
synonymy 198f., 237
syntactic component of a grammar 4ff., 416
syntactic disorders 281, 406ff.
syntactic illusions 403f.
syntactic parameters 342ff.
syntactic variation 338ff., 418
synthetic compounds 186

Tagalog 187f.
tag questions 307
tap 38
taxonomy 196, 206, 207, 208, 220ff., 239
Teheran 54
telegraphic speech in Broca's aphasia 245, 247, 411

tense 154, 285
tense vowels 42, 86f.
Texas 80f.
texts 279
theme 408f.
third person singular present morpheme, in acquisition 215f.; allomorphy 178; in SLI 251
tone 47f.
tone language 48, 373
Tongan 185
tongue twisters 126
topic (vs comment) 284f.
topicalisation 335
total suppletion 175, 179
trace of movement 323f., 327f., 335, 365ff., 397f.
transition problem in historical linguistics 66, 73ff.
Travis, L. 345
tree diagrams (see also labelled tree diagram) 163f., 177
Trudgill, P. 266
truncation 382f., 391
truth conditions 360ff., 370
Turkish 109, 180f., 183, 254
typing errors 133f.

Umlaut 188
underlying representation 93ff., 98, 107ff., 111ff.
underspecification, of functional categories in agrammatism 410; of functional categories in Child English 391; of phonological features 98, 111ff. 116
understood subject 311
uniformity in first language acquisition 7f.
Universal Grammar (UG) 7, 9, 97, 101, 263, 354, 376f., 385, 390, 391, 406, 417
uvulars 39

Valian, V. 383
variables in LF 362ff.
variables in sociolinguistics 17
variation, age and 266; interactional determination of 57f.; linguistic determination of 58ff.; morphological 264, 268f.; parametric 342ff., 375; phonological 21, 52ff., 133, 418; semantic 261; social

contact and 269f.; stable 266; stylistic 57f.; syntactic 338f., 418
velars 33
velum 32
verbs 147f., 153ff.; base form of 153, 170, 183, 287f.; -d form of 154, 169, 287f.; and derivational morphology 166f.; inflectional categories of 168ff.; -ing form of 154, 169f., 287f., 301; intransitive 155, 185; in language acquisition 212; -n form of 154, 169, 287f., 301, 333; propositional attitude 198; -s form 287f.; in taxonomies 196f.; transitive 155, 301
verb phrase (VP) 293
Vietnamese 180
vocal cords (vocal folds) 30
vocal tract 30
voice box (see larynx)
Voice Onset Time (VOT) 123f.
voicing 37; change as morphological process 188f.; s distinctive feature 95f., 201; in language change 67; and speech perception 123ff.
vowel change as morphological process 188
vowel length 84, 86f.
vowel reduction 93ff.
vowels 31, 39ff.; continuous perception of 122f.; in language change 69ff.; mergers 70f.; quality in 41; quantity in 41; splits 70f.

Wernike, C. 14
Wernike's aphasia 244, 248f., 252, 253, 406, 412f.
Wernike's Area 15
Wexler, K. 388
wh-parameter 379f., 384
Wisbech 76
words 165ff.; in aphasia 244ff.
word-association experiments 237
word-based inflection 184, 223, 246
word form 166, 177
word formation 150
word stress 46f.
writing systems 130, 131f.
written languages 27

Yawelmani 91
yod-dropping 69
Yoruba 41, 45, 47